Jo Draper's *Dorset, The Complete Guide* has lived-up to the expectations placed on it by one reviewer who described it as 'the most important and valuable book about the county to have been published for many years'. Since first being published in 1986 it has sold over 15,000 copies, which even by national standards would win it a place on any bestseller list. For a county guide to sell in such numbers is a tribute to what the historian Richard Ollard has described as 'the accurate and concise presentation of information, much of it learned and out-of-the-way . . . achieved without the slightest touch of the patronising or the pedantic.'

Jo Draper's credentials to be author of this guide could hardly be bettered. She lives in Dorchester, the county town, and was editor of the Dorset Natural History and Archaeological Society for fifteen years. Her other books include *Dorset Food*; *Dorchester, An Illustrated History*; *Hampshire, The Complete Guide*; and *Thomas Hardy's England*, the last of which was written with John Fowles.

The original edition of *Dorset, The Complete Guide* took Jo Draper three years to research and compile, during which time she visited every entry mentioned in the text – a task she has repeated for this new fully revised and corrected edition.

FRONTISPIECE *St Catherine's Chapel, Abbotsbury, looking west from above Rodden*

JO DRAPER

DORSET

The Complete Guide

THE DOVECOTE PRESS

For my father, John Kenneth Draper, 1925-1986

Flake tool, core-tool; in the small museum
Rare butterflies, green coins of Caracalla
Keep easy company with the fading hand
Of one who chronicled a fading world;
Outside, the long roads, that the Roman ruler
Rules himself out with, point across the land
To lasting barrows and long vanished barracks.

Stanza from *Wessex Guidebook*,
LOUIS MACNEICE

Roman road, west of Dorchester
from Unknown Dorset
Donald Maxwell 1927

First published in 1986 by
The Dovecote Press Ltd, Stanbridge,
Wimborne, Dorset BH21 4JD

ISBN 0 946159 40 8

© Jo Draper 1986
Reprinted 4 times
Revised and corrected edition 1996

Designed by Humphrey Stone
Photoset in Palatino by The Typesetting
Bureau, Allen House, East Borough,
Wimborne, Dorset
Film origination and assembly by
Appletone Graphics, Bournemouth, Dorset
Colour map provided by John
Bartholomew & Son Ltd, Edinburgh
Printed and bound in Singapore

1 3 5 7 9 8 6 4 2

Contents

The main MAP *and six pages of colour plates
fall between pages 112/113*

Using this Book

The main map, which forms the centre of the colour section in the middle of the book, shows the position of virtually all the entries in the alphabetical Gazetteer, and really forms the index. The letter bracketed after the entry gives the relevant square on which it can be found on the map. In addition, each of the towns has its own map, showing car parks and tourist information offices as well as features of interest.

The introductory Praise o' Dorset gives brief descriptions of each main area in the county and lists all the most interesting places in it.

The Lists at the back of the book give opening times and other information, including as a rough price guide all those places which charge admission, indicated in the Gazetteer by 'fee'.

For getting about the county the Ordnance Survey's 1:50,000 (the Landranger, which used to be the one inch) map is vital. Most of Dorset falls within sheets 194 and 195, but there are fringes of the county on 193, 183 and 184. For walking the larger 1:25,000 (the Pathfinder, the old 2½ inch) is better, especially as it looks as though one has walked further and also all the rights of way are shown. There is a useful, especially extensive sheet for Purbeck and South Dorset (Outdoor Leisure Map) which covers all the coast from Bridport to Poole, and much inland too. Modern editions of the 1:50,000 (and the Purbeck 1:25,000) give useful 'tourist' information in blue – viewpoints, houses, gardens and monuments open to the public, information centres and so on.

The system of grading used here is bound to be a problem: I will be the only person to agree with all the ratings. The top is fairly obvious and straightforward: most people would agree that Sherborne Abbey is ★ ★ ★ ★ and that many of the 19th century churches are not of great interest. It is the middle, the ★ ★ and ★ ★ ★, which are more controversial, and inevitably rather arbitrary. Broadly I have tried to reserve ★ ★ ★ ★ for those places which are worth travelling to see, and these, along with the ★ ★ ★ are listed both in the sections on areas and on subjects, so that they cannot be missed. Allowance has been made for quantity as well as quality, so that although Purse Caundle and Sandford Orcas are first class manor houses, they rate ★ ★ ★, behind all the larger houses, where by their very nature there is more to see.

19th century churches are dealt with in their own right, not dismissed as second-rate imitations, which may be regarded as heresy by some entrenched medievalists, but Dorset is a fine county to enjoy their variety and beauty.

I have had to confine myself strictly to Dorset, using blinkers when necessary – there are all sorts of interesting places just over the borders which are completely ignored.

I will be glad to hear of omissions and mistakes in this Guide, and they should be addressed to me via the publisher: Dovecote Press Ltd, Stanbridge, Wimborne, Dorset BH21 4JD.

Foreword

JOHN FOWLES

I remember once reading of a Dorset divided, like ancient Arabia, into three: into a desert part, a stony one, and a third termed *felix*, or fortunate. That last was bestowed mainly on West Dorset, with its green hills and combes and rich agricultural land; but today's traveller, less persuaded that farmability is the sovereign virtue in landscape, is likely to find the 'desert' (or East Dorset heathland) and the 'stone' (the Purbeck peninsula and Portland) quite as attractive as the part called *felix*.

In any case all modern Dorset can in one obvious way count itself happy. It remains the gentlest, the most classically balanced of the four South-Western counties; and yet with a quite astounding variety of landscape, both natural and manmade (in many cases, very anciently manmade). I suggested several years ago that it should officially declare itself 'green', with all that that adjective now means, beyond the colour: in short, be especially concerned to preserve and conserve itself — its architectures, its villages, its frequent solitudes, its rich natural life and landscapes. Such wishes, alas, are offensive to many of the living.

One must not museumize present reality and deny 'progress', or suggest that being allowed to make a profit, whatever the damage this causes, is not a prime good in society. I remain attached to my dream, even if I despair of its ever being made official policy.

The county is not least lucky in the fact that by far its largest conurbation, made up of Poole, Bournemouth and Christchurch, lies on its eastern fringe. No unwieldy city or even, by national standards, over-large town disturbs the rest of it. The county town, Dorchester, remains mercifully, and beautifully, small. It is still almost an eighteenth or nineteenth century provincial 'capital', ten thousand miles from London; and still a fitting home for its two most celebrated literary ghosts, those of William Barnes and Thomas Hardy. In much of the remoter Dorset countryside, this impression of a wise balance between human use and natural environment is even stronger. Little seems to have changed there since much older and less populated times. Of course a great deal has changed in social and cultural terms; nevertheless the county retains a remarkable number of out of the way and largely unmarred areas and places, where the past remains present to anyone with the smallest imagination. All the world on holiday craves the sea, nowadays; but not the least virtue of this book is its clear suggestion that true Dorset lies quite as much inland as on its overcrowded (at least in July and August) coasts.

I welcome this new guide to the whole county. It does not contain all there is to see, for obvious reasons, but I am sure it will become an indispensable handbook for all those (not only from outside Dorset) who wander in it. I know Jo Draper has indefatigably visited and revisited, and re-assessed, everywhere she describes in the writing of the guide; and no one has better credentials to be its author. Not only is she the editor of the annual *Proceedings* of the Dorset Natural History and Archaeological Society, where most of the county's serious scholarship appears; but she is possessed of a lively

The Marshwood Vale from below Pilsdon Pen

curiosity as a tourist herself, and is well aware that most visitors are *not* serious scholars, and need a concise friend a good deal more than the usual verbose and cliché-ridden 'official' guide.

Visitors to Green Dorset no longer have any excuse to say they don't know where to go or what to see. This is not simply a guide to the county; but like all good books, a guide to the greater freedom of anyone who reads it.

JOHN FOWLES

Praise o' Dorset

We Do'set, though we mid be hwomely,
Ben't asheämèd to own our pleäce;
An' wo've zome women not uncomely,
Nor asheäm'd to show their feäce:
We've a mead or two wo'th showen,
In the village,
At the tillage,
Come along an' you shall vind
That Do'set men don't sheäme their kind.

WILLIAM BARNES

Charles II declared that he never saw a finer county, either in England or out of it, and the chronicler who recorded his words thought his judgement might be relied upon, since Charles had seen more counties than most people — a delicate allusion to his toing and froing as a fugitive before becoming King. Natives (and perhaps even more emphatically newcomers) boast of Dorset's fine rural landscapes, diverse and beautiful coastline, and its small-scale towns. Visitors soon fall for the county's charms, perhaps prepared for them by Thomas Hardy's novels, or the poetry of William Barnes or Hardy.

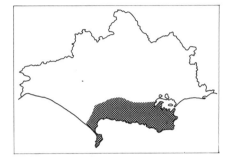

PORTLAND WEYMOUTH PURBECK

Towns: Swanage, Wareham, Weymouth.
Houses and Castles: Corfe Castle ★ ★ ★; Lulworth Castle; Portland Castle; Smedmore; and The Nothe Weymouth, all ★ ★ ★.
Villages: Corfe ★ ★ ★; Worth Matravers ★ ★ ★.
Gardens: Kingston Maurward ★ ★ ★.
Archaeology: The Ridgeway ★ ★ ★ ★; Flower's Barrow, T... ★ ★ ★.
Walks: All the coast, but especially Arne, Ballard Down, Durdle Door, Durlston Country Park, Kimmeridge Bay, Lulworth, Osmington Mills, Portland, Tyneham, Ringstead, St Aldhelm's Head, Studland, West Lulworth, White Nothe, Worth Matravers.
Churches, Medieval: Studland, Wareham St Martins and Worth Matravers ★ ★ ★;
18th century: Portland, St George Reforne ★ ★ ★ ★; St Mary, East Lulworth ★ ★ ★;
19th century: Kingston ★ ★ ★.
Museums: Timewalk, Brewer's Quay, Weymouth ★ ★ ★ ★; Portland ★ ★ ★; Mill House Clock and Cider Museum, Owermoigne; Wessex Water Museum, Sutton Poyntz; Wareham ★ ★; Corfe and Swanage.
Other: Sea Life Park, Weymouth ★ ★ ★ ★; Deep Sea Adventure, Weymouth ★ ★ ★; Monkey World, Wool ★ ★ ★.

The southern part of the coast encompasses what many would consider to be the finest scenery in Dorset. From the bleak windswept heights of Portland through the varied coastline of Purbeck the whole coast is fine walking country. The area is delightful for cycling or driving, but as there is (happily) no coast road the best way to see it is on foot. Some small parts of the coastal path which runs right along it are steep and strenuous (for example up through Arish Mell), but most of it is easy.

Portland is an odd place, bleak and almost treeless, nibbled away by quarrying and with cliffs almost all round. It is has a strange outlandish charm, but seen from the roads is far too developed and uncompromising to be called pretty. It should be explored on foot.

Weymouth is totally different — real picture-book seaside, with its wide shallow bay, sandy beach with donkeys, Punch & Judy and so on. The harbour is picturesque but still working, and both the seafront and town are full of elegant Georgian terraces, legacies from the days when Weymouth was the most fashionable seaside resort in the country.

The only other town on the coast is Swanage, which grew to a seaside resort in the later 19th century, having been little more than a village through which stone was shipped before. It too has a fine natural position in a sheltered bay, with the chalk hills beyond.

Between the two towns is a glorious length of wild coast whose swift geological changes give rise to a superb variety of scenery. Purbeck is even less of an island than Portland, although it often is called one. Like Portland this is an area where stone has been quarried since the Roman period, the Purbeck Marble and Kimmeridge shale being used decoratively, and Portland and Purbeck limestone for building. Many of the fields are walled in stone, and the villages are built from it. The later 19th century Kingston church was proudly constructed

Worth Matravers

completely from local stone, even down to the decorative marbles.

The structure of Purbeck is best seen and admired in the Tyneham valley and in Worbarrow Bay, where the Wealden clay valley is bounded on the north by the chalk and the south by the clays and limestones. In Worbarrow Bay the sea is eroding all three types. The villages of Purbeck are charming, with stone cottages and churches perfectly suiting the landscape from which their stones were won. Worth Matravers is perhaps the prettiest smaller one, while Corfe is virtually a small town, with the picturesque centre all stone, including the roofs. The medieval stronghold of Corfe Castle dominates the only gap in the chalk ridge, and looks out over the low heathlands to the north and Poole Harbour to the east. Just across the heath is Wareham, formerly a port on the River Frome, but now a market town with some handsome buildings still enclosed by its Saxon defences – grass-covered earthen banks. Lulworth Castle is a pretty 17th century mock castle, not war-like at all but now a shell.

Part of the heathlands and the coast between Lulworth and Kimmeridge are used by the Army as a firing range for tanks. The footpaths (and indeed the roads) between the two are closed when the range is in use, but are usually open at week-ends and in school holiday periods. Lulworth, on the edge of the range, can be overcrowded in summer with visitors to the stunning circular bay, but those who walk can soon lose the crowds. This is true all along the coast.

The coast between Osmington Mills and Lulworth is nearly as good as Purbeck, with the great chalk headland of White Nothe and rolling chalk downs behind, bounded by the lusher, more domestic landscape of the Frome valley, all green fields and cows.

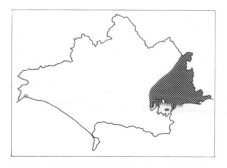

POOLE HARBOUR WIMBORNE BOURNEMOUTH CHRISTCHURCH

Towns: Bournemouth, Christchurch, Poole and Wimborne.
Houses: Kingston Lacy ★ ★ ★ ★; Merley House ★ ★ ★.
Gardens: Compton Acres ★ ★ ★ ★; Stapehill and Dean's Court, Wimborne ★ ★ ★.
Villages: Pamphill ★ ★ ★ ★.
Archaeology: Badbury Rings ★ ★ ★ ★; Hengistbury ★ ★ ★.
Walks: Avon Forest Country Park; Brownsea; Hengistbury Head; Studland Heath; the coast generally; Moors Valley Country Park, West Moors.
Churches, Medieval: Christchurch and Wimborne Minster ★ ★ ★ ★; Canford ★ ★ ★; **19th century:** Bournemouth, St Stephen ★ ★ ★ ★; Boscombe, St Clement; Bournemouth, St Peter; Colehill, Wimborne; Parkstone, St Osmund; Poole, St James, all ★ ★ ★.
Museums: Russell-Cotes, Bournemouth; Waterfront Museum, Poole; Stapehill Experience ★ ★ ★ ★; Red House, Christchurch; Scaplens Court, Poole; Priest's House Museum, Wimborne; and Southern Electric Museum, Christchurch ★ ★ ★; Shelley Museum, Boscombe; Tricycle Museum, Christchurch.
Other: Merley Bird Gardens; Natural World, Poole; Poole Zoo; Dorset Heavy Horse Centre, Verwood; all ★ ★ ★.

OPPOSITE ABOVE *Poole Harour from the western slopes of Godlingston Heath*
OPPOSITE LEFT *The Guildhall, Poole*
OPPOSITE RIGHT *Wimborne Minster*

Poole Harbour is one of the largest natural harbours in the world, with a shore line of 100 miles, so indented is its margin. The entrance is tiny – less than ½ mile across and crossed by a chain ferry. The contrast between the north and south sides of the harbour is starkest here, with to the south the unspoilt heathlands of Studland and to the north Sandbanks, totally covered with development, mostly hotels and houses built since the 1920's. All they have in common are the fine views and sandy beaches. They are typical of their areas: to the south, heaths and forests fill the area between Studland and Wareham, without even villages. Brownsea is the largest of the islands in the harbour, but there are several others in this wild landscape of peninsulas and mud-flats.

The north of the harbour was once heathland too, but is now built up right round the shore and stretching for miles inland. Most of this development dates from after the middle of the 19th century, with Poole the only medieval town. Poole, now the western side of a huge urban sprawl which extends for 15 miles into Hampshire, developed because the earlier port at Wareham, at the head of the harbour, became too small for sea-going vessels.

It is difficult to believe that the whole area between Poole and Christchurch was heathland, poor gravels and sands which were of so little value for agriculture that much of the area was not even enclosed until 1805, when an acre of land on the seafront at what was to become Bournemouth or Boscombe could have been bought for £5. In 1800 the area was described as 'a most dreary waste, serving only in the summer to support a few ordinary sheep and cattle, and to supply the neighbouring villages with heath for firing'. The only people who used this remote area were the smugglers, and the excise men trying to catch them. The few medieval villages were to the north and east in the fertile valley of the Stour, but such is the expansion of Bournemouth that they are now absorbed within it.

The phenomenal growth of Bournemouth from wild heathland in 1800 to a town of 78,700 people in 1911 completely altered the whole area, leading to the conurbation which runs for 15 miles along the coast from Sandbanks in the west to Highcliffe in the east, and stretches inland nearly to Wimborne. The decline of Poole was arrested by supplying raw materials for all this expansion. Today the area is totally different to the rest of Dorset, with the hundreds of acres of houses and huge shopping centres, and in the Poole area more than double the level of industry found in the rest of the county. More than half of the population of the county are in the Poole-Bournemouth-Christchurch area, and there is a thriving holiday trade as well. Poole's quay area attracts visitors, with its boats and nearby museums, and the sandy beach at Rockley Sands (the only one actually inside the harbour) is also popular, but the majority of holidaymakers are found on the sandy beach which runs all the way from Studland to Highcliffe.

The mudflats of low tides on the south of Poole Harbour are not attractive to bathers but the area offers superb walking, seabirds, and varied views.

At the eastern corner of the county is Christchurch, once a small town between the rivers Avon and Stour. The interesting old centre has the large priory church and a pretty river frontage. Christchurch Harbour is far smaller than Poole Harbour, but is the only undeveloped piece of this coastline, with the promontory of Hengistbury still heathland. Although the urban sprawl is approaching Wimborne, it is still separate, a handsome market town with a lovely church and interesting streets. Close to it is Kingston Lacy, with its sylvan park, and the extraordinarily unchanged estate village – Pamphill. Stapehill, also close to Wimborne, has many attractions including gardens.

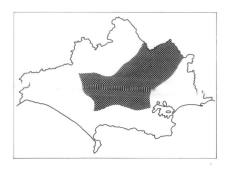

DORCHESTER
BLANDFORD
CRANBORNE CHASE

Towns: Blandford and Dorchester.
Houses: Athelhampton and Milton
Abbey ★ ★ ★; Wolfeton and Islington
House, Puddletown ★ ★ ★; Chettle ★ ★;
Cloud's Hill (T.E. Lawrence) and Thomas
Hardy's birthplace, the cottage,
Bockhampton ★ ★ ★.
Gardens: Athelhampton, Cranborne
★ ★ ★; Kingston Maurward; Minterne
★ ★ ★.
Villages: Cerne Abbas, Milton Abbas
★ ★ ★; Ashmore, Briantspuddle; Sydling
St Nicholas ★ ★ ★; many more in
Gazetteer.
Archaeology: Cerne Giant, Maiden Castle
and Hod ★ ★ ★ ★; Bokerly Dyke,
Hambledon, Knowlton; Maumbury;
Oakley Down and Rawlsbury ★ ★ ★.
Walks: Bockhampton; Bulbarrow ★ ★ ★ ★;
lots of footpaths, eg in the area between
Plush and Melcombe Bingham, Hilton,
Milton Abbas, Up Cerne, Stinsford;
Bokerly Dyke particularly, but see other
archaeology too.
Churches, Medieval: Bere Regis ★ ★ ★ ★;
Charminster, Hilton, Milton Abbas &
Winterborne Tomson ★ ★ ★.
   17th-18th century: Blandford Forum
★ ★ ★ ★; Charlton Marshall, West Stafford
and Puddletown ★ ★ ★.
   19th century: Moreton ★ ★ ★ ★;
Wimborne St Giles ★ ★ ★. The area
includes lots of charming ★ ★ churches
such as Woolland, or my favourite,
Winterborne Clenston.
Museums: Bovington Tank Museum and
Dorset County Museum, Dorchester
★ ★ ★ ★;
The Dinosaur Museum and The Keep
Military Museum, both Dorchester and
★ ★ ★; Blandford Town and Army Signals
Museum; Park Farm, Milton Abbas; and
Tolpuddle Martyrs, Tolpuddle.

Cranborne Chase from near Wyn Green

All this heart of Dorset is chalk – rolling hills, mostly rounded, but with steep scarps on the north overlooking Blackmore Vale. The higher parts were all once downland, described in the 1620's as 'all overspread with innumerable Flockes of Sheepe, for which it yields very good and sound Feedeing'. These sheep had created and maintained the downs, which have been largely ploughed up this century and used to grow corn. Nevertheless these rolling hills still have a particular distinctive and rather bleak character. The villages mostly sit in the valleys, and the roads either run along the tops of the spurs, and give wonderful views of the valleys either side, or run along the valleys through the villages. The most extreme example of the high road is the A37 from Dorchester to Yeovil, which sticks to the high ground for as long as it can, and passed through only one village (now by-passed!) between the two towns. In total contrast is the A352, Dorchester to Sherborne, which uses the valleys and has villages all the way.

The north east of the county was a chase reserved, like medieval forests, for hunting and named Cranborne Chase, after its centre. From the 11th century until it was abolished by an Act of Parliament in 1830 the needs of the deer and the hunters dominated, to the detriment of agriculture. The outer bounds stretched from Shaftesbury to Blandford and Wimborne in Dorset, Fordingbridge in Hampshire and Salisbury in Wiltshire. The central part, within the inner bounds, was smaller, but still covered 40,000 acres, about half of which was wooded. The preservation of the deer, estimated as between twelve and twenty thousand in 1828, was not beneficial to the farmers and nor were the deer poachers. This was especially resented because the ownership of the land was separate from Lordship of the Chase. The control was such that for 15 days either side of Midsummer, when the fawns were born, the Lord of the Chase could (and did) charge cheminage, a levy on every traveller through the chase to make up for the disturbance to the deer. The bridge at Harnham, Salisbury was chained off and antlers erected to show that cheminage was in force. Most of the deer were killed when the chase was abolished, but there are still woodlands, especially around Stubhampton, and the number of roe deer is currently rising.

On the higher parts of the chalk ridge are many hillforts almost all of which are accessible, and which all give superb views. Hod is perhaps the finest, although many would prefer Maiden Castle. The north-east of the country is particularly rich in prehistoric remains, with Bokerly Dyke right on the boundary, a fine group of barrows at Oakley Down, and Knowlton, a Neolithic enclosure with a church in it. Many prehistoric fields and

ABOVE *The Market Place, Blandford Forum*

settlements were preserved on the downs, until they were ploughed, but a few still survive, and one at Ringsmoor, Turnworth is accessible.

A great variety of pretty villages are found in the valleys like the Piddles and in the shallow Tarrant valley. The best are Sydling St Nicholas, Cerne Abbas and Milton Abbas. The last is the famous model village built in the late 18th century after a small market town was removed to improve the park of the mansion. Ashmore is the exception to the valley rule: it is the highest village in the county at 700 ft up on the chalk ridge. This has led to suggestions that the village which relied on its famous pond for water, is of Roman origin. Be that as it may, it is very pretty.

There are many interesting churches in the area, ranging from fine later medieval ones like Bere Regis to charmers like Moreton where the 18th and 19th century church is completed by modern engraved glass of the highest quality.

The two main towns – Dorchester and Blandford – are in the river valleys. Both are interesting: Dorchester is smaller than one would expect from its status as county town, but it is handsome, with fine museums, and shopping streets where everything is still on a sensible, human scale. It seems surrounded by

RIGHT *The centre of Dorchester*

prehistoric earthworks — Maumbury, Maiden Castle and Poundbury still survive, and the line of the town's Roman walls can still be seen and walked. Blandford is simply one of the most beautiful Georgian towns in Britain, small scale but nearly perfect, rebuilt after a large fire in 1732, and is all brick apart from the church.

Thomas Gerard noted in the 1620s that in this area 'the Gentelmen's houses are seated' in the valleys 'for avoiding those sharpe blasts which this Southerne parte is subject to'. This is still true, and he might well have included the villages which equally avoid the wind-swept uplands. Four houses are open to the public in this area — Chettle, an early 18th century brick house; Athelhampton and Wolfeton, both fine stone houses developing from the 16th century, and Milton Abbey, a huge later 18th century mansion set in a lovely landscape.

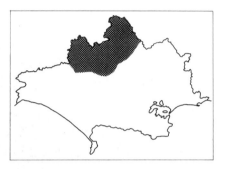

In 1906 Treves found this an enchanting and old-fashioned area, all small green fields and good hedges: 'everywhere there are cows, for the smell of cows is the incense of North Dorset' *(Highways and Byways)*. This remains true, and although all the hedgerow elms have been killed by disease there are still many oaks and good thick hedges. The fields still produce the proverbial patchwork effect, especially when seen from the chalk ridge to the south. A *Guide* of 1716 described it as 'Blakemore forest, once a place well wooded, as the Name imparts, but now almost naked'. The heavy clays of the vale were a

BLACKMORE VALE NORTH DORSET

Towns: Sherborne, Shaftesbury, Sturminster Newton.
Houses: Fiddleford and Sherborne New Castle ★ ★ ★; Sandford Orcas ★ ★ also Purse Caundle.
Villages: Okeford Fitzpaine, Trent and Yetminster and lots more listed in the Gazetteer.
Archaeology: Sherborne Old Castle ★ ★ ★
Walks: Belchalwell; Chedington; Fontmell Down; Duncliffe Hill; many footpaths shown on OS over the whole area.
Churches, Medieval: Sherborne ★ ★ ★ ★ Bradford Abbas; Marnhull; Trent; Yetminster ★ ★ ★;
17th century: Folke ★ ★ ★;
19th century: Sutton Waldron ★ ★ ★ ★.
Museums: Gillingham; Shaftesbury; Sherborne.
Other: Mills at Sturminster Newton ★ ★ ★; Melbury Abbas; Worldlife, Compton ★ ★ ★.

Sherborne, the Conduit and Abbey

The eastern edge of the Blackmore Vale from Shaftesbury, with St James in the foreground

medieval forest, preserved for hunting. Farming always existed too, and by the time Leland saw this 'flate vale of a greate compace environed withe high hills' in the 1530's it must have been very much as we see it today.

The vale, like the Marshwood Vale in west Dorset is a very much used domesticated countryside, nonethe less beautiful. The area is not completely flat — there are smallish hills like Duncliffe with its woodlands — but it does not have the quick changes of height found on most of the coast, in the west or on the chalk hills. The many winding narrow roads, thickly hedged, and a selection of good villages, make the area good for driving or cycling. Marnhull is a typically scattered village, albeit on a larger scale than most, and Okeford Fitzpaine, Trent, and Yetminster are more compressed, but equally attractive. Three of the finest manor houses in the county are in the north. Fiddleford is not lived in, and so is empty, but well worth seeing, while Purse Caundle and Sandford Orcas are still homes.

The only mansion in the north open to the public is Sherborne New Castle, an interesting mixture ranging from the late 16th to the 19th centuries. Close by are the ruins of the Old Castle, built in the early 12th century.

Sherborne and Shaftesbury are the two larger towns of the north. Sherborne is the prettiest town in the whole county, with a picturesque (but functioning) mixture of houses and shops, and in the centre the abbey church, Dorset's most beautiful church. Shaftesbury has a smaller list of attractions, but is rare in being a hill-town, with wonderful views. Sturminster Newton is small, with a pretty centre, and an interesting bustle on Mondays when its huge market is held.

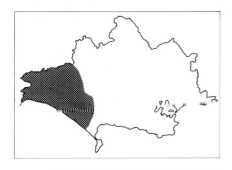

WEST DORSET

Towns: Lyme Regis, Charmouth, Beaminster, Bridport.
Houses: Forde Abbey (near Thorncombe) ★ ★ ★ ★; Parnham (near Beaminster) ★ ★ ★.
Gardens: Abbotsbury; Forde ★ ★ ★ ★; Horn Park and Mapperton ★ ★ ★; occasionally open Melbury House grounds.
Villages: Abbotsbury ★ ★ ★ ★; Evershot, Little Bredy, Melbury Osmund, Netherbury, Skoke Abbot, Whitchurch Canonicorum, all ★ ★ ★; Bride Valley see main map and Gazetteer.
Churches, Medieval: Abbotsbury; Beaminster, Whitchurch Canonicorum all ★ ★ ★; **17th-18th century:** Frampton ★ ★ ★; **19th century:** Bothenhampton; Fleet new church; Cattistock; Chideock, all ★ ★ ★.
Hillforts: Eggardon ★ ★ ★ ★; Pilsdon, Coney's Castle and Lambert's Castle ★ ★ ★.
Other Archaeology: Poor Lot (barrows) and stone circle Winterborne Abbas.
Walks: The Bride Valley; Chesil; Hardy's Monument; Kingcombe; The Spittles, the undercliff (both Lyme); Golden Cap and the rest of the coast each Wootton Fitzpaine footpaths in the Marshwood Vale. Too many to list.
Museums: Lyme Regis and Abbotsbury Tithe Barn ★ ★ ★; Bredy Farm, Burton Bradstock; Bridport; West Bay.

The west of the county is superbly diverse, with a coastline ranging from the bleak and private landscape of the Fleet behind Chesil Beach to the hump of Golden Cap and its dramatic sea-cliffs. Neither of the seaside towns is large — Lyme Regis is small and charming (if crowded in high season) and the even smaller Charmouth turns its back to the sea. The tiny West Bay is really an appendage to Bridport. Lyme and Charmouth are attractive, but Lyme is the more urban, larger and with a particularly good and varied seafront ranging from Regency cottages to the old harbour of the Cobb. The coast on either side of Lyme is as good as any part of Dorset's coast line, which is saying something. To the east the Spittles and Black Ven, and the great 5 mile run of the coast beyond Charmouth all belong to the National Trust and are superb, including Golden Cap with the highest cliffs on the south coast. Footpaths through all of this area give the most lovely coastal and inland views.

The Fleet, the strange partly salt-water lagoon behind the Chesil Beach, is a complete contrast. Only the eastern parts of the north shore are accessible, and then only via footpaths. The waters of the Fleet are calm, and the Chesil hides the sea. Combined with the small-scale hills inland the result is an unusual, rather monotonous landscape, which, however should be sampled, and is good for birds.

The village of Abbotsbury is just back from the west end of the Fleet and deservedly attracts thousands of visitors to see the stone-built village itself, the remains of the abbey, the abbey barn, the little chapel on the hill, the swannery and the sub-tropical gardens. The views from the hill above are good, and the eastward view from the road back over Portland and the Fleet are some of the finest in Dorset.

There are dozens of pretty villages inland, and only a few are mentioned here (see map and gazetteer for the rest). The Bride Valley is spectacular and charming, and deserves exploring from its head at Little Bredy down to the sea at Burton Bradstock. Close to the head of the valley is Hardy's Monument, with its famous views.

OPPOSITE *Lyme Regis and the Cobb*
RIGHT *Chesil and the Fleet, with Portland in the background*

Lewesdon Hill from Pilsdon Pen

On the edge of the chalk is Eggardon, perhaps the best of the Dorset hillforts, with stunning views across west Dorset. The inland towns are not large either – Bridport is a busy, handsome town, and Beaminster is so small and quiet that it seems a survival from an earlier age. Barnes famously admired the setting of the town 'Sweet Be'mi'ster, that bist abound / By green an' woody hills all round / Wi' hedges reachen up between / A thousan' vields o' zummer green'. The same effect on a much larger scale is given by the Marshwood Vale, enclosed by hills which give lovely views of the vale with its small well-hedged fields which seem always to be green. Three of the hills have Iron Age hillforts – Pilsdon Pen, the highest point in Dorset, Lambert's Castle and Coney's Castle, all of which belong to the National Trust. In the Marshwood Vale, and the hilly country to the east or west the roads are deep

Pilsdon Pen

and narrow, thickly hedged, and in the west even the main roads all give splendid views.

The two houses open to the public in the west are both gorgeous, and totally different. Parnham is a romantic large stone manor house, but Forde Abbey is a wonderful combination of bits of a medieval monastery mixed with superb quality mid-17th century alterations. Both must be visited.

As a total contrast the South Dorset Ridgeway offers a good high level walk, up on the chalk ridge, with hundreds of barrows.

Over the whole of the west are many small unspoilt and unselfconscious villages, and in the spring the roadsides are filled with flowers. Handsome stone cottages or farmhouses in the villages and amongst the fields. The west is a good area for walking, both along the coast and inland, and for driving or cycling because the views are constantly changing. Certainly off the main roads the lack of traffic makes cycling a pleasure even if there are lots of hills.

Gazetteer

ABBOTSBURY (H) A much-visited pretty picture-postcard village, all stone with lots of thatch. With the Swannery, the church and Abbey remains, the Abbey Barn Museum and the sub-tropical gardens, it is a good place to spend a day. Can be crowded in the high season.

Although set a little way back from the sea it was a fishing village, and traditionally on Old May Day the children of each boat crew made a garland of flowers which was taken out in the boats and thrown into the sea as an offering. The main street is of 17th and 18th century cottages in the local orange ochre limestone, some with dressed or carved stones robbed from the Abbey buildings. The centre has the school and other mock 'Gothic' buildings of the mid-19th century, and the Ilchester Arms, 18th century classical. On the street to the church is the Old Manor House with a pretty Elizabethan two-storied porch and just beyond a garden wall with 'trophies' of carved stonework taken from the Abbey. Modern cottages in local style and stone (some thatched) have been built, the largest area in Abbotsbury Glebe (1992-3), the eastern end of the village.

The Abbey buildings were mostly to the south of the church, but little remains today apart from the huge barn. Stubs of the outer gateway just south of the trophied wall, and further down the road is a 14th century inner gateway, adapted as a house. Beyond are the big pond and **Abbey Barn.** The thatched part is only half the original building which was 270 ft long, and dates from about 1400. It is one of the largest barns in England and now houses the Croker collection of agricultural bygones (fee:lists). The interior of the barn is even more impressive, with a simple 17th century roof and narrow windows. Half a dozen carts, and good thematic displays with lots of objects ★★★ .

Just above the barn is a pigeon house of such elaboration that it looks like a house.

The church of St Nicholas is the parish, not the abbey church. Inside it is high and light, with simple narrow 16th century

OPPOSITE St Catherine's Chapel, Abbotsbury
RIGHT Abbotsbury Church

pillars and rather domestic-looking clerestory windows of the same date above. The aisles fit oddly to the tower. In the south wall of the south aisle are strange round headed windows of the 16th century. The east window was obliterated in 1751 by a huge wooden reredos with splendid gilded Corinthian columns, jugs aloft and a table of commandments in the middle. Odd plaster vault of 1638 with strange angels and even some tortoises. Attractive early 17th century pulpit with sounding board. Most of the rest of the fittings date from the restoration of c 1885, apart from an 1808 curved gallery with 18th century Royal coat of arms. In the porch, the upper part of a shallowly carved effigy of an abbot of about 1200. Outside there are good gargoyles, and two medieval stone coffins with recesses for the head. Handsome 15th century tower, with an inscription just below the roof commemorating the restoration of 1808, and the doorway at the east end is dated 1638. In the graveyard on the south is a small part of a

wall of the Abbey church. From this point there is a good view of the Abbey barn, with Chesil Beach and the sea beyond, and up to St Catherine's Chapel. Below the church is the gable end wall of a monastic building of c 1500, standing alone.

On a bare hill to the south-west of the village is **St Catherine's Chapel,** well worth the 10 minutes climb to see, along with the views from the top. The hill is covered with strip lynchets. The small but monumental chapel was built by the Abbey in the late 14th century, and has an elaborate and unusual stone tunnel-vault. Here, one day a year, spinsters could pray for a husband: 'A husband, St Catherine;/A handsome one, St Catherine;/A rich one, St Catherine;/A nice one, St Catherine;/And soon, St Catherine!'

The chapel survived because it was useful as a sea-mark. From the top of the hill are splendid views back across the village, along the Fleet to Portland and west across Lyme Bay, with the Sub-Tropical Gardens in the foreground. Worth walking out in

ABOVE *The Abbey Barn, Abbotsbury*
BELOW *Abbotsbury*

St Catherine's Chapel from the churchyard

Portland. One of the best views in Dorset. Further along, beyond great trenches probably dug to extract ironstone, is Abbotsbury Castle, an Iron Age hillfort.

The Swannery is to the south of the village on the shores of the Fleet (fee: lists). A flock of 400-800 mute swans make their home here in the breeding season, and have done so since at least the 14th century. By 1716 it was described as 'a Curiosity which strangers often visit'. A remarkable experience to walk so close to the large birds on their nests, and to see the cygnets. They nest all over the place, even on the paths, on heaps of reed, and seem to do a lot of sitting about, even when off the nest. Small museum at the entrance, and a noticeboard explaining what the swans are up to. Around the Duck Decoy (a pond where ducks are attracted and then driven up traps or pipes, once used for food, now for ringing) are the reed beds, still cut and used for thatching in Abbotsbury.

★★★★ *Village, views, swannery, gardens. . .*
★★★ *Church and Tithe Barn Museum*

ADBER (A, near Trent) A small hamlet with no church, a few rather austere stone cottages and farm buildings, and good views over Somerset.

AFFPUDDLE (F) Small, down in the watermeadows close to the River Piddle, with forests and heath to the south. Some pleasant buildings, including the former vicarage of 1792. The medieval church of St Lawrence has a magnificent 15th century tower of flint and ashlar chequer work, with golden hamstone pinnacles,

front of the chapel as the view of the Fleet opens up. Several other walks around Abbotsbury are sign-posted from the village.

To the south-west of the village are the **Sub-Tropical Gardens,** 20 acres of enchanting woodland gardens. Being so close to the sea, and having shelter belts of evergreen oaks, the gardens are virtually frost free, so that many tender plants are grown, with unusual trees and shrubs. The whole valley is filled with trees of all sorts, including, in the lower part, mature oak. The garden is very good at all seasons, but breathtaking in the spring, with huge camellias and rhododendrons, and drifts of

daffodils in the orchard. Good in summer for old roses, and in the autumn for colour. Miles of winding walks, and a stream with ponds. Screaming peacocks (fee: lists). One of the four best gardens in Dorset.

Just down the road from the gardens is Chesil Beach (see entry) – a large hump of shingle with a good view along the beach. There are usually fishermen, and in storms the sea is terrifying. Currents can make the area dangerous for bathing.

The view from the top of the hill going west out of the village is stunning, with St Catherine's Chapel on its hill and Chesil with the Fleet behind stretching away to

Detail of the pulpit, Affpuddle

the mill, now interestingly converted to a house.

★★ *Church*

ALDERHOLT (C) in the heathlands which border the New Forest, was small and scattered until recently. Now modern houses fill the gaps between the 18th and 19th century small farmhouses and cottages. The area has never been good farming land so there was little medieval occupation. Lots of trees and wide verges. The centre is mostly early 20th century, and there was no church here until 1849. The nave of the church of St James is of that date, and odd, all brown heathstone with stepped gables and triangular-headed windows. The chancel is 1922. Inside it is rather barn-like, but with an elegant, austere pulpit.

South-west of Alderholt is Cranborne Common, a wet heathland reserve accessible by footpaths.

ALMER (F) A small low-lying hamlet, very flat and open. A row of trees leads up to the church of St Mary, small but with a heavy Norman doorway and north aisle, 14th century tower with the nave and porch rebuilt early in the 18th century possibly by the Bastards of Blandford. Almer Manor, glimpsed through the trees, is Elizabethan.

★ *Church*

ALTON PANCRAS (E) Runs alongside a little stream partly lined with thatched cottages with chalk hills running up on either side. The church has an odd dedication - to St Pancras. A common Dorset pattern - the main body of the church dating from 1875, and a 15th century tower. Two recent stained glass windows, one traditional in design 1956, the other 'modern' 1964 but both by Leonard Evetts. The manor house next to the church is 18th century, as are the gate piers through which the road to the church passes. Deer farm to the south.

ALWESTON, *see* **FOLKE**

ANDERSON (F) Noteworthy for the fine brick and stone manor house of 1620, barely visible from the road because of trees. The redundant church of St Michael was largely rebuilt in 1880. Pretty little valley.

ANSTY, *see* **MELCOMBE HORSEY**

ARNE (J) A tiny village in the middle of a large peninsula on the edge of the wildest part of Poole harbour. 1,200 acres of heathland area Nature Reserve, run by the RSPB. Only a part of the reserve is open to the public. Car park just south of the village, and a track leads to Shipstal Point, across

Dunlin, typical of the waders visible at Arne

gargoyles, and heraldic beasts on the lower stages. The body of the church is of a medley of dates from the 12th century up to the 1880's all combining harmoniously to produce a real 'village church' atmosphere. The large windows in the south of the nave and the chancel arch all *c* 1400. There are two late 12th century fonts — one from Turner's Puddle (see entry). Church treasures are the wooden fittings — pulpit and benches. The latter were restored in 1883, but retain much original work. An inscription on one records that 'Thes seatys were made yn the yere of owre lord god MCCCCCXLV' ie 1545. They have linenfold panelling and Renaissance foliage. The pulpit is rather more sophisticated, with figures, but of similar date. The screen between the aisle and nave is restored, but is basically 15th century, with modern painting. The reredos, the figures on the east chancel wall and the painted organ case are of 1952.

Behind the church is the River Piddle, and

Ashmore Pond

some of the very few fields of Arne, then through a wood and the heathland of the Reserve, to the shore of Poole Harbour, taking about ½ hour, longer if some of the well laid-out trails are followed. Well worth the walk for the marvellous views of Poole, across Long and Round Islands to Brownsea with the entrance to Poole Harbour beyond, and back landwards to Corfe Castle sitting in its gap in the chalk ridge. The many birds may best be watched from a public hide just north of Shipstal Point.

The little early 13th century church of St Nicholas is simple – and has no electricity. No tower, and the nave and chancel are one. Original lancer windows. From the altar window, the view is tremendous.

World of Toys (fee: lists). In the village. Small, but crammed with toys of all sorts from the 19th and 20th centuries. Musical boxes too. Worth seeing.★★

★★★ *For the views around Poole Harbour and the huge area of unspoilt heathland.*

ASHLEY CHASE (E) On the south side

of the Bride Valley, hidden by woods and only approachable on foot, are the remains of St Luke's Chapel, probably originally monastic, but now deserted and ruinous.

★ *Landscape*

ASHMORE (B) An isolated hill-top village high on the chalk, 700 feet above sea-level with woods around. It has been suggested that the large (75 yards across) pond at its centre is Roman in origin. This rarely dries out, and traditionally cakes were eaten in its bed whenever it did so. Now with dozens of predatory ducks, and a lovely Georgian rectory and 17th century cottage as a backdrop, which causes it to appear on many calendars. Despite this Ashmore is unspoilt and unselfconscious, with buildings of the 17th, 18th and 19th centuries, some of which (especially the early 19th century brick ones) are dated. Banded flint and brick Wesleyan chapel of 1855, slightly churchy looking. The church of St Nicholas was rebuilt in 1874, and has interesting 1930s corbels with carvings of hunting scenes, reflecting a way of life that once dominated all the villages in Cranborne Chase.

★★★ *Village, setting.*

ASKERSWELL (D) Not picturesque; stone cottages and farm buildings, mixed with too many bungalows. The tower of St Michael's church is 15th century, but the rest was rebuilt in 1858 (dated on the porch) and the fittings are all of that date except a fine 12th century font and a *c* 1320 stone which originally held a brass. Opposite is the village pound – an oval masonry enclosure used to 'pound' straying animals, whose owners had to pay a fine to get them back. A steep and gloriously overgrown footpath from the northern corner of the churchyard leads down to the village.

★★ *Landscape*

ATHELHAMPTON (E) A delightful late 15th and 16th century house with fine formal gardens (fee: lists).

The earliest part of the building is the hall and much altered service wing, started in 1493 by Sir William Martyn. The building has battlements, a two-storey porch and a graceful oriel window. Adjoining it is the west wing, in a totally different style, dating from 1525-50. A matching gatehouse was demolished in 1862. Behind the early house are imitation Tudor wings largely dating from 1895 and 1920. Inside the porch and at the end of the screens passage opposite are two original doors with wooden tracery. The spectacular hall roof is original, with all the timbers curving and moulded. The panelling, screen and gallery are mostly of the 15th and 16th century, but were brought here from elsewhere this century. The oriel window is as lovely inside as out, with delicate vaulting. The heraldic glass here and elsewhere in the hall is partly original. In the lower room of the west wing the ceiling is of c. 1900, and the 17th century panelling with eight portrait roundels of c. 1540 over the fireplace was placed here at a similar date. The best room upstairs is the State Bedroom, with a 15th century stone fireplace and 17th century panelling. The house is furnished throughout with a successfully eclectic variety of periods. Upstairs, there are some splendid 19th century pattern wallpapers. The east wing has been well restored after the bad fire of 1992. The formal gardens have vistas, walks, pools of all shapes and a great variety of shrubs, trees and plants, all laid out to such advantage that it is good at any season. Most of the design, the pavilions and walls date from the 1890's. To the west of the house is a wilder area, and a large 16th century circular dove-house. These were used from the medieval period to breed up pigeons for the table. The village is small, with a simple new church of 1861. To the east, off the bridleway, north, the ruins of Burleston church, now overgrown but soon to be restored.

★★★★ *Manor house and garden*

AVON FOREST PARK (G) Near Ringwood on the Dorset/Hampshire boundary, with good views east across the River Stour and south to Bournemouth from the car park at Matcham's. Woodland walks over about 500 acres from both that car park and another to the west, off Boundary Lane (run by Dorset County Council). Visitor Centre in the northern part, off the Wimborne – Ringwood road, and several marked trails.

★★★ *Walks, views.*

BADBURY RINGS (T) Iron Age hillfort belonging to the National Trust. Car park by the fort. The hilltop is defended by two ramparts close together, the outer of which encloses a barbican or defensive gate area on the west. Beyond these is a third, lower, outer rampart, probably a later Iron Age addition. The simple entrance on the west is probably original, but the direct route

ABOVE *Brick, stone and flint chequered cottages at Ashmore*
BELOW *Athelhampton, the hall*

cut through on the west is probably Roman. Although the fort does not give the high overview of the surrounding landscape which so many of the hillforts do, at 330ft it is as high as anything in the area, and in clear weather the Isle of Wight can be seen. The beech avenues leading to Kingston Lacy (see entry) are prominent. The fort was planted with Scots pine in 1761 to make it more prominent as a landmark, and these plantings are now being replaced by the National Trust. Good area of downland around the fort.

Badbury is close to the junction of two Roman roads. That from Dorchester to Old Sarum is seen running across to the west of the hillfort as a clear and large earthwork. To the north this crosses a north-south road which probably ran from Bath to Hamworthy (Poole). The earthwork of the road just clips past the hillfort, and in the angle between the fort and the continuation south-west of the road are the earthworks of a Roman settlement, probably the road station of *Vindocladia* named as being at a road junction hereabouts in the *Antonine Itinerary*. The three prominent barrows alongside the Roman road towards the south-west are probably Bronze Age. The history of the site after the end of the Roman period is obscure: we know it was used by an army in about 900, but this, like

ABOVE *The beech avenue, with Badbury Rings in the background on the right*
BELOW *Badbury Rings, showing the Roman road from Dorchester to Old Sarum running diagonally across the photograph, and, in the foreground, the crossing with the Bath to Hamworthy road*

the assembling of the Clubmen here in 1645 (see Hambledon) may merely be the very temporary use of an empty well-defended area. More romantically it has been suggested that it could be *Mons Badonicus* where we know from rather difficult to interpret Saxon written sources that the last of the Romans (or Romanised Celts) defeated the invading pagan Saxon hordes soon after 500 A.D., stopping their expansion apparently until as late as 650 A.D. The Romans (or Celts) may have been led by the legendary King Arthur. Ravens, magical birds always associated with Arthur, bred here until the late 19th century.

★★★★ *Hillfort*

BALLARD DOWN (K) Separates Studland and Swanage, and is worth ascending for the views of Swanage Bay on one side, and Poole Harbour and the coast to Bournemouth on the other. A path leads along the ridge all the way to Corfe (5 miles) or eastwards out to Ballard Point and Old Harry Rocks (see entry). The latter are more interesting from a distance: the walk along the cliffs from Ballard Point to Old Harry Rocks is rather dull. At the junction of the paths on top of Ballard Down is a large block of stone inscribed 'Rest and be thankful', and above Ulwell an obelisk commemorating the new water supply of 1892.

★★ *Landscape, walks.*

BATCOMBE (E) is a lovely overgrown combe surrounded by downs, with the village strung out along the little deep road. A few cottages, including a late 17th century one just north of the church, are built of clunch (hard chalk) and some of the monuments in the church are of the same material. The church is right in amongst the downs, with an excellent early 15th century tower with pinnacles and gargoyles. 'Conjuror' Minterne, a 17th century local squire and a 'white' witch, is supposed to have leapt over the tower on his horse, knocking one of the pinnacles off in the process. It has been replaced. Inside the tower are some rather crude but very effective memorials of the 16th-18th centuries. The nave and chancel arch are later 15th century, as is the nice stone screen (although considerably restored). The chancel was completely rebuilt in 1864.

At the side of the road running along the chalk ridge which overlooks the village is the Cross and Hand, an oval pillar

ABOVE *Batcombe from Batcombe Hill*
BELOW *The Cross and Hand, Batcombe*

29

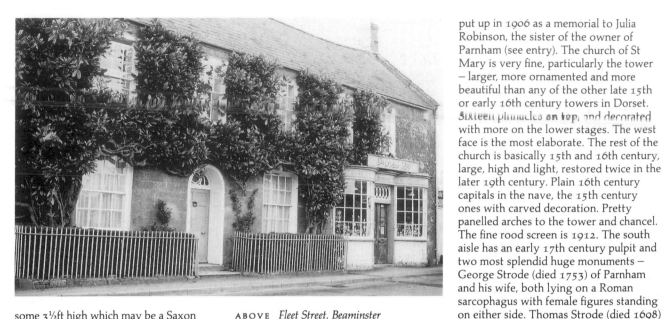

put up in 1906 as a memorial to Julia Robinson, the sister of the owner of Parnham (see entry). The church of St Mary is very fine, particularly the tower – larger, more ornamented and more beautiful than any of the other late 15th or early 16th century towers in Dorset. Sixteen pinnacles on top, and decorated with more on the lower stages. The west face is the most elaborate. The rest of the church is basically 15th and 16th century, large, high and light, restored twice in the later 19th century. Plain 16th century capitals in the nave, the 15th century ones with carved decoration. Pretty panelled arches to the tower and chancel. The fine rood screen is 1912. The south aisle has an early 17th century pulpit and two most splendid huge monuments – George Strode (died 1753) of Parnham and his wife, both lying on a Roman sarcophagus with female figures standing on either side. Thomas Strode (died 1698)

some 3½ft high which may be a Saxon boundary mark. The incised hand is not visible. Hardy's Tess swore never to tempt Alec again here, mistakenly thinking it was the remains of a cross. Just to the east is a picnic site with equally good views.

★★ *Landscape.*

BEAMINSTER (D)

Sweet Be'mister, that bist abound
By green an' woody hills all round,
Wi' hedges reachen up between
A thousan' vields o' zummer green,
Where elems' lofty heads do drow
Their sheädes vor haÿ-mäkers below

WILLIAM BARNES

This small town (pronounced Bemminster) does not figure largely in Hardy's novels, yet today it is the one place in Dorset where a good idea of the 19th century towns he wrote about, functioning as the centres for a large rural area, can be felt. The lack of recent development, the small friendly old-fashioned shops, and simply the scale of the place combine to make it a most attractive town to visit.

Virtually the whole town is built from local creamy orange limestone, and it is well worth exploring the side streets to see the handsome stone houses and cottages. A few 18th century houses have brick front walls. Many of the larger 17th and 18th century stone houses are in Whitcombe Road along with the Congregational Chapel of 1825. Fires in the town centre have left the Market Square with houses and shops of a mixture of dates. Several good shop fronts – the best is the late 18th century house and shop in Fleet Street. In the centre of the market square is 'Julia' a little market house

ABOVE *Fleet Street, Beaminster*
BELOW *Beaminster church*

Looking west from Belchalwell church

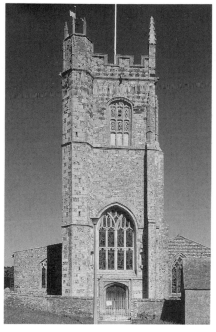

ABOVE *Bere Regis church*
BELOW *The roof, Bere Regis church*

stands proudly in a wig, and is more consciously classical. Lots of 19th century stained glass all around the church. In the north-west corner of the graveyard is a little almshouse of 1630, now the Strode Room. Two miles north of the town, on Buckham Down, is a picnic site with good views.

★★★ *Super town to visit; outstanding church.*

BEER HACKET (A) Very small, with some good stone cottages, and large industrial looking buildings by the railway. The small church of St Michael was mostly rebuilt in the later 19th century.

BELCHALWELL (F) A hamlet with lovely views, particularly from the knoll the church sits on – east to Hambledon Hill, south to the chalk escarpment and west into the Blackmore Vale. The church of St Aldhelm has a Norman doorway while most of the rest is 15th century altered in the late 18th century when the north aisle was rebuilt. The west arch of the aisle retains some original colouring. Pretty 17th century pulpit

★★ *Landscape.*

BERE REGIS (F) has an old fashioned main street, with most of the brick buildings dating from after a severe fire of 1788. Now by-passed, and recovering from having been part of the main road to the west. Attached at the west end is the picturesque hamlet of Shitterton, lots of thatch including a large 18th century

thatched brick farmhouse at the end of the road.

The church of St John the Baptist is one of the most visited parish churches in Dorset, with a stupendous wooden roof of *c.* 1475, easily the best in Dorset, and the tombs of the Turbervilles whom Hardy translated into D'Urbervilles for his *Tess*. Externally the church is remarkably pretty, with a 16th century tower in chequer work of flint and stone, perhaps the most attrac-tive in Dorset. The rest of the church is flint, limestone and brown heathstone in stripes, with the later 18th and 19th century repairs and additions in banded brick and flint. All the materials mix together well and demonstrate how far the church is from a good source of stone. Once inside, it is the roof of the nave which dominates – extraor-dinary, with huge carved figures of the Apostles at right angles, a vast head of a man on one boss, a structure of the greatest possible elaboration. The roof was prob-ably paid for by Cardinal John Morton, archbishop of Canterbury and chancellor to Henry VII. Morton was born in Bere Regis, and died in 1500 leaving

Tooth-ache, south arcade, Bere Regis

money for a chantry to be established in the church. He was described as wise and eloquent, but hard and haughty. The roof was restored and repainted in 1875. The same carver who then repaired this ceiling made the imitation one in the chancel. The 13 bench ends re-set in the backs of the Victorian seating are less obvious. One is dated 1547 and another is filled with the inscription 'ION DAV WARDEN OF THYS CHARYS'. The building history of the church is complicated. A tiny part of a church of about 1050 survives to the north east end of the nave, but the south arcade of *c.* 1160 is much more interesting, with chevron decoration, and heads of a monkey, kings, and other humans, two apparently with 12th century head-aches and another with tooth-ache. The eastern-most pillar has been rebuilt, but above it is a corbel with a little figure of a man in a cape, *c.* 1400. The arcade to the north aisle is later, *c.* 1200 and plain. The chancel is 15th century, with all the windows of that date except the east. The table tomb of 1596 is the only one in the church retaining its brasses — two kneeling figures, an inscription and a coat of arms. The north aisle is a medley of dates, with an early 16th century chapel at the east end, recently re-fitted. Set behind the altar as panelling, part of a 17th century pulpit. The decorative stained glass all around the church dates from the restoration of 1875. In the tower with its prettily panelled arch is the 12th century font, with interlacing arches and flowers. The south aisle is also a mixture of dates. The eastern-most window in the south wall is the Turberville window,

which John Turberville had built as his memorial (d. 1535) having been buried in one of his family's tombs. Both the 16th century Purbeck Marble tombs in this aisle were put up for Turbervilles and the glass in the window, although of 1875, contains their arms. Hardy's Tess and her family camped outside the Turberville window, building a tent from their furniture after they had been evicted from their cottage. Hanging in the porch are big iron hooks designed to pull burning thatch from roofs to prevent fire spreading.

The low wooded hill to the east of the town is Woodbury Hill, an Iron Age hillfort re-used from the early medieval period until the 1950's for a large fair.
★★★★ *Church.*

BETTISCOMBE (D) is a tiny hamlet on the northern side of the Marshwood Vale with a pretty little chert church (of St Stephen) rebuilt in 1862, re-using some medieval windows, and leaving the medieval tower almost intact. Hicks, the Dorchester architect, was the designer. Good high Victorian font and pulpit. Lovely landscape.

BINCOMBE (H) Tiny hamlet, mostly farms, one of which embraces the church. The rounded chalk hills rise behind giving it an enclosed feeling. Very clear strip lynchets. Almost all the buildings are in pale grey limestone, although more recent barns obtrude. The church door is dated 1799 inside. The church is a serene plain little building, mostly later medieval, with a rounded Norman chancel arch. The east wall and most of the fittings date from the restoration of 1862.
★★ *Landscape.*

Cornford Bridge, Bishop's Caundle

BINDON ABBEY, *see* **WOOL**
BINGHAM'S MELCOMBE, *see*
MELCOMBE HORSEY

BIRDSMOORGATE (D) A little settlement on the northern rim of the Marshwood Vale, with stunning views.
★★ *Landscape.*

BISHOP'S CAUNDLE (A) The main road runs smack through it, but there are several thatched cottages in the local limestone and a big farmyard. The church of St Peter and St Paul has a 15th century tower, and a nave of the same date partly rebuilt in 1864. The chancel is a good example of high Victorian taste, - carved stone reredos and elaborate candle-holder perhaps the best bits. On the north wall of the nave is a huge pompous memorial of 1815, and the Royal coat of arms of Charles II, dated 1661 (only a year after his restoration) and suitably inscribed 'Feare God, Honour the King'. The pulpit is very 1860's, but the handsome font is 15th century.

Almost a mile south of the village is the medieval Cornford Bridge, with niches for pedestrians to stand in.

BISHOP'S LIMEKILN (H) picnic place and car park on the road from Abbotsbury to Blackdown has superb coastal views round from St Catherine's Chapel, to Portland, and to White Nothe. Square stone 19th century lime-kiln in the corner of the car park, and a map showing walks to Abbotsbury hillfort (4-5 miles circular) and around the hillside above (2 miles).
★★ *Landscape.*

BLACKDOWN (H) is a tiny village with a small plain church of 1840 restored after a fire in the 1960's. Blackdown House (seen just along the road to Broadwindsor)

although much restored, is a large late 17th century house (the porch is dated 1679). The dormers are modern.

BLANDFORD FORUM (F) is the best, most complete, small Georgian town in England, with a superb setting. Water meadows all along the river, and to the south towards Bryanston a steep wooded slope known as The Cliff. Virtually the whole of the town centre, including the church, dates from 1732-60). Besides its architectural charm there are many interesting shops. 'Forum' does not mean there was a Roman town here: the 'market' part of its name was simple latinised.

Blandford's handsome buildings are the result of three factors. Three-quarters of the old town were destroyed by fire in 1731, and 480 families made homeless. Many towns suffered from disastrous fires when thatch was still common, but Blandford made much better use of the opportunity to rebuild than did most, because there was already a very capable firm in the town who combined the functions of builders, architects, joiners and much else (including funeral directors). Bastard & Co. consisted of two brothers, John and William, sons of Thomas Bastard who rebuilt Charlton Marshall (see entry) church in 1713. The brothers were appointed surveyors for the new town, built and designed some of the houses, the church and the town hall them-

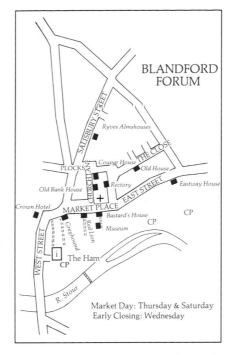

selves, and controlled, or at least influenced, the design of all the new build- ings. There has been little subsequent development to spoil their grand design. Most of the Georgian houses are of fine red brick, but variety is supplied by the stone town hall and church, the stucco of the Greyhound and the occasional use of bluish bricks.

ABOVE *The Red Lion and Greyhound, Blandford Forum.*
BELOW LEFT *The church and fire monument, Blandford Forum*
BELOW *The Town Hall, Blandford Forum*

Despite being built in rather dank greensand, the **church (St Peter and St Paul)** ★★★★ is an attractive plain classical building, with a more elaborate interior. It is not exactly as the Bastards intended it, nor indeed as they left it. They designed a steeple rather than the wooden cupola (which is contemporary) on the tower, but the most serious alteration is the chancel. Originally there was just a shallow apse, but in 1895 this was moved east and a chancel inserted. It matches well outside, but the interior is less happy. The gallery at the back of the church was added in 1794, and the organ is of the same date. The box pews have been shortened, but otherwise the fittings match the date of the church which was opened in 1739. The font has the air of a garden ornament, but the Mayor's chair (made by the Bastards in 1748) is very imposing. Like most Georgian churches, the interior is light, sophisticated and rather un-churchy.

Beyond the west of the church, in the market place, is the fire monument, looking like a miniature classical temple. It was designed by the Bastards and is dated 1760. The inscription records thanks to 'DIVINE MERCY, that has raised this Town, like the PHAENIX from it's Ashes, to it's present beautiful and flourishing State'. Above the churchyard are the Old Bank House and the triple-arched greensand entry to almshouses which have since been demolished. The Rectory at the other end of the path shows very clearly the partly glazed or vitrified bricks of which much of post-fire Blandford is built. The market place is all post-fire and survives remarkably well apart from the modern shop-fronts, the modern bank building west of the Town Hall and the 19th century stone bank opposite. The Bastard's own house (the Red Lion Inn) and the Greyhound are the best buildings in Blandford.

The present appearance of the large Crown Hotel, seen through the west end of the market place is neo-Georgian, as it was refaced in 1938. The side-streets are worth exploring. Coupar House in Church Lane is the most elaborate house, but fine post-fire buildings can be seen in Salisbury Street and East Street. A few buildings survived the fire, including the odd heavy brick-built Old House of about 1660 in The Close, and Ryves Almshouses of 1682 in Salisbury Street. The east end of East Street had been destroyed by fire in 1713, and new buildings there survived the great fire. The most attractive house, Eastway House, seems, however, to have been rebuilt about 1735. Behind the Bastard's House in the Market Place is Blandford Museum, with local history, archaeology etc. (Fee: lists).

In **Blandford Camp**, a large army camp to the north-east of the town, is the Royal Signals Museum. Free (lists). The museum covers the history of the army communications virtually up to the present day, including exhibits on the history of the regiments involved, much radio and telegraph equipment including the only surviving horsedrawn cable-laying wagon. Worth seeing.

BLANDFORD ST MARY (F) just over the river Stour from Blandford Forum, is dominated by the late 19th century buildings of the Hall & Woodhouse Brewery. Close to the river bridge is the impressive stone gateway to Bryanston (see entry) and a triangular green with older cottages. St Mary's church is in Lower Blandford St Mary cut off by the bypass. Mostly 19th century except the low 14th century tower. Pleasant flint and greensand chequering. Inside a fine monument to Francis Cartright (d. 1758) an architect/builder contemporary to the Bastards of Blandford. The scroll at the bottom of the monument shows the facade of Came House (built 1754) Winterborne Came, (see entry), near Dorchester, which he designed.
★ *Village.*

BLOXWORTH (F) An undulating wooded area with a few brick cottages and houses amongst modern development. The church of St Andrew must have been charming before the Victorians got at it. Its simple chancel was replaced by an over-elaborate, very serious one in 1870, with maroon Irish marble pillars, weak angels and so forth. It is wildly out of place and typical of the later Victorian equation of elaboration equals holiness. The rest is simple (although altered in 1870 – new pews etc.) 14th century tower, reset plain 12th century doorway, and most interestingly, a rebuilding in the later 17th century. The north wall of the nave, the Savage pew and the porch were built then, the south wall re-faced, and the simple wagon roofs put up. The shields of arms painted in the Strode pew are the same date, but the text on the tower wall is later 16th century. The 13th century font and the 18th century hour glass on the pulpit are virtually the only fittings which are not late Victorian. The Rev. Octavius Pickard-Cambridge who was responsible for the 19th century rebuilding was rector from 1868 until his death in 1917, and was a great authority on spiders, naming more than 800 new species and publishing *Spiders of Dorset*. Bloxworth House is a fine early 17th century brick house, occasionally open.

BOCKHAMPTON (E) Upper Bockhampton is a hamlet containing the cottage where Thomas Hardy was born in 1840, and where he lived for almost 30 years. The last part of the road to the cottage is closed to vehicles and the best approach is along a signposted path through deciduous woods from the car park (10 mins walk). The 66 acres of Thorncombe Woods and Black Heath are open to the public, with nature trails and good walks, which can be extended into the adjacent Puddletown Forest. The Roman road can be seen clearly running through the wood. Black Heath is the most westerly part of Hardy's Egdon Heath, and although small is a good place to see the contrast between the acid heather and birch covered heathland and the rich fertile river valley beyond. Heath originally extended right up to Hardy's cottage, but much of it is now covered with conifers. The cottage was built of traditional cob, brick and thatch by Hardy's great-grandfather in 1800 for his son. Thomas Hardy was born in the cottage in 1840 and lived there, walking the three miles to school and work in Dorchester daily until 1862, when he went to work in London. He returned to the cottage in 1867 and there wrote his first novel (never published). This was followed by *Desperate Remedies* (1871), *Under the Greenwood Tree* (1872) and *Far from the Madding Crowd* (1874) all written at the cottage and set in the immediate area. Hardy said that he found it 'a great advantage to be actually among the people described at the time of describing them'. He left the cottage in 1874 when he married, but was a frequent visitor, walking or cycling over from Max Gate until his death in 1928. Hardy recorded that his grandfather when living at the cottage helped smugglers. 'A whiplash across the window pane' warned him that tubs of brandy had been left outside and he took them in and stored them overnight. His wife made him stop, but even in Hardy's mother's time 'a large woman used to call, and ask if any of "it"was wanted cheap.' She was large because she had 'bullock's bladders' filled with spirits slung under her clothes. The cottage belongs to the National Trust and is open by appointment (fee: lists) and is well worth a visit, especially out of the busy summer season. The cool simple interior would be worth seeing even without the Hardy associations, as an example of an ordinary Dorset home of the 19th century. The outside of the cottage and the small garden are often accessible (lists).

Lower Bockhampton is a small hamlet by the river Frome, with the school (now a private house) which was the first that Thomas Hardy attended. Good walks west

ABOVE *Lower Bockhampton and the River Frome*
RIGHT *Bokerly Dyke looking north*

along the riverside path to Stinsford (½ mile) or on to Dorchester (1½ miles). The main A35 to the west of the Bockhampton turn runs through Yellowham Wood, still partly coppiced, and where the original of the keeper's house in *Under the Greenwood Tree* may be glimpsed. To the east a north-south road runs through Puddletown Forest, along Rhododendron Mile, in late May or early June ablaze with the mauve flowers of the bushes. It was deliberately laid out by the local estate, and originally entry was limited to those who were given tickets.

★★★★ *Upper Bockhampton, Hardy connection, landscape, walks.*

BOKERLY DYKE (C) is a defensive bank and ditch which runs for nearly four miles across the north-east corner of Dorset. Still impressive: originally the ditch was 5ft deeper, and the bank higher and steeper, and survives best to the south of the Roman road. Originally it extended to the north as well. The dyke was built early in the fourth century, and late in the same century was extended to block the Roman road. It runs across the chalk, an area which was probably open ground in the Roman period, while at each end is heavier ground which is wooded today, and was probably even more dense then, and therefore difficult for an army to traverse. The dyke must have been built by the Romano-Britons of Dorset as a defence against the

encroaching Saxons, and they seem to have been successful in keeping them out during the fifth and sixth centuries (see Badbury). Still the county boundary between Dorset and Hampshire, and best approached from the Hampshire side, where there is a car-park to the south of the main road for the Martin Down Nature Reserve. One can walk along the sinuous bank and ditch of the dyke for two miles in the reserve. To the north of the modern road is the Roman road from Badbury Rings to Old Sarum, showing as a clear earthwork. South west of the dyke the modern road follows the same line as the Roman.

★★★ *Landscape, archaeology.*

BOTHENHAMPTON (D) was a separate village, although it is so close to Bridport. There has been much modern expansion,

and even the old village street is somehow both austere and rather messy. Distinctive raised pavement along one side. The churches are interesting however. Right at the east end of the village are the chancel and tower of the old Holy Trinity. The little tower is 15th century and the chancel 14th century. The best feature is inside; a lovely oak reredos, and in fact a complete sanctuary – grey and white marble floor, altar rails and dado, of the early 18th century. The church is looked after by the Redundant Churches Fund and was beautifully restored in 1974. One cannot blame the parishioners for moving, because their new church at the other end of the village is so good and well worth seeing. From the outside it looks simple, if mannered, with no tower, only a little bell-cote. Inside is amazing: the nave has four stupendous parabolic stone arches rising from the floor

ABOVE *Bournemouth, looking east*   BELOW *Bournemouth, the central gardens*
LEFT *Bothenhampton new church*

almost to the ceiling, like huge wooden crucks. Designed by the well-known Arts and Crafts architect E. S. Prior in 1887, who used huge arches like these at his better-known church at Roker in County Durham, designed 15 years after Bothenhampton. The whole interior uses local materials in a simple, well-designed way (the iron screen of 1910 is a little fussy) and the east window by Christopher Whall (1895) fits in wonderfully. The simple roofs and bare walls combine with the overall design to produce a very lively, satisfying building. The gesso altar frontal (concealed under the cloth) has a lovely design of simple roses, and is an early work (1889) by the architect W. R. Lethaby. There is a slight but deliberate slope up to the chancel.

★★★ *The new church is well worth seeing for anyone interested in churches, or in 19th century architecture.*

BOURNEMOUTH (G) did not exist until 1810, when Lewis Tregonwell built a house at the mouth of the little River Bourne in the middle of the heathy wasteland between Christchurch and Poole. It was a haven for smugglers: in the late 18th century a man with a telescope saw from the school-room over Christchurch Priory a 'procession of twenty or thirty waggons loaded with kegs of spirits; an armed man sitting at the front and tail of each; and surrounded by a troop of two or three hundred horsemen' also carrying tubs, all coming from Hengistbury Head. 'The revenue troop were present, but with no other views and intentions, than those of perfect peace' since they were about to receive some of the tubs as a bribe. This was a regular route for smugglers.

Until the 1880s its growth was very slow. In 1856 Murray's *Guide* described 'the watering place of Bournemouth' as 'principally a creation of the last few years' consisting of 'an irregular cluster of villas scattered through the valley, the centre of which, a pretty fir wood, is laid out as a pleasure ground'. The pleasure ground is still there, and the pines (which are not natural but planted from the early 19th century) are now to be found all over the town. All the later 19th century guides refer to the softness of the air, filtered through the pine trees, and the mildness of the climate, which made the town an invalid's watering place, with the villas suitably secluded by trees. It was regarded as particularly suitable for those with tuberculosis, which is why Robert Louis Stevenson wrote *Kidnapped* whilst living in Alum Chine Road for three years from 1885, and why Aubrey Beardsley lived in the town from 1896-7, nearly dying of a haemorrhage in Boscombe Chine. After the railway arrived in 1870 (when the population was only 2,000) Bournemouth began to lose its exclusiveness. By 1881 the

population was 16,800, in 1911 it was 78,700 while at the last census there were more than 150,000 residents, and together with Christchurch the area had nearly one-half of the population of Dorset. (The other half of the population would probably still deny that the two towns are part of Dorset – they were moved from Hampshire in 1972). Bournemouth is the only city in the county, a vast conurbation with resort attached.

Today Bournemouth meets Poole from one direction and Christchurch from the other, whilst to the north and east the built-up area has engulfed several medieval villages such as Wick, Tuckton and Kinson and reaches nearly to Wimborne. The conurbation extends along the coast from Sandbanks on the west to Barton-on-Sea (Hants) in the east, 15 miles broken only by the still wild headland of Hengistbury (see entry). For modern holiday makers the attraction is the almost ten miles of sandy beach running from Hengistbury to Sandbanks, backed by a low sandy cliff for most of the distance. Cutting into the cliff and running back landwards are the chines,

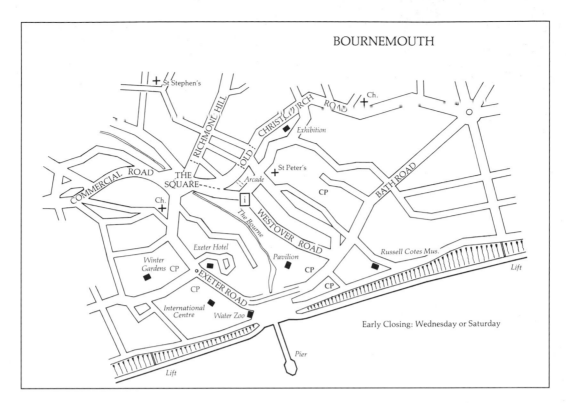

BOURNEMOUTH

Early Closing: Wednesday or Saturday

little ravines formed by small streams. The largest chine is that filled by Bournemouth itself. The others have been preserved from development, have paths and are full of trees. Bournemouth is famous for its sandy beach, smart shops, pretty gardens and pine trees. Recently it has become a business centre too, with huge new office blocks around the centre. Little remains of the original Victorian buildings of the town because there has been so much rebuilding, but many of the Victorian churches do survive. Two in the town centre – St Stephen's and St Peter's are of great interest, as is St Clement's in Boscombe. The Russell-Cotes Museum must be visited.

The best church in Bournemouth is **St Stephen's** (list) close to the centre. Sir John Betjeman said it was 'worth travelling 200 miles and being sick in the coach' to see the inside of this church, and even after that eulogy the building does not disappoint. Externally it has complex profiles, and the tower of 1907 which lacks its intended spire. Over the crossing in a little lead-covered spire flanked by little round towers with more spires. The whole church was designed by J. L. Pearson, one of the best later Victorian church architects, and this is one of his best works constructed from 1881-98. Inside, especially on a gloomy day when the dramatic sanctuary and colourful altar are spot-lit and the rest of the church illuminated only by flickering perpetual lights and votive candles,

it is a wonder. Not a huge church, but rich and stone-vaulted throughout. The two aisles either side add to the complexity, but the sanctuary is the climax, with shafts running everywhere. Beautifully placed triptych, and the whole sanctuary laced with wrought iron. The sanctuary and lady chapel floors are covered by costly marbles. The baptistry (of the 1890's) has an iron screen, marble font and superb oak cover. Good stained glass all round.

★★★★ *St Stephen's is a magnificently successful Gothic revival church, one of the two best in Dorset.*

St Peter's Church is also in the middle of Bournemouth, surrounded by enormous buildings, mostly 20th century. The original parish church of Bournemouth, built in the 1840's, was on this site, but nothing of it now remains. The present church (apart from the north aisle of 1851) was designed by G. E. Street from 1854-79, and was described in 1866 as one of the very best churches of that time. The pulpit was particularly admired— today it seems far too elaborate. Externally the tower and its spire, 202ft high, dominates, as does the chancel internally. From floor to ceiling it is rich, elaborate and expensive, with alabaster pillars, brass and iron screen, wonderful reredos and so forth. The south chapel has Morris glass in the little south window, and the rest of its decorations are 1907. The nave had painted decoration added in the 1870's. The whole church is a wonderful example of what the High

Church movement of the second half of the 19th century thought a church should be ★★★ . In the churchyard is a mortuary chapel and war memorial designed by Ninian Comper in 1925, and buried in the churchyard are Shelley's heart, his wife Mary Wollstonecraft Shelley (author of *Frankenstein* 1818) and her mother the feminist Mary Wollstonecraft Godwin author of *A Vindication of the Rights of Women* (1792). The memorial to Shelley intended for this church is in Christchurch Priory. His son lived at Boscombe.

Besides those already described there are more than twenty churches and perhaps nearly as many chapels in Bournemouth (including the wider area of Boscombe and so on) almost all dating from after the 1870's, and with the bulk 1880's to 1910's. Some are stone, and some brick and stone, but because of the limited date range there is not a great variety of styles. Only the more interesting ones are named here. St Michael and All Angels, Poole Road, has a good tower of 1900, with the body of the church dating from 1873. Nicely painted chancel inside. Charminster Road has two unusual and quirky churches opposite one another: St Alban stone, 1907, lined with brick inside and with a life-sized angel for font, and opposite the even odder Catholic church of the Annunciation, brick and stone, 1906 by Sir Giles Gilbert Scott with the central part raised up like an unfinished tower. St Francis further along Charminster Road is rendered, 1930s, in a

Bournemouth, the pier approach from the east about 1897

smoothed out Romanesque style. Pretty south doorway, with hall and vicarage to match the church.

On top of the cliff just to the east of the pier is the **Russell-Cotes Art Gallery and Museum.** The building was the home of Sir Merton and Lady Russell Cotes who gave the house and its contents to Bournemouth to be a museum in 1922. A strange late 19th century house of no particular style, all very richly fitted out (do visit the lavatories). The huge hall has a mosaic fish pond, and cases containing the variety of momentoes brought back from foreign parts by the owners. Upstairs is if anything even more overpowering: one cannot imagine writing anything in Sir Merton's study. Fascinating house, full of exactly the sort of collections one might expect: soap stone, Siamese ceremonial swords, lots of elaborate furniture and so on. Quantities of pictures, some very good. Outside there is a small garden. The new galleries are used to display temporary exhibitions and collections of ceramics etc. Outside on the terrace is a geological display. Must be visited to see both the house and collections (fee: lists) ★★★★ .

Because the short cliff is unstable the buildings of Bournemouth keep back from the sea, and so do not form a promenade. Either side of the pier cliff lifts (summer only) carry passengers up and down the cliff, and there are lots of zig-zags or steps for the more energetic. The view of Purbeck from the beach is lovely. Next to the pier is **Water Zoo** (fee: lists). Right in the centre on the cliff top are the Bournemouth International Centre (1984) and the pier (mostly recent). Neither of these, nor the Pavilion (1920s) a little way back in the Central Gardens, are pretty. The gardens are, although at the lower end they are extremely formal, with the River Bourne carefully restrained to a concrete bed, and all the fine turf protected behind railings. Good plantings of pine trees (and some squirrels), and these continue in the Central Gardens beyond the square (actually a roundabout). Meyrick Gardens are large and wooded, with many sports. The town centre runs from the square, and has little to do with the sea. The main shopping streets are Westover Road, Commercial Road and Old Christchurch Road, where there are many later 19th century buildings surviving above shop level, some with awful half timbering. A glass roofed arcade of *c.* 1870 leads to Gervis Place (another, much more elaborate and 1890's, in Boscombe). **Bournemouth Expo Centre,** Old Christchurch Lane has changing historical exhibitions.

Encased in the turreted Royal Exeter Hotel, Exeter Road, is the remains of the first house in Bournemouth, built by Lewis Tregonwell about 1810. The south-west part is the original, and the rest 1870's and 1880's. In and around the south end of Tregonwell Road, to the west, are other buildings with high pitched roofs, decorated barge boards and plain window surrounds which show what the buildings of Bournemouth looked like before the great expansion of the 1880's and 1890's.

The Russell-Cotes Museum, 1920

Durleston Court Hotel, Gervis Road has a plaque recording an unexpected resident - the comedian Tony Hancock (1924-68) lived there as a boy. His father owned the hotel.

The site of St Peter's School, **Southbourne,** to the west of Hengistbury was where C. S. Rolls of Rolls-Royce was killed in a flying accident in 1910, at an aviation meeting which was part of Bournemouth's centenary celebrations. He was the first pilot to be killed in Britain.

Boscombe developed from the middle of the 19th century. From 1851 Sir Percy

Florence Shelley (the son of the poet) lived in the manor house, which has a small museum devoted to Shelley housed in part of the building, the rest of which is the Art School. (Fee: lists). Amongst the houses and hotels on the cliff top road beside the sea is Shell House with an amazing shell garden. From 1808, with the discovery of a mineral spring, attempts were made to turn Boscombe into a spa. At the bottom of the chine is Boscombe pier rebuilt in the 1950's (fee). The rest of the little seafront is uniformly late Victorian. Tucked back from the main road of Boscombe is the brick church of Corpus Christi, 1880's with an odd tower of 1932. The finest church in Boscombe is St Clement's, St Clement's Road, designed by J.D. Sedding in 1871, and the tower added in 1890. The tower is pretty, with an unusual top, and the west side has a large window with very unusual Art Nouveau tracery. Fine quality High Church fittings of the late 19th century, include the brass lectern, the lady chapel altar and especially the huge stone reredos. Good glass in the west window.
★★★ *Church.*

Talbot village, to the north-west of Bournemouth is a series of plain but pretty 1830's style houses laid out along the main road as a model village for the labouring classes by the wealthy Miss Georgina Charlotte Talbot from 1835 until 1860. In the middle is the church of St. Mark, built in c. 1870 after Miss Talbot's death, with a pretty tower and a large 1980's extension at the back. Huge graveyard. Until recently this was an isolated settlement, but it is now enclosed by development. Bournemouth University (founded 1992) is close by.

BOURTON (A) is the most northerly parish in Dorset, with Wiltshire to the east and Somerset to the west. Much modern development, but scattered about the parish are quite a few late 18th or early 19th century small stone houses, resulting from the prosperity brought by the linen weaving industry which flourished here at that time. One of the mills survives on the River Stour nearly enclosed by more recent buildings. The church of St George is of 1878 with an attractive tower of 1903-6. 1992 stone in centre commemorates the opening of the bypass.

BOVERIDGE (C) is a tiny hamlet, in thick woodlands east of Cranborne. The little church of St Aldhelm is now a house. It was built in an odd Georgian style in 1838, of banded brick and flint.

BOVINGTON (F) has been used by the

Tanks from Bovington on the East Lulworth range

military since the First World War, and is now a huge army camp, surrounded by heathland scarred with tank tracks. The home of the Royal Armoured Corps, and the very popular Tank Museum (fee: lists). Almost 150 tanks and other armoured vehicles, including the first tank ever made, 'little Willie' of 1915. Besides complete vehicles there are shells, engines, guns, wireless sets and so forth, with displays of uniforms, medals and memorabilia of T. E. Lawrence who was stationed at Bovington (see Cloud's Hill). Also videos (of tanks). Fascinating to anyone interested in military history, and to children. The tanks used today can sometimes be seen from the public viewing enclosure at East Lulworth (south of the road from East to West Lutworth): notices at the Museum explain when this is possible.
★★★★ *Tank Museum.*

BOWLEAZE COVE (H) East of Weymouth and partly wild, partly seaside development, all small-scale and dominated by the long white vaguely Spanish building of Pontin's holiday camp. Many caravans, an amusement complex, cafe and so forth. The low clay cliff slips are ugly, but from the top of Furzy cliff are good views east to Redcliff Point, and west all round Weymouth Bay and Portland. On the top of the hill behind the houses the footings of a little Roman temple are preserved. This is Jordan Hill, and the river which borders the caravan sites is the River Jordan. From the temple is a good view north to the chalk lump of the Ridgeway.

BRADFORD ABBAS (A) A large village, mostly modern, but with a street of pleasant older houses running along in front of the church and down to the River Yeo. The church of St Mary is one of the most beautiful in north Dorset, particularly

Reconstruction of Roman Temple, Jordan Hill, Bowleaze Cove

externally where it is almost all of the 15th century, heavily battlemented and with very attractive windows. The tower is superb, with rounded corners, and, on the west side 11 niches, two still containing the original figures. The wooden door is dated 1717. Nearby is the battered base of a 15th century cross. Towards the eastern end of the handsome south front is an extremely pretty and unusual little porch and priest's doorway. Inside the church is less pleasing, mostly because in 1890 all the plaster was removed from the walls and the stone grouted with horrible dark grey mortar. However, apart from the 19th century chancel arch and organ chamber, virtually all the church is 15th century with characteristic windows and clustered plain pillars. Many fittings of this date survive as well. The bench ends (with 19th century benches) are excellent, especially those with poppy-heads and lively carved foliage made up into a reader's desk close to the stone screen. Even the main door is 15th century, with 17th century iron fittings. Between the chancel and the south vestry is a lovely deeply panelled arch, inset with a little doorway. Fine tracery in the glass-less window between the south chapel and vestry. The roofs have been much restored, but many of the angels in the nave are original, and the tower roof *(cont p.42)*

Archaeology

'The early history of Dorsetshire is vague, and unsatisfactory'. Written in 1803 this defines 18th century knowledge of a county which is covered with archaeological remains. A hundred years later a guide is prepared to say 'The remnants of primitive antiquity in this county are numerous and definite'; a great advance, although the understanding (and even dating) of the remnants still had a long way to go. We now know very much more, particularly with dating, but often it is only enough to make us wish we knew more. As Hardy wrote when he published the Roman burials he discovered when building Max Gate on the outskirts of Dorchester 'what kind of object did Dorchester form in the summer landscape? . . . how did the roofs group themselves, what were the gardens like, if any, what social characteristics had the streets, what were the customary noises?' We still cannot answer all of these questions.

We know when the town was started, lots about its defences, something of its streets, houses and public buildings, and from the cemeteries about the town we have the remains of the people themselves. Even drawing in parallels from written sources or evidence from elsewhere in the Roman empire, it is impossible to understand their lives. If Roman Dorset is another country (and a little visited distant one at that), the prehistoric period is worse, even more misty and remote.

However, Dorset is a very good county to see many types of remains left to us by our prehistoric forebears and this description is mostly limited to the more visible and visitable. The earliest people, the Paleolithic hunters and the succeeding Mesolithic hunter-gatherers, have left no monuments, only their flint implements, now to be seen in museums. With the succeeding age, the Neolithic, starting about 4,000 BC, comes farming, and in Dorset a good many substantial earthworks, some of which still survive. The most prominent are *long barrows*, used for the burial of parts of a number of people; *henge monuments* - circular earthworks with the ditch inside, probably for ritual use and the *Dorset Cursus* a strange six mile long monument, on the southern edge of

The Shapwick barrow being excavated in 1838

The Dorset Cursus, with ploughed out barrows foreground

Cranborne Chase, originally two banks and ditches about 100 yards apart, now mostly ploughed out.

Although the introduction of bronze may not have had the decisive effect on life suggested by naming the succeeding Bronze Age after it, it is this period (roughly 2,000-800 BC) which has left the uplands of Dorset littered with round barrows, where the dead were buried either as cremations in pots, or as inhumations. It seems likely that some at least of the small square fields known as Celtic date from this period.

The Iron Age produced the most visitable monuments in Dorset – the spectacular hillforts, of which there are 30 in the county. Some at least were occupied like towns: in the account of the Roman invasion given by Suetonius in his life of Vespasian (one of the Roman commanders of the invasion, and later Emperor) we are told that in the south Vespasian captured more than twenty *oppida*, and although that is not the Roman word for properly civilised towns such as they had at home, it certainly has urban overtones.

Many of these *oppida* must have been the hillforts of Dorset: we know that Maiden Castle and Hod were taken at this time because they have been excavated and evidence found. Hillforts were not the only type of Iron Age settlement – there were also open farms, and other smaller, simpler enclosures, but hillforts are the most prominent. Many of the so-called Celtic fields, now seen as small square earthworks, date from

Hod Hill, Iron Age hillfort with the Roman fort in the corner

this period. They only survive on the uplands, particularly the chalk, and although they probably existed elsewhere on the better, lower lands they have been obliterated by the succeeding two thousand years of agriculture.

If Iron Age Britain was anything like the life of the Celts on the Continent described by contemporary Roman writers they were brave, fierce, and warlike, and barbarous. Certainly the very construction of the hillforts suggests that society was not peaceful.

After the Roman invasion all the hillforts were deserted, and gradually the Iron Age inhabitants became Romanised, accustomed to living in towns and paying taxes. Many people still farmed the land of Dorset of course, and some small settlements changed little. Instead of hillforts the major legacy from the Romans are their roads, designed to make quick communication possible. Two of these in Dorset are still used by modern roads — three miles west of Dorchester the A35 turns to the south after following the Roman route, but the Roman road can be seen continuing straight on high on the ridge, as a minor road, up to the edge of the uplands near Eggardon. It continues on west but the exact route is lost in the valleys. The Roman road north from Dorchester is now (from Stratton) the A37, and this route also runs along the ridge. Ackling Dyke is found just to the east of Dorchester on the heath above Hardy's cottage, and crosses another Roman road close to Badbury Rings. These eastern roads are not used for the routes of modern roads, but survive patchily as earthworks, boundaries and minor roads. Ackling Dyke is particularly clear in the northern part of the county, and is perhaps best seen around Bokerly Dyke. This earthwork was probably built on either side of the Roman road in the fourth century, to defend it.

The Roman fort at Hod Hill, and the temples on Maiden Castle and Jordan Hill, Preston (Weymouth) are worth visiting, as is the Cerne Giant, which may or may not be Roman. Dorchester has not only the Roman defences and the footings of a town house, but also Maumbury, a prehistoric henge adapted as an ampitheatre by the Romans, and an aqueduct (virtually a ditch) 12 miles long which brought water to the town.

By 410 AD all the Roman army had left Britain, and the towns were told to look to their own defences against the barbarians (in Britain's case mostly Saxon) who were attacking the whole of the northern part of the Roman empire.

Sites to visit

Neolithic: *Henge monuments* - Maumbury (Dorchester), Knowlton; *Long barrows:* Ridgway, Pimperne, Grey Mare and her Colts (Kingston Russell); and Dorset Cursus.
Bronze Age: *Barrows:* Ridgeway, Poor Lot (Winterborne Abbas) and Oakley Down. *Stone circles:* Kingston Russell and Winterborne Abbas.
Iron Age: *Hillforts:* Abbotsbury, Badbury, Coney's Castle, Eggardon, Flower's Barrow (Tyneham), Hambledon, Hod Hill, Lambert's Castle, Maiden Castle, Poundbury (Dorchester), Pilsdon and Rawlsbury, Bulbarrow. *Promontory Fort:* Hengistbury.
Roman: *Temples:* Jordan Hill (Bowleaze Cove) and Maiden Castle; Dorchester; The Walks and Wall, Maumbury, Town house, and the aqueduct. *Fort:* Hod Hill. *Roads:* Thorncombe Woods (Bockhampton), Bokerly Dyke, Badbury Rings, A35 west of Dorchester, see OS 1:50,000 for routes. *Other:* Bokerly Dyke; Cerne Giant, Cerne Abbas.

The War Cemetery, Maiden Castle. Two Iron Age men killed fighting the Romans, one with a Roman arrow-head in his spine. In Dorset County Museum.

Bradford Abbas

Briantspuddle war memorial with Bladen Valley behind

has deep moulded beams. The 15th century stone font is of superb quality, with a bishop at each corner, and the pulpit is also pretty, and dated 1632. Crude, possibly medieval, chest with three locks.
★★★ *Village, church.*

BRADFORD PEVERELL (E). Pleasant small village. John Hutchins, the county historian, was born here in 1698. St Mary's church is all of 1850, designed by Decimus Burton in a 13th-14th century style. The spire looks elegant across the water-meadows. New Barn Centre, 1½ miles to the south along a bad track, has reproduction Iron Age round houses and small displays on the Celts.

BRADPOLE (D) now joins up with Bridport. Prettily set on small hills, with older cottages in the lower part. A plaque where Lee Lane meets the main road records Charles II's flight following the Battle of Worcester and his failure to find a boat at Charmouth. The church of Holy Trinity was completely rebuilt in 1845-6 in Early English style. The very odd spire was added in 1863.

BRIANTSPUDDLE (F) has no church (and is really part of Affpuddle) but this picturesque, but unusual village, has 16th-19th century thatched cottages interspersed with others from the early 20th century. Sir Ernest Debenham bought four farms in the area, and from 1919 to 1932 built model farm buildings and some 40-50 cottages, all in an 'Arts and Crafts' style. The most characteristic part is Bladen Valley, to the west of the main village – huge elaborate thatched cottages on either

side of a wide road in a park-like setting (the whole development was intended to turn at the end and return to the main road). At the entrance is a unusual war memorial by Eric Gill – a tall thin, smooth, pillar with figures of the Virgin and Child, and Christ with a reversed sword. In the village itself there are more 1920's cottages – the large building with louvres in the roof in the middle was the power and pump-house and on the road to Turner's Puddle (see entry) is a splendidly odd block, the Ring, originally the Central Dairy, where the milk from the model farms was processed. Opposite, much altered, is Cruck Cottage a 15th century cruck building. Sir Ernest Debenham was trying to reverse the flight from the land, and to prove that the country could produce all its own food. His cottages were huge – only couples with no children were allowed to live in 2-bedroom cottages. Bricks were produced on the estate, and concrete blocks made from the waste from the gravel pits (see also Milborne St Andrew).

Just south-west of the village is **Culpepper's Dish**, the largest of hundreds of swallow holes in this area on the edge of the chalk, probably resulting from acidic water produced by the heathland eating away the chalk. 100 yards across and very steep, more than 40ft deep, hiding full-grown trees. Opposite is a Forestry Commission car park and picnic spot which has fine views.
★★ *Village.*

BRIDE VALLEY (E-D) running from below Hardy's Monument (see entry) down to the sea at Burton Bradstock is

beautiful, and makes a lovely journey at any time of the year, with charming villages all along its length. See Burton Bradstock, Chalcombe, Little Bredy, Litton Cheney, Long Bredy, Puncknowle, Swyre.
★★★★ *Landscape.*

BRIDPORT (D) Prominent small hills surround the town. *Pinnocks' County History* of 1820 says: 'the general appearance of Bridport is respectable, the principal streets are broad and spacious, and the centre of the town is adorned by a handsome market house and town hall'. Today it is much the same, an interesting market town, rather old-fashioned, where chapels out-number churches, and the Georgian Town Hall is neatly placed to catch the eye (but almost to block the road). The back streets of the town are also picturesque, and there are dozens of alleyways, all worth exploring. Bridport was a small town by 1086, and in the 13th century the rope industry was established. This has remained the staple trade to the present day, with its most prosperous period in the 18th and early 19th centuries, the date of most of the town's buildings. Rope was originally made in long 'walks' which extended from the back of the houses, but later production became centralised in mills. Net-making was also undertaken and still continues, although many of today's products are in artificial fibres rather than the traditional hemp or flax. An old saying is 'to be stabbed with a Bridport dagger' i.e. hanged. The three main streets are solid with attractive 18th and 19th century buildings – houses in much of South Street, and a mixture of shops and houses in West and East Streets.

The Bride Valley from Portesham Hill

All three main streets swell towards the centre to make room for the market. At the south end of South Street is a strange stone building – the Chantry, looking like a fortified house, and dating from the 14th/15th century, with an original doorway to the two-storey porch (occasionally open, information from Bridport Museum). Nearby is the Quaker meeting house and almshouses, domestic looking stone buildings of the 17th and 18th centuries, with modern alterations.

The church of St Mary is mostly medieval, with additions of 1860, when John Hicks (the architect Hardy worked for) added 2 bays on the west end, and entirely rebuilt the chancel with its chapels. The church is full of rather heavy woodwork of 1860, and powerful, highly coloured glass of the later 19th or early 20th century. Overpowering Caen stone pulpit 1860. However the main part of the church is medieval – the earliest parts are the 13th century transepts, with huge (restored) 15th century windows. The central tower of 1400 produces a good crossing inside, with lovely slender pillars. Outside the whole yellow-orange hamstone church looks fine, especially the tower and porch (c. 1400), and it forms a charming group with the massive late 19th century Sunday School and church hall to the north.

Much further up South Street, past lots of small good 18th and 19th century houses, is the **Museum,** (fee: lists) an early 16th century stone house, with displays on the history of the town, rural bygones, local archaeology, ropemaking and netting etc. Set back from the street, nearby is the imposing Wesleyan Methodist Chapel of 1838, now the Arts Centre. At the junction of the three streets the Town Hall of 1785-6, with a fine clock tower and cupola of 1805. Opposite, in East Street is a beautiful 18th century shop front (late Beach and Barnicott) with 19th century scrolls and board above. Further along East Street is a rather odd United Reformed Church of 1859, with prominent porches either side, Opposite (on the north side of the street) is a very much more restrained chapel – the Unitarian of 1794, set back from the street. Beside it is the impressive ashlar Literary and Scientific Institute of 1834, now the (much duller-sounding) Public Library. West Street is well worth walking down too, and has a super conversion of a 19th century mill building at the end. Just before that is a large ivy-covered building, once a rope factory but now offices.

The Chantry, South Street, Bridport

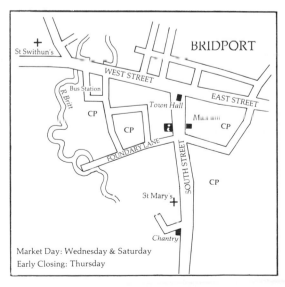

Market Day: Wednesday & Saturday
Early Closing: Thursday

South Street, Bridport

Looking up West Street, Bridport

Allington, at the extreme west end of the town, has the classical church of St Swithun, 'rebuilt and enlarged in the year 1827' (inscription on gallery). Big plain columns on the portico, and a plain attractive interior, like a chapel. Many modern fittings.

BROADMAYNE (H) Mostly on a main road, and although it retains some good cottages it is not picturesque. One of the cottages just behind the main road west of the cross-roads is dated 1732 and of brick -- rare so early in Dorset. The bricks are probably from the local kilns. The church of St Martin is unusual in having a south tower. Very plain –the lower part is 13th century and the top *c.* 1500. Inside, the church is heavily restored – the whole north part was rebuilt in 1865-6 by John Hicks of Dorchester for whom Hardy worked. The rather anaemic 1856 angels around the church were described at the time as having 'very striking' expressions on their faces.

BROADOAK (D) does have a lot of oak trees. Only a few farms and cottages in the Marshwood Vale with a little chapel-like stone church of 1865. Pretty area. Not to be muddled with the village of the same name in the centre of the county.

BROAD OAK (B) sits on a small hill near Sturminster Newton, a mixture of mostly 19th and 20th century buildings, with a small church of 1866. There really are oak woods to the east of the village.

BROADSTONE (F) Now virtually part of Poole, with modern development stretching over what was heathland. A few Victorian brick cottages in the middle, and still lots of trees. White brick church of 1888.

BROADWEY (H) is largely along the main road to Weymouth, but the more attractive part is Mill Street, leading down from the church to the river and Watery Lane beyond. Most of the buildings there are of pale local limestone, and the mill (18th century, heightened in 1846) is linked to the building opposite by a wooden bridge. The church of St Nicholas is entirely of the 19th century, with re-set Norman bits – main doorway, two good head corbels and the rather plain font. Apart from the Jacobean pulpit everything else is 19th century – and are as one would expect, but the attractive and complex imitation Norman chancel is unusual for its date – 1874. Imitation Norman was not fashionable then, and must have been designed to complement the real Norman doorway.

BROADWINDSOR (D) Large village with a strangely empty small square at its centre, which seems little changed since the 19th century. Some nice stone buildings,

Broadwindsor from the west

including a cottage with an inscription recording 'Charles the second slept here' in 1651 as a fugitive. He only escaped detection by a troop of soldiers because one of their camp followers gave birth to a child that night. The church of St John the Baptist is large and light. Although attractive, most of it dates from a severe restoration in 1868. The 15th century tower survived, and quantities of material from the old church were re-used. Good benefactor boards of 1795 and 1839, and the pretty carved panels with their surround on the pulpit are 16th century (the rest is modern). The super rather modern looking carved doors to the tower are of 1885, in memory of the vicar who rebuilt the church. Font *c.* 1200. Big primitive paintings of two prophets (17th century). From 1634-50 the Royalist poet and author Thomas Fuller, author of *A History of the Worthies of England*, was rector here, but in 1650 he was replaced by a presbyterian, John Pinney. Pinney and a wandering Anabaptist had a strange competition –

Brownsea Island with Sandbanks

a preaching match in a field close to the village, both preaching extempore on given texts. Pinney won. Just to the east, Broadwindsor Craft Centre, with interesting new 'vernacular' housing around it.

★★ *Village, church.*

BROWNSEA ISLAND (K) The largest island in Poole harbour, now belonging to the National Trust. Open all summer (April-Sept inclusive) and very easy to get to, with boats running from Sandbanks (next to the chain ferry) and from Poole Quay about every half hour from 10.00 a.m. The last boat off the island is 5.00 p.m. (ferry and landing fee: lists). The island, which is about 1½ miles long and less across, has had a colourful history from the time Henry VIII built a blockhouse here in 1545-7 as part of his coastal defences (see Portland Castle). In the 17th century copperas, used for dyeing, was produced on the island, and during the 18th century the blockhouse was transformed into an imitation Castle, and quantities of trees planted. A crenellated coastguard station was built in 1842 (now the tea-rooms). In 1852 a Colonel Waugh bought the island and made many changes, setting up a large scale pottery on the south side of the island to produce drainage and sewage pipes, and terracotta. He rebuilt the church, completed the reclamation of St. Andrew's Bay, refronted the castle and built the Family Pier. During his time the population of the

Brownsea Island, the Castle

island increased from 12 to 200. His bankruptcy in 1857 was hastened by his wife. When alone at the Castle she saw a boat approaching containing the Corporation of Poole (men who were also the local tradesmen). They were coming to ask Col. Waugh if he would be their parliamentary candidate but being deaf she could not understand them and shouted 'Only give us time and we will pay'. The next owner was a collector who embellished the church, Cavendish Bentink. The pottery ceased production in 1887. Although the castle burnt to a shell in 1896, it was reconstructed by 1901 and was bought by Mr. van Raalte, who entertained lavishly there. About 1910 a new industry started –

growing daffodils for sale as cut flowers. From 1927-1961 the island was owned by Mrs Bonham-Christie, who was virtually a recluse and who let the island become a wilderness. Two thirds of the island was burnt in 1934. On her death it was bought by the National Trust.

The best view of the buildings, all of them crenellated in fanciful mock-castle manner, is from the sea. Henry VIII's blockhouse is totally enclosed by the additions of the 18th and 19th centuries (Castle not open). The church of St Mary, a little way inland, has a pretty green in front of it: in the Edwardian period this was a golf course. The church, totally rebuilt in 1853-4, is pleasant, but dominated by its fittings. Cavendish Bentinck, owner of the island in the 1880's and 90's, embellished it with 16th century English panelling in the chancel, tower and chapel, and put up the wooden ceiling of about 1490 in the tower (itself the private family pew). The south chapel is filled by the recumbent effigy of Charles van Raalte, another owner of the island who died in 1907. Many of the other fittings in this very Victorian medley of the tower are 16th or 17th century Flemish (except the Victorian domestic-looking fireplace which has some old wood). The chancel is very Victorian too, with dark ceiling, altar with lots of different marbles, inscriptions and gaudy stained glass. Cavendish Bentinck is buried outside beneath a very classy Venetian well-head.

One can walk all round the southern part of the island, with lovely views over Poole Harbour, completely undeveloped on this side, in signal contrast to the north overlooking Poole, Parkstone, Sandbanks and so forth. The whole of the north of the island is a Dorset Trust for Nature Conservation reserve, around which there are guided tours every afternoon in July and August (other months check). The island is rich in wild-life – in the reserve is a large heronry, and many other species of bird, particularly waders, ducks and terns. A great varietyof habitats – mudflats, reed-beds, lakes, woodlands and shore, with sika deer on the island, and red squirrels. Baden Powell held an experimental camp on Brownsea in 1907, to see if his idea of the Boy Scouts would work, and today there are often scouts or cubs on the island. The resident peacocks are so tame that they save you the trouble of eating your sandwiches. The geese are more aloof.

★★★ *Island, setting, nature reserve, outing*

BRYANSTON (F) A small, mostly brick village, where all the buildings are late 18th century or later. The main part of the parish is taken up by Bryanston House, now a school, a vast brick and Portland stone mansion built in neoclassical style in the 1890's. Designed by Norman Shaw for Lord Portman, it was one of the last large country houses to be built. The house and the church of the same date are visible from the road into Blandford from the south, and the bypass, but the roads through the lovely woods and park are private. The impressive stone gateway at Blandford St Mary was probably designed by James Wyatt about 1770; the house he designed was demolished for the present mansion.

BUCKHORN WESTON (A) On the edge of the Blackmoor Vale, with nice late 18th and early 19th century houses and cottages, many colour-washed. Almost the

only original part of the church of St John surviving is the 14th century greensand porch, which has slumped to a surprising angle. The niche contains a blurred statue. Almost all the rest, including the pretty tower, was rebuilt in 1861 or 1870, in 14th century style. In the tower are six endearingly bad 18th century paintings, originally on the front of the gallery. 15th century font, and in the chancel a late 14th century effigy in a rather Robin Hood type tunic.

Between Buckhorn Weston and Gillingham is the little settlement of **Langham,** which has at its western end a tiny thatched church, built in 1921 as a memorial to those from the estate and hamlet who died in the First World War. St George's church stands alone, with fine trees. Designed by Ponting in simple Arts and Crafts Gothic with appropriate thatched roof. Simple and pleasing inside, with no electric light.

★ *Village.*

BUCKLAND NEWTON (E) Quite large, but scattered, in an area of pastureland and gentle hills. The church of the Holy Rood is rendered, which gives it an odd, foreign appearance. Restrained 13th century chancel (with east window of 1868), and very light nave and aisles, of the 15th century. The elaborate tracery in the aisle windows is original and unusual. Good woodwork – 15th century bench ends, a nice imitation medieval screen of 1930 in the tower arch, handsome plain 18th century pulpit, and very unusual 16th century poor-box, a wooden pillar decorated with carvings, (a little iron box with three latches drops into the top). The porch has a little stone vault, and set in the wall a much mutilated Norman Christ in Majesty. Just inside the church a small very lively carving of a warrior with a bow and spear is probably not local, but north European, 7th or 8th century. Below the church is a handsome Georgian vicarage, and above it is

Langham Church, Buckhorn Weston

the manor house, an early 18th century adaptation of a 17th century house.

★ *Village, church.*

BUCKLAND RIPERS (H) A small village north of Chickerell set on the side of an irregular small ridge which shelters it from sea-winds. The modern part is on the through road, and the church and manor house are at the end of a cul-de-sac. The tiny church of St Nicholas had a bad fire in about 1650, and much of it dates from 1655, including extraordinary chancel arch with its central pendant. The roofs, seating and east window in the medieval chancel are later 19th century.

BULBARROW (E) is the second highest point in Dorset (902 ft), on top of the chalk escarpment giving the longest view in Dorset, north over the Blackmoor Vale and into Somerset including Glastonbury and the Quantocks in clear weather. Shaftesbury is visible, sitting on its hill. A stone giving directions of towns and features in the car park is useful to identify others. Just to the north of the car park is Ibberton Hill picnic site.

★★★★ *Good area for walking.*

BURSTOCK (D) is a small stone-built village, very agricultural. The church of St Andrew has an attractive setting and a good 15th century tower. The body of the church was heavily restored in 1877, and the porch and chancel were built then. The resulting Victorian interior is pleasant.

★ *Village.*

BURTON (G) Moved from Hampshire in 1972, and a typical New Forest edge settlement with a few thatched cottages and much modern building. Some Georgian brick, including the huge Burton Hall (1750) right in the village street. Dull brick church of St Luke, 1874.

BURTON BRADSTOCK (D) A large pretty village, just back from the sea at the end of the Bride Valley, with many thatched cottages built from the local stone in the 17th and 18th centuries. A few Georgian houses have fronts of the more expensive brick, and the side and back walls of stone. In the centre is a little grass triangle, with a seat around a tree, a memorial of 1902. Beside the pleasant plain Wesleyan Methodist chapel of 1825 is an L-shaped cottage retaining some stone mullioned windows, dated 1635. At the east end of the village Grove Mill has an inscription recording that it was the first flax-swingling mill in the west of England, built in 1803 and using machinery to separate the flax fibres. A spinning mill to

the south of the church worked from 1794-1931, providing alternative employment to the traditional occupations of fishing and agriculture.

The church of St Mary is attractive and mostly of the late 14th or early 15th century. The central tower is handsome internally with four matching panelled arches. The chancel has seven intricate late 15th century French carved wooden panels with flowing tracery incorporated into later desks. The arcade and south aisle were rebuilt in 1897 with E. S. Prior (see Bothenhampton) as architect. Mannered and attractive. The simple stained glass and the sea-green panelling was added and painted at the same time and commemorates in inscription the restoration and enlargement of the church in the 'thirteenth hundredth year since Columba died and since Augustine came to Canterbury' i.e. 1897. Rather crudely painted 18th century testament boards at the west end of the church and much 20th century woodwork elsewhere – behind the altar with fine lettering, and in the north transept, and the pulpit (all 1930's) and the seagull lectern of the 1960's. Many good memorials including a naive *Memento Mori* in the north transept. The porch is late 14th century, with a contemporary niche.

Bredy Farm Museum is two miles to the east of the village (fee: lists), with a collection of farming bygones in a barn, a wood-turner working and a saw mill.

Burton Beach has a National Trust car park, and just to the west a road with limited parking leads to the cliff top. The Dorset Coast Path leads along the top of the cliffs to West Bay (see entry), or eastwards towards West Bexington (see entry). The pebbly beach is the start of Chesil Beach (see entry), here attached to the land. Cliffs behind, and although there are good views, the beach is not safe for bathing. Another car park on the beach just to the east, and a break in the cliffs just west at Burton Freshwater.

★★ *Village.*

CANFORD MAGNA (G) Partly modern development, partly an old estate. The estate (and parish) was huge, stretching from Wimborne to the old town of Poole, so that the elaborate Victorian estate cottages found in the village can be matched over a wide area. The big house (now a school and not open) is a fairy-tale mixture of 19th century buildings: a mock-Tudor house of 1825 was bought by the Guests, of Welsh iron-founding fame, and enlarged from 1848 by Sir Charles Barry with towers and turrets. Embedded within the building is the late medieval 'John of Gaunt's Kitchen'. The house can be seen clearly from the south end of its playing fields and from the Wimborne by-pass. Of the last owner of the house, Hilaire Belloc wrote: 'Grant, O Lord eternal rest / To thy servant, Ivor Guest / Never mind the where or how / Only grant it to him now'.

Just to the west of the church a suspension bridge carries a footpath over the river, which leads onto Wimborne. The church is on the edge of the house's grounds, and is accessible. It is complicated and interesting but not beautiful. The long chancel is a rare survival – the nave of the late Saxon church. The simple arches at the eastern end are original, as are the remains of two windows (one cut by a later arch). The other arches are not original, but some are Norrman. In about 1200 the nave with its pretty doorways and arches was added, turning the earlier church into the chancel, and a little tower was built in the north at the same time. Several small Norman windows survive in the nave, augmented by larger 14th century ones. The south chapel and south aisle of the chancel were also built in the 14th century and the chancel arch is of the same date. In 1876 the nave was extended westwards with pretty detailing, the east window rebuilt and the circular openings in the nave walls added. Good monuments from the 18th-20th century, some to the Guests, the family of Lord Wimborne who lived in the big house from 1846 until the 1920's. The good quality seating must have been put in by them, perhaps in the 1860's. The church is often used by Canford School, giving it an unusually intensively inhabited feel. The flying organ on the gallery was added for them.

★★★ *Church*

CATHERSTON LEWESTON (D) Lies behind Charmouth and consists almost entirely of a huge mock-Tudor manor house of 1887, whose monster gate piers also guard the road to the church, which is a period piece– 1857 imitation of 1300. Externally it is a jig-saw puzzle of chert, inside elaborate font, pulpit and sanctuary, and good stained glass, all of the same date as the church.

★ *Landscape.*

CATTISTOCK (E) A happy mixture of brick and stone cottages, especially in the centre, the triangle in front of the church where thatch and nice window mouldings identify the old ones from the more recent. The baying of the famous Cattistock hounds can still be heard around the village.

Cattistock has one of the finest 19th century churches in Dorset. Its stunning tower should convert anyone who thinks that 19th century Gothic architects merely copied medieval buildings. The body of the church of St Peter and St Paul was virtually completely rebuilt by Sir Gilbert Scott in 1857. The north and south transepts are 15th century, but the interesting and pretty apse and the south aisle are 1857, with a fine stained glass window by Morris with a

starry blue background at the west end of the south aisle. The north aisle and tower were designed by Sir Gilbert Scott's son, George Gilbert Scott, in 1874 in a much freer style, starting from local buildings like Charminster but producing a final form of great beauty and individuality. Externally the tower is stunning, huge and visible for miles around. Internally it is sumptuously painted, and forms a rich baptistry with a huge (c. 16ft high) elaborate font cover. The upper part of the tower suffered from a fire in the 1940's and was rebuilt by the Arts and Crafts architect J.S. Brockerly (1879-1955) in the early 1950's. He is buried in the churchyard.

★★★★ *Church, village.*

CAUNDLE MARSH (A) West of Bishop's Caundle, sparsely settled, but marshy no longer. Lots of oak trees and good hedges. The small church was rebuilt in 1857, with elaborate windows in the chancel. The new font, lectern, altar rails and pulpit are all of Ham stone. Simple tomb of 1587 by the altar.

CERNE ABBAS (E) A flourishing small market town until the railways reached Dorset. Cerne was left off the routes, and has fossilised since the 1840's. Its handsome streets, the church, the remains of the Abbey and the Giant make it one of Dorset's most popular villages. The two main streets – Long Street and Abbey Street – preserve a great variety of houses dating from the 15th century to the 19th, with some simple shop fronts of the early 19th century still surviving. In Long Street there are stone-mullioned cottages of the 17th century; the New Inn whose unusual tall stone mullions probably date from around 1700; buildings of banded flint and stone; and super Georgian brick houses, some set back from the street. Round the corner into Abbey Street, opposite the church, are the remains of a row of houses about 1500 – rare survivals. The one at the south end retains the elaborate original door surround, and all have the upper storey jettied out. Some were altered in the 18th century: the odd-looking little pieces of stone wall on the frontages are the party walls. Abbey Street is the most picturesque part of the village, with a stream alongside the road.

The church of St Mary the Virgin is almost entirely 15th century, and very attractive. The fine west tower is of around 1500, with smooth corners, rather plain finials, and a figure of the virgin and child set in a niche. Inside is very light and rather plain. 15th century nave, aisles and stone screen, the latter reset in the 19th century with a new top. The chancel is earlier, basically c. 1300, but the east end was

rebuilt in 1639 just before the Civil War (dated lower left). Elaborate pulpit dated 1640; colourful font cover 1963. Painted on the walls are robust 17th century texts with charming simple borders. Between the tower and body of the church is a rustic screen, dated 1749. Outside, the south porch, with its terrific battlements, is dated 1696 on a charming datestone.

At the head of Abbey Street is the duck pond and the sombre but attractive Abbey Farm, which was burnt and largely rebuilt in the middle of the 18th century, but which contains material from the abbey. The south wing with buttresses may have been part of the abbey gatehouse. A pretty path on the left leads round along the mill stream and out to Duck Street. On the right, at the end of a graveyard amongst lime trees, is St Augustine's Well, a rather magical spring surrounded by the restored medieval walls, which feeds the pond and the rivulet along Abbey Street. According to legend, St Augustine asked local shepherds whether they would prefer their thirsts to be quenched by beer or water. They piously preferred the latter and he struck the ground with his staff and produced this spring.

In the ground of **Abbey Farm** (fee: lists) are two of the surviving abbey buildings. First, on the right, what may have been the guest house – a two-storey late 15th century building with its original door and many original windows, including a

Cattistock church

The Giant, Cerne Abbas

Tithe Barn, Folly St, Cerne Abbas

simple oriel. Further on in the garden is the porch to the Abbot's Hall, an elaborate late 15th century building with two stories above the doorway. On the front is a superb two storey oriel window, elaborately decorated, and inside fan-vaulting. The abbey church was probably where the detached graveyard is now, and the striking earth-works to the north of the graveyard may have been part of the Abbey. It is possible to walk through the beech trees up to the Giant to the north-west, but it is now not possible to walk over him as he is fenced in.

The best place to see the **Giant** is from a lay-by just north of the village on the main

road. He is 180 ft high cut through the turf to the chalk. His date is uncertain: he could be Hercules with his club (and recent investigations have shown that he originally had a cloak over his left arm as Hercules should) and therefore Roman, or he could be more recent. There is no mention of him in the extensive medieval documents for Cerne, or indeed until the 18th century. Chalk figures need regular maintenance or they grow over, so that if he is Roman he must have been scoured out many times. Many 18th and 19th century illustrations of him omitted his most prominent feature, and the local clergy opposed the cleaning of 1868 because

they thought it would corrupt local morals. Above him is his 'frying pan', the Trendle, originally probably a prehistoric enclosure but re-used as a tree plantation in the 18th or 19th century.

Just north along the main road is the Workhouse, a large faintly classical building, one of twelve built in Dorset in the 1830's.

★★★★ *Village, church, abbey, Giant . . .*

CHALBURY (G, near Horton) A tiny hamlet in an area of deep narrow roads, with lots of trees. The church stands so prominently that as, Hutchins the county historian recorded, 'a very high Elm tree'

Abbey Street, Cerne Abbas

The Abbot's Hall porch, Cerne Abbas, before restoration

standing by the church was used as a landmark because it could be seen from the Channel 'and might be plainly discerned from the hills that lie above Yarmouth in the Isle of Wight'. It was broken in a great storm of 1703. Remarkable views on three sides of the church, with Horton tower prominent (see entry). The little church is white-washed, with a red tiled roof, and although the chancel and parts of the nave are 13th century the overall impression is 18th century, since along the south side all the windows (and the porch) are of that date. The west end has outside a classical window surround. The 18th century also dominates the interior – box pews, a simple triple decker pulpit, and a garden-ornament type font. The oddest feature is the (again 18th century) chancel arch which looks more like part of a house or carriage than a church. A very attractive church, with an interior of rustic classical charm.

★★ *Church, setting.*

CHALDON HERRING or East Chaldon

(J) still largely consists of thatched cottages at its west end, while around the church are more substantial houses and a snug village hall converted from a school. Only the north wall and tower of the original church survive – both are 14th century, and the rest dates from 1878. 1940 collage by the children of the village and Elizabeth

ABOVE   *View west from Chalbury churchyard*
LEFT   *Chalbury church*

Muntz. Plain apart from the roof and the inscriptions over the doors and windows inside. The amazing font presumably dates from 1878. The village is associated with the three Powys brothers – T. F. Powys (1875-1950) lived here from 1904-1940, and the area (particularly High Chaldon, the hill to the west of the village) is the setting for many of his books including *Mr Weston's Good Wine*. Llewelyn (1884-1939) lived in an outlying cottage south of the village for 14 years and John Cowper Powys (1872-1963) was also here for shorter periods. Other writers and artists were attracted to the place while they were here, including David Garnett, Sylvia Townsend Warner, and the sculptor Elizabeth Muntz (the latter two buried in the churchyard) whose stone head of T. F. Powys is in the Dorset County Museum, Dorchester. Elizabeth Muntz's inscribed

'Wayside Carving' (1985) at Chaldon Herring

memorial to Llewelyn Powys is ½ mile back from the sea, on the ridge 1 mile north-east of White Nothe, close to the O.S. trig pillar at 178 m (on O.S. 1:50,000). On the same inland path, parallel to the sea, are modern (1985) sculptures. Three stone 'cupboards' with 'fossils' in are only 50 m east of the Powys stone, and ½ mile further east on the down slope are four huge wooden ears of wheat. The narrow ridge to the north of the village has a line of six well preserved barrows called the Five Maries (it is not respectful to count these things correctly) which stand up clearly on the skyline.

★ *Village.*

CHANTMARLE (E, north of Frome St Quinton) is a large and beautiful stone manor house of the early 17th century, just visible through the trees and not open to the public. At the entrance are two huge 20th century imitation cottages, which served as lodges.

CHARBOROUGH PARK (F) Conceals a large house with its little church. Visible from outside is the tower, built in 1790 as an ornamental folly, and rebuilt after being struck by lightning in 1838, one of the models for the tower in Hardy's novel *Two on a Tower*. The lengthy brick wall and huge entrance gates along the main Dorchester/Wimborne road (one surmounted by a lion, the other a stag) were built in 1841 after the owner of Charborough Park had managed to get the Dorchester/ Wimborne turnpike road diverted further from his house. From 1905 the family's surname has been Plunkett-Ernle-Erle-Drax.

The Stag Gate, Charborough Park

Charminister church

CHARLTON MARSHALL (F) spreads untidily along the main road between Poole and Blandford, and although it backs onto the River Stour it is not pretty. The church is however. Apart from the bulk of the tower which is 15th century, the whole church was rebuilt and re-fitted in 1713 (dated inside and out), almost certainly by Thomas Bastard (father of John and William who rebuilt Blandford after the fire) The outside of the building is handsome, with classical door and window surrounds, chequered flint and stone walls, and an odd top to the tower – the crowded pediments and pinnacles seem to have pushed the

Charlton Marshall church

rather squat tower into the ground. Underneath the tower are restored village stocks. Inside is even more interesting: the north aisle is divided from the nave by serious classical arches, but the fittings are much more lively. The pulpit of 1713 has fine geometric marquetry, classical drapes, putti (like those on the reredos) and a pelican right on top. The reredos completely fills the east wall: it has pediment upon pediment, putti all over the place and huge jugs, but it is not improved by the 20th century stained glass window. The south doorcase matches the reredos, and on the wall opposite is the monument to the man who paid for the re-building – Dr Charles Sloper, the rector. There are several good (and large) 18th and 19th century monuments. The 1713 font is of the garden-ornament type (and very similar to that in Blandford church), with a superb wooden cover. Parts of the seating in the nave are made from the 1713 box pews, more of which are on the walls as panelling. The organ and the screen around it, the lectern and choir stalls are later fittings. Well worth seeing, even if it means pursuing the key to the rectory at Spetisbury.

★★★ *Church*

CHARMINSTER (E) Neat and prosperous with a wide variety of cottages and houses, including some banded with flint and stone. Several cob walls. St Mary's church has a superb 16th century tower, a good 12th century nave and interesting monuments. The tower was built with its elaborate finials and gargoyles by Thomas Trenchard of Wolfeton House (see entry) in lovely orange Ham stone about 1525, and his monogram can be seen repeatedly on the external buttresses. Inside, the nave has stout Norman pillars carrying pointed arches with nail-head ornament. These arches are Transitional; ie their style and decoration is Norman, but they have the pointed arch of the succeeding gothic style, Early English, rather than the round

Norman arch like the slightly earlier chancel arch here. Chancel 1838, and north aisle later 19th century. The early 16th century stencilled decoraton of strawberries on the wall close to the chancel arch is an unusual survival. In the south chapel two elaborate Purbeck Marble tombs of the 16th century, and a gorgeous monument (recently repainted) with the kneeling figure of Thomas Trenchard's daughter Grace, who died in 1638. A path at the north-east corner of the churchyard leads out to the river Cerne.

★★★ *Village, church.*

CHARMOUTH (D) Almost a small town, consisting largely of one steep street lined with a great variety of buildings. At the east end the large apparently Georgian Queen's Arms is actually an early 16th century house, refronted in the 18th century, and there are other smaller cottages of the 17th and 18th centuries. Many of the buildings running up the hill date from the 19th century, when Charmouth was becoming a resort. Lots of bow windows and some very attractive large stuccoed villas. Despite being ½ mile back from the sea, it has a sea-side holiday feel in the summer. The church of St Andrew was rebuilt in 1836-8, quite pretty externally, and plain inside. Virtually

no chancel. Bright stained glass and an elaborate reredos.

Many car parks at the beach (fee). The Charmouth Heritage Coast Centre has a display on the local fossils, natural history etc., in the upper floor of the old Cement Factory, right on the beach. Good coastal views.

CHEDINGTON (D) Attractive small village with many 17th and 18th century stone houses and cottages – much of the village is lovely orange Ham stone. The largest house (now a hotel) was built in the 1890's. Manor Farm (dated 1634) is one of the best houses. The views from the village and the roads along the ridge are tremendous. The church of St James (now a private house) was totally rebuilt in 1841.

Wynyard's Gap This narrow prominent ridge covered with beech trees, a notable view point, was given to the National Trust in memory of the men of the 43rd Wessex Division who died in Normandy in 1944: a memorial stone at the end of the ridge on the south side of the main road. The steep path is well worth climbing (5-10 mins) for the superb views from the top – east back into Dorset, and most extensively north-west into Somerset. Also possible to walk south through the beeches to Chedington.

★★★ *Views, landscape*

CHELBOROUGH (D) consists of East Chelborough, really just farms, and West Chelborough, the larger but more remote part, with lovely views north and west towards Castle Hill which has the damaged earthworks of two small medieval castles. Little green hills all around, some nice stone buildings, well wooded. Good walking country. The church of St Andrew's tower is dated 1639 on the parapet, an uncommon period for church building. The rest is mostly 15th century, drastically

ABOVE *Chesil and the Fleet, looking east from above Abbotsbury*
BELOW *Wall memorial, West Chelborough*

restored in 1894. Fine 12th century font, altar rails of 1763 and a touching wall memorial of the early 17th century, apparently to a woman who died in child-birth and who lies in bed with a swaddled baby tucked into the blanket. The seating of 1894, the 1935 pulpit and the remains of the 18th century pews used as panelling are all stripped to the bare wood.

★★ *Setting*

CHESELBOURNE (E) Scattered along a small chalk stream and tucked into a shallow valley. The church of St Martin has walls mostly of flint with stone dressings, and is entirely medieval (although, of course, restored, in 1874). Very plain tall tower. 14th century chancel with simple windows. The 13th century south aisle has plain pillars with Purbeck marble tops and bottoms. The west window is also 13th

The Emma Marie *wrecked on Chesil, 1903*

century. The north aisle with all its windows and door is late 15th century, and in the churchyard is the base of a large cross of the same date. Nice plain pulpit of *c.* 1630 and good Elizabethan brasses.

★ *Village, church.*

CHESIL BEACH (H) is a huge ridge of shingle which runs from Portland to above Abbotsbury, some 8 miles, joining Portland to the mainland and cutting off a long lagoon of partly salt, partly fresh water, the Fleet, which is only open to the sea at Small Mouth, the eastern end. The stones on Chesil are naturally graded from large pebbles at Portland to much smaller ones at Abbotsbury, and locals can tell their position by the size of the stones. Alongside the Fleet are some of the specialized plants that can survive on shingle, including Sea Beet, Yellow Horned Poppy and Sea Pea. It is an ornithologists delight, and the birds include herons, reed and sedge warblers, and over-wintering wildfowl – best seen from the coast path along the south-eastern part, or at Abbotsbury Swannery. Good views of the whole length of Chesil can be gained from Portland or Abbotsbury Hill; closer views *(cont p.54)*

Beaches

The Dorset coastline varies from steep cliffs reaching down into the sea with no beach at all, to long sandy beaches or shallow bays. Most of the coast is safe for strong experienced swimmers, apart from Chesil, where there are strong and erratic currents. Local warning signs should be scrupulously observed. Weymouth is a fine beach for children, with its wide, very gently shelving bay, with lots of shallow water. The mostly sandy beach offers all the traditional seaside amusements – donkeys, ice cream and so on. Lyme Regis and Swanage are also good. The longest sandy beach is that which runs from Studland right through to the county boundary at Highcliffe, through Sandbanks, Boscombe, Bournemouth, and Southbourne. It is backed by the built-up areas of those places, but to the south over the harbour mouth at Studland there are only dunes and the natural landscape. People in a state of nature are also (reputed) to be found here.

Less developed shingle beaches are also to be found in Purbeck, if one is prepared to walk. Mupe Bay and Worbarrow Bay can be used when the Army Ranges are open, and St Oswald's Bay is always open, but sometimes very crowded. West Lulworth is popular too, and Kimmeridge, which is perhaps visited more for rock pools than bathing. The only beach in Poole Harbour is Rockley Sands, which is sandy – the rest are mudflats. Hengistbury Head can be quieter than the rest of the eastern beaches, but Christchurch Harbour behind is not attractive for swimming. The Fleet, behind the Chesil Bank is not suitable either, and the western end is a nature reserve.

ABOVE *Bathing at Lyme Regis in 1819*
BELOW *Weymouth in the high summer*

The west Dorset beaches are West Bay, Eype's Mouth, Seatown, Charmouth and Lyme Regis. All the beaches make good walks, but care must be taken with the tide – people have been drowned through not realising the danger of being swamped. All the Dorset cliffs are unstable and eroding, and whilst one has to take the chance of falling rocks striking one whilst walking along, the danger can be lessened by not sitting directly underneath cliffs. All the undeveloped Dorset coastline has been designated Heritage Coast, which means that besides having additional protection from undesirable development, all the coastal footpaths are signposted or marked, leaflets explaining many areas are available and guided walks are conducted in holiday periods. Details of walks and the leaflets can be obtained from the Tourist Information Offices.

from the coastal path which turns inland towards the north-western end. Good sea fishing off the Beach, but walking along it is exhausting and bathing treacherous.

★★★ *Landscape.*

CHETNOLE (F) Strung out along the road, with stone cottages, some new houses, lots of trees and good thick hedges. To the east of the church is a fine brick house, Chetnole House, built about 1760 with brick stables of the same date. Across the field to the north are several stone farmhouses. The church of St Peter is the usual amalgam – 15th century tower, with, inside, carved stone figures in the corners holding up buttresses, late 13th century nave with one original lancet window accompanied by larger 15th century windows, north aisle and chancel of *c.* 1860.

CHETTLE (B) A very unspoilt village, lying in the hollow of a small valley on the edge of Cranborne Chase, with big hedges and many brick cottages of the 17th and 18th centuries, including one particularly good row of brick and thatch. Several smaller houses of the 19th century, but the most interesting building is Chettle House, built about 1710 by the architect Thomas Archer for George Chafin, MP, and Ranger of Cranborne Chase. The house (fee: lists) is high quality red brick with stone dressings, very mannered, with curved ends, not large but charming. Edward Castleman, a Wimborne solicitor and the promoter of the first railway through Dorset, bought the house which was in a poor state in the 1840's, and restored it. The drawing room is a monument to his taste, and many of the fittings in the house date from his time. The exception is the splendid double staircase which is 1710. Over the doorways in the hall are carvings by the famous Victorian sculptor and painter, Alfred Stevens, born in Blandford in 1818. His best known work is the Wellington monument in St Paul's Cathedral. The smallish pretty, formal gardens around the house are open, and close by is the little church of St Mary which, apart from the 16th century tower, was rebuilt by Castleman. Externally it has wide bands of flint and greensand, and internally it is a period piece of the 1840's, with everything, from the stained glass and the odd glum heads holding up the roof to the heavy communion rails and screen, of that date, including the simple Portland stone font and pulpit. The original wooden 17th century pulpit was cut up and made into two chairs and kneelers, still in the church. Outside is Castleman's memorial, a draped urn.

★★ *House*

CHICKERELL (H) Mostly modern development (Weymouth suburban), but some earlier buildings remain towards the centre, and around the church it still feels quite 'villagey'. Many of the 19th century buildings, e.g. the Methodist church of 1865, are in the rather bright red brick produced by the local brickyards, all now closed, although the tall square chimneys and other buildings of one of them survives to the south-west. Opposite the church is a fine 17th century stone cottage with mullioned windows. The medieval church of St Mary has a north aisle added in 1834 with iron pillars like pipes between it and the nave. The aisle is so big as to make the church square. The big west gallery is 1834 too. Nice pulpit dated 1630. A Purbeck Marble slab has the outline of a 15th century priest, simple and charming. Norman font.

Bennetts Water Gardens (fee: lists) are lakes and ponds formed by the clay digging, with a huge collection of water lilies. ★★

CHIDEOCK (D) On the main road, and suffers from it, but plenty of 17th and 18th century houses in the local stone. Very hilly. The medieval, but restored, church of St Giles is in the middle of the village and contains the black marble effigy of a recumbent knight in armour dating from the 16th century. In the graveyard is a strange Byzantine chapel-like building in the form of a Greek cross, with a finely carved figure of Christ on the Cross. This is the mausoleum for the Welds, built by Charles Weld (who carved the stone figure) in the 1880's. He was also responsible for the design of the Catholic Church, ½ mile to the north. The road passes the earthworks which are all that remain of Chideock Castle (now distinguished by

a large (modern) wooden cross), and a gateway made from whale bones. The Catholic church of Our Lady of Martyrs and St Ignatius is a great surprise: richly decorated inside, and in form like an early, Byzantine church. It was built from 1850-72 by Charles Weld who lived in the adjoining early 19th century manor house. The site was that of a barn where Catholic services had been held in secret in the 17th and 18th centuries, when Catholicism was virtually illegal. The present church is a magnificent medley of Byzantine, Gothic and even Baroque. The Sanctuary (added in 1884) is particularly strange and successful. Charles Weld carved the capitals and painted the altar, roof and walls himself. An unexpected rather alien church.

★★★ *Catholic church.*

CHILCOMBE (D) Clings to the north side of the Bride Valley, with lovely views from the narrow, mostly unfenced, road. The fabric of the little church is basically Norman (as is the font) with 14th and 15th century alterations, all restored. Good 17th century monuments and chairs, and an odd wooden panel, perhaps a reredos, foreign, 17th century, decorated partly by carving and partly burnt poker work. The church shares a farmyard, with a stone Georgian house, a wonderfully positioned little hamlet.

★★ *Setting*

CHILD OKEFORD (B) A big village, with several modern estates and many 19th century houses. Many trees. Good 18th century houses and Victorian farm buildings, mostly brick, up by the church which has a tower of *c.* 1500 made of big blocks of greensand, but the rest is 1850 or 1879. The chancel was lined with patterns of marble in 1911, producing an over-rich

Child Okeford from Hambledon Hill

effect something like a 1930's bathroom. On display is a 1568 bible. The vicar in the 1560's was the author of the famous hymn 'All people that on earth do dwell', known as The Old Hundredth. The bare green slopes of Hambledon (see entry) lean over the village from the east.

CHILFROME (E) A hamlet with an enviable setting – watermeadows, hedges and trees, with Cattistock church tower in the distance. Only a few cottages, farms and a couple of larger houses, and now, sadly, modern development. Small church of the Holy Trinity, once 13th century but now mostly mid 19th century.
★★ *Setting.*

CHRISTCHURCH (G) has a pretty High Street, attractive river frontages to the Stour and Avon, and perhaps the best medieval church in the county. The town grew from a Saxon settlement on a small ridge set in marshland at the head of Christchurch Harbour. The present town centre was a burgh or defended settlement from at least the early 10th century, and it is likely that there was a church here from an even earlier date. We know that a Saxon church was demolished in 1095 to make way for the present building. In the 12th century a castle and the Constable's house were built, both surviving as ruins, and although it was never a large or rich town, Christchurch slowly developed through the medieval period. Never a big port, but fishing was quite a large industry until the 19th century. Inevitably Christchurch was caught up in the general development of the area as Bournemouth grew, and it is now part of an urban sprawl which spreads along the coast from Poole into Hampshire. Called Twinham in the Saxon period, meaning the place between the waters.

The High Street has some nice 18th century brick buildings, and towards the north, a remarkably restrained brick Town Hall of 1859, looking Georgian, now in front of a modern shopping precinct. The spire of the late 19th century Congregational church shows well although it is in a side street. Lying across the end of the High Street is the great grey block of the Priory Church, and just outside the church gates is a large Georgian brick house and several smaller ones. Bridge Street is well-named as there are three separate bridges – first the little one over the mill stream, then a larger, basically later medieval one, over one arm of the Avon and finally Waterloo Bridge of 1816. The **Castle** now seems very small, but it may have once had a bailey to the north-west. It was constructed from about 1100, but the two massive walls on top of the mound are the remains

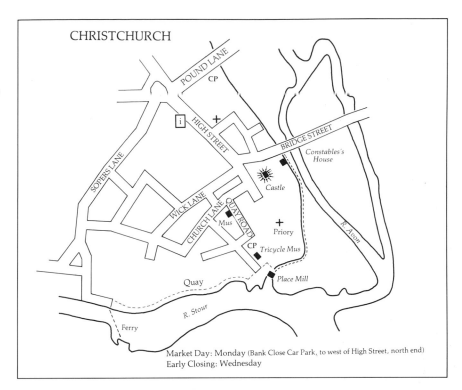

CHRISTCHURCH

of a keep of c. 1300. Beside the mill stream is the roofless Constable's House, built in the 1160's (not for a constable) as a hall for the Castle, with much original window detail surviving, and a chimney with a garderobe (lavatory) tower beside it. On Bridge Street are some more fine Georgian brick buildings.

A network of paths runs around the Priory, and along between the river and the separate mill stream, leading to the gardens south of the church. The priory buildings stood here, and are now all gone apart from precinct wall and Priory Cottage to the west of the church, which was at the entrance. Inside there is now only a large brick Georgian house (and the church). Right on the river is **Place Mill**, which originated in the medieval period and which has recently been restored. The interior is open to visitors (summer only, fee: lists), and is worth seeing for the machinery and the huge undershot wheel. The river front close by is a popular area, with motor boats for hire, ferries to Wick, Hengistbury, Mudeford and Tuckton, a bandstand and so on. Off the car-park to the south-west of the church is a small museum devoted to tricycles (fee: lists). The Red House Museum, Quay Road, is in an early 18th century red brick building once the parish workhouse with extensive displays of local history, bygones (especially toys and dolls), a costume gallery, and a small aquarium with local fish. Many local sites including Hengistbury have their archaeology and local

history explained here. Garden also open (fee: lists).
★★★ **The Priory church** survives because it became the parish church after the Priory was dissolved in 1539: it is the longest parish church in England. Apart from admittedly extensive restoration and patchings the whole building dates from the Norman period and the late medieval. The most important (and attractive) external feature is the north transept, Norman and covered with decoration. The 15th century tower seems small in relation to the bulk of the church. The impressive porch, higher than the aisle it joins, is 13th century, although much was renewed by Ferrey in the 1830s, and the vault is entirely his. Inside, under the tower, is the fine memorial to the poet Shelley, intended for St Peter's Bournemouth (see Bournemouth). The nave, crossing and transept are all Norman, the nave with characteristic heavy round arches and smaller ones above, many decorated. The vault was inserted in 1819, very sympathetically to the building. Restored 12th century wall arcading in the south aisle, and cutting off the choir and chancel from the nave is a stone screen or pulpitum in 14th century style, actually mostly 1848 restoration. The chancel, Lady chapel and the east end are 15th century, with chancel completed early in the 16th century. All vaulted, with a particularly elaborate one in the chancel. Around the ambulatory are chantries and tombs, including that of John Draper, the last prior, fine with a Renaissance *(cont p.58)*

Building Materials

Dorset's building materials range from the world-famous Portland stone to mud (cob). Almost every type of material is represented in the county including a very varied selection of stone, although timber framing and early brickwork are uncommon. Until the 19th century materials were not usually transported any distance for humbler buildings, so the cottages and farmhouses reflect the local geology, while more prestigious buildings like churches and large houses may not. In areas where building stone was found whole villages used it, like Corfe Castle where even some of the roofs are stone, but on the chalk or clay it is more complicated.

Milton Abbas shows the variety on the chalk. The humblest buildings, the 24 cottages of the new model village, are built of the cheapest material – cob, and an attractive mixture of brick and flint walls with stone dressing was used for the alms houses. At the top of the scale, for the two churches and the mansion house, stone is used, all brought from some distance. The medieval Abbey church is Chilmark and Ham stone,

ABOVE *Banded flint and limestone dated 1573, with door and window mouldings of better stone, Puddletown*
BELOW *Timber framing of c. 1500 with flint and limestone below, Cerne Abbas*

Limestone for walls and roof, Corfe Castle

both high quality and brought from outside the county, with the less good Marnhull stone and local chalk for the walls of the vaulting inside. The 18th century mansion has facades of Portland stone, with the courtyard walls of the house banded with the local flint, probably to match the surviving portions of the Abbot's hall rather than an economy in this case. The 18th century church in the village is a compromise. It uses Greensand (transported only a short distance) for the walls, and Ham Stone for the dressings. The quality of many of the buildings in Milton Abbas is unusually high, but the variety of materials used is not.

Portland Stone was used only locally until the 17th century, but since then so much has been exported that it is said that there is as much in London as there is left unquarried in Portland. It has been used for high quality buildings in Dorset, but confusingly the same stone was mined in some quantity in Purbeck, and is known as Purbeck-Portland. Both types are very hard, and therefore expensive to work.

Many other limestones ranging from grey through to orange in colour, but not of the superlative quality of Portland, have been used locally. For example, quarries at Marnhull, Sherborne, and in Purbeck supplied their areas with good building stone, and from Purbeck came stone roofing slates, used in many parts of Dorset, and the Purbeck Marble. This is not a building stone but of shelly limestone which will take a polish and has been used for decorative work since the Roman period.

Greensand of various qualities is used in the Shaftesbury area, and for churches in central Dorset. On the Chalk, stone was often eked out by being banded or chequered with the native flint, a durable building material, but one which requires stone or brick for any openings. Occasionally the Chalk itself was used, but it is really too soft for external use. In the west of the county the Blue Lias was used, but it is not a very good building stone needing to be clad with slate to be weather-proof. The dark brown Heath-stone was also used where it was found on the heathlands of south-east Dorset.

The lovely golden orange Ham Hill Stone was brought from Somerset for high quality buildings, particularly churches, from the medieval period, and Chilmark stone from Wiltshire was also imported.

Chert, which looks like flint but has a rougher

Cob at Moreton

surface, has occasionally been used in the west of the county: Thorncombe has many chert buildings, including the church. Flint and chert are both sometimes knapped to produce a flat surface. Timber framing is not common in Dorset, but it can be seen in several towns and in some villages in east Dorset, with brick infilling.

Bricks were occasionally used in the county from the early 16th century, but they were commoner from the 18th century for larger houses and in the towns. There are only a very few wholly brick cottages, mostly in places where bricks were actually made. In areas without stone, flint and brick banding was very common in the 19th century, and occasionally the more expensive brick with stone dressings is found.

The humblest building material was cob – mud mixed with chalk or clay and straw, built up as a wet mixture for about 2 feet, left to dry, and another layer added. Limewashed externally it lasts well if looked after, and if, as in the old saying 'it has a good hat and a good pair of shoes'. In Dorset the shoes were usually a few courses of stone footings and the hat, thatch. Cob walls have to be very wide to bear the weight of the roof, and it is this width which gives away cob buildings which have been faced with brick. Many surviving cob buildings have been rendered with cement.

Dorset was the home of Eleanor Coade, who in the late 18th century developed perhaps the best artificial stone ever invented, Coade Stone. There are not many of her products in the county, but only too many modern imitations of stone, often used for buildings which differ from their brick equivalent only in the material used. Most of the quarries and brick kilns which supplied materials for Dorset's buildings up to the middle or end of the 19th century no longer exist, and from the mid 19th century building materials most commonly used in Dorset changed to the ubiquitous brick and slate, ending hundreds (if not thousands) of years use of local materials.

ABOVE *Fine quality Portland stone ashlar used widely on Portland, with limestone roofs, Fortuneswell, Portland*
BELOW *Example of limestone, heathstone and flint*

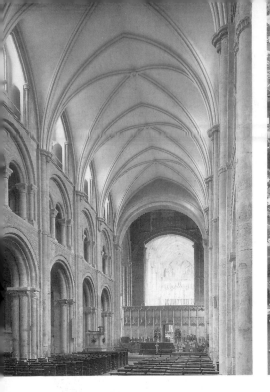

The nave, Christchurch Priory

Christchurch from the air

Lady FitzHarris monument, Christchurch

motif in the friezes. Highly decorated Lady chapel. Spot-lit above the south aisle at this end is the miraculous beam, once the object of pilgrimages. The medieval builders found that a vital beam was too short: when they returned the next morning it was miraculously not only the right length but in position. At the end of the north aisle are two alabaster figures of 1461, and the superb chantry chapel for Margaret, Countess of Salisbury. She was the last of the Plantagenets, described by Henry VIII as 'the most saintly woman in England'. He made her governess to his elder daughter, Mary, but she fell from favour and was executed in 1541 at the age of 70 and buried in the Tower. She had had this beautiful tomb made in the 1530s, probably by a Florentine sculptor. Lovely friezes, and a superb fan vault inside, all showing the newly fashionable Renaissance influence. The chancel is wonderful, up a few steps from the aisles, and with windows, walls and ceiling all blending together. The reredos is of about 1350, remarkably complete even to the figures. Fine Regency memorial by Flaxman to Viscountess FitzHarris (d. 1815), sitting with her children. Beyond is a more conventional mock-medieval effigy of 1876. The wooden stalls in the choir are 1520s, re-using some earlier misericords which have figures of jesters, tumblers and others. In the north transept is an altar made by the famous Gothic Revival architect Pugin in 1831, when he was only 19. All around the church is bright pleasant 19th century

stained glass, and good wall tablets, mostly of the 18th or 19th centuries. **St Michael's Loft Museum** (fee: lists) is in a large room over the chancel, the superb views of the town, harbour, Hengistbury Head and so on, worth the many steps up. Small collection relating to the church. ★★★★ .

On the east side of Bargates is the **Southern Electric Museum ★★★** (fee: lists) in a little power station of 1903. The building is surprisingly elaborate inside, especially the ironwork, and houses many of the machines used for generating and distributing electricity since the late 19th century. Also many domestic appliances, including the earliest washing machines. Well worth seeing. Limited opening times.

CHURCH KNOWLE (J) is a real Purbeck village, with a variety of buildings in the local limestone. Perhaps the prettiest is Church Farm. The church of St Peter is basically early 13th century, with chancel and small east window of that date, as well as the triple chancel arch. The nave and both transepts were altered in the 1830s when the north aisle and gallery were added. The alterations are very tactful; lancer windows were used, and the windows in the south of the nave were lengthened rather than being replaced. The new roofs are very odd, and have features of several styles and methods of roof-construction. Plain pulpit of about 1840. The monument to John Clavel is in very good condition, and is unusual in that it retains all of its brasses — one of John who

ordered it in 1572 (and who died in 1609) with his two wives either side of him. The plain tower was rebuilt in 1741. Display of local photographs in the gallery. MGFT Animal Sanctuary (fee: lists)
★★ *Village, church.*

CLIFTON MAYBANK (A, just south of Yeovil) is hardly a village today. The great Elizabethan home of the Horseys was mostly demolished in 1786, a fate shared later by the church. Sir John Horsey owed his rise to being steward of Sherborne Abbey at the Dissolution, but the family's fall was rather more gradual (see Sherborne Abbey) – Decorative bits of the house were distributed all over the place, including the splendid west front, re-erected at Montacute, Somerset. A small part of the house remains here, much altered in 1786, but with the characteristic 16th century octagonal shafts at the corners, now shorn of their pinnacles.

CLOUD'S HILL (F) is a small cottage which T.E. Lawrence (of Arabia) used from 1923, when he was stationed at Bovington Camp nearby and which he adapted in the 1930's to make a permanent home. An odd house, dominated by books and music, and making no allowances for humdrum domestic needs like hot food. He died in a motorcycle accident only weeks after leaving the RAF in 1935.

The little cottage is rather prim and Victorian outside, set in amongst rhododendrons, but inside Lawrence's alterations dominate. Over the entrance is a Greek inscription which Lawrence freely translated as 'Why worry?'. The ground floor has a bathroom (only visible from outside), and a combined book-room/bedroom, now with many photographs taken by Lawrence, and others of him. Upstairs is the paneled music room with wooden shutters, huge gramophone, and wrought iron candlestick and fender made for him by the local blacksmith. The other room has a ship's bunk, and his larder – glass domes to cover bread, cheese and butter. Cloud's Hill now belongs to the National Trust. Well worth seeing, but

T. E. Lawrence at Bovington Camp in 1924

Robert Goodden, Over Compton church

can be crowded because it is so small (fee: lists). See Wareham, Moreton and Bovington.

★★★ *Cottage, heath.*

COLEHILL (G) has become a large, rural-looking suburb of Wimborne, and is mostly modern, with the most surprising

church (of St Michael) designed in 1893 by Caröe. Although its brick and half-timbered style is alien to Dorset it is an interesting building which is either successful or irritating according to taste. Very contrived small tower. Inside is as good as outside, slightly crazy 'cosy' imitation Tudor, with a bare brick and plaster chancel, complex timber aisle, brick niches, timber tracery in the windows and lots of leaded lights. The alabaster font and somewhat 'Rococo' lectern have a rather different flavour. Highly recommended for those interested in churches or architecture. Well worth chasing the key to the vicarage nearby.

★★★ *Church, an oddity.*

COMPTON (A) is two villages, Over Compton on the side of the hill, and Nether Compton in the valley. Both have many golden orange stone buildings set beside narrow winding roads. A prettily wooded valley leads from the main road to the church and Compton House, which is now used by Worldlife (fee: lists). Displays on butterflies and conservation, with many exotic species flying around in natural environments. Upstairs is Lullingstone Silk Farm, with a display on silk production, from the egg to the yarn. The house was rebuilt in fashionable Tudor style in the

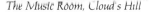
The Music Room, Cloud's Hill

19th century, but many much simpler 18th century outbuildings belonging to the earlier house survive. The gardens are also open. Close by, and best approached from the drive to the house, is the village church. Externally it is pretty, with an early 15th century tower, but internally it is most unusual. The new chancel of 1877 is normal enough, and so are the admittedly pretty 15th century windows in the nave and the Jacobean pulpit. The unusual features are the north chapel, the little baptistry on the south side and the nave fittings, all 1820s. It is unusual to find a church being built and fitted in such a traditional way in the Regency period. This was the work of Robert Goodden whose robust life-sized statue dominates the north chapel. It was erected in 1825, three years before his death and by his orders it remained boarded up until a year after his death. **Nether Compton** has, below the church, a village green created in 1895, with a single house of 1893 in a very Arts and Crafts manner on the far side. Many 17th century cottages, and 1880's ones (several dated) with brick door and window surrounds. Otherwise everything is of stone, including the 'Gothick' school of 1843. Lots of trees. The church, although mostly medieval, is not exciting. Some 13th century details but it is mostly 15th century, restored heavily in 1885. Unusually it retains the stone screen of c. 1500, but in a chancel arch of 1885. Nice early 17th century pulpit.

★★★ *Worldlife, house, church.*

COMPTON ABBAS (near Powerstock) see **WEST COMPTON**

COMPTON ABBAS (B) is small with winding roads and a lovely position in the lee of Melbury Hill. Many plain buildings in the local greensand. Fontmell Down (see entry) lies a steep walk to the south-east. It has two churches: the 15th century greensand tower of the original is in East Compton encircled by downs. Manor Farm next door is a pretty 18th century farmhouse and some of the farm buildings are of greensand too. The main village is on uneven ground, with lots of cottages scattered about, many still thatched. The church of St Mary (1866) is nearer the centre of the main village, and has a lovely view from the south doorway. Pretty broach spire. Good apse with big foliage capitals, and an even larger one to the south aisle, the latter surprisingly classical. The Norman font has running foliage, possibly re-cut in 1866.

★★ *Village, churches, setting.*

COMPTON ACRES (K) A contrast to the other great gardens of Dorset, being almost entirely formal, although set within heathland and pine trees. The visitor is directed through a series of theme gardens, carefully screened from one another by thick hedges or trees. Mostly constructed between the wars, around a large house built in 1914, and after restoration following wartime neglect were opened to the public in 1952. Now very popular. First a small 'Roman' garden, then herbaceous borders lead on to the larger Italian garden with its long formal pool. After the palm court and wishing well come the rock and water gardens, with twisting paths, contrived bridges, and lots of fish including vast carp. Now the house comes into sight, with a good view across Poole Harbour and Brownsea Island from the terrace. The heather garden and a stand of cactus follow, but perhaps the best garden is the last – the Japanese. All the vistas through or across this are breath-taking, although one doubts that any Japanese garden is like this. Entertaining tea-house at one end. Teas available in another part of the garden. Good all year but perhaps best with bulbs, rhododendrons etc through the spring but could be rather too formal and contrived for some gardeners (fee: lists)

★★★★ *Garden.*

COMPTON VALENCE (E) Small, isolated, attractively set, with luxuriant trees and shrubs. The church of St Thomas of Canterbury has a 15th century tower; the rest was rebuilt, with Benjamin Ferrey as architect, in 1838. His church is interesting if rather odd because it is very early Victorian Gothic revival, using the Decorated style with a polygonal apse (later quite common): and because, as Pevsner says, the new church is allowed to look like a real medieval church in scale and materials, most unusual at that early date. Good simple pews in an almost 'Arts and Crafts' manner. The brass of c. 1440 in the floor by the font is Thomas Waldon, priest, who had earlier rebuilt the church, including the surviving tower. Of interest to architectural historians.

★ *Church, setting.*

CONEY'S CASTLE (D) (National Trust) is a small hillfort in the Marshwood Vale. Car park on north side. Deep ditch on the SE side, splendid views, good trees, bluebells etc., and it makes a pleasant picnic spot. The fort probably dates from the middle of the Iron Age, and the smaller enclosure on the south is probably a barbican to defend a gate.

★★★ *Landscape, walks.*

COOMBE KEYNES (J) still has lots of thatched cottages, some in a super puddingy mixture of grey limestone, dark brown heathstone and brick, randomly arranged in the 18th century and more formally in the early 19th century. Several farmyards converted to dwellings. The little redundant church of the Holy Rood was designed by John Hicks in 1861, preserving only the medieval tower. Hick's masonry is a lot more organised than in the medieval.

★ *Village, setting.*

CORFE CASTLE (J) deservedly attracts many visitors to the superb castle and the pretty little town clustering at its foot. Almost all the buildings in the town, and all the castle, are of the local grey limestone, and many of the cottages have stone roofs as well. The **Castle** (fee: lists) is in a classic position described in 1643 as being 'seated in the fracture of a hill.' It covers the whole of a natural mound in the only gap in the ridge of chalk which separates Purbeck from the rest of Dorset. There were buildings (which do not survive) on the top of the mound by the late Saxon period, and by tradition it was here that King Edward was killed by his step-mother in 978. After a year at Wareham his body was moved to the more important church at Shaftesbury, where it caused many miracles. William the Conqueror bought the site for the castle, and by 1080 had built an enclosure wall around the inner bailey, right on top of the hill. Subsequent building campaigns up to the late 13th century enclosed the whole mound with a stone wall, and added very high quality buildings suitable for its use as a Royal castle. Right at the end of its life, the castle was held by the Royalists in the Civil War, was beseiged, and finally fell. Its present tattered appearance is due to the thorough slighting by the Parliamentarians in 1646. Up to the middle of the 19th century ravens bred here. New displays close to the way in.

The entrance is over the ditch (partly natural) on a mostly medieval stone bridge. The gatehouse of the 1280's leans outwards, having been undermined in 1646, but this is nothing compared to what has happened to the towers around the curtain wall. These semi-circular buildings with little arrow-slits look as though they are still sliding down the steep banks of the defences, having been persuaded to move in 1646 by a combination of undermining and gunpowder. The outer bailey had been enclosed by the curtain wall (with its towers) gradually through the 13th century. In the 16th century there was a stable built against part of the wall, and guns were ranged along the upper part. The south-west gatehouse (over another ditch, dug in 1207) has been spectacularly damaged so as to make it useless – the left

ABOVE *An interesting but not wholly accurate 18th century reconstruction of Corfe Castle*
BELOW *Corfe Castle from the west*

hand part has dropped 8ft leaving a ragged gap between the two halves of the building. Despite this the two halves survive very well, and there are still portcullis grooves, arrow loops and many other details surviving in the shattered building, which was constructed about 1250. Originally a long covered stairway ran from here right up to the keep, the tall building above. The outer walls defending the area are 13th century, replacing earlier wooden palisades. The Butavant tower on the west corner had in the bottom an underground dungeon which could only be reached by a ladder.

The highest part of the inner bailey is defended by a curtain wall of 1080, and contains the 12th century keep, standing to its full height but damaged, and beyond it the 13th century house built for King John called the Gloriette. The Keep was built very early in the 12th century, and despite

the removal of the north side much architectural detail, such as round-headed windows and blind arcading, survives. One or two square headed openings which date from the alterations of the 16th century. On the south side it is still possible to walk through a passageway which has small chambers off it. One of these was a garderobe (lavatory) and the other probably a guard room. The stairway up from the south west gatehouse led to this passage, whose floor is the stub of the 1080 curtain wall. The king's hall would have been in the first floor of the keep, but in the 13th century a much more domestic King's house, the Gloriette, was built of a very high quality ashlar to the east of the keep. This also had a hall on the first floor, of which the fine doorway and parts of the windows, all with pointed arches, survive. Below was a vaulted undercroft, and to the south of the main block the barrel vault of

the undercroft to the solar range survives. Towards the north edge there is a wall with squared headed windows, part of a 16th century building.

On the slopes of West Hill 300 yards south west of the castle and almost level with it are the 'Rings', the ditches and banks of a medieval earthen castle which are now almost covered with scrub and rather difficult to distinguish without a map. Probably thrown up as a base for besieging the Castle in 1139 during the Anarchy, and used as a gun platform by those besieging the Castle in 1643 and 1646. The Civil War and the Anarchy were the only times the castle saw any fighting. From the earliest times until 1572 it was a Royal Castle used by the king and his court on their journeys around the country, and it was a particular favourite of King John's; he stayed there while hunting in Purbeck. It was also used to house the Royal prisoners. The most romantic episode in the history of the Castle is perhaps the Civil War, when Lady Bankes ('a heroine with a Constancy and Courage above her sex' according to her monument in Ruislip, Middlesex) the wife of a man who had bought it in 1635, held the castle for the Royalists with a garrison of five men and her maids, against a siege in 1643, and then lost it in a second siege (1646) when Parliamentary troops managed to enter the Castle disguised as reinforcements, assisted treacherously by one of the garrison. The castle was looted, and lists of the property which the Bankes tried to get back give some idea of the richness of the furnishing of the Castle – 7 or 8 sets of fine tapestry hangings, another set of blue damask and one of green leather decorated with gold had been used to cover the walls, and there were satin cushions for the windows along with crimson damask curtains. The Parliamentarians reduced the Castle so that it could never be defended again. It has reminded a splendid ruin ever since.

The town of Corfe grew up below the Castle, and prospered from the 12th to the 14th century with the stone trade. Purbeck Marble, a shelly limestone capable of being polished, was very popular in the 13th century, and was brought from the Purbeck quarries to be worked in Corfe. In West Street deposits of marble chippings up to 12ft thick have been seen, the result of stone working. Purbeck Marble was mostly used in churches for small pillars, fonts, altars, tombs and other decorative purposes, all internal because the stone weathers badly. Some traditions of the Company of Marblers – the guild of the quarriers – survive. On Ash Wednesday a football supplied by the most recently married man should be dribbled from Corfe

Corfe Castle village from the north-west

to Ower on Poole harbour, and a pound of pepper presented to the lord of the manor for the rent of the road. Although the marble trade declined the limestone quarries continued, and besides general building stone the mushroom-like legs and capstones for granaries were made and sent all over the country. In 1852 they cost 4s (20p) a pair round and 3s (15p) square.

Corfe was a rotten borough – one of the tiny places which elected MPs. Bribery was rife – in 1784 £30 was given to the voters and large quantities of beer. In 1831 Corfe had a population of 1,700, Manchester 182,000, yet Corfe had 2 MPs, Manchester none. The 1832 Reform Act deprived Corfe of its parliamentary representation.

The centre is the Square with the superb Greyhound Hotel, its columned porch dated 1733. The Bankes Arms is of the 1920s, but almost all the other buildings are of the 17th or 18th centuries. Opposite the Greyhound is a house whose projecting bay was used as the Mayor's robing room. 1920s signboard with King Edward, by Francis Newbury. Along West Street is the little Town Hall, with stone for the ground floor and brick for the upper. It was built in 1774, and now houses a small museum (free: lists).

The church of St Edward (king and martyr) has a good stout 15th century tower with particularly big and good gargoyles and a pretty west doorway. The rest of the church was rebuilt in 1859 in 13th century French Gothic style, with wonderfully odd

capitals, and quantities of Purbeck Marble columns in the chancel. Interesting 1940s woodwork, particularly the handsome font cover, the screen to the north chapel, chandeliers and very plain lectern. On the east gable a statue of King Edward, 1931 by Francis Newbury of Glasgow School of Art.

About 1½ miles north west of Corfe is **The Blue Pool,** a small lake created in the 19th century by clay digging, surrounded by pine woods and sandy heathland, and many paths lead around it. The pool grows no weed, and so can be a very clear blue. Small museum. (fee: lists).

Close by is Furzebrook Rail terminal, where the oil extracted in the Arne peninsular is loaded on to trains. Next door is a ball clay works.

The Swanage (see) railway has now reached Corfe, with steam trains running from Corfe and Norden to Swanage. Car parking at Norden.

★★★★ *Village, castle.*

CORFE MULLEN (F) splits into two very different parts: the south is modern, and joins up with the suburbs of Poole, while the northern is still villagey, with houses of a variety of dates. It was always a dispersed village, with several centres, typical of the heathland. The church of St Hubert has a stout 14th century tower of dark brown heathstone. The rest of the church is medieval, apart from the north chapel – and south transept which are of 1841. The roof of the south transept was carefully

matched to that of *c.* 1480 in the nave. Both have pretty bosses. The two cheerfully painted mid 19th century galleries look like those in a chapel. 15th century Purbeck marble font, and up by the altar a nice little brass of 1437 with the figure of a man.

★ *Church.*

CORSCOMBE (D) Splendid views over Somerset from the upper road and many good stone cottages. Interesting landscape of little hills. The church of St Mary has a pretty porch, elaborate doorway and plain tower, all 15th century. Almost all the rest is 1875. Thomas Hollis (1720-74), republican and benefactor of many universities including Harvard lived here, and renamed some of his fields to suit his convictions – Republic, Revolution, Toleration and so on, and called one of his coppices Stuart so he could have the pleasure of beheading it. He had advanced ideas about diet and would consume no butter, milk, sugar, spices, salt or alcohol.

CORTON (H) is well hidden. A concrete road which looks as though it leads only to a farm descends through a tiny pass in a hill near Portesham, with bare limestone on either side. The hamlet sits on the side of the hill, consisting of a few cottages, a grey limestone farmhouse and a little chapel. The farmhouse has 16th century round-headed windows under elaborate labels, and square-headed 17th century ones. Several of the farmbuildings are

Corton

limestone too, including small out-houses and the arched base of a granary. Geese and chickens wander about. Glorious views. The tiny chapel of St Bartholomew has an early 13th century chancel with its original stone altar and a 16th century doorway. It was a free chapel, that is not subject to the bishop's jurisdiction. After a period of neglect it was reconsecrated in 1897, when the west end was rebuilt. The roof is also of that date, and is now painted a cheerful green.

★★ *Setting.*

CORYATES (H) consists of a few pretty cottages, near to a gap through the hills. Close to Corton.

CRANBORNE (C) is in a pretty, well-wooded area, and the village, once a small town and the centre of Cranborne Chase, now seems a backwater, which is what it became after it was left off both the turnpike roads and the railways. All brick, unusual in Dorset, with a few thatched cottages of the 18th century, and more formal houses of the same date, some with patterns in glazed (vitrified) brick. Half a mile to the south-east is a very overgrown motte and bailey castle, of which little is known. Cranborne Ancient Technology Centre (by appointment: fee: lists) has Iron Age round houses, animals and so on.

The large church of St Mary and St Bartholomew is built of different stones and flint, giving a variegated appearance, 15th century tower. The Victorian porch has reset inside a fine mid 12th century doorway with pretty zig-zag decoration. The 14th century nave has arcading of alternate octagonal columns and composite shafts (with the central one of Purbeck Marble); with its 15th century wagon roof and faded 14th century wall-paintings it

gives a good general impression of a later medieval church. (Bright 19th century painting). The pulpit is surprisingly early – early 15th century – with pretty tracery like that used for windows. Many good 17th and 18th century monuments, some with figures. The chancel was totally re-built in 1875, and has an elaborate chancel

Cranborne Manor from the south

arch, with a rood screen. The general effect is a bit cold and outsize. To the west of the tower are some finely lettered Cecil gravestones (including one of 1934 carved by Eric Gill and that of the writer David Cecil) and a lovely view of the manor house can be seen through an iron gate a little to the south.

The Manor House gardens (fee: lists) are huge, delightfully designed and planted, with more than ten different enclosed gardens – by the river, courts either side of the house, a knot garden, herb garden and so on. Magical, with trees all around. One of the four best gardens in Dorset. The manor house is not open, but can be seen from the garden. Beautiful tiny brick lodges (early 17th century) are part of the entrance court. Facing the house, the central part of the main house is a most unusual survival – a house built for King John (*c.* 1208), which he used when hunting in Cranborne Chase. The two lower stories of the left hand tower and the centre block are all of this date. Following the acquisition of the house by Robert Cecil, 1st Earl of Salisbury, it was altered in the early 17th century – the left hand tower was given another storey, the right hand (cont p.65)

Castles and Forts

To be logical this should begin with the great series of Iron Age hillforts in Dorset, dealt with more fully under archaeology. They are not castles, but they are certainly forts, built with defence in mind. The most spectacular castle in the county is Corfe, famous for its position, the picturesque ruins and the pretty village at its foot.

Despite the deliberate destruction of the 1650's, Corfe is the most interesting (as well as the prettiest) castle in the county, with the remains of a huge curtain wall and towers along with the buildings in the bailey. Christchurch still has its medieval castle and the 12th century house which belonged to it, but neither are anything like as impressive as Corfe. Although Sherborne Old Castle was defensive, it was not a Royal Castle like Corfe, but a combination of castle and house built by a Bishop of Salisbury in the 1130's. It also was pretty thoroughly ruined after the Civil War, so that only fragments of the main buildings are left. Sherborne New Castle is a castle only in name, like Highcliffe, Durlston and Lulworth, which are all undefended, and which are houses merely using the name of castle romantically. East Lulworth Castle is the only one which even looks like a castle.

Three small forts were built in the 1530's for coastal defence — at Sandsfoot and Portland to defend Portland and Weymouth Harbour, and at Brownsea to defend Poole. The one at Brownsea has disappeared and Sandsfoot Castle is falling into the sea, but Portland survives, now encircled by Portland Harbour and right next door to a helicopter base. On the top of Portland above the castle is the Verne, built as a fort in the 1860's to defend Portland Harbour. It is not open (it is now the Prison) but its massive stone lined ditches can be admired. The fort on the Nothe at Weymouth of the same date is open, and is a fine example of a mid 19th century artillery fort.

The Keep Military Museum in Dorchester shows the history of the Devonshire and Dorset regiments and other military formations right up to the present day, and the Tank Museum at Bovington and the Army Signals Museum at Blandford illustrate the much more mobile aspects of modern warfare, in contrast with the defensive castles and forts which earlier armies have left in Dorset.

★★★★Corfe ★★★ The Nothe (Weymouth), Portland and Sherborne Old Castle.

ABOVE *Portland Castle*
BELOW *Sherborne old castle with the new castle beyond*

Keepers of Cranborne Chase in the 18th century

tower was built, and both given corbel tables matching the 13th century one. All the windows (apart from the 13th century arrow-slits) are early 17th century, along with the beautiful naively classical loggia entrance with signs of Zodiac above. A larger loggia on the other side, above a terrace and a walled white garden. The left hand end is a new wing of 1647, which looks out over lawns.

★★★★ *Manor house and garden.*

CREECH GRANGE (J) is a handsome stone house lying under the northern flank of the Purbeck Hills, and the glimpse from the road is of its 1840's mock 16th century front. The chapel is not accessible. The road up the chalk ridge gives wonderful views of the 18th century south front designed by Francis Cartwright of Blandford. On the top of the ridge is Creech folly, stone arches meant to mark the end of the southern vista from the house, but now hidden from it by trees. The Bond family lived there from the 17th century, one of whom founded Bond Street, London, in the time of Charles II.

CROSSWAYS (H) north of Warmwell consists of recent housing developments, and seems to be surrounded by gravel pits. It is in a very pretty, well-wooded area however.

DEWLISH (E/F) Peaceful and uncluttered, with many flint and brick banded buildings. Above the church is a handsome stone and flint manor house of *c.* 1632, with opposite a rather jolly 19th century building – an imitation of the 17th century, now the village hall. Down by the river is a fine large brick farmhouse of *c.* 1700. The church of All Saints is of a mixture of dates – the

main doorway is re-set Norman, the north aisle 16th century with attractive panelled arches. Quite a lot of 17th century woodwork – the pulpit and re-used panelling in the chancel and north aisle. Large decorative oil lamps. Huge monument to Sir John Michel who died in 1886. Behind the church are the earthworks of a medieval settlement and its fields. To the south parkland around the big house.

In 1814 a field mouse digging in the chalk revealed a deposit of sand – rare in this area. It was used as a sand-pit for some years, and in 1884 after the discovery of some teeth it was excavated and the remains of several elephants found, dating from 350,000 years ago.

Creech Grange, the east front

They seem to have fallen into the fissure in the chalk.
★ *Village.*

DORCHESTER (E) is the county town, and although it is small its long history gives weight to this status, which has often been challenged by other Dorset towns. It has only one-tenth the population of Bournemouth, but whereas Bournemouth only started in 1810, Dorchester was urban by 100 A.D. Dorchester (or *Durnovaria* as it was then called) was the only Roman town in Dorset, but Hardy's claim that the town 'announced old Rome in every street, alley, and precinct' is heartily exaggerated. The only obvious features surviving from the Roman town are the Walks, laid out along the line of the Roman walls and on top of the Roman bank in the 18th century. The footings of a Roman town house are exposed in Colliton Park, but the best place to see Roman Dorchester is the County Museum, where many Roman mosaics are re-laid on the floors. The town was probably completely deserted after the Romans left, because the Roman street pattern was lost and a new one superimposed. Little is known about the succeeding Saxon town but by Domesday (1086) it had 172 houses and soon afterwards a Castle (now completely gone) was built. Dorchester was never a large town, but continued to grow through the medieval period. Like all towns with thatched buildings, fires were a regular occurrence, and destroyed many of the medieval houses in the 17th and 18th centuries. The town today still has many handsome 18th century buildings, and in many respects is still the Casterbridge described by Hardy in his *Mayor of Casterbridge* and other novels. In 1716 its situation was described as 'delightful, being on a rising Ground, and opening at the South and West Ends unto Sweet Fields and Spacious downs'. Today it is a little more hemmed in, but on the north, river, side there is no transition between town and country, just an abrupt change.

Right in the centre of the town, at the junction of High Street and South Street is **St Peter's**, the only surviving medieval church in the town. Once inside one feels miles away from the bustle. The whole church, with its pretty tower, is basically 15th century. Inside the porch is a re-set late 12th century doorway, with lots of decoration, which would originally have been round-headed. The church was restored by the Dorchester architect John Hicks in 1856, and his new assistant Thomas Hardy (aged 16) drew the plan of the restored church now on display in the south chapel. 1856 east window, but most of the chancel fittings, including the alabaster reredos, were added in the 1890's. Heavy 17th century communion table and fine 'crown of thorns' iron candlesticks 1976. Typical 15th century panelled arches lead to the north and south chapels: in the north one, almost squeezed out by the organ, is the re-set monument to Sir John Williams and his wife (erected 1617). Their figures kneel on either side of a sarcophagus, with a big arch over. Lying on the window sills of the south chapel (not their original position, but they look very comfortable) are two later 14th century effigies of men in armour, cross-legged. The roofs of the nave, aisles and chapel are basically 15th century. At the west end of the north aisle is a superb massive monument to Denzel, Lord Hollies, erected in 1699, twenty years after his death. He lies, a corpulent Roman senator with a 17th century wig, and two weeping putti below. He was a member of parliament for Dorchester before the Civil War, fought for parliament, but survived the Restoration of the monarchy to become a privy councillor to Charles II. The fine pulpit is probably that used by the Rev John White, rector from 1606 to 1648, a famous Puritan who helped to found the colony of Massachusetts in America, and is buried under the porch. Under the tower is a fine painted Charles II coat of arms inscribed 'Feare God, Honour the King', brought here from All Saint's Church. By the doorway is a monument of 1599 to an earlier Thomas Hardye who founded the town grammar school.

Between the Dorset County Museum and

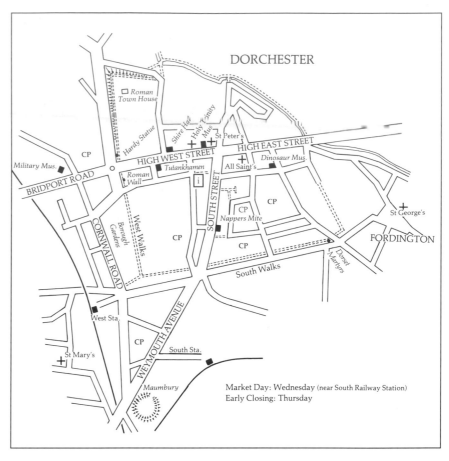

St Peter's Church is the statue of William Barnes, the Dorset poet, erected in 1888 two years after his death.

Opposite St Peter's is the Corn Exchange of 1848, one of three buildings in the town centre designed by Benjamin Ferrey. His building was plainer, with the lower storey having open arcades. The amusing, rather fussy, clock tower was added in 1864, and the complex doorway on High East Street later still. Ferrey also designed the handsome All Saints's Church (1843), no longer a church, but whose huge spire is still a prominent landmark.

Just up High West Street from St Peter's is the **Dorset County Museum**, ★★★★ (fee: lists) in mock-medieval style, erected in 1884. It is the best museum for the archaeology, natural history and geology of Dorset. Displays on Thomas Hardy, William Barnes, local history and so forth. Large gallery for temporary exhibitions. The Victorian Gallery, part of the original museum of 1884, has relaid Roman mosaics on the floor, and splendid cast iron-work now painted in the colours the architect intended. Reconstruction of Thomas Hardy's study. The archaeological display, centred around Maiden Castle, clearly explains Dorset from Paleolithic to Roman times. Natural History and

The monument to Denzel, Lord Hollies, St Peter's church, Dorchester

66

High West Street, Dorchester, in 1860

Military Museum, Dorchester

Geology, including dinosaur footprints, fossils of all sorts and a display on oil in Dorset.

Opposite the Museum are the only timber framed buildings surviving in Dorchester in anything like their original state. Judge Jeffries and the shop next door are basically 17th century, although the shop fronts have been altered.

Holy Trinity Church just up the hill was also designed by Ferrey (in 1876) but is not such an attractive building as All Saints. Since 1976 it has been the Roman Catholic church. Inside good stained glass of 1900 in the south aisle and chapel and a very elaborate gilded wood reredos of 1897.

Above Holy Trinity is Shire Hall, built in 1797 of Portland Stone, with the Old Crown Court, where the Tolpuddle Martyrs were tried in 1834. Usually open (free: lists) – entry is through Agriculture House the council offices next door. Agriculture House was built in a very successful mock-Georgian style by Crickmay in 1883, and inside the surviving original decoration (eg the doors) is faintly Japanese. The late 18th century fittings of the Crown Court make it look rather like a church, with the judge's seat instead of an altar. The Court is owned by the TUC and was restored by them as a memorial to the Tolpuddle Martyrs in 1956. Guided tours including the cells underneath in summer (fee lists).

The further reaches of High West Street (and indeed High East Street) still have lots of pleasant town houses of the 18th and early 19th centuries, some stuccoed, and some brick in several different colours – red, brownish and pale yellow.

Tutankhamun, The Exhibition, High East Street (fee: lists). Smallish, with reproductions of many of the famous objects from the tomb. The full-size reconstructions of the ante-chamber stacked with grave-goods and of the removal of the inner coffin are good. Plenty of background material.

South Street is now the main shopping street, and apart from the north end with the handsome Antelope Hotel of the early 19th century and the Georgian brick buildings opposite (one with a pretty shop window of the same date), this is the area of the town which has most changed, with quite a lot of recent development. Towards the south end is Napper's Mite, now shops but built in 1616 as an almshouse. The pretty street frontages were rebuilt imitating the original in 1842. Opposite are two town houses with inscriptions recording that William Barnes and Thomas Hardy worked there in the 1860s. At the corner of South Street and South Walks is a rare survival – a hexagonal letter-box dating from between 1866 74.

The Military Museum just over Top o' Town roundabout is in the impressive Victorian (1879) Keep, in front of the depot barracks. The army left the barracks in 1958, and some of the buildings have been demolished. The surviving stone and brick buildings date from the 1860's and 70's. The Keep Military Museum ★★★ fills the two upper stories of the Keep, with displays on the Dorset and Devon Regiments and their volunteer units. Their postings (and the displays) are a list of our wars over the last 250 years – India, Egypt, Gibraltar, South Africa, France, Mesopotamia, Crimea, Burma, America and so on. The local volunteer companies from the Militia and Yeomanry through to the Home Guards are also represented as are the more recent postings of the Devonshire and Dorset Regiment. Huge view, right over the town and beyond, from the roof. (fee: lists).

The Dinosaur Museum ★★★ (fee: lists) in Icen Way has three large rooms and a video hall displaying just about everything to do with dinosaurs. The displays include wonderfully awful jokes, eg What do dinosaurs have that no other animals have? (baby dinosaurs). Some of the computer/videos in the displays are rather difficult to read, but children love the museum.

Behind the huge block of County Hall (started in 1938) are the excavated footings of a **Roman town house**. There are two ranges of buildings, both probably built in the fourth century. The southern is the simpler, and may have been the kitchen block. Close by is the well, 33 ft deep. A little covered verandah ran alongside part of the south range, with its roof supported on columns, one of which has been restored. In the more sophisticated west range, every room had mosaics, now removed apart from the one under the little lean-to. Beside the mosaic is a restored window surround, found collapsed but complete during the excavation. Passageways ran under the floor and up the walls to carry hot air. The bramble covered hole just to the west of the buildings is a huge stone-lined pit, Roman but of uncertain use. The Roman defences (now topped by trees) run close to the town house on two sides.

Apart from the three main streets the finest feature of Dorchester is **the Walks**. The remains of the Roman bank and wall were levelled in the 18th century and planted with trees. These are still maintained today, so that there is a tree-lined traffic-free walk encircling the centre of the town. Starting at Top o' Town, at the top of High West Street, the view down Colliton Walk is good. Just to the south is the only remaining part of the Roman wall, a short length of rough walling which is in fact the core of the wall, with the facing stones long gone. It was probably built on top of the defences about 300 A.D. To the north, over the road is Eric Kennington's fine statue of Thomas Hardy put up in 1931, three years after Hardy's death.

Colliton Walk runs along the top of the defences and the road beneath is in the Roman ditch. Around the corner North Walk fades out before the thatched Hangman's Cottage: the Roman defences continued but have been obliterated, partly by the medieval Castle, whose site is now used by the Prison. The path continues along the riverside, with the fine 18th century Prison wall with its gatehouse above. Eventually the bottom of High East Street is reached, and passing through Salisbury Street the Roman defences are regained, bordered on the east by Salisbury Field, a recreation ground. Near the road junction are three strong figures, bronzes by Elisabeth Frink showing Dorset Martyrs – those persecuted for their religion. It is on the site of the gallows. South Walks is formed from chestnuts, glorious in bloom. Across the bottom of South Street the name changes to Bowling Alley Walk, and round the corner is West Walks, with the Borough Gardens on the west. Good Victorian plantings, fine cast iron bandstand and clock.

On the southern outskirts, beyond the 1880 brewery and the market is **Maumbury Rings,** ★★★ originally a Neolithic henge monument, but adapted by the Romans as an ampitheatre and finally used as a fort in the Civil War. The outer banks are thus Neolithic with Roman heightening, and the ramps inside are 17th century. Walking along the banks the views are urban, with both railway lines very close,

but from inside the town could be miles away.

To the west of the town is a 19th century extension, with streets of Victorian villas and terraces. In the middle is St Mary's, built rather belatedly in 1910-12. Arts and Crafts Gothic, mostly fairly simple but with an elaborate doorway. Inside, lots of bare plaster and stone, traditional woodwork and 1920's stained glass.

Fordington on the south-east of the town was not a suburb, even though its High Street starts from the bottom of Dorchester's. It was once a village although so close to the town, and the two were always in rivalry. Hardy described Fordington in the 19th century when parts had a population density equal to that of Manchester, and Mill Lane was a synonym for poverty, vice and degradation. The open fields of the village encircled Dorchester and were not enclosed until 1874, so that all the farmhouses and cottages were in the village. Many have been replaced or refaced, and those around the Green are mostly early 19th century. Below the church is a rendered house with stone mullioned bay window of the 17th century. The church stands on a prominent site, overlooking the Green. Apart from the 15th century tower, the Norman tympanum and some of the fittings, St George's is a dull, forbidding church, over-enlarged from 1907 in an unattractive hard imitation of the perpendicular style. The tympanum of St George assisting the Crusaders above the south doorway (inside the porch) is lively and attractive, and set at a low enough level for close viewing. It dates from around 1100, and is part of an earlier building reset here in the 12th century. The two fat pillars just inside the door are 12th century as well. Under the tower inside (by the 18th century Bavarian wooden doors) is part of a Roman tombstone, dating from the 1st or 2nd century A.D., dedicated to Carinus, a Roman citizen, aged 50. Roman burials have been found all round the church (and indeed along virtually all the other Roman roads out of Dorchester), and this tombstone was found during the 20th century rebuilding of the church. The glowing stained glass window in the south transept is by William Morris. The whole of the eastern half of the church dates from the rebuilding of 1907-25. An attractive stone altar of c. 1390 now in the north aisle was imported from Salisbury Cathedral in 1959: the top is modern. The austere stone pulpit is dated 1592, 1833 and 1912: the earliest is the date of construction, and the others dates of restorations or changes of position. Externally the 15th century tower is the glory: the little turret top roofing the

Thomas Hardy by Eric Kennington, Top O Town, Dorchester

stairway on top of the tower was added in 1900: Thomas Hardy was so disgusted by this alteration to the original skyline that he resigned from the church's restoration committee. On the north of the extensive churchyard, on the side of a little terrace overlooking the river, is an attractive carved stone commemorating the German soldiers who died in Dorchester Prisoner of War camp in the 1st World War.

Max Gate (fee: lists) is the house Thomas Hardy designed for himself right on the outskirts of the town in 1885 and his home for over 40 years. Parts of the ground floor open, including the Drawing Room. Garden also open.

★★ *more for anyone interested in Hardy.*

Poundbury, ★★ on the north west of Dorchester, is a small, simple hillfort, which originally had a double rampart all round, except perhaps on the north where there is a steep slope down to the river. This northern side of the hillfort has been cut away by the Roman aqueduct, which has also clipped the north-east corner. The aqueduct was an open channel, 12 miles long, bringing water from Notton, 6 miles upstream, to Roman Dorchester. The length was necessary because the channel had to keep to the contour line in order to maintain height and thus hugged the sides of all the little valleys on its route (seen very clearly in Fordington Bottom, less than a mile to the west of Poundbury). It probably entered the town at the highest point, Top o' Town, and is estimated to have provided 13 million gallons of water a day. The aqueduct can be seen from the hillfort continuing north-west as a pronounced shelf in the hillside. The rail-

Dorset Martyrs by Elisabeth Frink, South Walks, Dorchester

Modern 'vernacular' at Poundbury, Dorchester

way tunnels underneath the fort, and on the west and southern sides the outer rampart was adapted during the Second World War to provide a defence against tanks. The view over the water meadows immediately below is pleasant. No features show inside except one big Bronze age barrow on the south. Poundbury is also the name given to the Prince of Wales' new development on the western edge of Dorchester. Very pretty locally-styled houses.

The DORSET CURSUS (B/C) is one of Dorset's most famous and earliest prehistoric monuments. Two parallel ditches and banks, 3-400 ft apart run for 6¼ miles across chalk downland of north-east Dorset. Constructed in the Neolithic period, about 3,000 B.C., and has a long barrow incorporated within it, and more aligned on each end. Very impressive from the air, but less so on the ground. The south-west end and two long barrows can be seen from the road at Thickthorn Down (just off the A354), and it also survives as an earthwork to the north on either side of the B3081 at Bottlebush Down. Elsewhere ploughing since the Iron Age has turned it into a crop mark. Its original purpose is obscure.

DRIMPTON (D) The small church of St Mary is dull (built 1867), but the village has a few good stone buildings and much modern. Netherhay is prettier with the plain stone Methodist Chapel of 1838. Netherhay Farm is dated 1638.

DUNCLIFFE HILL (B) is prominent from all over north-east Dorset. It lies 2 miles west of Shaftesbury and is formed of two rounded hills (one 700 ft high) of Greensand covered with deciduous woodland. Footpaths lead up into it from most sides and in clear weather it offers panoramic views of Devon, Somerset and Wiltshire, as well as south across the Blackmore Vale to the Purbeck Hills.
★★ *Walks, landscape.*

DURWESTON (F) has many brick houses built by the Portman estate (Bryanston) but up by the church there are older, thatched cottages. The church of St Nicholas has a nice 15th century tower with two big statues of 1994 in the niches: the rest was rebuilt in pretty chequered flint and greensand in 1846. Part of an inscription of 1455 from the tomb of a rector is re-set around the doorway outside, and above the door inside is an amusing 15th century carving of St Eloy, the patron saint of blacksmiths. Being a saint he has detached one leg from the horse so that it is easier to shoe. The horse stands patiently awaiting its return on three legs. Other blacksmiths must have envied him this facility.
★ *Village.*

EAST BURTON, *see* **WOOL**
EAST CHALDON, *see* **CHALDON HERRING**

EAST CREECH (J) is small, with rather austere stone cottages, mostly thatched, and a good pond. The area is well-wooded, and sits up under the great chalk ridge which bounds Purbeck. The roads up from the village are spectacular.
★ *Landscape.*

BELOW *Duncliffe Hill*

ABOVE *The pump, East Holme*
RIGHT *Lulworth Castle burning in 1929*

EAST HOLME (J) is tiny, with a few plain cottages close to the ford, and Holme Priory and the church standing rather apart. Well-wooded. The footpath across the park to the church is signposted, and passes in front of Holme Priory, a fine late 18th century house on the site of a small Cluniac Priory. The Priory church survived as the parish church until 1715. A new parish church was built in 1865 to the designs of John Hicks, and is one of his more elaborate churches. Now it has a faintly seedy air, which somehow suits this fine example of high Victorian taste. Built from local materials — dark brown heathstone quarried close by, Purbeck limestone roof, and Purbeck Marble shafts inside. The painted decoration inside is by Miss

Doorway, East Lulworth

Selina Bond of the Priory: her daughter was the second baby to be christened in the new church, its churchwarden for 46 years, and organist for 70.
★★ *Landscape, buildings.*

EAST LULWORTH (J) Picturesque small village, with thatched cottages in grey Purbeck limestone or brown heathstone (and occasionally striped with both).

Lulworth Castle (fee: lists) is the shell of a large house built from 1608 as a fanciful imitation of an idealised castle, set in a thousand acre park. Square, with round towers at each corner, the building had little decoration apart from pretty little shell-headed niches. It was gutted by fire in 1929, and has recently been partly restored. The view from the top of the tower is stupendous.   Interesting walks are marked around the park, leading to the lake and the lodges and through woods. Close to the Castle is the chapel of St Mary of 1786, the first free-standing Catholic church to be built in England after the 16th-century Reformation. Catholicism was virtually illegal, and the personal permission of George III was necessary — he is supposed to have made the condition that it would not look like a chapel. Externally it succeeds in this, but inside it is calm and classical, with a big dome (painted in 1988) and a decorative scheme based on the original carried out in the 1950s. A very interesting building. Just to the west is the new brick house (1970s) which replaced the Castle. The parish church of St Andrew is close to the Castle,

and has a late 15th century tower. The rest was rebuilt by the Dorchester architect John Hicks in 1854: the drawings were by his assistant, the young Thomas Hardy. The village was originally around the church, but was moved from 1790 to improve the park. Just to the west a viewing area for the tank demonstration ground.
★★★ *Castle, park, chapel.*

EASTBURY, *see* **TARRANT GUNVILLE**
EASTON, *see* **PORTLAND**

EAST ORCHARD (B, near West Orchard) has a plain and simple church of 1860 and a few scattered farmhouses, partly brick, partly stone. Dairying area.

EAST STOKE (J) parish spreads across the flat wide valley of the River Frome, but most of the small settlement is along the main road. The little Victorian church of St Mary is now a house.

EAST STOUR (B) is a big village, but mostly modern. Nice austere early 19th century stone farmhouse next to the church. Christ Church was totally rebuilt in Norman style in 1842, solid and chunky with a square tower in the middle. Only the 12th century font, and a fine 18th century wood-carving of a pelican (re-used as a lectern) survive from the earlier church. Neo-Norman was fashionable in the 1840's — there is another church nearby at Enmore Green, Shaftesbury in the same style and by the same architect, and Melplash of 1845

is also neo-Norman. Henry Fielding, the author of *Tom Jones* lived here as a boy from 1710, and returned in 1734 for a couple of years, during which he spent the whole of his inheritance from his mother. The house he lived in has gone.

EDMONDSHAM (C)

Woody and prettily set, once part of Cranborne Chase. Lots of old brick houses and cottages, and a big iron pump dated 1884, with a big iron wheel. Many of the large beech trees are swagged with mistletoe. The church of St Nicholas is partly 12th century (north aisle) with a 14th century tower. Many of the windows and the chancel date from a restoration of 1862. Finely carved 18th-century grave slabs in the north aisle, and handsome Royal coat of arms, 1788. Behind the church is **Edmond-sham House** (fee: lists) whose gardens are also often open. The centre of the house dates from 1589, and is tucked in between larger scale wings of the early 18th century with round gables. Inside the house has been altered several times. An impressive 17th century staircase survives, and pleasantly classical rooms. Interesting furniture, paintings, textiles and so on. Portrait of John Tregonwell who survived a fall from Milton Abbey church tower in the 17th century. Also a portrait of Lewis Tregonwell, founder of Bournemouth.

The setting of the house, with its fine trees, is serene and very English. Interesting garden, at its best in April, and a big walled organic fruit and vegetable garden. Good outbuildings, including a little Victorian octagonal dairy and a big stable block of 1864.

Upper Farm (fee: lists) has many sorts of farm animals, mostly in a real farmyard.

Good duck pond. Very good for small children.

★★ *Village, House, Upper Farm*

EGGARDON (D)

A lonely place, with much atmosphere, and with perhaps the best views of any hillfort in Dorset, encompassing the distant sea. The easiest way into the 20 acre hillfort is diagonally south across the field to the south of the road at the east end. This leads to one of two Iron Age entrances, and joins other footpaths (see OS). The view changes completely on this side: the road side is in the uplands, with a pretty wooded view, especially from the continuation of the road which runs crazily along the top of outer rampart of the fort (and continues to be spectacular as it descends to Powerstock). Once on the south or west of the hillfort, over the hump of the hill, all is changed. Eggardon is on the edge of the chalk and looking out over west Dorset, a magnificent prospect of fields, farms and villages, bounded by the sea. The hump back of Golden Cap is clear, with beyond the white chalk cliffs of Beer (Devon). To the north-west is Pilsdon Pen (see entry) one of the hillforts on the edge of the Marshwood Vale. Around most of the hillfort are three ramparts and two ditches: on the south side these have been damaged by landslips, and then repaired, presumably during the Iron Age. The south part of the inside of the fort seems never to have been ploughed and has a great variety of humps and bumps, the clearest of which is a barrow sliced through the middle by 'excavation', perhaps in the 18th century when questing antiquarians would open several barrows in an afternoon, seeking their treasure. Just to the north of

the barrow is a large octagonal earthwork traditionally thought to be the result of tree planting by a smuggler owner of the fort as a seamark for his ships. The other linear earthworks may be field banks predating the hillfort. Just to the west of the fort, down the side road to Wynford Eagle (see entry), is a roadside picnic area.

★★★★ *Hillfort, views, landscape.*

EVERSHOT (E)

Rather remote (although large), with lots of trees; interesting and little changed from when Hardy knew it, and used it for part of *Tess* – the cottage (cont p.74)

ABOVE *Eggardon hillfort*
BELOW *Tess Cottage, Evershot*

Medieval Churches

There is no point in pretending that Dorset is a good county, on a national scale, for medieval church architecture. This does not mean that the churches are not interesting to visit. Many are in beautiful positions and have interesting fittings or associations. The most spectacular medieval churches were not originally parish churches – Sherborne, Christchurch, Milton Abbey and Wimborne were all monastic foundations, converted after the Dissolution of the monasteries in the 1530's to parish churches.

Saxon churches can be in a great variety of styles. Very few survive in the county and those which do are late, ie 10th or 11th century. The most complete is St Martin's Wareham, and St Mary's in the same town contains strange memorial inscriptions which seem to date from the 7th-9th centuries, very rare survivors. A very few others such as Canford or Winterbourne Steepleton include some late Saxon masonry with the characteristic Saxon 'long and short' work; alternating long and narrow stones marking the corners of the building. None are as interesting as St Martin's. Of the few surviving pieces of Saxon sculpture (mostly crosses with interlace) the most impressive is the strange font at Melbury Bubb, with large animals amongst the interlace.

Norman churches are far more standard than the Saxon, but they also can have rampant ornament. The characteristically robust circular pillars carry round-headed arches, and the small windows are round headed too. Many decorated Norman doorways survive in the county, with splendid zig-zag carving, and occasionally carvings in the panel beneath the arch and above the door (the tympanum). Chancel arches can be multiple, like Powerstock, and very impressive. Studland is a Norman parish church which survives in a remarkably unaltered state, and the charming tiny Winterborne Tomson is another. All the fine large churches have varying amounts of Norman architecture surviving, most notably perhaps the exterior of the north transept at Christchurch, but with fine quality work elsewhere at Christchurch and at Wimborne and Sherborne. There is little *Transitional* architecture in Dorset, with only Charminster and the nave at Wimborne showing the combination of pointed arch and Norman style of decoration typical of the period. *Early English,* the full flowering of the pointed arch style (most famously seen in Salisbury Cathedral) of the 13th century is not largely represented either, although the huge north porch at Christchurch and much of Whitchurch Canonicorum are good and attractive examples of this style, much more slender than the Norman. The following style *Decorated* (c 1290-1350) is even more poorly represented. Milton Abbas is a large but perversely rather plain example.

The succeeding *Perpendicular*, which is like Decorated in having far wider windows than the earlier styles, is found all over the county. The name of the style comes from the main upright stone divisions within the windows (mullions) which are upright (or perpendicular) for their full height, rather than flowing or curving as in Decorated. Perpendicular starts about 1350, and the majority of the surviving medieval churches in the county are at least partly of that date.

Many have panelled arches, that is arches with decoration on the underside of the arch, and these are seen at their most complex in Sherborne Abbey which also has the other characteristic feature of high class Perpendicular churches – fan vaulting. The fan vault in the choir there is the first large scale one in England, and the nave and crossing were later vaulted as well, adding the finishing touch to the finest church in the county. Dorset has many fine Perpendicular towers, dating from the late 15th or early 16th century and often these are all that survived the 19th century 'restoration' mania. Beaminster is possibly the best, but there are many others – St Peter's Dorchester, Bradford Abbas, Piddletrenthide and so on.

By far the finest church in the county is Sherborne Abbey ★★★★. Wimborne Minster, and Christchurch are also very good (★★★★), and the most interesting medieval parish church is probably Bere Regis (★★★★) with its famous wooden roof of 1475. Abbotsbury, Beaminster, Bradford Abbas, Canford, Charminster, Hilton, Milton Abbas, Studland, Trent, Wareham (St Martin's), Whitchurch Canonicorum, Winterborne Tomson, Worth Matravers, and Yetminster are all listed as ★★★ in the gazetteer, and are all worth visiting, but there are dozens of others which are nearly as good, churches of great character which have grown up over the centuries, often with fine fittings and beautifully placed in their landscape.

OPPOSITE *Sherborne Abbey*
BELOW *Christchurch (north transept); Bere Regis (nave roof carving)*

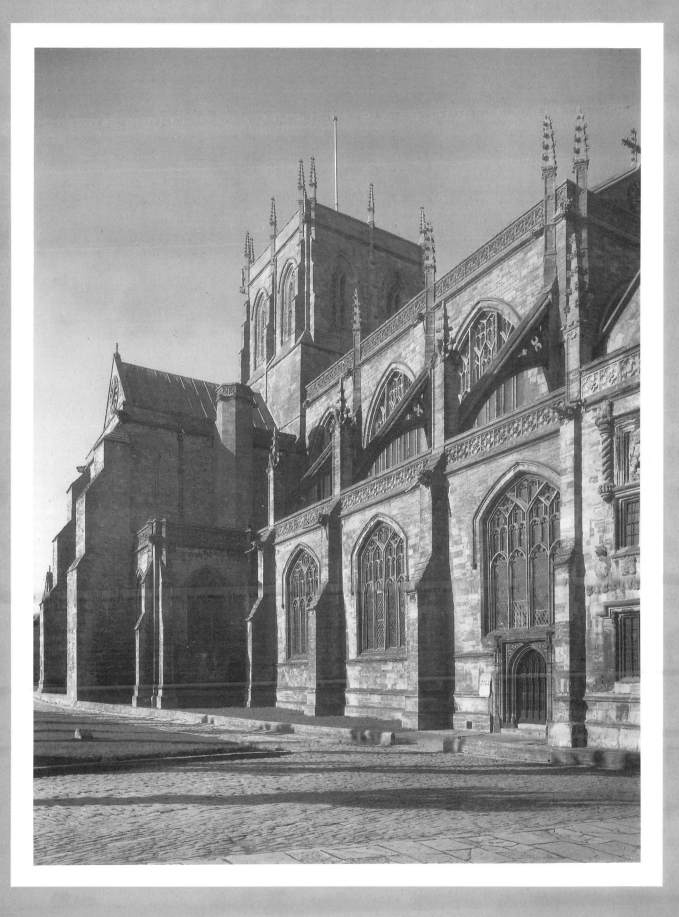

west of the church is where she breakfasted. From the church steps is a view right over the whole village to the green fields beyond. The rather urban and austere village street shows a wonderful variety of architecture, from rather heavy later Victorian imitations of 17th century buildings (mostly at each end of the street) through large and small Georgian houses to proper 17th and 18th century cottages, including an inn with a nice projecting bay supported on posts. The church of St Osmond has a north arcade and tower of the 15th century. The rest was built in imitation in the 1850's and 60's to such good effect that it is difficult to tell the old and new apart. One of Jane Austen's favourite poets – George Crabbe (1754-1832) was rector here from 1783-7.

★★★ *Village*

EYPE (D) A small village close to the sea approached down a deep, and leafy narrow lane. The church of 1865 sits on a prominent lump. The rather plain stone cottages are a little way back from the sea, but caravans close to the shore slightly mar the rural setting. Car-park (fee) down by the shingle beach. Good sandstone cliffs either way, but especially to the west, with the imposing Thorncombe Beacon (508 ft). The Dorset Coast Path can be taken eastwards to West Bay or westwards to Thorncombe Beacon and beyond, with inland footpaths offering an alternative route back. The road west from the village, through Upper Eype, has good inland views and scenery.

★★ *Landscape.*

FARNHAM (B) is quiet, secluded, and decidedly pretty, especially the middle of the main street where a succession of white painted thatched cottages stand with their gable ends to the street. Other cottages are spotted or banded in flint, stone and brick, and many are thatched. Farnham and nearby Minchington (which is in a lovely valley) are full of trees. The Museum Hotel is a reminder of the archaeologist Pitt-Rivers who encouraged visitors to the Larmer grounds and King John's House nearby (but in Wiltshire), and to the Museum which was ½ mile to the south of the village. The Museum was built in 1832 as a school for gypsies, and Pitt-Rivers converted it in the 1890's to a museum for his excavations, and for antiquities from other countries. In 1899 over 12,000 people visited and to provide accommodation and refreshments the Old Ash Inn was extended and renamed the Museum Hotel. The Museum is now converted to houses, but a gallery at the Salisbury and Wiltshire Museum (in Salisbury) displays the work of Pitt-Rivers, including much material from the Farnham Museum. One of Pitt-Rivers' anthropological collections can be seen, just as he left it, in the Pitt-Rivers Museum, Oxford. The church of St Lawrence is basically medieval, with a tower over the porch of *c.* 1500, and an economical north aisle added in 1835 with simple iron pillars like pipes supporting the arcade. The chancel is more elaborate and dates from 1886. Two fonts, one medieval, the other unusual late 17th century classical with a minute bowl. Two well-bordered texts on the west wall are of *c.* 1700.

★★ *Village, setting.*

FERNDOWN (G) is huge and mostly modern, with some pine trees surviving from the heathland. St Mary's church of 1933 is stone, in a rather smoothed out compendium of medieval styles, and with good modern (but traditional style) woodwork.

FIDDLEFORD (B) (just east of Sturminster Newton) has a pretty selection of cottages on the main road, and right down by the River Stour is one of the earliest manorhouses in Dorset, (free· lists) The hall and solar wing were built in the 1370's or 80's, and have heavy complex wooden roofs of great beauty. That in the hall has great cusped beams forming circles in the upper half and arches in the lower, while the beams in the apex form lovely shapes, again curved and cusped. The solar roof has arches and then a complex arrangement of beams in the upper half. It is difficult to realise the great age of these roofs – they have been here for 600 years. The hall was shortened in the 17th century, which makes it feel more cosy. The 16th century fireplace was re-set in the wall – the original fire was central and open, with the smoke finding its way through a louvre in the roof. None of the windows in the hall are original, for like the rest of the building it was remodelled in the 16th century, and the windows date from then. The screen across the west end of the hall is modern, the upper part survives in 17th century panelling. Off the passage are three fine 16th century doorways, with shields bearing the initials T W and A for Thomas and Ann White who owned the building in the first half of the 16th century and who remodelled it. Underneath the solar are storage rooms, much altered in the 16th and 17th centuries. On the first floor is the solar itself, the private room of the owner of the house, as opposed to the hall, the public room. As well as its superb 14th century roof, there are the remains at the north end of the original 14th century window.

The pump house, Farnham

The manor house, Fiddleford, before restoration

Solar roof, Fiddleford manor house

Lower Fifehead Farm, Fifehead St Quintin

Pack-horse bridge, Fifehead Neville

Running off the hall and solar is a long 16th century addition (not open). Just up the river is a little mill, with an inscription dated 1566 stating 'He thatt wyll have here any thynge don/Let him com fryndly he shal be welcom.' A footpath leads on across footbridges with several channels and a weir.

★★★★ *Despite being unfurnished, a house which must be seen.*

FIFEHEAD MAGDALEN (A/B) sits on a slight rise overlooking the Stour and has many houses and cottages in the local limestone, mostly 19th century. The church of St Mary Magdalen is surrounded by trees, and is largely 14th century, including the rather plain tower. The folding door is dated 1637. The north chapel was built in 1750 to house a vast monument on its north wall commemorating six members of the Newman family, with busts on top and medallions for daughters below. Four 18th century brass chandeliers in the nave, still with candles. The font is an odd marriage of a 15th century top, with an 18th century base and wooden cover. 1973 stained glass in west window.

★ *Village, church, setting.*

FIFEHEAD NEVILLE (A) Scattered, prettily wooded and with good hedges. The Fifehead villages are named after their assessment at Domesday – five hides. The little late medieval church of All Saints was extensively altered and made classical in 1736 when new windows were added, and a porch with a date stone were added (keeping the 16th century door). The

windows have much of their original plain glass. At the same time the tower was demolished and replaced by a simple bell-cote. The chancel is 1876, as are the roofs. Good monuments, including one to Robert Ryves 'a constant and sincere lover of the Royal family for which he suffered much in ye time of rebellious Persecution' and who died in 1658, two years too soon to see the restoration of Charles II. The churchyard is dominated by a vast 18th century table tomb of the Brune family. The chancel window surrounds are interesting outside – the western one in the north wall is 18th century Gothic revival with coarse heads, a great contrast to the delicate 1876 ones, but the 18th century ones, crude as they are have much more medieval 'feel'.

To the west of the village is a tall stone pack horse bridge over the river, with two pointed arches. It is medieval in origin, although restored. Very pretty. Just to the south is **Fifehead St Quintin**, a tiny settlement with a lovely farmhouse. Lower Fifehead Farm has lots of additions, but the core of the building, in stone, is probably 16th century. One wing has stone mullioned windows with rounded heads, and most unusually, those on the upper floor have cable-moulding on the hood-moulds. The barn next to the farm is dated 1881, largely, in the bricks.

★★ *Village, church, setting.*

FISHPOND (D) A very small village perched on the side of a hill with lots of extremely narrow and confusing lanes on

Fishpond

the edge of the Marshwood Vale. The countryside is well-wooded and charming – a good place to get lost. The view from the churchyard down to the sea through a wide valley is breath-taking, and only marred by a huge pylon. The tiny, white-washed church of St John the Baptist was built in 1854, is plain outside and in, with a fine east window of stained glass, 1967 and abstract.

★★ *Landscape.*

FLEET (H) is a 'small, romantic village' (1860 guide) in two parts: a few cottages and the remains of the old church, and the houses clustered around the new church. The former was made famous by J. Meade Falkner's novel *Moonfleet* (1898) a stirring tale of smugglers in the mid-18th century. The village and most of the medieval church described in *Moonfleet* were destroyed by the great storm of 1824 when the sea broke through the Chesil Bank, and all that remains of the

church is the chancel, which was repaired after the storm. There are several brasses to the Mohun family inside: it was in their vault that the smugglers' kegs were hidden in *Moonfleet*. The houses in the tiny valley are rather dolled-up, but the landscape of the novel endures – bleak and small scale, with the strange semi-saltwater lagoon of the Fleet and then the huge shingle bank of Chesil holding back the sea. It is possible to walk from Fleet along the lagoon to Moonfleet Hotel, but not very exciting. Parking near the old church is difficult and discouraged: it is easier to park by the new church and walk down.

The new church of 1829 was built in a safer position after the great storm. Park-like setting with huge beech trees by an ivy bordered stream. The building is magical – fairy-tale revived Gothic, all of one piece, looking like a model or a toy put down in the wood. The interior is less exciting (the chancel arch was made wider

Church screen, Folke

in the 1890's), but it has some pretty mock-medieval plaster in the chancel (and a good neoclassical monument of 1818). The plaster ceiling of the nave is peculiar. The churchyard is surrounded by impressive iron railings and two gates, all with flames on top. The whole area is pretty, well-wooded and good for walks.

★★★ *New church, landscape, walks.*

FOLKE (A, Alweston) is in a low-lying clay area with lots of trees, good hedgerows and, on the outskirts, hazel coppices (some overgrown) with oak trees above. The main (and more modern) part of the village is to the north and called Alweston.

The old village is small, isolated, mostly of stone and with drystone field walls. The church and manor house stand together. Large manor house with a reset 15th century doorway and window over, while most of the rest is 17th century. This is a normal enough date for a manor house, but, unusually, the church is also 17th century. It was totally rebuilt in 1628, and the shape is broadly that of a late medieval church, but even externally the windows look odd, with their stepped hood moulds.

Inside is even more Jacobean, with fluted pillars supporting arches ornamented with little flowers. Wood dominates. Stunning timber screen with great S scrolls on top, echoed by a smaller one in the north aisle. Communion rails, and table, pulpit and reading desk are all early 17th century but the most distinctive fitting is perhaps the font, also 1628, with a huge scrolly stone base and an even scrollier wooden lid. Some of the bench ends with their pretty shell pattern are original, although re-arranged a bit in the restoration of 1875.

★★★ *Very pretty, and unusual date for a church.*

Fleet, the old (bottom) and new churches

FONTMELL DOWN (B) off the high road between Blandford and Shaftesbury is a spur of chalk downland preserved by the National Trust and managed as a nature reserve by the Dorset Trust for Nature Conservation. Lots of flowers and butterflies on its 149 acres, and an Iron Age cross-ridge dyke is preserved within it as a substantial earthwork. This is one of several in the area. Their purpose (apart from being land boundaries of some sort) is uncertain, but they are often found in areas without Celtic fields, ie where there was no arable, and so probably relate to the organisation of grazing grounds. The down gives good views of the Blackmore Vale to the west and the continuation of the chalk scarp to the south-west. Car park to the north beside the road.

★★★ *Down, walks, views.*

FONTMELL MAGNA (B) A big, pretty village with houses and cottages in greensand, brick and timber-framing, some of them dating from the 17th century. Meadows and streams one side and high chalk downland the other. The church of St Andrew has only the lower part of the tower surviving from the medieval church: the rest was rebuilt elaborately in 1862. The parapet outside is copied from an original section now reset on the north aisle: it is reported to have had the date 1530 still surviving in the 18th century. The 1862 church has 'bold capitals of Bath stone, alternately floriated or representing angels' according to a contemporary newspaper which also admires the pulpit 'elaborately wrought in Caen stone being covered with tracery and having canopied niches containing figures of the four Evangelists'. Too elaborately wrought for current taste. Good carved corbels. All the stone carving is by Boulton, a London carver. Unusually the chancel is rather plainer than the rest. The 12th century font has running foliage and very dead looking birds and a nice 17th century cover. Under the tower is an early 16th century screen with two good roundels containing profiles. Mid 19th century eagle lectern, unusually made of cast iron. In the churchyard is a memorial cross to Philip Salkield, son of a rector, who won the VC in the Indian Mutiny of 1857 during the Siege of Delhi. The clock plays a tune every 3 hours.

To the east the road leads through Springhead and up into the hills through woods, very fine all the way.

★★ *Village, church.*

ABOVE *Looking west from Fontmell Down*
RIGHT *Springhead, Fontmell Magna*

FORDE ABBEY (D) is a beautiful house, with many surprises, surrounded by a large and interesting garden. In 1141 twelve Cistercian monks returning from an unsuccessful attempt at setting up an abbey in Devon were offered the manor of Thorncombe by Adelicia de Brioncis. Instead of continuing back to the mother-house in Surrey, they stayed here and built a monastery. The only buildings surviving from this earliest phase are the chapter house (now chapel) and the dormitory range behind it. The Abbot's hall and cloister were built just before the Dissolution of the Monasteries in 1539. It then became a house, the church and other buildings were demolished and the great staircase and saloon added in the 1650's. From 1815-1818 the house was let to the philosopher Jeremy Bentham.

The chapel, basically the 12th century chapter house, has nice scalloped capitals and stone vaulting, and is embellished with good 17th and 18th century woodwork. The pulpit has its own little window. Outside the battlements have two rainwater heads dated 1713.

The house is entered through the three storey porch, high quality with a little fan vault inside. Around the top is a Latin inscription meaning 'Made in the year of Our Lord 1528 by Thomas Chard, Abbot'. He was the last abbot, and his name and insignia are found in several places on his buildings. The porch leads to the great hall, unfinished when the Abbey was dissolved in 1539. It must have been very light before the north windows were blocked. All the stonework (apart from the 18th century fireplace) is 1530's, the ceiling 17th century and the panelling early 18th century, all combining harmoniously. Leading off the hall is the great staircase, heavy, elaborate and handsome, dating

from the 1660's. The plaster ceiling is dated 1658. At the top is the most magnificent room of the 17th century alterations: the saloon, far removed from the austerity one might expect from the Commonwealth period – the huge elaborately coved ceiling and panelling make it odd and impressive. The Duke of Monmouth was entertained here in 1680, which caused the ruin of the family after Monmouth's fall in 1685. The very fine Mortlake tapestries were given to a later owner of the house by Queen Anne.

The Monk's refectory has its original 15th century roof. The library fittings are 19th century Gothic, and the partition was made from Breton bedsteads at the same date. In the Prideaux suite of rooms are more 1650's ceilings. A plainer 17th century staircase returns one to the ground floor, and to the surprising view along the surviving side of the cloisters. It is difficult to know whether to first admire the architecture or the splendid plants which always line it. The cloisters were built in the early 16th century, with superb windows, echoed by stone panelling on the inner wall. At the eastern end is a wooden door which imitates the stone windows exactly. The plaster vaulting is 18th century. Part of the inner wall is removed to show the little Purbeck Marble columns of an earlier structure.

The Dorter was the monk's dormitory and dates from *c.* 1200. The upper storey was altered in the 19th century to form servants' bedrooms, but thirteen original lancet windows remain. The lower part (currently the tea-room) has original stone vaulting, with plain, modern-looking pillars. Outside the arches over the Great Drain can be seen at the north end of the building. The 'Monk's Kitchen' at the back of the house is basically 15th century.

ABOVE *Forde Abbey*
BELOW *The saloon, Forde Abbey*

The Gardens (c.40 acres) are entrancing. Although full of wonderful plantings, they are still natural – as well as millions of daffodils there are sweeps of bluebells, wind-flowers and even some native orchids. Ponds and cascades are mixed with a bewildering variety of beautiful trees. The ponds are fed by water brought nearly 2 miles by an artificial leat. They were the monastic fish ponds, adapted in the 18th century to make formal water gardens. Impressive bog garden. Arboretum. Good at all times of the year, one of the four best gardens in Dorset (fee: lists).
★★★★ *House and gardens*

FORDINGTON, *see* **DORCHESTER**
FORTUNESWELL, *see* **PORTLAND**

FRAMPTON (E) A completely lop-sided village, with lots of attractive cottages on one side of the main street, and nothing on the other. The owner of Frampton Court (demolished) removed in about 1840 all the cottages on one side to improve his park. One of the lodges to the big house is on the east side of the village. Some thatched cottages, some flint and stone banding. The church of St Mary is an oddity. The tower corners are two huge columns, one on top of the other, with pinnacles above. This classical body with a medieval hat was built in 1695. The body of the church seems wider than it is long – the chancel arch and south arcade are of about 1500 with initials and figures in the foliage of the capitals, but the mock-medieval aisles gained their present appearance about 1820. The Victorian fittings are splendid, particularly wall tiles, the font (given in 1858), the reredos and the ugly roof of the nave. The treasures of the church are the monuments, especially those of the Browne family. The most unusual is to Robert Browne who paid for the tower – an elaborate classical window of 1734, with the inscription below. Those in the north aisle are mostly of the 18th century, but reset in the chancel (itself 1862) are monuments of 1627 and 1634.

★★★ *Church for its odd date and style of tower, rich monuments and 19th century fittings.*

FRIAR WADDON (H, near Portesham) is really only a large farmstead, with stone buildings of the 16th-late 18th centuries.

FROME ST QUINTIN (E) is partly on an abrupt hill, and has mixed stone, brick and flint cottages and farm buildings. In the centre is a very distinguished brick house, Frome House, built in 1782 with a lovely Portland Stone porch (large 1913 addition). The little church of St Mary is in the middle of fields, with no driveway to it. It is simple and basically 13th century.

★ *Village*

FROME VAUCHURCH (E) A tiny settlement close to Maiden Newton right down by the River Frome. Sylvia Townsend Warner (1893-1978), the short story writer, novelist and poet, lived here for 40 years. The church is small, basically Norman with a 19th century chancel – the widened arch retains simple Norman decoration. Charming interior, narrow and homely, with pale walls, dark pews and roof. Fine early 17th century pulpit.

★ *Landscape.*

GILLINGHAM (B) is on the edge of the Blackmore Vale, and was once the centre of the Royal Forest of Gillingham. The town is not pretty, but at its best at the northern

Purn's (or Parham) Mill, near Gillingham, by John Constable, 1826

end. Until the railway came in 1859 it was very small, but after that several large industries developed, including production of a hot red brick, much in evidence about the town, and also in Bournemouth. Stone buildings too.

The church of St Mary the Virgin (lists) is in the prettiest part of the town. Apart from the 14th century chancel, the whole large church is of 1838-40. Between the north chapel and the chancel are original pillars with ball-flower decoration, and in the north chapel is a handsome monument to two brothers, Thomas and John Jessop 1625. The monument to Mrs Frances Durdoe (1733) is superb, with three female figures. On the north side of the chancel is a heavy baroque wall monument made by the Bastards of Blandford. The south chapel is fitted as a memorial to a soldier who died in the First World War. In the chancel the darker bench ends are the original 15th century ones – the others and much of the seating dates from 1840, The reredos is also a memorial, made in 1925. At the end of the north aisle is a fine Coat of Arms of 1618, and at the west end of the south aisles are fragments of a Saxon (probably 9th century) cross with pretty interlace. The 1840 tower was remodelled in 1908-9.

Gillingham Museum (fee: lists) is in the new part of the town, Chantry Fields to the south-west off the new relief road, with local history, etc.

GLANVILLE'S WOOTTON or Wootton Glanville (E) in the Blackmore Vale has lots of trees, but most of the houses are recent or 19th century. The church of St Mary has a short tower of *c.* 1400, with the nave and chancel mostly dating from a severe restoration of 1876. The earliest and best part of the church is the south chapel, endowed as a chantry chapel (where masses were said daily for the dead) in 1344. Lovely windows (each different) in the Decorated style, only found rarely in Dorset, embrasures for tombs, and a good archway and doorway to the nave. Medieval tiles re-set in one tomb recess and on the eastern part of the floor, the rest is reproduction. 13th century effigy. The showy large monument of 1679 on the west wall of the chapel is mostly painted clunch (hard chalk).

★★ *Landscape and church.*

GOATHILL (A) is tiny and rural. The church of St Peter was basically rebuilt in the 19th century. ½ mile south is a mid 19th century ornamental lodge to Sherborne Castle, with a ludicrously large thatched roof (*see ill. on next page*).

GODMANSTONE (E) lies along the little valley of the River Cerne, with many flint buildings banded with stone or brick and the so-called smallest inn in England – the single storey Smith's Arms, built of flint and thatched, once a smithy. To the south,

The Lodge, Goathill

at Forston, a perfect early 18th century brick house.

The church of Holy Trinity is surrounded by trees, and has a good view over the downs. It too is stone and flint, with a most amusing doorway which is either an 1848 copy of a Norman original, or possibly partly original, with the surface re-cut – a horrid Victorian habit. Imitation 'Norman' door. Rather wonky 17th century chancel arch with Norman pillars (base on the south side is part of a Roman altar with inscription). 16th century nave, with a good stout angel corbel on the south-east. All around the church are various sized square-headed 15th and 16th century windows.

★ *Village.*

GOLDEN CAP (D) The centre of a large estate owned by the National Trust, and all

accessible for walking. The Cap itself has the highest sea cliffs on the south coast (618 ft) and gives wonderful views both along the coast and inland. The name comes from the capping of Upper Greensand, here as in some other places, golden orange. If it is clear Start Point can be seen to the west and Portland is almost always visible to the east. Inland views are also fine, with Pilsdon Pen hillfort visible beyond the Marshwood Vale. The distant prospects are rivalled by smaller, closer views. 18 miles of footpaths, some along the coast, some inland, are within the National Trust area, and it is a superb place to walk, with many flowers, butterflies and so on. Only traditional farming methods are used on many of the fields so there is no spraying – the difference in the spring and summer between this area and those using more 'advanced' methods is enormous. The easiest way to reach the top of Golden Cap is the footpath from the NT car park at Langdon Hill, south of the main road between Chideock and Morcombelake, but it can also be approached on foot from Seaton on the east or from Charmouth to the west. On the west there is a car park at Stonebarrow, reached by a very narrow lane (full of bluebells) off the main road just east of Charmouth. The information centre is in an old radar station by this car park. Right in the middle of the estate, and only accessible by foot, is what remains of the village of Stanton St Gabriel, which declined after the main road moved north. Only the ruins of the little church, a farmhouse and one cottage. A very peaceful place.

★★★★ *Walking.*

GUSSAGE ALL SAINTS (B) All the Gussage villages take their first name from the stream which seems to mean 'gush of water'. This one has pleasant brick and cobb cottages along its leafy main street, including one with timber framing and a few with thatch. The church sits prominently at one end, on the side of the tiny valley. Although it looks Victorian because it has uniform windows and is so square and regular, it is in fact a large 14th century building, with pretty greensand windows, and flint walls with odd pieces of greensand and dark brown heathstone. The interior is impressive, with cusped arches inside the windows. In the 1860's it was given a new chancel arch, and new roofs, with complex supports. The ornate Victorian work contrasts with the much more attractive 14th century building. 18th century mahogany cased organ of high quality, once in Westminster Abbey, and a decorated 14th century recess in the north wall, which may originally have been a monument, or an Easter Sepulchre. Good plain 14th century font.

★★ *Church.*

GUSSAGE ST ANDREW (B, just southwest of Sixpenny Handley) Just a small flint church hiding behind a large farmhouse on the eastern edge of the county. The farmhouse is partly early 17th century brick and greensand with flint banding, and partly 18th century brick, and makes a fine courtyard to the road with stables and out-buildings. The chapel of St Andrew is small, all medieval and

Golden Cap and Seaton from Eype Down

interesting. The 12th century nave has one little window of that date. 13th century chancel with two simple lancets at the east end. The straight lines imitating masonry in the nave wall paintings are late 12th century, and superimposed are scenes from the Passion, in shades of red and yellow, painted in the late 13th century: damaged, but worth seeing. Below is a 16th or 17th century inscription. Nice 17th century pulpit and 18th century chandelier, still in use, as despite having an electric organ the church is lit by oil lamps.

★ *Church.*

GUSSAGE ST MICHAEL (B) has few buildings earlier than the late 19th century, although most of the church of St Michael is medieval. There is a plain round arch of the 12th century inside under the tower, while the aisles are slightly later – early 13th century – with big fat pillars and pointed arches. Most of the rest is 15th century, but the chancel is by Street, 1850's, with a complex reredos typical of his work.

★ *Church.*

HALSTOCK (D/E) Some good stone cottages and a few fine Georgian stone houses, all in a lush green landscape. The church of St Mary has a 15th century tower, while the nave of 1845 is by Pugin, the famous Gothic revival architect, and the chancel 1872. The chapel is dedicated to St Juthware, a Saxon saint who carried her head to the altar after she had been beheaded, inspiring several Dorset Inn signs of The Quiet Woman. She was probably martyred at Halstock.

HAMBLEDON HILL (B, Child Okeford)
The most impressive Iron Age hillfort in Dorset, with multiple ramparts enclosing the whole of a high spur of the chalk. Prominent for miles around, and from the top there are wide views north and west across the Blackmoor Vale, and south-west along the chalk escarpment. Footpaths lead up to it from the east and west. The interior is unploughed, so hut circles and platforms show clearly in the grass. In the middle is a Neolithic long barrow, predating the hillfort. To the east were a series of Neolithic enclosures, now largely ploughed out. Two ditches across the fort indicate that it was built in three successive stages. The only excavations on the hillfort were in the 19th century, when Iron Age and Roman material

The slopes of Hambledon Hill

was found, but the Neolithic enclosures to the east have been extensively excavated recently, showing that they were part of a complex Neolithic landscape including some 2 miles of outworks and enclosing more than 160 acres.

The Clubmen made their last stand on Hambledon. These were country people who resented the 'un-natural' Civil War and the depredations of the soldiers of both sides, and banded together armed only with clubs (hence the name). Their banners were inscribed 'If you offer to plunder or take our cattle, be assured we will bid you battle'. They were particularly strong in Dorset, and after being harried by Oliver Cromwell some 2-4000 of them fought against him (and his army of 1,000) here in August 1645. The Clubmen were routed and most of them fled. (See also Iwerne Courtney).

★★★ *Hillfort, views.*

HAMMOON (B) A small low-lying hamlet. Once home, or ham, of the Mohun family. Just along from the church is the manor house with a superb late *(cont p.84)*

Churches 1540-1800

After the Reformation and the dissolution of the monasteries in the 1530's no new churches were built (and only a few additions made to existing buildings) until early in the 17th century, but many fittings, particularly wooden ones, were added. Puddletown is a good example of this, with much early 17th century woodwork still surviving. This lack of later 16th century churches is the national pattern, as is the paucity of the 17th century ones. Up to about 1750 most of the new church building was because the medieval had fallen down, or was threatening to do so. Folke is an interesting new church of 1628, in simplified medieval style, and the new tower of 1695 at Frampton is a compromise between medieval and classical. Apart from some fittings, Dorset churches were not at the forefront of fashion in the 17th or 18th centuries. The small church at Charlton Marshall is restrained classical and 1713, and the fine, much larger church at Blandford is slightly out of date for the 1730's, but still very good. St George Reforne, Portland, is also by a local architect and although it was designed in the 1750's it is in a style current in London some forty or more years earlier. It is still a superb church, especially combined with its early 19th century fittings and tombstones. The Catholic church at East Lulworth is classical of 1786 and very fine.

★★★★ Blandford; St George Reforne, Portland;
★★★ Charlton Marshall, St Mary East Lulworth, Folke, Frampton, Puddletown, West Stafford.

BELOW *St George, Reforne, Portland* ABOVE RIGHT *Moreton*

Churches: the Nineteenth Century

Dorset has a fine selection of 19th century churches in a wonderful diversity of styles. None are huge, but for quality the best will bear comparison with the best in the country. There has been a tendency to regard 19th century churches as inferior imitations of the medieval, somehow spurious, and so not worth looking at. This is nonsense. The 19th century churches can be as interesting (or as dull) as any earlier period. Those which are either total rebuilds, or new churches on new sites, are often interesting because the whole building, its fittings and sometimes even decoration, are all of the same date providing a type-fossil of what a church was intended to be at the time.

Up to about 1840 most of the churches were Gothic revival, but in a rather playful manner, using plaster for vaulting for example, producing some very pretty churches. The smaller ones are the best – Fleet of 1829, Winterborne Clenston of 1840 and Moreton where the 1840's extensions match the charm of the 1776 original (completed by the superb modern engraved glass). Sutton Waldren is rather later (1857) but just as good. St James, Poole is on a much larger scale, but is 1820 and not at all serious.

A revival of the Norman in the 1840's left Dorset

with several churches in that style, the best of which is Melplash, but increasing study of medieval architecture brought a far more serious approach to church building. Scholarly architects derided the use of one material to imitate another, so that if a roof was to be vaulted it must be stone, not plaster. By some curious logic Decorated architecture was deemed to be the most 'Christian' although as the century went on more variety was allowed. Monkton Wyld (1848) and Woolland (1857) are fine Dorset examples of what was regarded as 'correct' church architecture, and Monkton Wyld is full of fine quality fittings. These churches can be very rich, and even though they are carefully detailed from surviving medieval examples they are not simply copies.

The diversity of the later 19th century is well represented, especially since the addition of Bournemouth to the county. St Peter's, Bournemouth, and St Clement's, Boscombe, are both fine, but St Stephen's, Bournemouth is magnificent, probably the best 19th century church in the county. It could be rivalled by Cattistock, whose tower of 1874 is as good as any of the medieval ones.

Kingston, Purbeck, is a complex and very successful Early English style church, designed in the 1870's. Colehill is much more unusual, a brick and half-timbered church of 1893, rather alien to Dorset. Bothenhampton of 1887 is a very engineered church, with huge parabolic arches running from the floor to the apex of the roof.

Two earlier 20th century churches are of great interest: the partial rebuilding and elaborate refitting of Wimborne St Giles in 1908, and the far more modern St Osmund's, Parkstone (Poole), brick and Byzantine.

Most of the 19th century churches mentioned were designed by London architects who produced churches all over the country. The best known local person working on church restoration was Thomas Hardy, who worked for the Dorchester architect John Hicks from 1856-62 and 67-72. He later deplored the drastic alterations made by architects, who, he said thought they needed to pull churches down to effect a thorough 'restoration'. Hardy designed part of Turnworth church, which is rather French in style. The most spectacular of Hicks churches is North Poorton, which demonstrates the fine stone carving of Benjamin Grassby, whose work is found in 45 Dorset churches.

There were other local architects of course, and the unusual, almost Byzantine, Roman Catholic church at Chideock was designed by the client himself, Charles Weld.

★★★★: St Stephen, Bournemouth; Cattistock; Moreton; and Sutton Waldron.
★★★: St Peter's, Bournemouth; St Clement's, Boscombe, New Holy Trinity, Bothenhampton; Chideock Roman Catholic church; Colehill; Fleet; Kingston; St James, Poole; St Osmund, Parkstone, Poole and Wimborne St Giles.

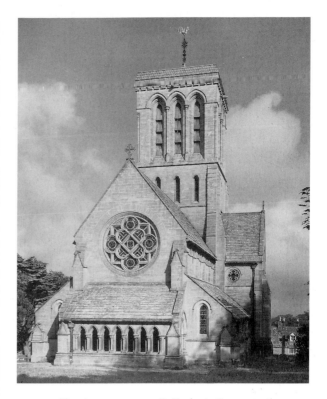

ABOVE *Kingston*   BELOW   *St Stephen's, Bournemouth*

16th century porch and two-storey bay window, both in a rather naive classical manner. Most of the rest of the house is 17th century. The church of St Paul is mostly 13th century, and the chancel has a simple east window of that date with interesting stained glass of 1959. Behind the altar is a stone reredos of about 1400, brought here in 1945. The nave roof is of the mid 15th century, carefully copied in the western extension of 1885. The wooden door with its huge lock-box is 15th century too, and the carved pulpit is dated 1635.
★★ *Setting, manor house,*

HAMPRESTON (G) Still rural, although close to the Bournemouth conurbation. The church of All Saints had its north side rebuilt in the 1890's, and new windows in the nave at the same time. The chancel and tower are 14th century, with a pretty window of that date under the tower and a 15th century east window in the chancel, which also has fine corbels holding up the roof. Elaborate monument of 1630 to a priest. The medieval feel of the church is rather destroyed because all the plaster is stripped off internally.
　　Knoll Gardens (fee: lists) 4 acres, densely planted with rockeries and so on. Rather suburban.
　　★★ *Garden.*

HAMWORTHY (F) The commercial docks of Poole are technically in Hamworthy, adjacent but across the river. They are not accessible. Flying boats used the harbour in the Second World War, and it was an important embarkation point for D-Day ferries to France. The area developed after the construction of the bridge across to Poole in 1835, so there are Victorian buildings on the main road from the bridge. The rest is 1920's and 30's ribbon development, with more recent infilling behind. Between the modern library and Herbert Carter Secondary Modern School, on the main road, is a distinguished mid 17th century brick manor house, unusual in Dorset; big gables and pilasters on the front wall.

HARDOWN HILL (D, Morcombelake) Belongs to the National Trust, and is worth climbing for the splendid views, especially west towards Lyme Regis. Good heathland with dense heather and furze.
　　★★ *Views, landscape.*

HARDY'S MONUMENT (H, Blackdown) A popular view point, centred on a 72 ft high Portland Stone tower (looking rather like a factory chimney) commemorating Admiral Sir Thomas Masterman Hardy (1769-1839) the hero of Trafalgar ('Kiss me,

ABOVE　*Hammoon manor*
RIGHT　*Hardy's Monument, Blackdown*

Hardy'), not the novelist. Hardy lived at Portesham until 1781 when he entered the Navy and the monument was built after his death. If it's really clear it is possible from this elevation of 780 ft to see the Devon coastline and also to Bulbarrow in north Dorset. Even in normal weather the views are very good, with the Chesil and Fleet to the south, the variety of the Dorset coast to the east, and wide views inland. Around the monument and along Bronkham Hill to the south east the rough bracken has not been reclaimed, so many barrows survive (see Ridgeway). Conical sink or swallow holes, some small and some infinitely deep (and fenced off), are natural, produced by acidic water eating away the chalk underlying the gravel.
　　A mile to the west of Hardy's Monument is the Valley of the Stones, with very marked Celtic field systems on the sides of the valley – a series of small square fields showing as earthworks. The stones which litter the area are sarsens, occurring naturally on the surface. Prehistoric man used large sarsens for stone circles like those nearby at Kingston Russell and Winterbourne Abbas.
　　★★★★ *Views, landscape.*

HAYDON (A) Small, with many rockfaced Victorian stone buildings, including a vast parsonage. The small church of 1883 looks like a chapel. On the outskirts are some very unspoiled farm buildings, and on the main road a Victorian lodge to Sherborne Castle.

HAZELBURY BRYAN (E) is so scattered that the different parts have different names. Most of the modern development is in **Kingston,** but some farms (stone or

Georgian brick) are spread over the typical Blackmore Vale landscape of pasture and small hills. The church and school are in **Droop.** The church of St Mary and St James has a stout 15th century tower, with a wooden door dated 1827 in nails. This defines the date of the whole building – the entire church was built in the second half of the 15th century, and then was repaired and altered in 1827. Some original painted and stained glass survives in the upper parts of the windows. Even the main wooden door is 15th century, including all its fittings, apart from the ring handle inside. The roof is 15th century, with bosses and mouldings. The church was restored in 1904, late enough for it to be a proper restoration, and the chancel was refitted in 1937. The 1782 pulpit has an unusual sounding board, hanging by a chain. In the porch are two painted boards of 1840, one of which had the name of the village removed in 1940 lest it assist invading Germans. Beyond the church are ponds, and beside the road a 19th century almshouse restored in 1934.
　　★★ *Church.*

HENGISTBURY HEAD (G) and the long thin sandspit beyond form almost two sides of Christchurch Harbour. The Head is high and heathy, and is a nature reserve. It has a complicated history, recently investigated by a series of excavations. On what is now cliff there were Lower Paleolithic and Mesolithic hunters camps dating from 12,500 and 7,500 years ago, when the coastline was much further south. Neither these nor the Neolithic activity in the area are visible on the ground, but some of the 13 Bronze age barrows are. An early Iron Age settlement was abandoned in the 6th

century BC, and when occupation resumed about 100 BC Hengistbury was a port, trading with the Continent. Italian amphorae, Breton pots and raw purple glass are amongst the imports which have been found here, and exports perhaps included slaves. It was probably to defend the port that the prominent Double Dykes were constructed, cutting the Head off from the mainland. The port declined after about 50 BC, but the site continued to be used as a small agricultural settlement until the end of the Roman period. Cars are not allowed inside the Double Dykes, but 'land trains' run from the large car park to the sandspit, and ferries run around the harbour, calling at the centre of the spit from Mudeford, Tuckton and Christchurch. Pretty views from the Head both over the Harbour and along the coast. The sandspit has a spine of two rows of chalets almost up to the exceedingly narrow mouth of the harbour (see Mudeford).

★★★ *An interesting place for walking, along either shore or the top. A good escape from Bournemouth's urban sprawl.*

HERMITAGE (E) is in the extreme southern part of the Blackmore Vale, with lots of cows and trees. Flat, but the chalk ridge dominates the southern skyline. Very scattered, with a rather odd little church probably built in the 14th century for the unofficial Augustine monks from whom the village name is derived. Much altered in the 17th century, and perhaps partly rebuilt in 1800, leaving the windows looking rather naked with no tracery. Lovely setting, close to a 19th century stone farmhouse.

★★ *Landscape.*

ABOVE *Hengistbury Head and Christchurch Harbour looking west*
BELOW *Highcliffe Castle*

HIGHCLIFFE (G) The most easterly parish in Dorset, with a wild slipping short cliff to the sea, and lots of groynes to try to halt the erosion. Nice coastal views, including the Isle of Wight. Mostly recent houses, all well-wooded, with a shopping street parallel to the sea, but back from it. Highcliffe Castle, built in the 1830's in a Romantic Gothic style, is enhanced by the inclusion of real late Gothic French features such as the very elaborate oriel window above the porch and the windows to the

right of it. An odd but attractive building, on a large scale. The hall by the road looks like a church. The house burnt in the 1960's, and is being restored. The inscription round the top is a quotation from the Roman poet Lucretius: 'Sweet it is, when on the great sea the winds are buffeting the waters, to look on from the land on another's great struggles'. A park around the house, with the woodland and small garden south of the house open to the public (car park; fee in summer) and with a winding path leading down to the mostly sandy beach. The combination of cliff, trees and beach is picturesque. The church of St Mark in Hinton Wood Avenue was paid for by the owner of the Castle, but it lacks the Castle's eccentricity. Largely of 1843 and plain.

★★ *Castle.*

HILLFIELD (E) A secluded scattered hamlet on the lower slopes of the chalk escarpment, with a large view over the Blackmore Vale to the north. The tiny isolated church is probably 13th century, but it was greatly restored in 1848, with unusual stained glass of that date in the chancel. The bench ends are odd, and their date uncertain. 17th century has been suggested, but 19th century seems more likely. The benches in the chancel are conventional 15th century. Franciscan friary away to the west.

★ *Church, views.*

HILTON (F) shares the superb landscape of its neighbour Milton Abbas. Wooded hills frame the church on its prominent knoll in the centre of the village. Some good cottages, a few thatched, and a stream, but it is the wider landscape which dominates. Apart from the 19th century chancel the church is of the 15th or 16th centuries – the south wall is dated 1569 externally. This is an extension – the earlier porch has been left half inside the church. Presumably it was too good, with its stone fan vault, to demolish. Inside, the north aisle catches the eye – it is almost all window, brought here from Milton Abbey after the dissolution of the monasteries in the 1530's. 15th century wooden roofs. In the tower are twelve large painted wooden panels of the late 15th century, also taken from Milton Abbey, which show the apostles. Very pretty pulpit constructed from 16th and 17th century panels. Handsome 15th century tower.

★★★ *Setting, church.*

HINTON MARTELL (F/G) Leafy and quiet, with several brick and thatch cottages, including one of the 18th century with timber-framing. In the middle is a rather odd fountain, last rebuilt in 1965. The church of St John was rebuilt in 1870 in a mixture of flint, brown heathstone and limestone, in a style typical of the period. Much painted decoration. Thomas Hardy was working for Crickmay at the time the new church was designed, and may have had a hand in it.

HINTON PARVA, *see* **STANBRIDGE**

HINTON ST MARY (B) is well-known for the fine Roman mosaic pavement with a head of Christ found there in 1963, and now in the British Museum. The village is particularly good off the main road, with many cottages of the local pale stone, some of them still thatched, and Dalton's Farm, a classical 18th century farmhouse. Behind the church is the pretty 17th century manor house extended in the 18th century. The church of St Peter has a late 15th century tower, with the rest of the church dating from 1846. Nice monument to Thomas Freke, who died in 1642 and built part of the manor house. Just along the road, south from the church, are the 16th century stone stables of the manor house, with many buttresses, and beyond a tithe barn of *c.* 1500, much altered in the 1930's to form a theatre.

★ *Village.*

HOD HILL (B) (National Trust) has the largest internal area of any hillfort in Dorset. Because it is not so prominent as its neighbour Hambledon, the extensive and pretty views from the top come as a surprise. Access is from the side road running from Child Okeford to Iwerne Stepleton, to the west end of the fort. From

Head of Christ, Hinton St Mary Roman mosaic

the same point a woody path leads round the base of the river cliff at the foot of the hill and on to Stourpaine. A stiff 10 minutes' climb leads up to one of the Roman entrances to the fort. This corner was re-used as a Roman fort from immediately after the Roman conquest in 43 AD up to about 51 AD. Excavations have shown that it was used by a legionary detachment of 600 men (foot-soldiers) and a cavalry unit of about 250. It is very difficult today to imagine all these men and horses living in a disciplined military manner on this windy hill, a real outpost of the empire, although their earthworks cutting off the corner of the hillfort still have a neat, regimented look. The Iron Age hillfort is four or five times the size of the Roman, with original entrances on the north-east and south-west, and another added by the Romans in the middle of the east side. The Iron Age ramparts round the outer edge of the fort are double except on the west where there is a steep cliff. The quarry pits inside the rampart, dug to provide material to heighten them, are clear, but vegetation obscures the unploughed south-eastern segment where many hollows of Iron Age huts and pits survive. The ploughing of the rest of the interior from the middle of the 19th century produced quantities of Roman and Iron Age objects, now mostly in the British Museum. During excavations ballista bolts were found in the area of the largest hut enclosure (probably that of a chieftain) suggesting that the Romans bombarded it deliberately. The interior is not flat so the

views change as one walks round the fort. Hambledon Hill (see entry) is only a mile away to the north, but obscured by a rounded shoulder of chalk with a big yew wood. The flowers on Hod are very good, particularly in early summer, and there are many butterflies.

★★★★ *Hillfort, views, natural history.*

HOLDENHURST (G) On the edge of Bournemouth, which is creeping closer. Although by-passed, and indeed a *cul-de-sac*, a main road rushes past. Pretty little village green, with some nice cottages and a big late 17th century brick farm-house, all alongside more recent housing. The church is a replacement of 1834 and 1873.

HOLDITCH and LOWER HOLDITCH (D) are hamlets with chert buildings like Thorncombe. The lanes are pretty, the verges filled with wild flowers.

HOLNEST (A/E) is so widely scattered about the lush low-lying southern part of the Blackmore Vale that it hardly seems a settlement. The church sits in the fields, with next door (but some 150 yards south) Dunn's Farm, a 17th century stone building with a later brick extension, still with stone mullioned windows. The later medieval church of St Mary has a very varied external outline due to lots of additions. The chancel is 1855, and the interior is attractively all painted white.

★★ *Surrounding landscape.*

ABOVE *Pig Oak, God's Blessing Lane, Holt*

HOLT (G)The centre of the Royal Forest of Wimborne mentioned in Domesday. The area is still well-wooded and has scattered settlements with many brick houses and cottages of the 18th and 19th centuries (including the delightfully named God's Blessing Green). The church of St James was repaired in 1493 because of the 'great distance' from Wimborne: 'In winter [the road] is so noxious and muddy that the inhabitants of the hamlet are unable to get to the church without grave and tedious labour'. Rebuilt on a larger scale in brick and a very simple style in 1836, and a rather more complicated chancel added in 1889. Fine early 17th century pulpit brought here in 1858, from Wimborne.

HOLT HEATH, *see* **WHITE SHEET HILL**

HOLWELL (A) Two separate settlements, one with mostly 19th century and later buildings to the south called Barnes Cross (with the oldest letter box still in use in the country, 1850's), and right by the river to the north, the original medieval settlement with the church, a large early 18th century rectory and a few stone cottages, called The Borough, a perfect little hamlet. The handsome church of St Lawrence is a well preserved late 15th century building (apart from the chancel of 1885). Good tower and battlements all round. The windows are pretty, and inside the high arches to the north aisle have angels holding inscribed scrolls on the capitals. The roofs are 15th century too – a barrel vault in the nave, and a much more elaborate coffered wooden roof in the north aisle. An inscription on wood records that 'Ion

BELOW *1850's letter box, Holwell*

Chaffie gave a Tree to ye Erecting of this Gallery 1734': the gallery is gone but the inscription remains.
★★ *Landscape, church.*

HOLYWORTH (H, Ringstead) only a couple of farms and cottages, but preserved to the east of Holworth Farm (and visible from the road) are the remains of a particularly good deserted medieval village, partially excavated in 1958 and

probably occupied from the 12th to the 15th centuries. A roadway and square plots for houses can be seen, with garden or small field divisions behind.

Amongst the houses on the cliff-top is a tiny weather-boarded church, St Catherines-by-the-sea. The Holworth road is private and it is best to park at Falcon Barn (see Ringstead). Upton Fort to the west is 1902 and Second World War.

HOOKE (D/E) A pretty village. Near the centre is a large pond lined with trees. On the west side is Hooke Court, 17th century with later additions. The church of St Giles reverses the common pattern in Dorset churches – unusual 19th century tower with the rest late medieval. The tower was designed by Crickmay, a Weymouth architect, in 1874, when the chancel arch was also rebuilt. Most of the windows are 15th century, apart from the early 16th century south chapel, with a fine arch, intricately and formally decorated. 15th century font, and a niche of the same date containing a stone carving of St Giles (1878) by Benjamin Grassby the Dorchester carver.

The Working Woodland (fee: lists). Between Beaminster & Hooke on the B3163. A 330 acre mixed wood, used from 1983 to experiment with uses for smaller timber, now often wasted, including a display building. The woods themselves are open to the public. 'Sculptured' small wood entrance. The main walk leads through beech, ash and conifers – fine at all times but magical in late spring with bluebells under beech.
★ *Village, church.*

HORN PARK GARDENS (D) 1½ miles north of Beaminster, Good formal gardens around the house (very fine Neo-Georgian of 1911) with a huge view across the Beaminster valley to the hills and sea beyond. Wonderful setting on small hills, with a woodland garden, a very rich natural meadow, and bluebell woods.
★★★ Close by is the Horn Tunnel, built in 1831 to take the road through a steep hill. Like a railway tunnel.

HORTON (G) A scattered parish with some good 18th century brick cottages and houses, in low-lying, rather flat area with lots of trees and big hedges. The church of St Wolfrida (a later Saxon Abbess here) has a little tower and tiny spire of such high architectural quality to suggest that Vanbrugh, who was working at Eastbury close by when the tower was built in 1722-3, was the architect. In c. 1720 the only surviving medieval walls (the chancel) were refaced in brick and given new *(cont p.90)*

Cottages and Farmhouses

Dorset's cottages are, quite rightly, famous. Grouped together they make up picturesque villages, while isolated examples almost seem part of the landscape. Local materials and simple detailing make the cottages and farmhouses look as though they have grown, rather than having been built. The cottages of the farm labourers and the farmhouses of their employers can be identical in size, but usually farmhouses are larger, and have more elaborate doors and windows. Farmhouses are not necessarily out amongst the fields, but are often found in the villages. Large, functioning farmyards are still often found in the middle of many Dorset villages.

Most cottages are not as old as their owners and admirers assume: humble medieval buildings do not survive, partly because they were so slightly built. A few partly medieval farmhouses or small manor houses still survive, and so do a few 16th century cottages, but they are difficult to distinguish externally from the great majority which date from the 17th to 19th centuries. The traditional cottage is built of local materials, stone where available, cob or brick if not, with a simple plan, only one room wide, which gives them their distinctive profile. This narrowness was designed to make the most economical use of timber in the roof, an economy extended when thatch was used for roofing since between the main timbers really thin wood (sometimes like peasticks) could be used, as the timbering does not need to be absolutely level for thatch. The alternative roofing — stone slates — was doubly expensive because it was very heavy, needing heavier roof timbers as well as the expensive stone. Cottages were mostly thatched.

Cottages built by small farmers or other tradesmen for their own occupation ignore all the changes in architecture, and are extremely conservative, presumably on the rural principle of 'what was good enough for my grandfather is good enough for me'.

From the middle of the 18th century a new type of cottage appears, consciously picturesque, not built by farmers or labourers, but by large estates and the rich. The most ornate were often built as lodges, and there are a few of these in Dorset. Lyme Regis has one, and several more seasidy versions. Deliberate neatness and regularity is found in the model villages, rebuilt on more sanitary lines by the large estates. Milton Abbas is a good example, with 24 identical plainish cottages in its one street. Early Victorian estates also built Romantic cottages for the workers, usually in a Tudor style. At Little Bredy virtually the whole village was rebuilt to the designs of an architect in the 1840's, along with the farmyard, church, and a village school carefully disguised as a cottage. The Tudor style, sometimes all stone, sometimes brick with stone dressings, remained a popular style for estate cottages until the later 19th century, and they are usually easy to distinguish from the originals by their mass-produced, rather mechanical air, and because they are symmetrical, something no traditional cottage or farmhouse builder bothered about. Often they have the arms of the owner of the estate, or the date, emblazoned on them, and all the cottages on an estate may be in a matching style.

The later 19th and early 20th century cottages are usually more cheaply built, partly because of the agricultural depression. From the 1920's olde worlde cottages became desirable second (or even first) homes for town dwellers, and steadily the homes left unwanted because of the mechanisation of agriculture were bought up by retired people, or those who worked outside the village. From the 1920's reproduction traditional cottages (some very large) were also built, particularly in villages close to the sea, and at Briantspuddle and other nearby villages, where they were part of one estate's attempt to halt the drift of agricultural workers from the land. 1990s vernacular reproduction cottages like those at Abbotsbury or Poundbury seem convincingly real.

The attractiveness of old cottages today, restored, weather-proof and warm with running water and drainage, should not blind us to the miserable lives of many who lived in them in the 19th century, and earlier. Farm labourers in Dorset were some of the worst paid in the country, because there was no competition from factories for their labour. Trying to keep up Victorian standards of cleanliness — white pinafores for children and so on, in an overcrowded damp cottage was a pitiful task. Most labourers and their families had barely enough money for food and shelter, and the overcrowding was terrible. Evidence given to the Royal Commissions into agriculture gives concrete examples. In 1843 a family of 11 lived in a two room cottage in Stourpaine. The one bedroom had just enough room for three beds in each of which 3-5 people slept. The total wages for the family per week were 16/6. It was described as 'not an extraordinary case'. The cottage was damp: 'the matter constantly escaping from the pigsties, privies etc is allowed to find its way between the cottages [which are] surrounded by streams of filth'. Hardly surprisingly there had been typhoid fever in the row.

TOP LEFT *Umbrella Cottage, Lyme Regis, early 19th century seaside romantic.* CENTRE LEFT *Estate cottages, Canford mid-19th century mock Tudor.* BOTTOM RIGHT *Farmhouse at Stoke Abbot, dated 1751 and 1762.* TOP RIGHT *West Lulworth, with Gothic windows.* CENTRE RIGHT *Partly 16th century cottage of mixed pale and dark stone at East Lulworth.* BOTTOM RIGHT *Traditional style at Kimmeridge dated 1848.*

windows. The nave was rebuilt at the same time, and the north transept was added in 1755. Thus externally it is virtually entirely 18th century, with attractive, if plain windows. Inside it is not so exciting although oddly L-shaped. Fine mid-18th century reredos, two stone effigies of *c.* 1300 and good 17th century monuments: one under the tower of Henry Hastings, the eccentric squire who died in 1650 aged 99 (*see* Woodlands). The church was restored late in the 19th century and the 18th century box pews have been re-arranged. Nearby the long low Abbey House may be a remnant of the abbey.

Horton Tower is a big triangular folly of brick, six storeys high, built in the mid 18th century by a local land-owner, Humphrey Sturt, to watch the hunt from when he became too old to ride to it. It is prominent from miles around and now restored for use as a transmitter for mobile phones.

★★ *Church, tower.*

HURN (G) a small village, mostly brick with some 18th century buildings, lots of trees and too many fast roads. ¾ mile west is Hurn Airport, a large regional airport, where the planes can be observed from the new terminal buildings. Alice in Wonderland Maze and Family Park, with herb garden, farm animals and a superb maze. Good for small children.

★★ Christchurch Motor Museum, Matchams have Vintage Cars.

St Catherines's Hill 1 mile south-east. Only 163 ft high, but a good view point. Heathland, birch and pine, with earthworks marking the site of the medieval chapel of St Catherine. On a clear day the Isle of Wight can be seen.

IBBERTON (F) A village in a classic geological position – on the junction of the chalk and clay, the spring line. The village is a typical rural mixture with a small stone and flint banded manor house dated 1666 and 1686, some thatched cottages, and many 19th century brick or brick and flint banded buildings. The roads, even in the village, are winding and well-wooded. The church of St Eustace (a very unusual dedication) is up a steep narrow path, and sits in a superb position on a ledge in the chalk hillside overlooking its village, surrounded by trees. The church was lucky not to be demolished: by the end of the 19th century it was so dilapidated it could not be used (see photograph in the church). In 1892 services were transferred to a temporary corrugated iron church down in the village (which survives as a village hall). Luckily the church was properly restored in 1903, rather than rebuilt. The chancel walls still lean at amazing angles.

The church is mostly 15th century, with simple windows and a little 17th century porch. Good monuments. In the east window of the north aisle are two areas of Elizabethan stained glass, both pretty, one with the arms of Elizabeth I.

★★ *Position.*

IWERNE COURTNEY (B) (also known as Shroton) has a lovely setting in a wide valley, with many trees. On one side of the church are some stone cottages, rather formal-looking, and on the other a huge stone and thatched barn. The bulk of the village along the street consists of thatched cottages with recent development, partly around a new village green. The church of St Mary is very unusual because it was rebuilt in 1610 in true Gothic survival manner, ie not as a revived style as in the 18th century, but in the living Gothic tradition. The windows are lancet-shaped with plain tracery, and the aisle arcades are simple. The west part of the south aisle is an extension of 1871, and the roofs are all replacements of that date. Chancel dated 1610 outside, but greatly altered inside in 1872 and given a more elaborate window. The terracotta reredos with sheaves of wheat mixed with more medieval motifs was made locally. The seating is all 1871, and the porch is very much of that date. The north chapel is 1610, with monument to the man who paid for the rebuilding of the church – Sir Thomas Freke. It has inscriptions all over the place, fat awkward-looking (but charming) angels and lots of shields of arms. He died in 1633 and his wife in 1641, but the monument was not put up until 1654, after the most dramatic

ABOVE *Cutting silage near Horton Tower*
BELOW *Ibberton church*

episode in the history of the church. After the Clubmen were defeated on Hambledon Hill (see entry) in 1645 the 400 of them who failed to run away were imprisoned in this church. Oliver Cromwell decided that they were 'poor silly creatures' and set them free. Around the monument to Freke are two wooden screens of 1610, perhaps originally placed around the family pew. Very fine, delicate in the lower parts and

Looking out over the Blackmore Vale from near Iwerne Minster

chunky above. An elaborate helm, partly 1560 and partly 1650 hangs on one wall of the chapel.

★★ *Church, village.*

IWERNE MINSTER (B) A large village, combining old cottages and late 19th century rather mechanical red brick and half-timbered buildings, many of them quite large. These were (of course) built by the local estate, and the 'big house' of 1878 (designed by Alfred Waterhouse) is now Clayesmore School. Only its red-brick stables are obvious from the road. To the south of the church is a far better imitation half-timbered (and complicated) building – the Homestead, built as a village club in 1921, by a well-meaning landowner who turned the village into a model village (painted shop-signs, agricultural experiment) and who even dressed the village girls in red-hooded cloaks. At the north end of the village is a pump dated 1880 under its own little roof. The church of St Mary is a fine medieval building with many little Norman windows. The 14th century tower has a 15th century spire – one of only three medieval spires in Dorset. Norman north aisle, with fat pillars and two little original windows. West part of the south aisle Transitional – Norman with pointed arches. The north transept is 13th century with two reset Norman windows, and between them a fine capital, Purbeck Marble with a stiff-leaf capital. Most of the rest of the church is 14th century, apart from the complex south chapel of 1880 (by J. L. Pearson) with its stone vault and so on. Super 1920 glass in east window.

★★ *Church.*

IWERNE STEPLETON (B) has no village, but a large 17th century house (altered in the 18th century and with pavilions of the same date either side) in a lovely park and woodland setting which the road makes a long curve to avoid. Beside the house, hidden in the garden, is a small partly Norman church. Stepleton was the home of Peter Beckford (1740-1811), author of *Thoughts on Hunting*. 'Never', it was said, 'had fox or hare the honour of being

Chapman's Pool, Purbeck

chased to death by so accomplished a hunter . . . he would bag a fox in Greek, confine a hare in Latin, inspect his kennels in Italian, and direct the economy of his stables in exquisite French'. He is buried in the churchyard.

KIMMERIDGE (J) Sensibly placed a mile or more back from the sea, with lots of snugly battened down stone and thatched cottages. Some are 19th century, despite their traditional appearance, one being prominently dated 1848 (damaged by fire 1995). The church seems smaller than the vast mock-tudor parsonage of 1837 next to it. Very humble church, long and low with no tower. Plain 12th century doorway, and virtually everything else 1872.

Toll on the road to the sea and a good car park at the end of it. Kimmeridge Bay is wide, flanked by short cliffs of dark shale, and with horizontal ledges of the same rather depressing rock and limestone, good rock pools but no 'real' sandy beach. It has an odd atmosphere and was once called 'The Haunted Bay'. The Bay lies within the Dorset Trust for Nature Conservation's Purbeck Marine Wildlife Reserve – one of the first 'underwater' reserves in the country. On the east the cliffs rise higher, with Clavel Tower very prominent on top, built as a folly in the 1820's by the owner of Smedmore (now ruinous). Kimmeridge Bay seems an unlikely site for industrial

Smedmore House, Kimmeridge

activity, but in fact there have been many attempts to use the shale, ranging from the manufacture of shale bangles, inlays and even table legs in the Roman period to a glass furnace in the early 17th century using the shale as fuel (where the boat park is now) and 19th century attempts to win oil from the shale. All except the first failed, but the green tanks on the cliff beyond the row of shale miners' cottages are part of a well extracting oil, but from far deeper in the ground than the shale. The history of the area, its natural history and marine wildlife are explained by a display in one of the fishermen's huts. The stone jetty and so on are the legacy of the earlier industries. In the background on the west is the high ridge of limestones.

To the east of the village is **Smedmore House** (fee: lists), a lovely smooth Portland stone house set amongst trees. The beautiful entrance front with its two large bays was built in 1761, and the detailed estimate for building it is on display in the house. This new part cuts across an earlier west front and the two fronts together enclose 'a little newe house' of the early 17th century, built by Sir William Clavell so that he could be close to his glass-works and other industrial attempts at Kimmeridge. He 'beautified it with pleasant gardens' according to a contemporary, and Smedmore still has lovely gardens with lots of trees, and some charming contrasting small walled gardens. The little entrance courtyard with its medley of small roofs contrasts with the organised elegance of the front of the house. In the late 18th century kitchen block is a small museum with dolls, a little archaeology and so forth. Inside the main house, which has a satisfying lived-in air,

are lots of 18th century fittings and furniture.

★★★ *Village, Bay, Smedmore, walks.*

KINGCOMBE (D/E) Higher and Lower Kingcombe are hamlets on the River Hooke, very unspoilt and rural. Only a few cottages, and at Lower Kingcombe a famous Nature Reserve, created in 1987 to preserve the unimproved grassland and unaltered old-fashioned field systems. Fascinating walks around the 400 acre reserve, giving a glimpse of the landscape of the past, filled with butterflies, plants and so on.

★★★★ *Walking country and natural history.*

Kingston

KINGS STAG (A) Despite the medieval sounding name, a recent settlement, starting in the early 19th century along the main road. Some brick and thatch. The tiny stone and thatch Mission Room of 1836 is now a house.

KINGSTON (T) An attractive village sitting on a high ridge with a marvellous view of Corfe Castle (and a nice 1800-ish pump), is built almost entirely from Purbeck stone: most of the cottages are 19th century. It is dominated by the new church of St James, with its large tower, built by the well-known Victorian architect, G.E. Street, for the 3rd Earl of Eldon from 1873-1880. Early English in style, of great richness, and very grand. The stone (including the Purbeck marble for the shafts and pillars) was all quarried locally, but the result still seems alien. 'The oak for the roofs and stone slates have been brought from his Lordship's Gloucestershire estate' and all 'was erected without the aid of contractors by Lord Eldon's own men' reported a contemporary newspaper.

No expense was spared, and it is magnificent, but hardly a small village's church. The quantities of wrought iron were designed by the architect, and the stained glass is all contemporary. Well worth seeing. The new church replaced one of 1833, which still survives, although now private. Elegant tower.

South of the village, and visible in its valley from the footpath to Houns-tout cliff, is the big house, **Encombe.** Huge, long and low, 18th century with later alterations, in

Kingston Lacy, (above) *the south front and* (below) *the Spanish Room*

a glorious setting with man-made lakes to the south. Obelisk of 1835 put up by Lord Eldon, owner of the house, in honour of his brother, Lord Stowell.

★★★ *New church, village, views of Corfe Castle.*

KINGSTON LACY (F, near Wimborne)

Perhaps Dorset's grandest house, set in a lovely park (fee: lists).

The neat rectangle of the house sits quietly in its perfect setting, looking somehow smaller than rumours of its collections suggest. The house was built between 1663 and 1665 for Sir Ralph Bankes, whose father had owned Corfe Castle, which was slighted and made uninhabitable at the end of the Civil War. The house was originally brick with stone dressings, and had mullioned and transomed windows. These survive only on the west front where the outbuildings make a courtyard, because in 1835 William Bankes employed Charles Barry (architect of the Houses of Parliament) to alter the house. He encased the house in stone, added the large chimneys at each corner, altered the dormer windows in the roof, and changed the windows on the other three fronts to sashes. He also added a *porte cochère* (a sort of carriage porch) to the north (entrance) front, and lowered the level of the ground there, moving the entrance to the basement floor. On the east front he added a complex loggia, and on the south a partial third storey. The central, ground floor window on this south side may be 1650's. Barry also put back the central lantern, which had been removed sometime in the 18th century. Inside Barry altered the house to fit in a grand marble staircase which William Bankes had bought in Italy. This Bankes, an eccentric, a traveller, connoisseur and collector was really responsible for both the house and its contents as we know it today. He was a contemporary of the poet Byron at Cambridge, and friends with him ever after. Byron called Bankes 'the father of all mischief'. Bankes bought the staircase in Italy on his way back from the Middle East. From 1841 he lived in Italy having fled England to avoid prosecution as a homosexual, but continued to send back furniture and fittings for the house until his death in 1855. The complex entrance hall was inserted by Barry to lead to the staircase, which runs right up through the house. In the niches on the first landing are huge 1850s bronze figures of Sir John and Lady Bankes (holding the key of Corfe Castle which she defended) and Charles I, all three of them with concealed radiators beneath. On the first floor are the only two rooms with surviving late 18th century decoration — the Library and the Saloon.

The latter was the great hall of the 1650's house, given its painted ceiling, fine fireplace, and moulded cornice in the 1780's. The lush purple marble niches were inserted in 1854. The room is filled with magnificent paintings, including two portraits by Rubens and one by Titian, acquired by William Bankes in Italy.

The Spanish Room is overpowering, lined with tooled and painted Venetian leather and full of paintings (with labels in their own frames) many of which William Bankes bought in Spain in the 1810's. Everything seems to be at least half gilded, even the ceiling which is from a Venetian palace, and cut down to fit this room. The doors with paintings of the labours of the months and the pretty inlaid marble panels were commissioned for this room when it was fitted out in the 1840's. The whole interior, but especially this room, has been compared to London Clubs – hardly urprising since Barry designed The Travellers and Reform Clubs at much the same time. The Dining room has late 19th century panelling, but the rest of the decoration is 1830's-50's. Between it and the Spanish room is the coffee loggia, a strange tiny square room lined with alabaster.

The drawing room was lined with pink damask in 1898. Many portraits, including 55 miniatures painted early in the 19th century in imitation of 16th century originals. The library dates from the 1780's and is more restrained than the other rooms. The keys of Corfe Castle are here, never given up despite defeat. Many portraits including five by Lely. The only bedroom on this floor is staggeringly elaborately furnished, with the most horrible and impressive bed, made for William Bankes in Venice but not delivered until after his death in 1855. Upstairs the white bedroom is very feminine of 1897. Small display of Egyptian material.

The service rooms for the house are in 18th century buildings around the courtyard on the west, including the laundry and kitchen. Beyond are the harsh red brick stables of 1880, which house the tea room in loose boxes and stalls. Beyond the south front is a vast lawn, with six imitation Venetian well heads, made in the 1840's, and an Egyptian obelisk of the 2nd century BC, set up here in 1827. An Egyptian sarcophagus of the 14th century BC, looks rather lost islanded in grass. The ha-ha to the park is guarded by five small guns. The grounds contain a replanted Victorian fernery, a cedar avenue, a limewalk and so on, but the most memorable part is the park itself, wrapping right round the house and with woods beyond. Super trees and a herd of handsome Red Devon cattle.

★★★★ House, park.

Knowlton, the church in the henge

Lodge Farm (fee: lists) just north of the big house, at the start of the avenue, is an extraordinary survival, a small but very solid house of the late 14th century, which survived unknown as a farmhouse until recently. The front has three 14th century windows at first floor level. This is the most interesting part inside too, with a solar or private room and a hall. The solar has a doorway which originally led to a garderobe (lavatory) tower, and is separated from the hall by a thick medieval wooden screen. The hall is open to the roof, as it would have been when built.

★★ *Small but very interesting.*

KINGSTON MAURWARD (E) Between Stinsford and Upper Bockhampton (see entries) is Kingston Maurward House, a large classical house built early in the 18th century in brick, and encased in stone following a visit by George III in 1794 who is supposed to have remarked to the owner, 'Brick, Mr Pitt, brick.' It is the Knapwater House of Hardy's *Desperate Remedies.*

Kingston Maurward Farm, Animal Park and Gardens are all around the house, with many varieties of livestock. All four Dorset sheep breeds are here, and smaller animals for children to touch. In another area are labelled crops. The large formal gardens of the big house are also open. Interesting Edwardian layout, with herbaceous borders, pools, roses. Less formal slopes down to a romantic lake and a classical temple of 1720. Nature trail round the lake, and a walled garden.

The old house at Kingston Maurward is seen clearly from the lake, a tall stone house of the 16th and 17th centuries.

★★★ *Gardens, with Animal Park*
★★★★ *For a family afternoon out.*

KINGSTON RUSSELL (E) Flanked by hills in the Bride valley and now consisting largely of the house, seen clearly from the road. The west front is early 18th century, while the east has some late 17th century windows. The small blocks on either end are additions of 1914. The forebears of the

Dukes of Bedford lived here in the 16th century.

KINGSTON RUSSELL (H) stone circle is remarkably isolated. Footpaths lead to it from all sides. The easiest way to get there is from a footpath north of the back road from Abbotsbury to Hardy Monument, a fairly level 1½ mile walk, with views of the ridges either side. The path passes close to the Grey Mare and her Colts – a long barrow (Neolithic) whose large sarsen stones are now exposed. The barrow was opened early in the 19th century and human bones were found – long barrows were communal or at least multiple graves. The stone circle is not impressive: the stones are recumbant, and the largest is only 8ft long. They delineate a rather oval circle 80 ft across, and probably date from the Bronze Age, about 4,000 years ago. It is a very small scale and simple version of Stonehenge, built for religious or ritual purposes.

★★ *Stones and position.*

KINGTON MAGNA (A/B, near Gillingham) has farm houses and cottages of the 17th and 18th centuries, but much modern development. The church of All Saints sits in a magnificent position on the side of the little escarpment, with a wide view to the west. Immediately below is a re-used spring-fed medieval fishpond. The church has a fine 15th century tower. The rest was rebuilt in a rather smooth mock-medieval style in 1862. Leafy corbels in the chancel, and very characteristic partly painted and partly carved reredos. Nice Charles I coat of arms.

★ *Landscape.*

KINSON (G) Now a suburb on the north of Bournemouth. To the north however are the remains of the village, right down by the River Stour, with the church of St Andrew, all dark brown heathstone. The tower is Norman, the rest 1890's. The tower was used by smugglers for storing brandy-kegs and a gravestone in the churchyard records Robert Trotman 'murdered' in 1765 by the revenue men 'A little Tea one leaf I did not steal/For Guiltless Blood shed I to GOD appeal/Put Tea in one scale human blood in tother/And think what tis to slay thy harmless brother'.

KNOWLTON (G) is a deserted medieval village and a remarkable collection of Neolithic henge monuments. Only one of these survives as an earthwork, and inside it is the parish church. The henge is virtually circular, and has a bank with a decent sized ditch inside. It is not totally clear what Neolithic henge monuments were used for, but it was certainly not simply for living in. They may have been religious, or possibly different henges were used for different purposes. This one is most unusual in having been re-used as the site of a church, and it doubtless owes its survival to this. To the south-east is a huge barrow (covered in trees) which has two ditches around it (not visible). An even larger henge, now mostly ploughed out, encloses the farm and the road junction, and there are two more similar ones just to the north-west, also ploughed out. Many Bronze Age round barrows, smaller than the big one, in the area. The henge is impressive but too low-lying for grandeur. The little church inside was abandoned late in the 18th century when the roof fell in. Its tower is 14th century and the nave and chancel 12th century. The deserted village spreads along the valley of the River Allen. A peculiar place, with these two disused monuments superimposed.
★★★ *Monuments*

LAMBERT'S CASTLE (D) (National Trust) in the Marshwood Vale is an early, simple and slight hillfort with two entrances. Some of the ramparts have been re-used as field banks, and made higher, and there are other field banks running across the fort. The car park is ½ mile to the south-west of the fort, and has lovely trees.
★★★ *Landscape*.

LANGHAM, see DUCKHORN WESTON

LANGTON HERRING (H) Despite the addition of some 'executive housing' on the outskirts, the centre of the village is remarkably unspoilt. Almost everything is of a local yellow stone, and although many of the buildings are 19th century a few 18th century cottages survive, occasionally still thatched. The roads are narrow and parking is difficult. There are good footpaths from the village down to the Fleet and inland. The church of St Peter has the smallest possible tower, probably 18th century. The rest of the church is medieval but rather disguised by 19th century restoration. In the fields to the north of the village are several limekilns used to produce lime for fertilisers. At the road junction is a little medieval cross.
★★ *Setting*.

LANGTON LONG, BLANDFORD (F) A long name for a small hamlet on the Stour close to the larger Blandford but separated by the by-pass. The church was demolished in 1861 and replaced by a new one in an attractive Perpendicular style built of small squared flint and stone banding. The tower is of note, with elaborate pinnacles and gargoyles. Lots of wall monuments, and a 15th century brass. The single-storey lodge next to the church was probably built *c.* 1840.
★ *Setting*.

LANGTON MATRAVERS (J) Long and thin (hence its name), less picturesque than Worth Matravers, but full of local stone buildings from the 18th to the 20th centuries. The church of St George was rebuilt by the Weymouth architect Crickmay in 1876 on such a large scale that his nave is actually taller than the 15th century tower (once used as a smuggler's store). Inside it is pleasant, with squat pillars between the nave and aisles, and lots of Purbeck Marble in the chancel, with everything in Early English style.
★★ *Setting and village*.
Coach House Museum, just to the north of the church (fee: lists). The history of stone quarrying and mining in the area, with many interesting objects, photographs and so on. Smallish. ★★
Putlake Adventure Farm (fee: lists) offers farm animals, farm trail etc.
Sunnydown Farm, 1 mile west, will soon have on display the rare and recently discovered Purbeck limestone preserving the footprints of huge 4-legged dinosaurs, 140 million years old. Mammal and amphibian material too (fee: lists).

LEIGH (E) has some good stone farmhouses like those of neighbouring Yetminster (see entry), eg one behind the church, and others near the medieval cross (modern top). The church of St Andrew has a 15th century tower with good gargoyles, but the rest is mostly restoration of 1854. In the back of the nave are 16th century benches, some with scrolled finials. At the highest point in the parish, on the exact top of a hillock are the remains of Miz Maze, a slight hexagonal earthwork about 25 yards across. The county historian Hutchins recorded that this was neglected by the 1770's, but prior to that, it was the custom for the young men of the village to

Bridehead from the cricket ground

scour out the trenches and pare the banks once in six or seven years, with the day passed in rustic merriment and festivity. Quite a lot of these turf mazes existed in the medieval period – no trace of the maze survives here, only the enclosing earthwork.
★★ *Village*.

LILLIPUT see **POOLE**

LILLINGTON (A) is a tiny hamlet, but the middle is crowded with a farm, farmyard, and, right up to the church, a big stone barn of about 1600, tactfully converted to a house. The churchyard has a good view, with a medieval fish pond, now used by ducks. The church of St Martin is a variety of dates – 15th century chancel and fine tower, 18th century south chapel and the rest a mixture from the 13th century onwards. All was restored in 1848. The wooden **main** door is 15th century. Inside, the church is limewashed and attractive. Good stout 15th century font with a 17th century wooden cover.
★ *Village, setting*.

LITTLE BREDY (E) is at the head of the Bride valley, and the descent into it from the east is tremendous by either of the two roads, some of the best inland scenery in the county. Clumps and plantations of trees everywhere, with the bare grassy downs showing above them. Lots of flowers in spring, especially cowslips. The village is magical – visitor's cars are not allowed in, and so it is quiet, and somehow

ABOVE *Mock-medieval cottages at Little Bredy*
BELOW *Litton Cheney church, wood engraving by Reynolds Stone*

old-fashioned. In fact all the decorative thatched cottages (apart from the 17th century one by the church) are 19th century, built in imitation of the earlier local style. Even the village hall (once the school) was built to look like a cottage. The church of St Michael and All Angels was largely rebuilt in 1850 with Benjamin Ferry as the architect. The best materials were used, including Caen stone, and the end result is attractive. Ferry added an appealing miniature spire to the 14th century tower. From the churchyard it is sometimes possible to walk through part of the beautifully wooded grounds of Bridehead, up to the sparkling lake formed by damming the springs which are the start of the river. The house of 1837 can be glimpsed from the road.

★★★★ *Well worth visiting for its gorgeous setting.*

LITTON CHENEY (D/E) has wriggly roads, 17th and 18th century stone and thatched cottages, and little streams rushing alongside. In the church of St Mary only the 14th century porch, and the 15th century chancel arch and west tower survived a drastic restoration of 1877, which, although possibly leaving some walling from the medieval church, restored and altered all the detail. Good 17th century monuments. Between the church and the large 18th century rectory (with rooks above) is the fine gravestone (1979) of the wood engraver and artist Reynolds Stone, who lived at the one-time rectory and whose lettering can be seen in the tablet to Alexander Harper inside the church and the low tomb of Oscar Hilton in the north-east corner of the graveyard.

★★ *Village, setting.*

LODERS (D) has a handsome village street, all stone, dating from the 17th-19th centuries. One house has a datestone of 1786. The church of St Mary Magdalene was from 1107-1410 the priory church and is all medieval, although restored in the 19th century, ranging from the 12th to the 15th century, mostly mixed together. The north side of the chancel shows the variety — the easternmost window is *c.* 1400, the centre one a lancet of the 13th century, and the westernmost 12th century with a blocked doorway below. Perhaps the prettiest part of the building is the south chapel, 15th century and elaborate. Bell of 1461 on display. To the north of the church is Loders Court (late 18th century) whose splendid gardens surround the church (see also Uploders).

★★ *Village, church.*

ABOVE *Net making at Loders in the 1940's (see Bridport)*
BELOW *Sir Thomas and his wife, Long Burton*

Mangerton to the west is a hamlet set in the steep little green hills which characterise this area. Deep woody lanes and big stone walls. Plain stone buildings. **Mangerton Mill** is open to the public (fee: lists), and is being restored after twenty years of idleness. Small, with a collection of household and agricultural items. Nice lake behind.

LONG BREDY (E) is on a tiny stream, and has good cottages, a fine large 18th century house and, up towards the church, a huge later 18th century house which was once the rectory. The church is slightly to the north of the present village, surrounded by open grassy downs, in great contrast to the wooded village. Alongside it are what were originally the 19th century school and school-house (very Hardyean). The body of the church was drastically restored in 1863, but the early 15th century tower survived. Many of the fittings are of the 1860's – the multicoloured font was described in 1863 as 'very rich . . . fair medallions of Staffordshire alabaster are let in'.
★ *Village, setting.*

LONG BURTON (A) runs along the main road with several 17th century stone cottages, some Victorian ones and a lot of modern development. The church of St James has a rather plain 13th century tower – the rest of the church is 15th century, apart from the north aisle of 1873, and more interestingly, the little north chapel of the early 17th century. This was built for two sets of lavish table tombs with five effigies between them. They are the parents of Sir Leweston Fitzjames and his wife's parents, along with a grandfather. The latter was brought here from Gloucestershire because Eleoner was refused permission there 'to repayre and erect these remembrances'. The men have different faces, but the women are identical. Beneath one is a rather grisly set of bones with a pick axe and shovel. All have recently been repainted. The early 17th century wooden screen which originally protected them is now in the tower arch. Over the south doorway is an unusually large Royal coat of arms dated 1662, with suitable injunctions for the start of the restoration of the monarchy – for example 'Curse not the King, noe not in my thought. Eccles X'.
★ *Church.*

LONG CRICHEL (B/F) is quite lengthy, all spread out along the single road in a shallow valley. Most of the buildings apart from the church are of brick, including 19th century estate cottages in a great variety of styles, but with some later 18th century

Lyme Regis, looking east from the Cobb

houses. The church of St Mary is unusual for its date – it was built in 1852, but looks like a much freer Gothic Revival building of twenty years earlier, and even then it would not have been run of the mill. The 15th century tower survives from the medieval church, with a large doorway cut in 1852. The 1852 nave is long and narrow with no aisles, original stained glass and oddly proportioned windows. The roofs are odder still, especially in the transept and the chancel. The apse is pretty, and prettier still externally.

★ *Setting and church.*

LONGHAM (G) Thin and busy, with several Georgian houses. The south end is dominated by the Bournemouth Water Company's works, and a nice 18th century bridge over the wide River Stour. At the road junction at the north end is the United Reformed Church, a pretty pale brick building of 1841 with a tiny steeple.

LOSCOMBE (D) (between Mapperton and Melplash). Tiny and remote hamlet, set in a steep little valley. Deep narrow lanes, and an easy place to get lost. Nature Reserve of unimproved pasture: the whole area feels very unchanged and old-fashioned.

★★ *Landscape.*

LULWORTH, *see* **EAST and WEST LULWORTH**

LYDLINCH (A) A typical Blackmore Vale

village, mixed brick and stone, with some more recent houses. The church of St Thomas Becket is mostly late medieval, with the inevitable 15th century tower. Inside it has a 19th century feel, particularly because of the early 19th century pulpit and gallery, supported on wooden pillars painted to look like stone. Part of the tracery on the front of the gallery are made (very unusually) from cast iron. The painted coat of arms is dated 1686, the year after the Monmouth rebellion. 15th century glass with angels feathered all over above the pulpit. Late 12th century font with an interesting cover made in 1978. In the base of the tower is a painted notice dated 1746 exhorting the bell-ringers 'Put off your Hats, your Belt and Spur's. . .' These are Barnes' 'Lydlinch bells 'An' v'ok did come, a-streamen slow / Along below the trees in row, / While they, in merry peals, did sound / The bells vor all the naighbours round'.

Lydlinch Common, west of the village, is wild and wet, with surprisingly high undergrowth, sometimes gypsies, and nightingales. The road east is still carried over the River Lydden by an army bridge of 1942: the bridge was doubled over the river for army traffic.

★ *Common, church.*

LYME REGIS (D) A charming seaside town worth visiting to see the Cobb, the town itself and the views. Also in the centre of an excellent area for walking. Good for days out (crowded in high season). In the middle of the 16th century, Leland described it as 'a praty market toun

set in the rootes of an high rocky hill down to the hard shore', and it is still the hillyness of the place that surprises (and exhausts) visitors, and which provides the lovely varied views. There are references to Lyme from the 8th century, but it does not seem to have developed into a town until the 12th century. The Cobb, the town's artificial harbour, was probably built about 1250 and after that Lyme developed as a town and port, with its most prosperous period being from about 1500-1700. In the late 18th century it was rescued from its decline by the new fashion for sea-bathing. The town became a resort, described early in the 19th century by Jane Austen in *Persuasion* (1818). Many villas were built on the outskirts of the town, which even had an assembly rooms (demolished 1927). There are three separate, although adjacent, parts of Lyme – the town itself; the seafront; and another part by the Cobb with the port buildings – commercial or coastguard, now mostly used for the holiday trade. The land to the east and west of Lyme is unstable, so most of the buildings are in the valley of the little river Lym.

From all over the town there are superb views along the coast east past Golden Cap to Portland. Looking down Broad Street there is the surprise of the sea behind. The town has many good 18th and early 19th century buildings, some with pretty doorways. Towards the top of Broad Street, the main shopping street, there are even some thatched houses. Below the early 19th century inn, the Three Cups, the lowest part of Broad Street was rebuilt after fires in 1844

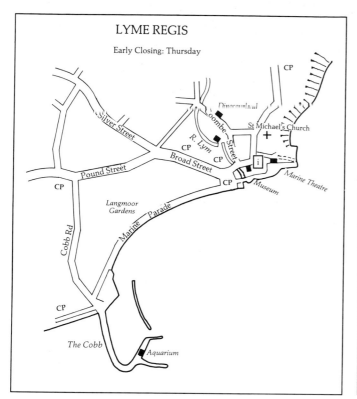

LYME REGIS

Early Closing: Thursday

Madeira Cottages, Lyme Regis

and 1889. The Royal Lion Hotel was built in 1844 on the site of a much older inn. The bookshop still has the imitation Victorian fascia and decoration put up for the film of *The French Lieutenant's Woman* (1970).

Just to the east of the bridge over the Lym (which is substantially medieval underneath) are the Guildhall, a rather odd building of 1887, and the purpose-built museum of 1901 in 17th century Dutch style. Beyond, overlooking the sea, is Gun Cliff, where the guns to defend Lyme were kept from the 16th century.

The Museum (fee: lists) ★★★ contains superb displays of fossils from the famous fossil-rich Lias between Charmouth and Lyme, including fish and good beasts like Ichthyosaurs, alongside the much more common ammonites and so forth. Displays explain the local geology and illustrate the landslips either side of the town. Also local history, archaeology, natural history etc., with an interesting collection of photographs, paintings and prints of Lyme and the area around. The building is a warren with little staircases, a gallery and a tiny central lantern. Lyme's promenade has been extended east by the construction of a new sea wall, combined with sewage works (1994). Handsome new walls and a little tower, all well designed to fit the irregular coastline.

The **church of St Michael** is large. The entrance is through the nave of the earlier church, which has been shortened (the west

end is 1933). Parts of the arcading of *c.* 1210 are exposed. On the floor and walls are inscribed stabs of the local blue lias. The elaborate 19th century font has an amusing cover dated 1846. The innermost doorway has a 12th century arch leading to the big new nave of *c.* 1500, parts of which are heavily restored. The carving on almost all of the capitals is modern. Much fine woodwork — some Victorian (the eagle lectern, screen, seating and so on) and some 17th century — the pulpit with its fine sounding board is dated 1613, and the magnificent gallery 1611. Good memorials, particularly from the later 18th and early 19th centuries.

In Coombe Street is the fine classical chapel of 1755, now used as a museum — **Dinosaurland** (fee: lists). Models of dinosaurs, and many local fossils including large ichthyosaurs, fish and so on. Some of the original chapel fittings survived 19th century restorations and can still be seen. Near the top of Silver Street the Roman Catholic church of St Michael and St George, basically of 1835 in Early English style. Off Mill Lane is the little Leper's Well Garden overlooking the (upper) millstream and the river, and higher up is the picturesque Sherborne Lane, very narrow and steep with some good 18th and 19th century building. The Town Mill, tucked in the middle of the town, is being restored. Its long leat dates from 1370, and the buildings are 17th century onwards. Along

Pound Street are late 18th and early 19th century houses (many now hotels) built here for the views. The most interesting is Belmont, on the corner of Pound Street and Cobb Road, built about 1785 as a summer villa for Eleanor Coade, the London manufacturer of an artificial stone. The front of the house is bedecked with her products.

At the bottom of Broad Street the road leads round to the Marine Parade along the sea to the Cobb ½ mile away. Towards the town end of the Parade are some superb seasidey houses, the best of which are the Madeira Cottage row of *c.* 1840. Library Cottage further along is of the same date, with earlier lead drainpipes taken from another building in Amiens, France. On the slopes behind are the Langmoor Gardens, a public park.

The Cobb is Lyme's wonder — it was first built in the 13th century as an artificial harbour, completely detached from the land, constructed of oak piles enclosing huge loose stones. It was joined to the land by 1756, and was rebuilt in Portland Stone in the 1820's, giving it its present appearance. It is not only a harbour — it protects the town from marine erosion. In normal weather it is a pleasant stroll to the end of the Cobb, with even better views back across the town, and along the coast, but in storms waves crash over it. There have been warehouses on the central part since at least the early 18th century and they now house an aquarium (fee; lists), which has live local fish, usually including conger eels, flat fish, lobsters, crabs and so on, and displays of rock pool fauna. Historical display too. Close by are 'Granny's Teeth', steps to the upper walk made from protruding stones, which are supposed to be where Louisa Musgrove fell in *Persuasion*, but sadly they seem not to have been built until after Jane Austen's visits in 1803 and 1804. The inner harbour seems to be on far too small a scale for Lyme ever to have been a large port, but it was (in 1677 it was the 14th largest port in England) and up to the mid-19th century ships were built here as well. There are usually fishermen with boats for hire, either for fishing, or for trips around the bay, at the landward end of the Cobb. A nucleus of buildings grew up by the Cobb after it was joined to the land. Big warehouse of the early 1830's, and the pedimented building was the Custom House, built in 1844. Just up the hill are buildings with traditional slate-covered walls, and behind the beach to the west is a row of late Victorian houses, appropriately named Ozone Terrace.

To the west of the town is the Undercliff (like the town, part of the setting of John Fowles' novel *The French Lieutenant's Woman* (1970). A strange area of overgrown landslips, mostly well-wooded and very wild. It is a National Nature Reserve, and walkers are restricted to the one footpath which runs through it. There is only one public access to the sea and none landward until Axmouth, Devon, is reached, 6 miles away. A serious walk. To the east is a much smaller Dorset Trust for Nature Conservation Nature Reserve, the Spittles, with good views back over the town and a nature trail walk. The landslips below the Spittles and Black Ven beyond can be very dangerous. Cliff walk above Black Ven, part of the Dorset Coastal Path, to Charmouth. Walkers should be very careful about being cut off by the tide on walks along the shore to the east of Lyme (see notices in the town).

Half a mile to the west of the town centre, south of the main road to Seaton, is Umbrella Cottage, a delightful seaside folly of about 1810, polygonal with a thatched roof.

The three **LYTCHETT (F)** villages are in a lovely landscape, with small scale valleys and hills, many little woods and some heathland. Lytchett may mean a grey wood, which seems appropriate.

Lytchett Heath is also known as Beacon Hill, a small settlement with lots of heathy woodland and rhododendrons. In a

Maiden Castle from the south

clearing, circled by a stone wall and insulated from the roads by trees, is the odd, small church dedicated to St Aldhelm. Built in 1900, with two distinct styles of masonry for the walls, a squat tower and a corbel table under the roof with heads like those made from pumpkins.

Lytchett Matravers has some thatched cottages, but most of the large village is recent. The church of St Mary is isolated to the north-west of the village, and is a typical village church, having grown through the centuries. Unusually for Dorset it is almost completely medieval. The tower and chancel arch are all that survive from the church of *c*. 1200. The chancel has windows of the 14th and 15th centuries, with the east windows of *c*. 1500 matching those of the nave and north aisle, which were both rebuilt in 1500 too. Just inside the church is a small inscription on a brass plate set into the floor recording that Margaret Clement paid for much of this rebuilding. She died in 1505 and her will survives; her legacies included 3/4d to the curate of 'Litchet' and 'every priest at my dirge and masse 8d and every pore body 1d.' Her windows are distinctive, with round heads in a square surround. The fine Purbeck Marble font is the same date. Lots of Purbeck Marble in this church – eight slabs in the floor and a table tomb in the north aisle of *c*. 1500 besides the font. Up by the altar is a little brass of a late 15th century priest in his shroud. A much larger brass in the north aisle has lost its unusual heraldic centre, but the inscription (in French) around the edge survives. It is probably the grave of John, Baron Maltravers, who died in 1365 and who lived up to his bad name – he was implicated in the murder of Edward II at

Berkeley Castle in 1327, and later accused of treason over another matter.

Roundels of 16th century glass reset in the north aisle, and parts of a barrel organ. The lovely primitive coat of arms for George IV described him as IIII.

★★ *Church.*

Lytchett Minster is small and rural, with many estate cottages. The church (whose dedication is lost) has a brown heathstone 15th century tower. The rest was rebuilt in 1833 in pale brick. Originally it had simple windows, now mostly elaborated. Inside a very short chancel and a gallery of 1833.

MAIDEN CASTLE (E) is the most massively defended hillfort in Dorset. Although its internal area is smaller than for example Hod Hill, and it lacks the high overview given from Eggardon or Hambledon, in many ways it is the most impressive, and certainly the best known since it is the only hillfort to have been excavated on any scale. Sir Mortimer Wheeler's excavations in the 1930s have been supplemented by more modern excavations.

Man's activities on this highest point of the ridge start with a Neolithic causewayed enclosure, of which nothing can now be seen on the ground because the earliest Iron Age enclosure was on roughly the same circuit. After the camp's ditches had been filled an enormously long earthwork (1790 ft), probably a bank barrow, was constructed. It is the longest Neolithic 'barrow' known. In the right conditions it can be seen as a shallow earthwork running from the inside of the west gate on across three-quarters of the interior of the fort. The area was deserted in the Bronze Age and was used, like the rest of the chalk

A reconstruction of the Romans storming the eastern entrance of Maiden Castle

ridge, as a suitable site for barrows. There is one in the south-west quarter of the fort, and many more can be seen on the chalk ridge to the south, pimpling the skyline (see Ridgeway).

The Iron Age hillfort started with a small enclosure on the eastern knoll, virtually coinciding with the Neolithic causewayed camp. This had a single rampart, still visible running across the middle of the interior. Later the defences were extended to enclose the whole of the hilltop, more than doubling the area of the fort. A pronounced kink on the south side inner rampart shows the junction of the original with the addition. This early phase of the hillfort enclosed the same area as it does now, but with only a single rampart. Later in the Iron Age the two outer ramparts were added and the two entrances made more elaborate. The sequence of construction of the hillfort and indeed the existence of the Neolithic phases was elucidated by Wheeler's excavations, but his most dramatic find was the famous war cemetery at the east gate. Thirty-four people were found buried with grave-goods, many of them damaged by sword cuts and one, the most famous, with a Roman iron arrowhead embedded in his spine. They must be the last defenders of the hillfort, defeated by the Romans in 43 or 44 AD. It is possible that occupation continued in the hillfort for a few years after the conquest, before or while the town of Dorchester was being established, but it is also possible to interpret the archaeological evidence to suggest that it was used as a fort by the Roman army. In the second half of the fourth century a Roman temple was built inside the hillfort, the footings of which are exposed. Nearby is a neat square depression, a modern dew pond. Walking around the ramparts gives good views of the town of Dorchester in the river valley to the north, and the Ridgeway to the south.

★★★ *Hillfort.*

MAIDEN NEWTON (E) is either a small town or a very large village, which although not picturesque (like Cerne Abbas for example) mixes pleasant older buildings with the new. Big base of a medieval cross in the middle. The church of St Mary is interesting, basically medieval. Externally the small 12th century north doorway has good zig-zag decoration, and beneath the tower the chancel arch has scalloped capitals of the same date (the arch itself has been restored). Much of the rest of the church is 15th century, including the porch with its attractive wooden door of about 1600. A much decayed simpler wooden door surviving in the blocked north doorway is probably medieval. The keystone of the arch over it has a high quality medallion enclosing a seated figure, and a similar medallion with a horseman is reset over the south doorway. Both are 12th century.

★★ *As a nice medieval parish church.*

MANGERTON, *see* LODERS

MANSTON (B) village has moved right away from the church and big house, which stand together by the River Stour. Manston House was damaged by fire in 1857, and despite its classical Georgian appearance most of it is 19th century. The neo-Norman mausoleum, looking like a tiny temple dates from 1857. Some of the earliest cremations in modern times (ie since the Saxon period) were carried out here in a private crematorium. In 1882 Captain Hanham of Manston House cremated two relatives at their instructions and he himself was cremated in 1883. It was then uncertain whether this was legal, and the first public crematorium did not open until 1885.

The church of St Nicholas has a nice 15th century tower in creamy stone, with a pretty inserted doorway dated 1534. The nave is 14th century with 17th century windows with simple tracery, and the north aisle and chancel are 13th century, with lancet windows. In the chancel is an unusual half-column memorial of 1689.

★ *Setting.*

MAPPERTON (D) Set in an area where complex geology gives rise to lots of little hills and valleys, just to the east of Beaminster. Mapperton is not a village, but a large and handsome stone manor house with a few dependent buildings (Garden open. Fee: lists). The house forms part of a courtyard, completed by the little church and a sophisticated pair of stables, one dated 1670. The charming main front is mid 17th century with a balustrade on top, a pair of two storey bay windows and a two-storey porch. The church forms one side of the courtyard, mostly 18th century with unusual round-headed windows of 1704, perhaps designed to go with the

ABOVE *The south front, Mapperton*
BELOW *T. F. Powy's cottage, Mappowder*

house. To its south is a little 17th century pigeon house, still in use. To the north is a huge croquet lawn, enclosed by high walls. This side of the house was remodelled in the 18th century, but the corners of the 16th century house survive, with piers running up each corner and heraldic beasts on the top. Marvellous view from the croquet lawn down the little valley, and across the formal gardens constructed in 1926; with an orangery built in 1966 and below two long pools with carp and on one side large trees. Down the little valley are paintings of trees and shrubs, a miniature park, in happy contrast to the formality above. A lovely garden enhancing a beautiful setting. Just up the drive is the parsonage of *c.* 1700. Surviving accounts record that stone was dug from the Parsonage orchard for the walls, but the stone for dressings was brought 10½ miles from Ham Hill. 6d was charged for 'ale given to the Carters at Bargaining for Carriage of the Stones from Ham Hill'. The house was originally thatched.

★★★ *But would be* ★★★★ *if the garden were bigger.*

MAPPOWDER (E) On the edge of the Blackmore Vale, with some stone cottages, and a pretty church. The novelist T. F. Powys spent his last 13 years living in the little house by the church gate. He attended the church frequently, and is buried in the churchyard. The church of St Peter and St Paul is virtually all of the late 15th century (restored), apart from the chancel which was rebuilt in 1868 in a matching style. Handsome tower. In the nave a 15th century 'green man' – the head of a man with leaves coming out of his nose. In the south aisle is a tiny 13th century effigy of a knight originally put up over a heart burial. 12th century font. Good 17th century monuments in the tower.

★★ *Landscape and church.*

MARGARET MARSH (B) is a scattered low-lying hamlet in the Blackmore Vale with several farms at least partly of the

King's Mill Bridge over the Stour at Marnhull and (right) *the notice on the bridge*

16th century. The church of St Margaret was rebuilt in 1872, with only the 15th century tower surviving from the earlier church.

MARNHULL (A/B) A large scattered village, with, amongst some modern development, many fine farms, cottages and farm buildings of the 17th and 18th century in the local creamy limestone. This is one of a string of villages on the band of drier limestone which runs through the middle of the Blackmore Vale. Senior's Farm, immediately west of the churchyard is of *c.* 1500 with some surviving traceried windows and a doorway of that date. Rare survival.

The church of St Gregory (lists) is complicated but attractive. Fine 15th century tower with odd little 18th century pediments on the top, a repair after a collapse in 1718. 1881 chancel with a pleasant east window by Morris and Co. 15th century chancel arch with angels holding shields. Close by is a brass of 1596 with a superbly misunderstood naive classical surround and verse including 'For love that he vnto this parrishe bore / Ten povnds he gave a stocke vunto the poore / which frinds of his in trust shall styll retayne / With them and their assignes to remayne'. The three

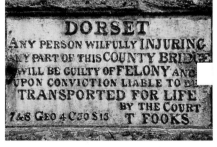

Marnhull church

ABOVE *Pope's Farm, Marnhull*
BELOW *A cottage at Melbury Abbas in the 1920's*

alabaster figures are a knight and his two (matching) wives, *c.* 1470. A marvellously bright little beaded bag dated 1640 is displayed. The text partly obliterated over the chancel arch is 18th century, whereas the skeleton and figure of a man painted at the other end of the church are 16th century. Nave and aisles later medieval (south aisle 1852). The west arch to the north chapel has capitals with very fine 16th century angels, one carrying an inscribed scroll, in a different style to the earlier ones on the chancel arch. Norman capital below with heads. The roof of the nave is one of the best in the county, deeply coffered with carved patterns in the heavily moulded squares, dating from about 1520. The wagon roof in the north aisle is the same date. Finely carved wooded Charles II arms in tower screen. The weather-vane, dated 1745, is now inside the church. Good memorial to John Warren, parish clerk, d 1752. . . 'Who smoked all his life, / And so did his wife / And now there's no doubt / But their pipes are both out.'

★★★ *Tower, effigies, roof.*

MARSHWOOD (D) spreads along the rim of the Marshwood Vale. The unusual church tower was rebuilt in 1841 and the body of the church in 1884, all in chert. Inside there are very stylised capitals and shiny marble columns to the chancel arch and east window. The little school opposite was built in 1843, and is chert too. Lovely view from the churchyard.

MARTINSTOWN, *see* **WINTERBORNE ST MARTIN**

MAUMBURY, *see* **DORCHESTER**

MELBURY ABBAS (B) is a small, strung out village on a slope, set against large hills, with several houses and a large farmyard in the local, rather dank greensand. To the north the road runs through a deep overgrown cutting in the greensand. The church of St Thomas was totally rebuilt in 1852 in a classy mock-medieval style. Odd tower, complex windows, and inside it is high and spacious with a heavy elaborate roof.

Good varied angel-corbels and pretty tiles in the chancel and baptistry, which has an amazing 1852 font and cover.

★ *Village*

MELBURY BUBB (E) near Chetnole. Tiny village tucked up under a well-wooded hill. The Bubb part of the name comes from a family who owned land here but the Melbury is obscure. Next door to the church is a lovely stone manor house, mostly Jacobean. The church of St Mary has a *(cont p. 106)*

Farming

Dorset Horn sheep

Outside the urban south-east of Poole/Bournemouth, Dorset is still a rural and agricultural county, even though only some 5,000 people are directly employed in agriculture. The landscapes are hardly ever 'natural', but the end product of thousands of years of agriculture. We cannot reconstruct the earliest (Neolithic) agriculture in any detail, but from the later prehistoric period small square fields still survive, outlined by banks in what is now pasture. Lynchets, mostly of the medieval period, abound in the county, long flat strips carved along the hillsides which probably indicate that the flatter ground, so much easier to cultivate, was either insufficient (which seems unlikely) or difficult to keep fertile because the farmers did not have a good understanding of crop rotation and manuring.

Most of Dorset followed the well-known open field pattern in the medieval period, where one field was allowed to lie fallow and recover each year. These were steadily enclosed from the 16th century to the 19th century – Fordington around Dorchester was still not enclosed when the railways cut across it in the 1840's and 50's, and parts of the open fields are still being cultivated on Portland. Although the end of the open fields (and rights to common lands) was bad for the majority of small farmers, it made possible selective breeding of animals (impossible when they were all herded together) and better control over crops. Enclosure, and the reclamation of wastes or common lands produced the lovely patchwork of fields in the valleys and lowlands.

The chalk downlands were made and maintained by the large numbers of sheep kept in the county. Before artificial fertilisers all farms had to have animals to keep the land fertile. Sheep fed all day on the downs, and were penned on the arable at night, thus using them as walking dung-carts. The manure from other animals was as carefully used, but had to be carted to the fields. The number of sheep in Dorset declined from a peak of half a million in 1850, to 1983 when there were only 160,000 sheep and lambs in the county.

Much of the downland they created has been ploughed up and is used to grow corn, which would have been difficult before the introduction of artificial fertilisers as the soil on the chalk uplands is poor and thin.

Dairying has always been present in the county, but it was given a great boost from the middle of the 19th century by the railways, because milk could be delivered to the large towns by rail before it went off, impossible before. This increased the number of cows kept in the areas where grass grew well – the Marshwood and Blackmoor Vales and the rich river valleys. Hardy's *Tess* shows the dairying industry after this expansion. The number of cows in the county has increased enormously this century, more than balancing the decline in sheep. There are now over 260,000 cattle and calves in Dorset, almost half of them dairy cows, more than three times the number in 1924. In many rural areas there are more cows than people: for example Mappowder parish has more than 1,000 cows and only 195 inhabitants. The dairy cows are almost all the black and white Friesians, but there is more variety in the beef cattle, with the pale Charolais and the reddish-brown and white Simmental and Hereford all found within the county.

In the river valleys water-meadows were set up to

Dorset farm labourers in 1846

Horse and cart near Wimborne in the 19th century

Threshing tackle being driven by a steam engine

provide early grass for sheep or cows — intricate networks of ditches and runners fed water all over low-lying fields, covering them with a thin sheet of water which had to be kept moving. This prevented the grass from being frosted and made it grow earlier. The technique was developed in the 17th century and went on in use until superseded by new strains of grass early this century. Relics of the water-meadows can be seen in many areas, especially along the River Frome.

Pigs and poultry, once kept by every cottager, are now specialised businesses, and are usually kept inside, although there are many 'free-range' pigs in the county, and still some farmyard hens and geese. Dorset has some unusual farms — because of the pure water from the chalk, watercress is grown around Waddock Cross and Cranborne, and there are several fish farms producing trout. Farmhouse cheese is still made on a small scale, and sheep or goat milk cheeses also.

The number of animals kept in Dorset has changed drastically this century, but there has been more change in the way the ground is worked. For example until the early 19th century the corn was harvested in much the same way as it had been since the medieval period or even earlier. It was cut by hand, stooked to dry, loaded on to carts, stacked in ricks, and then throughout the winter thrashed by hand. The first change in this primeval process came in the 1830's with the introduction of threshers powered by horses. The steamdriven thresher came in during the 1860's, and we have a graphic description of a harvest at this time from Hardy in *Tess of the D'Urbevilles*. Despite the application of modern machinery to the removal of the corn from the ear, most of the rest of the processes were carried out laboriously

by horse drawn machinery or by hand. From the 1940's combine harvesters have 'combined' the jobs of the reapers, stookers, and threshers, and carried out all these jobs actually in the field. This is perhaps the most spectacular advance of mechanisation, but machine milking, automatic feeding systems, muck spreaders, fork-lift trucks and so on have altered every job in farming. Artificial fertilisers and, more recently, the EEC intervention process have altered Dorset's agriculture, particularly with set-aside, but what remains the same are the skills of animal husbandry and soil cultivation, which despite the paraphernalia of modern machinery are as vital today as they have been for thousands of years. The weather and the seasons still control the rhythm and results of farming, and the farming controls the appearance of much of Dorset's landscape.

Manor Farm barn, Lillington, in the 1920s

ABOVE *Melbury Bubb from Bubb Down*
LEFT *The Saxon font, Melbury Bubb*

good 15th century tower with decorative shafts springing from half angels, and elaborate wide frieze. The rest of the church rebuilt in 1851, is still lit by oil-lamps, and heated by a coke stove, and has a well-fitted, well-used feeling to it. Attractive late 15th century glass in the upper parts of the windows. The Saxon font is hilarious: beautifully carved with animals and interlace decoration, but re-used here upside down (presumably deliberately), probably originally part of a shaft.

★★ *Landscape, church, font.*

MELBURY OSMUND (E) Picturesque, unspoilt and quiet. Many oak trees. Well worth walking down from the church to the watersplash, and even beyond to admire the 17th century thatched stone cottages. The church of St Osmund 'being ruinous was totally taken down and rebuilt on the same Foundation' in 1745, leaving only the internal tower arch from the medieval church. The new building was paid for by Susanna Strangways Horner, as recorded on the tablet in the chancel, itself rebuilt in 1888. The rest of the church (apart from the fittings) is hers still. Very plain, much prettier outside than in, with a stylised ashlar south front and heavy battlements designed to be admired from the village street. Thomas Hardy's parents – Jemima Hand and Thomas Hardy – were married here in 1839, and the area is the setting for *The Woodlanders*.

★★★ *Village.*

MELBURY SAMPFORD (E) A huge house, seldom open to the public. The grounds are occasionally and are well worth seeing, with lake, and glorious parkland with specimen trees, and fallow deer. The house is best understood from the south (lake side). On the right is the Tudor house, with its central tower. The gable ends of this early house form the end bays of the classical late 17th century facade. To the left is the library of 1872 and beyond that a huge tower (with wing behind) by Salvin of 1885. Nearby is an octagonal Tudor pavilion or garden house. The church is only accessible when the grounds are open, and is also

worth seeing, basically 15th century, with a very elaborate chancel fitted out in 1878. Nice crossing tower with two superb 1460s alabaster effigies of knights. Other good monuments too.

★★★★ *House, landscape.*

MELCOMBE HORSEY (E, Higher Ansty) is also known as Melcombe Bingham, and to complete the confusion the house is Bingham's Melcombe. The village is now almost a mile from the church and manor house, leaving the humps and bumps of a deserted medieval settlement in the fields to the south of the church. Most of the village is fairly recent, and runs into Ansty, a similar settlement. The most imposing building is Ansty village hall, converted from an 18th century malthouse, part of a large brewery established here in 1777 and used until the 1940's. Higher Ansty is remote, with thatched cottages

The road to the church is also the drive to the house and is private. One can park at the gates and walk to the church passing the superb manor house. Wonderfully English scene, green valley with downland above. Partly late medieval, but most prominent on this side is the gatehouse, built early in the 16th century, and brought up-to-date about 1730 when the windows were made classical and converted to sashes. The house belonged to the Bingham family from the 13th century up to 1895.

The church of St Andrew is mostly of the 14th century with a pretty window in the tower, and a similar imitation one as the east window in the chancel of 1844. In the south porch a niche with graffito and the date 1589 (16th century vandals). The south chapel is dedicated to the Horsey family and has a Jacobean wooden screen. Lots of Bingham family memorials in the north chapel. The pulpit was purchased from the

ABOVE *Melbury Sampford from the lake*
BELOW *The gatehouse, Bingham's Melcombe*

Bastards of Blandford for £10 in 1723. Good 17th century wooden communion rails and benches in the chancel. Fragments of medieval glass survive, particularly in the south chapel, where the east window has two figures labelled JERONIMO and AUGUSTINO for Sts Jerome and Augustine.

★★★ *House, church, setting.*

MELPLASH (D) runs along the main road and is not picturesque. Christ Church was built on a new site in 1845 as a memorial to a vicar of Netherbury who had died of cholera. His nephew employed Benjamin Ferrey as architect, and he produced an imitation Norman church with the tower looking the tiniest bit like a water-tower. Handsome and successful with realistic Norman detailing. The nave was made into a hall in 1976.

★★ *Church.*

MERLEY (F/G) A large modern suburb of Wimborne, with to the west Merley House, a mansion of the 1750s where the large 18th century walled kitchen garden is used for **Merley Bird Gardens** (fee: lists). The aviaries are set in nice plantings. Water garden. Vast selection of birds from colourful macaws, parrots, parakeets and so forth, to ravens and owls including snowy owls. Penguins too.

Merley House, restored and now housing a large display of models, toy trains, cars and so on (fee: lists). Externally the house is stark, but handsome. It was built between 1751-1759 for Ralph Willet who made a fortune in the West Indies from sugar and slaves; he is believed to have designed the splendid rococo plasterwork of the interior himself. Four wings were demolished early in the 19th century. The important rooms are on the ground floor, with fine plaster ceilings. Good staircase, the handrail veneered with emphatically grained *lignum vitae* (literally 'tree of life', so called because it was believed to cure venereal diseases) imported from the West Indies. Displayed on the ground floor is a huge collection of model cars and trains (more than 4,000), some of the latter in model landscapes and running.

Disconcertingly, a caravan park encircles the house, coming right up to the front door, but the house (and its models) are well worth visiting. ★★★

Delph Wood. Just south of Merley on the Wimborne-Poole road (F/G). 1½ mile nature trail around 24 acre woods with a bog, ponds, etc. Car Park.

MILBORNE ST ANDREW (F) is in the bottom of a valley, with steep hills either side. A pleasant mixture of cottages and houses from the 17th century onwards in the variety of materials one expects from a village on the chalk. The church is in a pretty position, surrounded by trees. Usual (but

Milton Abbas from the air

nonetheless attractive) 15th century tower, and a really pretty 12th century doorway, with the upper part of the arch striped in orange-yellow Ham stone and white Purbeck limestone. Inside, the font and the reset chancel arch are also 12th century, but the rest is mostly restoration and rebuild of 1878, with Street as the architect. The windows, the plain north aisle and the elaborate chancel with its fittings are all his. Nice Purbeck Marble tomb of 1527, good series of wall monuments, and a brass chandelier in the north aisle dated 1712. Close to the road south about 1 mile from the village is **Weatherby Castle**, a small Iron Age hillfort now partly covered with conifers, and on top an obelisk of 1761. Just to the east are large farm cottages and a dairy which were part of Sir Ernest Debenham's Bladen Farms, built in the 1920's as are the similar cottages a mile to the west of the village (see Briantspuddle).

★★ *Village, church.*

MILTON ABBAS (F) is famous for its village street, abbey church, and mansion. The house (fee: lists) and the abbey church sit together in a lovely valley close to a lake, with low wooded hills all around. The abbey church is accessible all the year round. Until 1780 the area to the southeast of the abbey church was the town of Milton Abbas, which grew up around the 10th century abbey. Joseph Damer (later Lord Milton, 1st Earl of Dorchester) had the whole town demolished because he disliked its proximity

The house and abbey church, Milton Abbas

to his great house, and moved those inhabitants he could not drive away to the model village still surviving ½ mile away. Only one thatched cottage of the old town survives up under the hill, and part is under the lake.

The Abbey was founded by King Athelstan (925-39), but all the earlier buildings were destroyed in a great fire of 1309. The present huge 14th and 15th century church is only the chancel, tower and transepts. The eastern chapels have been demolished, and the nave was never built. John Tregonwell, son of the owner of the house, aged 5, and after the fashion of the day still in petticoats, fell 60 ft from the top of the church tower. His petticoats acted as a parachute and he survived unharmed, dying in 1680 aged 82.

The porch is of 1865, when Sir George Gilbert Scott restored the church. Because there is no nave, the west door leads straight into the crossing. On the right the south transept has a superb 14th century window, Decorated style with flowing tracery and superb stained glass by Pugin (1847). The north transept window (left) is early 15th century, and Perpendicular. South transept has simple vaulting of 1500, while the crossing tower has much more elaborate vaulting of the same date, like that of Sherborne Abbey. The north transept is mostly of *c.* 1500, and enshrines a lovely white marble monument to Caroline Damer (1775) lying on a sofa with her mourning husband (Lord Milton – the builder of the house) beside her. The table tomb was designed by Robert Adam and the effigies are by Carlini.

Monument to Caroline Damer, Milton Abbey

The window behind was re-glazed and the marble floor laid at the same time. Behind is a mock-medieval brass of 1841. Life size angels with a little basin beneath them form a strange font (1880's).

The aisles and presbytery are 14th century, with simple vaults supported externally by elegant flying buttresses. The north aisle contains a good selection of monuments: Baron Hambro (1877) very Victorian late medieval; Sir John Tregonwell (1565) who bought the abbey at the dissolution, Purbeck marble tomb with twisted columns and a brass; and a monstrous one on the east wall of 1704, with an uncomfortable recumbant figure. The elaborate wooden object suspended in the presbytery was once thought to be the model for a steeple, but is in fact a rare survival of a pyx-shrine, a tiny hanging cupboard used to keep the consecrated bread (the host) in.

The tiles, most of the seating, and the arcading in the two westernmost arches of the presbytery are 1865. Six later medieval misericords on the north side, and a few more on the south with a little original woodwork. Sober alabaster altar in south aisle designed by James Wyatt during his 1789 restoration and pretty, elaborate 14th century piscina and sedilia (between the aisle and presbytery) with some original colouring.

Next door to the church is Damer's great mansion of 1774, designed by Sir William Chambers in a rather uninspired imitation Gothic to go with the church. The north and west fronts are in Portland stone. On the south side the Great Hall of the abbey survives, incorporated into the 18th century house. Externally much restored, internally largely original, with elaborate high quality woodwork. The heavy (restored) screen, is dated 1498 and the stonework of the hall has the same date (north end). Handsome hammer-beam roof. The bay to the left is

original too, with a much simpler (restored) 15th century ceiling. The fireplace is 17th century and there is re-set 16th and 17th century heraldic glass in the windows. From the courtyard the austere and very un-medieval symmetry of the 18th century house can be appreciated, with the porch of the 15th century abbots hall (18th century top) forming the centre of one side, flanked by 19th century corridors. The rooms along the west front of the house form a splendidly decorated suite designed by William Chambers and James Wyatt in the 1770's. All the rooms have elaborate door-cases, white marble fireplaces, and fine plaster ceilings, some with an attractive central feather motif. One room has large portraits (including George I and III) set into the walls, and another original shelves, possibly for displaying china. The staircase leads up to the Ball Room and its ante-room which are even more richly decorated with classical ceilings.

From the gardens a long flight of grass steps (not now used) lead up to **St Catherine's Chapel,** crossing the road by a bridge. The easiest way to reach the chapel is by a slip road on the left of the road from the Abbey to the village and then 3 mins walk. The chapel is directly in line with the abbey church, but 300 yards to the east, and both owe their construction to a vision King Athelstan (925-939) had here. Nothing survives of the Saxon buildings. The doorways are Norman – that on the south has a contemporary inscription granting 120 days indulgence to pilgrims who visit it. The two little windows at the west end are Norman. The interior is plain, with three large circular candle-holders, and in the chancel many rather faded later medieval tiles removed from the abbey in the 19th century. The west end (visible from the

house) was rebuilt in the 18th century.

Fanny Burney visited the village in 1791 and despite thinking the houses too good for 'the Poor' admired the then brand-new village 'built by his Lordship, very regularly, of white plaister, cut stone fashion (ie cob), and thatched'. It is still regular, a village built all at once in the 1780's, although most of the houses are now single dwellings instead of double. In the 19th century they were very over-crowded – it is said that 36 people lived in one of the cottages. Woods rise either side of the single sloping street with its evenly spaced thatched cottages, which are almost professionally picturesque. The almshouse of 1674 (opposite the church) was moved here from the old town. The new parish church was designed by James Wyatt in 1786, and externally it is still a charming 18th century Gothic building (even to the gates) but inside is mostly 1888 (when it was extended to the east and south), with a plain 13th century font with 18th century cover, and tables of commandments etc, of 1830. The fine glass in the east window is of 1970.

A mile to the north is **Park Farm Museum** (fee: lists) with farming bygones, photos etc., some tame animals, a large collection of chimney pots and a picnic area. To the south-west, on the road to Ansty Cross is **The Rare Poultry, Pig, and Plant Centre** (fee: lists), with a multitude of different breeds of poultry (including turkeys), all ten British breeds of pig and other animals. Large range of thatched farm buildings opposite.

★★★★ *House, churches, village and setting.*

The grass steps, Milton Abbas

Milton Abbas, the village and church

MILTON-ON-STOUR (B) has a new church of 1868 set rather apart from the small village which is largely Victorian. Nice spire, internally pleasant with quietly painted roofs and stylized leaf capitals.

MINTERNE MAGNA (E) Lush, beautifully wooded parish wedged between the hills. The small late medieval church of St Andrew has an early 17th century north chapel and a tower of 1800, heightened when the whole church was later restored. The monuments are splendid – to the Napiers (1693, 1695 and 1725) in the north chapel and General Charles Churchill (brother of the Duke of Marlborough) of 1714 in the nave with martial trophies above and below.

  Minterne Gardens, around the big house (fee: lists), have miles of woodland walks, with a great variety of trees rhododendrons, acers, azaleas and many more. Below the house in the most beautiful parkland is the lake, with the streams below it running through woodland and mixed paintings. Well worth fully exploring. The house (not open) is odd: it was rebuilt on the foundations of a Victorian house in 1903-6 in a medley of styles – the modern looking tower on the east front houses a water tank.

  ★★★ *Gardens, especially May.*

MONKTON WYLD (D) A small hamlet in a gloriously wooded area of small hills and valleys, right on the Devon boundary. A church was built here on a new site in 1849, with a 120 ft spire and an attractively elaborate plan. All chert with Caen stone dressings. Worth searching the hamlet for the key to see its rich Victorian interior. Chancel especially fine, with painted ceiling, rood screen, elaborate

wooden fittings and brass gates, coronas (candle holders) and so forth. Attractive stained glass and painted organ of 1872.

  ★★ *Church, landscape.*

MORCOMBELAKE (D) sits under Hardown Hill, and has a little chapel-like church of 1841. Moore's Biscuit factory is open to the public (lists), and one can walk through the bakery seeing their famous Dorset knobs and other delicious biscuits being made.

MORDEN (F) Scattered, with cob or brick cottages and brick farmhouses. Opposite the church is a brick farmhouse whose lower storey is 18th century with a nice brick door surround. The church of St Mary has a thin tower, and was totally rebuilt in 1873. Very odd in style - a combination of Tudor (windows) and

The gardens, Minterne Magna

The chancel, Monkton Wyld

classical (the capitals inside), more like an 1830s church. Very light-hearted, with heavy traceried wooden door, large clerestory, and pretty (if incorrect) tracery in the windows. Reset from the old church is the monument of Thomas Earle (1597), a large figure kneeling in over-size bloomers looking as if he expects a present. He was once owner of Charborough Park. East and West Morden are tiny, woody and remote.

  ★★ *Landscape.*

MORE CRICHEL (F) A large 18th century

Monument of Thomas Earle, Morden church

mansion (Crichel House) in a park with a lake. Many parkland trees. Only the brick stables of *c.* 1800 are visible from the road. The nearby Victorian timber-framed building on the road is a saw mill, and there are several estate houses around in a similar, alien style. The village was destroyed in the 18th century to create the park, and the inhabitants moved to Newtown, to the south, where there is a neo-Norman entrance to the mansion, of 1874. To the south west, down a short walk in the neighbouring hamlet of **Manswood,** is what is claimed to be the longest single stretch of thatch in the country – The Buildings. 120 yards long, and covering 11 cottages and a post office stores.

MORETON (F) An interesting, unspoilt, 'rural' village in woodland close to the heath with a **gorgeous** church and the grave of Lawrence of Arabia.

BELOW *The Buildings, Manswood, More Crichel*

ABOVE *Trinity Chapel window, Moreton church, engraved by Lawrence Whistler as a memorial to a pilot shot down during the Battle of Britain in 1940.*

On the main road are a couple of estate cottages and a former school house, all with intricately latticed windows. Off the road, north of the church is an eccentric thatched building (now PO) with a good street of thatched cottages beyond, some brick and some cob (now cement rendered) with heathstone footings. Beyond the PO is a footbridge over the River Frome, wide, shallow and picturesque. The track beyond leads to Lawrence's cottage (see Cloud's Hill), two miles away.

T.E. Lawrence was killed riding his motor-cycle near Cloud's Hill in 1935 and was buried in the new burial ground on the south of the village, where his handsomely lettered gravestone can be seen (the famous effigy in Arab dress is in St Martin's Church, Wareham). The classical gateway to the burial ground was once part of the entrance to the kitchen gardens of Moreton House. Within it are two inscribed marble tablets taken from the obelisk which can be seen on Fir Hill to the south-east, erected in 1786 to the memory of James Frampton, who lived at Moreton House, opposite the burial ground. The front of his house facing the road dates from 1742-5.

The Framptons were also responsible for the rebuilding of the medieval parish church, demolished in 1776 and replaced by a charming Georgian 'gothic' building. This was enlarged by the addition of the north aisle and porch in the 1840's, and the interior was remodelled at the same time. Miraculously the 1840's work was in the same light-hearted style as the original. Externally 1776 dominates: the south front with the tower rising from the middle of the facade, the door with 'JF' (for James Frampton) and '1776', a lovely parapet frieze of roundels, and the elegant (but very un-medieval) tracery in the windows all combine to produce the most charming facade. Similar windows in the apse, and in the north aisle rebuilt after a bomb destroyed it in 1940. The interior is mostly 1840's including the ribbed ceiling and the stone shafts for the vaulting, shields at the top of the walls, fanciful stone reredos, fine encaustic tiles, amusing font, cast-iron royal coat of arms, pulpit, communion rails, lectern, and most of the pews. The private pew for the Frampton family contains monuments to many of them: a good brass of a kneeling Frampton in armour of 1523 has an additional small brass recording that it was moved in 1733 'from a decayed marble monument in this Isle'. The marble monument to James Frampton's first wife, Mary (1762) is delicately carved with a border of tiny flowers.

The surprise, and the treasure of the church, is the engraved glass in all the windows. The bomb of 1940 destroyed all the glass in the church, and in 1955 the five apse windows were fitted with clear glass engraved by Lawrence Whistler. The other windows were engraved by him between 1974-1984. All are based on the theme of light – the apse has candles, the north aisle the sun, the vestry lightning, and so on. Each window deserves close scrutiny, and the overall effect is magical; the engravings seem to float on the treey views.

★★★★ *Church, windows.*

MOSTERTON (D) Not to be confused with Misterton, only 2 miles north, but across the border into Somerset. Not so attractive as many of the West Dorset villages, but lovely countryside. The church of St Mary was rebuilt on a new site in 1833: internally plain, like a chapel, with a large gallery retaining its original fittings A startling but good stained glass window of 1975 includes a combine harvester and a tractor.

★★ *Church, unusual date.*

MOTCOMBE (B) Sprawling and large, once part of the Royal forest of Gillingham. Many of the buildings are 19th century, but some older ones remain, all in greensand or brick, or a mixture of both. The village hall of 1925 is a splendidly spotted brick building, and next door to the church is a pretty greensand school dated 1839 with an oriel window, hood moulds and so on. The church of St Mary was rebuilt in 1846 in a rather ordinary Perpendicular style. Preserved from the earlier church are an attractive niche now containing a fragment of a statue with a small figure under the skirts of a larger one (both 15th century) and a heavy 13th century font with a plain 17th century cover.

MUDEFORD (G) Marred by modern development, but Mudeford Quay, which protrudes out into the mouth of Christchurch Harbour, is much visited, with a large car-park (fee). Good views all round, and usually boats to watch and salmon netting in season. Ferries run across the mouth of the harbour, on to Hengistbury Head (see entry) and up to Christchurch, Wick and Tuckton. Lots of pleasure boats moored here, and fishing boats work from the Quay, which still has an 18th century feel.

★★ *Setting, boats.*

NETHERBURY (D) Attractive, large village (in 1841 the population was over 2,000) set across the valley of the River Brit just south of Beaminster. Deep lanes. Many older buildings in the local orange stone. The area was once known for its orchards and flax growing.

The church of St Mary overlooks the village and although restored in the 19th century, is mostly later medieval with fine arcades. Battered 12th century font, and even more battered alabaster figure of a knight with canopy above and angels below, c. 1480. The pulpit is Jacobean, exceptional quality with lots of carving and inlaid panels with a simple pattern. The thin screen is 1910, and the benefactors board painted on the wall is a nice

example of 1852. Good glass of 1844 in the east window. Rare Victorian kneelers like bee skips.

★★★ *Village.*

NETHER CERNE (E) A beautiful hamlet consisting of a large house, a farm, a few cottages and a church. Flint and stone banding predominates. Nether Cerne House opposite the church is partly 17th century with mullioned windows, and partly 18th century. The church of All Saints (redundant) is basically medieval, but was heavily restored in 1876. The body of the church is late 13th century, with a fine original window in the east wall of the south chapel.

★★ *Hamlet*

NETHER COMPTON, *see* **COMPTON NETHER**

NORTH POORTON, *see* **POORTON**

NORTH WOOTON (A) has two churches, neither of them in use. The ruined old church stands in the fields, with just the tower surviving, and the new church of 1883 is now a house. A very scattered hamlet, with several good stone and thatched cottages on the main road.

NOTTINGTON (H, Broadway) runs across the valley of the River Wey. The strange octagonal building in its centre was built in 1830 over a spring, which had been discovered early in the 18th century, a time of great popularity for spas. This was quite an expensive one to use: in the 1830's it cost 2/6 a week to drink one glass of water a day, while baths ranged from 1s to 3s. Its popularity faded out during the 19th century, and by 1911 it was a laundry.

OAKLEY DOWN (C) The finest group of Bronze Age barrows off the Ridgeway, in the north-east corner of the county. Visible from the main road (A354) and from a footpath which runs along Ackling Dyke, the Roman road to the west. The Roman road cuts through one of the large disc barrows which Stukeley, the 18th century antiquarian noticed as one of the first proofs that barrows were earlier than the Roman period. The whole group consists of 31 barrows. The area in pasture includes three large disc barrows, with a ditch and bank of large diameter around one or two central mounds. Many were opened by Sir Richard Colt Hoare of Stourhead early in the 19th century. He found some inhumation burials and more cremations. Some burials had grave goods.

★★★ *Barrows.*

ABOVE *The River Frome at Wareham*
BELOW LEFT *Marine Parade, Lyme Regis*
BELOW RIGHT *Lighthouses at Portland Bill*

OPPOSITE ABOVE *The Central Gardens, Bournemouth*
OPPOSITE BELOW *Hardy's birthplace, Upper Bockhampton*
ABOVE *St James and the Blackmore Vale from Shaftesbury*
BELOW LEFT *The Custom's House, Poole*
BELOW RIGHT *Christchurch Priory*

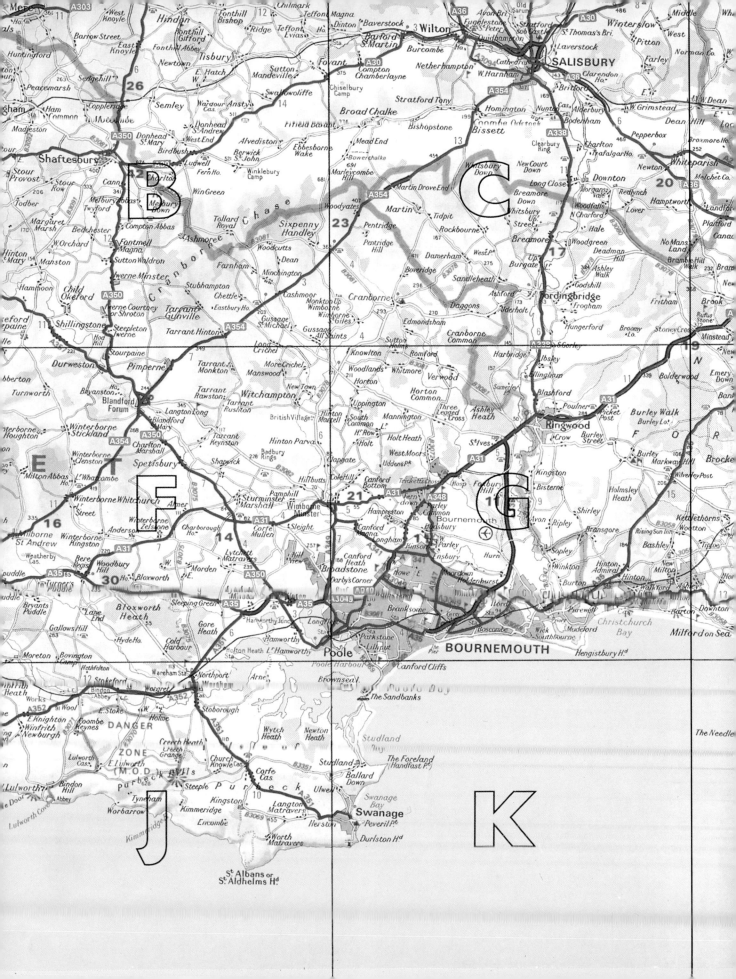

TOP LEFT *Kingston Lacy.* TOP RIGHT *Forde Abbey*
CENTRE LEFT *The Market Place, Blandford Forum.*
CENTRE RIGHT *Cranborne Chase*

BELOW LEFT *Little Bredy, the Bride Valley.* BELOW RIGHT *Nether Cerne*
OPPOSITE TOP *Looking north from Bulbarrow.*
OPPOSITE BELOW *Durdle Door*

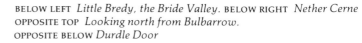

ABOVE *The Fleet, Chesil Beach and Portland* . BELOW *Looking east from Pilsdon Pen*

OBORNE (A) A small village, with thatched cottages and a stream beside the road. The chancel of the original church (1533) survives at the south end of the village, and a new church of 1862 at the north end. Very simple apart from elaborate chancel arch, stone pulpit and font.

OKEFORD FITZPAINE (B) Very pretty and, uncommonly for Dorset, lots of 18th century brick cottages, some with timber-framing, and many still thatched. West of the church is an especially good group, including St Loe's Farm, much restored 16th century, with a wing of 1638 in thinly banded flint and stone. Opposite the church is the mid 18th century rectory whose fine brick wall runs right round the large garden (18th century rectors in Dorset seem to have done themselves very well). The church of St Andrew has an odd tower, built in the 15th century but incorporating the arch and window of the earlier, 14th century tower. As a result the 14th century window is recessed in the new wall, and the walls are extra thick. Why the 14th century work was not demolished is a puzzle. Inside the tower is

ABOVE *Old Harry Rocks with Bournemouth beyond* BELOW *Timber framing and brick, Okeford Fitzpaine*

used as a baptistry, tiled and with the strangest of fonts – triangular, with three angels. This dates from 1866 when the body of the church was virtually rebuilt by John Hicks of Dorchester. Parts of the 15th century north aisle survive, and he copied this on the south. Chancel 1866 too, with good large angel corbels. The 15th century stone pulpit was a font in 1866, and was then given a new stand, stairs and statuettes in the niches. Plain 17th century

benches in the north aisle amazingly survived the restoration. Good view of the village from Okeford Hill, where moss was once gathered for sale in Covent Garden.

★★★ *Village*

OLD HARRY ROCKS (K, The Foreland) are the most easterly point of Purbeck: the land runs level to almost vertical chalk cliffs known as the Foreland or Handfast Point, some 100-180 ft high, with narrow promontories and detached stacks, the thinnest of which is Old Harry Rocks. Erosion is still active: Old Harry's Wife (another stack) collapsed in 1896 (and local fishermen are reputed to have painted a black mourning band around Old Harry afterwards). St Lucas Leap, the gap between the land and the largest stack, was only breached in 1921. The waves have cut arches through the base of others. The ghostly pealing of bells is still supposed to be heard in gales: a ship carrying bells for a Poole church foundered here because of the crew's blasphemy. On a clear day, the Isle of Wight can be seen, with the chalk cliffs of the Needles which once joined the chalk here. In fact Old Harry is probably best seen from a distance, although there are cormorants, black-backed gulls and other birds, and the walk from Studland is pleasant.

★★ *Views, walk.*

OSMINGTON (H) off the main road, picturesque, with a narrow street and thatched stone cottages (including brand new ones on the outskirts). To the north of the churchyard are the ruins of the 17th century manor house. The church of St Osmund is pretty, but mostly dates from 1846 when the nave and chancel were rebuilt, incorporating the original north arcade and chancel arch. Typically the tower is 15th century. Behind the altar is a plain memorial to the Rev John Fisher who died in 1832. He was a good friend of the painter John Constable, who spent his honeymoon in Osmington. Also in the chancel is a strange early 17th century monument, bravely classical but with inept lettering declaring that 'man is a glas: life is as water that's weakly walld about; sinne brings in death; breaks the glass; so runs the water out; finis'.

To the north of the village (and seen from the main road) is a figure of George III on horseback, cut into the chalk in 1815 as a compliment to the king who spent summers at Weymouth.

★ *Village.*

OSMINGTON MILLS (H) The first place along the shore east from Weymouth accessible by road. The view across Weymouth Bay to Portland is superb. The shore is wild and rocky, and the approach road through the little valley pretty. The row of tarred former coastguard cottages, a 'Smugglers' Inn and several other older buildings, are all now outnumbered by bungalows and caravans. The walk along the shore towards Ringstead (see entry) and back along the cliffs is pleasant and easy.

★★ *Landscape.*

OVER COMPTON, *see* **COMPTON**

OWERMOIGNE (H) has some pretty cottages around the church, which was rebuilt in 1884 with rather odd square windows. Only the small 15th century tower (used by smugglers in the 18th century as a store) survives from the original church. Heathland to the north.

Mill House Cider Museum and Dorset Collection of Clocks (fee: lists), about half-way between Owermoigne and Crossways. A dozen cider presses and half-a-dozen apple mills on display, some of which are used in early winter to make traditional cider. A video shows all the processes the rest of the year. Marvellous

Cottage on Pamphill Green

place to see this traditional Dorset farm industry. The Clock Museum has many Dorset clocks (and a chinese bed), well worth seeing. ★★★

PAMPHILL (F) One of Dorset's most unspoilt villages. Three commons or greens unite scattered 17th and 18th century brick and timber framed cottages. Undulating ground ornamented with trees and thick hedges. Much thatch. The estate village to Kingston Lacy, hence the oak avenue bisecting Pamphill Green planted in 1846, and St Stephen's church at the north end, built in pretty Arts and Crafts Gothic in 1907. To the west of Pamphill Green (with curved gables) is the 17th century manor house, built by a steward to the Bankes estate. To the south is Little Pamphill Green, and Gillingham's School and almshouses (now Pamphill First School) built in 1698, with originally the school in the higher, classical centre part and four single-room almshouses on either side. Cowgrove Common to the east has a good duck pond, and right on the west, on the main road into Wimborne is the chapel of St Margaret and St Anthony, tiny, all brown heathstone, restored in the 19th century and 1990s. Attached are cob and brick cottages of the 17th and 18th century, almshouses which replaced the medieval leper hospital. National Trust car park off Little Pamphill Green, park there and walk the village to see it properly.

★★★★ *Setting, village.*

PARNHAM HOUSE (D) A superb manor house (fee: lists) in a beautifully wooded setting ½ mile south of Beaminster, with gardens, mostly laid out 1910-14, all enclosed by woodland or parkland.

The Elizabethan house was altered in the 18th century, but in 1810 John Nash turned it back into a 'Romantic' manor house. Now the home of John Makepeace's Furniture Workshops, where stunning modern furniture is made. The east entrance front is enclosed with a court laid out in 1910, with decorated stone walls and roses. Golden orange three storey porch with pretty pinnacles and parapets added by Nash. The fine coat of arms is 17th century. In the hall the screen of about 1600 and fireplace with 15th century woodwork were brought from elsewhere. At the far end the three doorways are original, but restored. Nash added the central window on the east side. The timber ceiling is 16th century, and there is mid 17th century coloured glass in the two outer eastern windows. The hall is used to display recent work by John Makepeace and his students. The drawing room has good late 17th century woodwork – three door surrounds, panelling and a magnificent over-mantel with swags of fruit and flowers. Two splendid modern glass chandeliers. This room and the next were altered by Nash, with new windows. The Library, refitted in 1910, has mechanical imitation 16th century panelling and plaster. The bookcases are used to display tools and woodwork. The staircase is early 17th century, brought here in 1910, and is decorated with charming wall-paintings of

The east front, Parnham House

1935. Upstairs the bathroom has gorgeous 1920's tiling. The Strode bedroom has a huge four-poster bed by Makepeace, a 17th century carved overmantel and 1910 panelling. The Oak Room, where good teas etc, are to be had, has fine 16th century panelling placed here in 1910, and elaborate plaster above in 16th century style but of 1910. The colourful glass ranges in date from the late 16th to mid 17th century.

The terrace to the south of the house is of 1910-14 and has gazebos in imitation of 17th century ones at Montacute. Lawns and trees stretch away, with the little river Brit and its wooded bank on one side and parkland on the other. Good old-fashioned roses, daffodils and many other plants. The park is the burial place of William Rhodes-Moorhouse, the first airmen to be awarded the Victoria Cross (1915). To the north of the house are the stables and so on, remodelled 1910-14, and now used as workshops (one open). Over the bridge are the long herbaceous border and woodland walks, with at the end 1½ times life size fibre glass figures of Morecombe and Wise (1977) in bright blue suits. A good afternoon out.

★★★ *House.*

PENTRIDGE (C) At the end of a lane, and thus quiet and isolated, despite the proximity of the main road (A354). To the south-east is Pentridge Hill, with extensive prehistoric field systems. The cottages are mostly brick, banded with flint, and are all well-spaced and grown in with lots of trees. Up by the church a couple of cottages and the village hall face what is almost a village green. The church of St Rumbold was rebuilt in imitation Decorated style in 1855, pretty externally with elaborate windows, flint and greensand walls, and tower with a tiny spire. Nice thick timber porch. Inside is not so pretty. A tablet (of 1902) to commemorate a local great-grandfather of Robert Browning, the poet.

★★ *Landscape.*

PIDDLEHINTON (E) Thatched cottages and farm buildings mix with modern development along the narrow shallow valley of the River Piddle. The church of St Mary has a lovely setting, with trees all around. Good 15th century tower with big pinnacles. Most of the church – the chancel and much of the nave – is early 16th century but the north aisle was added and

the nave extended in 1867, when the rest of the church was restored. The chancel is stripped down to bare stone and flint, and has a late 15th century sedilia which looks just like a settle, and a plaster vault of about 1800. A wall brass has the figure of a merry looking parson who died in 1617. Nicely carved leaves on the capitals south of the nave.

★★ *Village, church.*

PIDDLETRENTHIDE (E) gets its extraordinary name from being on the little River Piddle, and its assessment for thirty hides at Domesday. It straggles along the little valley – a rather severe late Victorian Methodist chapel and its schoolroom at one end, the parish church at the other. In the middle is a pretty flint school of 1848, with simple 16th century iron gates from the tomb of Lady Margaret Beaufort in Westminster Abbey. Pretty 17th and 18th century cottages of banded stone and flint, and later ones of banded flint and brick. The church of All Saints is huge, with its fine tower dated 1487 by an inscription over the west doorway. Inside the 15th century porch a good Norman doorway, with zig-zag decorations. The nave and

The school gates, Piddletrenthide

aisles are of *c.* 1500, wide and light. Lots of decorative late 18th and 19th century monuments (and hatchments). The church furnishings are mostly of 1852, when the building was restored and the chancel virtually rebuilt. Close to the altar is an early example of Victorian-style Gothic, the monument to John Bridge, a London silversmith and jeweller who came from the village. He died in 1834, but the mock medieval monument is so far ahead of its time that it looks later Victorian.

★★ *Village, church.*

PILSDON (D) has the narrowest possible roads between high hedges down the side of the Marshwood Vale. Pilsdon Pen hillfort is in the background. Tiny settlement right down in the valley, with beyond the church a large 17th century manor house whose front appears to be all window. The little church of St Mary is undistinguished Victorian. Wild daffodils abound.

PILSDON PEN (D) Iron Age hillfort (National Trust), car park in the lay-by to the south. Not so many trees as Lambert's or Coney's Castle, but the best views — it is the highest point in Dorset (277m, 908 ft). Well worth the stiff 10 minutes climb up. To the south-east is the Marshwood Vale, and to the north the Axe valley: on clear days the Mendips can be seen. Double ramparts enclose the whole hilltop and probably date from the late Iron Age. Excavations in the 1960's revealed late Iron Age huts, and parts of a probably medieval

rabbit warren. The rectangular mounds inside the fort are pillow mounds, constructed for rabbits to breed in, and the square earthwork in the centre is perhaps also part of the warren. The earthworks visible just inside the northern end are probably the remains of an earlier rampart which was abandoned. Entrance in the north is probably the only original one.

★★★ *Hillfort, views.*

The Brace of Pheasant, Plush

PIMPERNE (F) A village with lots of brick buildings of the 18th and 19th centuries with flint banding, and several long cob boundary walls, most of which have been cement rendered, but which retain their tiny tiled roofs. St Peter's church has a mid 15th century tower, but the rest of the church and the top of the tower date from 1873-4. Nice Norman doorway with zig-zag decoration reset as the entrance and another simpler arch reset inside. The aisles seem oddly low, with strangely horizontal windows, but the interior is interesting, with strongly carved capitals to the pillars. 12th century font with elaborate, apparently 19th century top.

★ *Church.*

PLUSH (E) A happy tiny hamlet, perfectly sited amongst the downs, with an isolated and remote atmosphere. The little church was designed by Benjamin Ferrey in 1848, and is prettier outside than in. All the fittings apart from the 12th century font are 1848.

★★ *Landscape.*

POOLE (G) developed as Wareham declined: the river at Wareham was silting up, and as ships became larger Poole's deep-water harbour was more suitable. From the 13th century Poole became a port and fishing town, and by 1433 it was larger than Weymouth, and the biggest port in Dorset, the home of a famous privateer or pirate, Henry Page, who so enraged the French that they raided Poole in 1406 in retaliation. The medieval town was

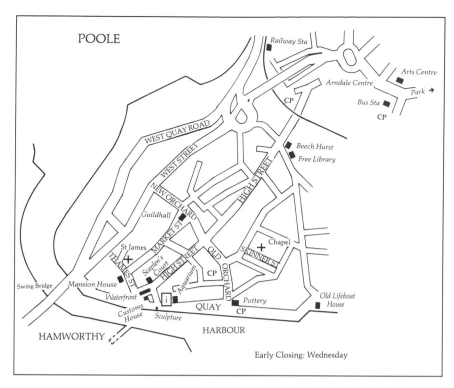

POOLE

Railway Sta
Arts Centre
Arndale Centre
Park →
Bus Sta
CP
CP
WEST QUAY ROAD
WEST STREET
Beech Hurst
Free Library
HIGH STREET
NEW ORCHARD
Guildhall
MARKET ST
Chapel
St James
Scaplen's
Court
OLD ORCHARD
SKINNER'S ST
THAMES ST
HIGH STREET
Aquarium
CP
Swing Bridge
Mansion House
Pottery
Old Lifeboat
House
Waterfront
i
QUAY
CP
Customs
House
Sculpture
HARBOUR
HAMWORTHY

Early Closing: Wednesday

The Guildhall, Poole

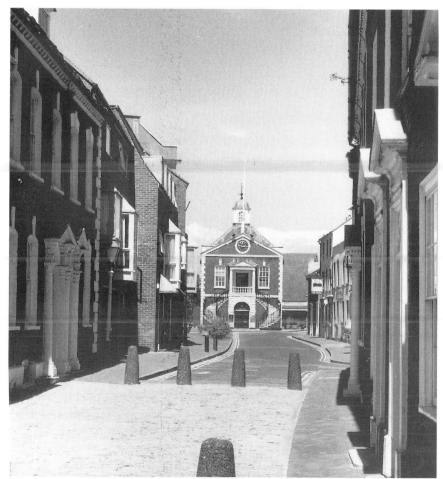

confined to the south-west of the present railway line, a tiny area in comparison to the town of today. From the beginning of the 17th century Poole was one of the main ports of the Newfoundland trade – a three-cornered route whereby ships went out to Newfoundland loaded with salt and provisions, brought salt fish back to the Mediterranean countries and finally came home with wine, olive oil and dried fruits. This trade declined in the early 19th century, but from the 1890's the growth of Bournemouth stimulated coastal trade at Poole with the import of building materials and so on, which led to a revival.

The Quay, and the area immediately behind (with St James church) is interesting to explore, with two good museums. Outside this area much of the town has been rebuilt. One of the most conspicuous new buildings is by the railway station and belongs to Barclays Bank. Because there are no distinct divisions between the storeys its twin towers look higher and larger than they really are.

Unlike Lyme, Weymouth, and Swanage, Poole did not become a resort in the 18th or 19th centuries, but Rockley Sands, Canford Cliffs and Sandbanks (see entries: all parts of Poole) have now become holiday resorts. Canford and Branksome Park developed as garden suburbs to Poole from the 1880's. All around the town were 'barren dreary heaths', now covered with suburbs. Hamworthy (*see*) with its docks did not develop until after the first bridge was constructed across the harbour in 1835. Upton (*see*) is even later.

Poole's older buildings have suffered dreadfully: between 1950 and 1972 over half the buildings dating from before 1850 were demolished, many of them Georgian town houses of great charm. In 1975 part of the town centre was declared a conservation area, and the demolition halted within it. Now this south west end of High Street, Church Street, Market Street and the areas around are smart, with new houses and flats mixed in with Georgian ones.

St James Church was totally rebuilt in 1820 on a large scale. Outside it is rather austere, Purbeck limestone with two tiers of windows along the sides, but inside it is spectacular – frivolous Regency Gothic, with all the plaster work repainted about 1970 in very pleasing colours. The plaster vault is supported on clusters of great pine pillars which are supposed to be masts of Newfoundland pine, and which were once plastered and painted to look like stone. This is the sort of building the serious Victorians despised – the church was called 'Carpenters' Gothic in 1857, lacking 'the exquisite beauty, effect,

117

ABOVE *St James's, Poole* BELOW *The Customs House, Poole*

and correctness' of Gothic buildings being erected by the 1850s. Huge galleries all round. The mahogany and gilt reredos of 1736 comes from the earlier church, but the combination Gothic and classical portable font is of the same date as the church, and is a very unusual piece, looking a little bit like a stove. Many of the monuments came from the earlier church, and are decoratively arranged in the spaces between the windows. Most of the windows are plain glass, but in the south wall is an interesting stained glass window of 1961.

★★★ *Church (lists).*

Some of the best 18th century houses are around the church – West End House set back to the west is a particularly elaborate early 18th century one. Off the south-west corner is the Mansion House, one of the largest houses built by the prosperous merchants of Poole. This one is of 1800, rather plain, with large round-headed arches to the lower storey. More good 18th century houses, some with fine door-cases, along Church Street, which turns into Market Street and gives a fine prospect of the Guildhall (1761), with its two curving flights of steps leading to the upper storey. The lower storey was originally open, and used as a meat market.

Sadly St George's Almshouses in Church Street, have been so drastically restored that little of the medieval building remains.

Poole Quay from Hamworthy Docks, showing the Harbour Office, Customs House and Waterfront Museum

The northern two-thirds of the High Street is a pedestrian precinct. Around the junction with Lagland Street is a fine group of buildings. First a bank, a rather plain town house of 1800, then in complete contrast just up Lagland Street the Free Library and Art School of 1887 (now offices) in an intricate brick and stone style, a jubilee celebration, and set back from the road, Beech Hurst, a real mansion house of 1798 with large palm fronds in the pediment. Strangely, the upper part of the High Street, where there are now no cars or lorries, is bisected by a railway line.

The Quay was the centre of Poole's prosperity from the Middle Ages, and although most of the business is now carried out from Hamworthy (opposite) there are still ships and boats tied up here and boats plying to Brownsea (see entry) or offering trips around the harbour. The wooded hump of Brownsea and the undeveloped hills of Purbeck fill the horizon. The best part of the quay is towards the western end, where the Town Cellars (now the Waterfront Museum), the Customs House and Harbour Offices form a fine group. The Customs House was rebuilt after a fire in 1813, reproducing the original

building of the late 18th century. Its sophisticated brickwork contrasts with the chunky stonework of the town cellars, built in the 15th century as a warehouse. Plaque recording the many D-Day ships which left from the Quay. The Town cellars were originally longer: Thames Street was cut through the building in the late 18th century, and a small part remains on the far side of the street. The new gable ends were built in brick. Beyond, in Thames Street the King Charles pub is a late 16th century building much restored, once the haunt of smugglers.

The Waterfront Museum ★★★★ is a superb display in an interesting building, tracing the maritime history of the town, with a big new extension into a huge early 19th century warehouse. Reconstructed street of shops enlivened by models, history of scouting, smuggling, etc. Highly recommended. Just to the west is the Fisheries Office and H.M. Coastguard built in 1822, with an open collonade along the front. Big new (1991) metal sculpture - Sea Music, with platforms built around it giving good views. At the corner a 1990 tile frieze with panels of Poole's maritime history. Round the corner, at the end of the quay is the town bridge, the third on the site, built in 1927 and typical of its date, with green copper cladding. It is opened at specific times for pleasure craft, and on

demand for commercial ships and boats. Just behind the Waterfront Museum is **Scaplen's Court** ★★★ basically a house of *c.* 1500, worth seeing for itself (fine kitchen), and also for its displays on the domestic life of the people of Poole. 19th century warehouses which once served the port survive beside the Waterfront Museum and along the quay to the East. One of them houses **Aquarium Complex** ★★★, an aquarium and serpentarium, with a large selection of fish, lots of snakes (all very lazy and including large cobras), crocodiles and alligators (fee: lists). Upstairs is what is thought to be the largest oo gauge model railway in the world. **Poole Pottery** has been on the quay at Poole since the 1870s, although early production was mostly tiles. Today there is a large factory shop, a museum showing products from 1900 on, and so on. Tours around the factory (fee: lists). Well worth it to see all the processes of pottery production. In Skinner Street, to the north of the Pottery, is a fine Congregational chapel of 1777, with a large classical porch added in 1833. At the eastern end of the Quay a little lifeboat station of 1882, now a museum with the lifeboat of 1938 which was used at Dunkirk (free: lists).

Poole Park to the east of the town centre, originally called The People's Park, was opened in 1890 by the Prince of Wales on land given by Lord Wimborne *(cont p. 122)*

Gardens

No-one has ever dared to call Dorset's landscape a garden: its windy uplands, bare heathland and rocky coastline are too austere for that. The fertile wide valleys like those of the Frome and Stour are the only areas to approach the cosy simile. From the 18th century many of the great houses had great parks, now enclosed for ornament rather than for the preservation of deer, and one of the most attractive is that of Kingston Lacy, which barely has gardens at all, but has a huge park, full of trees and so ringed by woodlands that it seems to be a forest clearing. Handsome cattle and sheep ornament the view.

One of the greatest gardens – Abbotsbury – has lost its big house, which was burnt down this century and never replaced. The garden flows down a steepish little valley close to the sea, well protected from frosts. It is charming both in the higher, more formal parts, and in the wilder plantings along the tiny stream. Magnificent all year, but best in spring with camelias (some quite large trees) and sheets of daffodils. Forde Abbey in the west has a superb garden around it, with ponds, a water staircase, good plantings and trees. Its style ranges from a fine herbaceous border alongside the canal, to a bog garden by the upper lake, with many rare trees everywhere. Many daffodils.

The extensive gardens at Cranborne Manor in north Dorset are totally different, with lots of separate gardens and walks, all exquisitely designed, often in a very bold, decisive way, such as the pinks which totally fill the long borders under aged cordoned apples in the White Garden. Many scented plants, lots of bulbs. Horn Park has a lovely setting, wild areas and interesting plantings.

Athelhampton is formal, with topiary enclosures, a lime walk and lots of small pools. Informal areas too, but it is perhaps the most architectural garden in the county.

Compton Acres, Poole, is presumably Dorset's most popular garden since it has the most visitors. Formal gardens, 'Roman', 'Italian' and so on and less formal areas like the woodland garden, are totally separated from one another by hedges, with good views over Poole Harbour at intervals.

Mapperton has formal and informal parts, with a walled croquet lawn, a large (and hidden) 1920's formal garden, and plantings continuing in a more informal way down the tiny valley. Minterne, in central Dorset, is famous for its rhododendrons, grown here since the 1870's, with a superb woodland garden with a winding stream, and a great variety of plants. Stapehill Gardens have been created since 1990, with a huge rock garden and lake, and so on.

Although the rural society which produced the true cottage garden has gone, the happy tumble of shrubs, perennials, herbs and simple annual flowers (often with vegetables as well, or fruit bushes) is still sometimes found. An aversion to lawns, except for paths or small patches under fruit trees, is another characteristic along with an apparently total lack of design. Hollyhocks and climbing roses are the most characteristic plants, along with a determination not to give the weeds room to grow. Another rural speciality – the austere totally vegetarian garden is also seen occasionally, with very straight rows of brussels sprouts by the front path in winter, and a greater profusion and variety in summer.

Many Dorset gardens are opened under the National Gardens Scheme, and lists are available from the tourist offices. Sometimes whole villages band together and open a selection of their gardens for a week-end offering fascinating tours for gardeners, with a great variety of sizes and styles of gardens to be seen. They are always well advertised locally.

Most of the towns in Dorset have pleasant parks, but the best is the Central Gardens Bournemouth, which

OPPOSITE *Compton Acres, Poole*
ABOVE *Mapperton*
BELOW *Cottage vegetables at Nettlecombe, near Powerstock*

runs along The Bourne, a little stream, right through the middle of the town. Fine permanent plantings such as the rock garden and wonderful bedding.

★★★★ Abbotsbury Sub-Tropical Gardens, Athelhampton, Compton Acres Poole, Cranborne, Forde.
★★★ Kingston Maurward, Mapperton, Minterne and Dean's Court, Wimborne. See also: Bennets Water Gardens Chickerell; Knoll Gardens, Hampreston; Smedmore, Sandford Orcas.

Branksome Chine

(who lived at Canford). The park curves round part of the bay cut off by the railway and adapted as a shallow boating lake. Good plantings, and lots of wildfowl with particularly tame Canada Geese. Poole's municipal buildings are to the north-east, 1929 and very classical with 1980s extension with stone frieze.

Branksome always seems more like part of Bournemouth than of Poole. This is especially true of the lower part, Branksome Park, which like Canford (*see*) was developed as a posh residential area from about 1880, with large houses in huge plots. Still well-wooded, although many of the large houses, and even some of the hotels, have been replaced by blocks of flats. Branksome Chine runs right down the middle of Branksome Park, a wooded ravine with paths running through it. In the 18th century it was part of a regular smugglers route inland to Kinson. Sir John Betjeman wrote 'I walk the asphalt paths of Branksome Chine / In resin-scented air like strong Greek wine'. Where the chine meets the sea there is a little formal park. Although visitors are no longer recommended to take compasses with them to explore the paths in the chines, as they were in the middle of the 19th century, the chines make good walks. R. L. Stevenson wrote *Kidnapped* and lived for two years in the 1880's on Alum Chine, the next one along. He was one of many TB sufferers who then came to the Bournemouth area for their health. Alum Chine has a serious looking suspension bridge to take pedestrians across

it. The cliff-top also makes a good walk, since its instability keeps development back from the edge.

Lilliput, on the edge of the harbour, is named after *Gulliver's Travels* (1726) by Jonathan Swift, because there was a famous local smuggler called Gulliver. 1930s small shopping centre, and housing all 1920s on. Lots of yachts, and good views from the only wild part of the shore – Evening Hill.

Parkestone is a suburb of Poole, and Lower Parkestone's shopping centre does indeed have a small park in the centre. Most of the buildings are Victorian or later, with two very good late churches. **St Osmund's** is almost certainly the best 20th century church in Dorset. It was the last church designed by E. S. Prior (whose other church in Dorset – Bothenhampton (see entry) was one of his early works). St Osmund's is really strange, a rich Byzantine beauty in variegated brick. The west front is superb, with a huge 'modern' rose window and decorated arch. The chancel had been built in 1904 by another architect, and the rest was designed by Prior in 1913. All the elevations are interesting, and the interior is as good. The dome and barrel vaults of the aisles are of concrete (some of which have had to be rebuilt). The sanctuary is both classical and theatrical, with terracotta pillars behind, and 18th century ironwork. The south aisle has a marble altar by Prior, with behind a severe and attractive screen by MacDonald Gill, Eric Gill's brother. The crossing capitals are terracotta like the rest, but more elaborate and with odd large angels added. The fittings are attractive, particularly the bronze lectern (1926). The stained glass is Prior's patented, thick and handmade in pale colours and abstract designs.
★★★ *A church for anyone interested in architecture.*

St Peter's ★★ is more conventional, but also interesting. A huge and sophisticated stone church basically of 1880-1900 designed by J. L. Pearson. Cathedral-like, with lovely stiff-leaf capitals to the clustered shafts. High nave with the wooden vault running right through the chancel as well. Pearson also designed St Stephens, Bournemouth, and this church has much more in common with the high quality (and high church) buildings there than with rural Dorset. Superb fittings including a thin wrought iron rood screen.

Like adjacent Bournemouth there are several other churches of the late 19th century, but all rather dull compared with the two described. Alderney, now an industrial suburb to the north-east of Poole, was the home of the artist Augustus John from 1911-27, although his mistresses and

The 1860s pulpit, North Poorton

children spent more time there than he did. They rented a large bungalow (demolished 1927) set in the then undeveloped heathland.

POORTON (D) Divided into two hamlets – north and south, both sparse and remote. North has a large 17th century stone farmhouse and a few cottages, all thatched, and the church of St Mary Magdalene which was totally rebuilt in 1861-2 by John Hicks, for whom Thomas Hardy was then working. All of a piece, with good imitation medieval tiles and other characteristic fittings, including complex pulpit

Cottage, North Poorton

Portesham House, once home of Admiral Sir Thomas Masterman Hardy

Bottom Combe Quarries, Portland

and a tour-de-force of large capitals with local flora, birds and even animals, supported by rather droopy angels: all the work of the Dorchester carver Benjamin Grassby. The 19th century font is an instructive contrast with the earlier one near it. Well worth seeing as an example of local Victorian Gothic.

★★ *Church.*

PORTESHAM (H) A pleasant village with the chalk hills rising behind. On the main road a pretty 18th century house where Admiral Sir Thomas Masterman Hardy lived (see Hardy's Monument). Many stone cottages and the Manor House in the middle. Landscaped pond. The church of St Peter is basically medieval, unspoiled despite restoration. Inside are 17 medieval stone brackets with carved heads, angels and so on. Good 17th century inscriptions including one (re-cut) set in the south wall externally, referring to the civil war.

★★ *Village.*

PORTLAND (H) A strange, bleak block of limestone jutting out into the channel, almost treeless and with cliffs on every side. Well worth visiting to see the quarries, Portland Castle, museum, the views, St George's church and the Bill, and just for itself, its own distinctive landscape. This is best seen from the coast path, running round most of the island. Hardy described it as 'a huge lump of freestone', and quarries have nibbled away, extracting the fine

white Portland stone since the 17th century. Not really an island, as it is linked to the mainland by Chesil, a 15 mile bank of shingle, but until 1839 and the construction of the first bridge visitors had to cross Smallmouth by ferry. Oyster farm by the bridge. The big car park by the road across was made as a marshalling area for the Americans at D-Day. A memorial stone to the half million men who passed through Portland in 1944-45 is in Victory Road, Fortuneswell. Chesil Beach Centre (free: lists), small with a good display on the natural history of the area

Beside the road across is Portland Harbour, constructed from 1849-1903 to enclose a huge area of deep water. Portland Prison (now a Borstal) was established in 1848 to provide the labour to quarry the stone for the vast breakwaters. A harbour had long been proposed, but the great storm of November 1824 when many ships were wrecked (and one actually thrown on top of the Chesil Bank near Portland) speeded plans. Its ceremonial stone is inscribed 'These are Imperial Works and Worthy Kings', (Alexander Pope) . The harbour was built for use by the Navy and commercial ships, but today it is mostly used by the Navy, whose huge fuel tanks dominate the road to Portland. The Navy is scheduled to leave before 2,000, so the harbour is likely to alter drastically.

Apart from Fortuneswell and Easton the villages are small with a few old cottages and much modern development.

Fortuneswell (and **Chesil,** the lower part) should be picturesque, clinging to the side of the steep hill and with the sea below, but except when seen from above, they are not, even though most of the buildings are of Portland Stone. Too many are rather mean Victorian buildings, and the whole layout ignores the sea. The harbour side at Castleton was once pretty, but has been engulfed by the naval installations. Older cottages are scattered about in Fortuneswell (some with the distinctive Portland stone porches), and some good 18th century houses (including a rather fine derelict

Wakeham, Portland

ABOVE   *The Chesil and Portland Harbour from Portland Heights*
BELOW   *St Andrew's church with Rufus Castle beyond*

BELOW   *Portland Museum from Pennsylvania Castle entrance*

Chesil Beach at Portland

one) but overall it is like the rest of Portland – bleak. The church of St John the Baptist was built in 1840, and is attractive externally, with a nice narrow tower. Inside, the dominating feature is a huge organ of 1896, recently brought here.

Portland Castle ★★★ is signposted from Chesil. A fascinating building now in an extraordinary position, well worth visiting. Surrounded by the helicopter base and naval docks, with the later (and much grimmer) fortress of the Verne on the hill high above it. Portland Castle was therebefore any of them, before even the harbour. Along with Sandsfoot Castle on the Weymouth side it was built in about 1540 to protect Weymouth Harbour from attack by sea, part of a series of forts built by Henry VIII along the south coast through fear of invasion by Catholic Europe to re-establish the Pope's supremacy in England, destroyed by Henry's Reformation. This invasion did not happen, and the only time the castle saw fighting was during the Civil War, when it changed hands several times. Many of the windows were altered in 1703, or from 1816-70 when the castle was used as a house. The entrance is in the lowest level, where the gunners lived and the stores were kept. The next floor has the first of three gun platforms, with five gun ports. These have little arched chimneys above to allow the smoke and fumes from the guns to escape. The stone doorways are original and so are many of the window surrounds, particularly on the top floor. The top storey was the governor's lodgings, and had more guns on the roof. Inside is a good display on the history of these Henrician castles,

small neat fortresses which were up-to-date fighting machines, loaded with firepower. By the entrance is a crenellated house, converted from a brewhouse early in the 19th century. There was a moat which has now disappeared. Helicopters can be viewed from the car park. Running steeply up the hill to the south is the incline part of the Merchants Railway of 1826, which carried stone down to piers of Castleton.

Portland Heights, (well-placed car park) **★★★** gives perhaps the best view in Dorset, with the naval and helicopter base in the foreground, long views along Chesil bank to the west (across Torbay if it is clear) and north to the Ridgeway. The wall to the hotel is full of large ammonites and piles of fossil trees, found during quarrying.

The road to the Verne, built as a fort in 1860-72, crosses over the steep cuttings of two of the later 19th century railways for carrying stone. The Verne's defences are impressive – deep stone-lined ditches, which were one of the quarries for the stone harbour. High Angle Batteries close by with big earthworks of 1892.

Grove is dominated by the Borstal (originally the Prison). At the west end is the church of St Peter, a huge church of 1870-2 built by convict labour in, unusually, Romanesque style. Not exactly pretty, but rather impressive. The mosaics in the entrance narthex and the chancel were laid by female convicts. Massive horrendous pulpit carved from a single block of Portland stone. Next door is the Vicarage of 1885 in rather watered down Romanesque and then the school of 1870, completely Romanesque. The austere but good Alma Terrace (Battle of Alma 1854)

leads along the massive Borstal wall with, round the corner, the gate to the original Prison of 1848.

St George Reforne (lists) stands isolated to the west of **Easton**, a superb but eccentric church of Portland stone built in 1754-66, with interesting early 19th century fittings. From the outside the nave looks like a house, with pedimented transepts in the long facades. The tower is much more elaborate and contrived. A tablet in the chancel records 'Thomas Gilbert, of this Island, Gent, Architect and Master Builder of this Church', and this seems to be the only building he designed. Inside is very plain, with complicated pilasters. The box pews, three galleries, pair of pulpits and so on are all early 19th century, painted in pleasant greens and greys. St George's is now redundant. Many interesting gravestones, some commemorating shipwrecks, in the huge graveyard. **★★★★**

Portland Stone Centre has been used each summer since 1983 for a display of modern sculpture, much of it constructed or carved from the stone of the quarry itself. Fascinating simply to walk around the ravines of the quarry. Superb view from the cliff-top, below which are the tips of waste stone from the quarry.

Easton has a huge Methodist Chapel of 1907 with turrets, and the attractive All Saints Church, built in 1914-17 to the design of the Weymouth architect Crickmay in medieval style, the Portland stone of its walls exposed inside with a variety of dressed finishes. The church of St Andrew at **Southwell** was built in 1878, as a memorial to those who died in

The distinctive and now rare Portland sheep, part of the small flock on the Island

the wreck of the ship *Avalanche.*

From the centre of Easton a wide road lined with stone buildings mostly of the 19th century leads towards Church Ope Cove. This is **Wakeham,** and at the south end is Portland Museum. ★★★ Part of it is Avice's Cottage, dated 1640, the house where the heroines of Hardy's novel *The Well-Beloved* (which gives a good picture of Portland) lived, given as a museum in 1930 by Marie Stopes. The simple stone cottage is still thatched, with lumps of petrified wood from the Portland beds outside. In a

new gallery is a fine display on the history of Portland, one cottage has temporary exhibitions and the other is furnished downstairs, with further displays above. Well worth seeing.

Just along the road from the museum are the remains of Rufus or Bow and Arrow Castle, dating from the late 15th century and perched on a huge lump of Portland stone. (Not open). A path leads down to the tiny bay of Church Ope Cove, and another up to the ruins of the medieval church of St Andrew, abandoned as unsafe

in the mid-18th century. Above is Pennsylvania Castle, with pretty rounded towers, built to the designs of James Wyatt in 1800 for John Penn, governor of the island and grandson of the founder of Pennsylvania.

Portland Bill ★★ is the low nose at the end of the island, sticking out into the Channel. Like Land's End it is much visited but hardly picturesque, with a huge car park. On either side of the road to it are the remains of strip cultivation, some of which are still used – a rare survival of medieval farming methods. On the left is the old lower lighthouse of 1788, now used as a bird observatory where censuses of migrating birds are taken. Right on the end of the Bill is the lighthouse still in use, built in 1905, 135 ft high. Sometimes open and worth seeing. On the ground floor are the compressors that produce the monstrous blare the lighthouse emits in foggy weather, while 153 steps up is the massive, revolving, many-lensed light itself, and in clear weather good views (if you are tall!). Also preserved in the ground floor is an inscription from the 1788 lighthouse which was 'For the Direction and Comfort of NAVIGATORS For the Benefit and Security of COMMERCE. And for a lasting memorial of BRITISH HOSPITALITY to All Nations'. In front of the lighthouse is a large stone inscribed

The lighthouse and Portland Bill

'TH 1884' for Trinity House – a sea-mark. To the right are ledges of stone, one known as Pulpit Rock, protruding into the sea, with ugly MOD fences and buildings beyond. On the east are 1930s cafes, and huts, some of them fishermen's. The sea in front of the Bill is the Portland Race, very dangerous for shipping, but particularly attractive from the land at night, illuminated by the lighthouse.

★★★★ *For whole place, and again for St George, Reforne.*

POUNDBURY, *see* DORCHESTER

POWERSTOCK (D) Large, straggling and attractive stone village in an area of tiny steep hills and valleys, many of them wooded or with small overgrown orchards. The church sits on one of these hills, and gives a breathtaking view over the village, with its mixture of 19th century houses, school and farm-buildings, and 17th-18th century stone cottages. The church of St Mary has a very fine Norman chancel arch, with three ornamented pillars either side supporting three superimposed arches. Good Victorian Gothic chancel (1850s) with a stone reredos, painted decoration, pulpit and tiles. 14th century nave, but roof and aisles rebuilt in 1850s too. Late medieval doorway with figures in niches, very good. Impressive 1991 semi-abstract stained glass in baptistry.

★★ *Village, setting.*

Powerstock Common 1½ miles northeast of the village, with a small car park off the Eggardon-Toller Porcorum road close to a railway bridge for the now defunct Bridport line. A bridleway and forest tracks provide access to this very varied nature reserve. It includes ancient oak woodland with hazel coppice, heathy grassland, a length of disused railway line and areas of conifer plantations which are being cleared to favour the establishment of deciduous woodland. Good views west and south.

To the east, overhanging the road from Eggardon are the earthworks of Powerstock Castle, humps and bumps of a small medieval castle apparently set inside a small Iron Age hillfort. Very muddly. ½ mile south-east is **Nettlecombe** virtually a separate hamlet with stone and thatch cottages cramped together in picturesque huddle still in the same overgrown landscape of small-scale hills and valleys. One especially fine cottage is dated 1698 and has original mullioned windows.

POXWELL (H) A tiny village, and although it lies along a main road, still pretty with the downlands behind. At the north end are four pairs of thatched Portland stone cottages, all built in 1843

Poxwell Manor

by the local land-owner, along with a conduit (looking like a pump) which is dedicated by him 'for the use of the Poor of his parish of Poxwell'. The manor house where he lived (not open) is one of the handsomest in Dorset, rather plain, of Portland stone and about 1600. The brick wall around the garden with its tiny charming hexagonal gate-house is dated 1634. Its combination of soft red bricks and white Portland stone dressings is unbeatable. Hardy used this house as Oxwell Hall in *The Trumpet Major.*

★★ *House.*

POYNTINGTON (A) The long hill flanking the village marks the Somerset border. Very green and rural, plenty of superb stone buildings. In the centre is the manor house of about 1500, with a large original arched gateway beside the road, and several cart sheds. Above the path to the church is a much altered late 14th century court house. Below the church a 17th century barn converted to a house. All Saints is a medley of dates. Norman door, 14th century porch, tower, nave and south aisle. Nice stout octagonal pillars to south aisle. Rather mutilated late 14th century effigy of a knight in armour, and a good Jacobean alabaster wall monument with three kneeling figures. The two bright paintings of arms are also 17th century memorials. The decorated openings in the south wall were probably for tombs. The very showy chancel is of 1863.

★★ *Setting, church.*

PRESTON (H) has been nearly overwhelmed by modern development and caravans, but there is a little of the older village left in the centre, including a few stone cottages. The church of St

Andrew has lovely flower borders along the path leading up to it, but the handsome 16th century tower looks out over a sea of caravans and recent development. A couplet on one bell reads: 'See in what a state the rich they live Nothing unto the poor they give.' The church is all of the local limestone, and dates mostly from the 14th-16th centuries, with a 16th century arcade of thin pillars. Most of the fittings date from the restoration of 1855, but up by the altar is a kneeling figure (with a replacement head) with an inscription: 'THE VICAR HERE INTOMBED LYES/WHOSE PATRON HIM DOTH ETERNIS/YT HIS FYR WORKS OF CHARITY/ MAY NOT WITH HIM STILL BVRIED B 1614'. Two interesting stained glass windows, both of 1949 – the east window and in the north wall of the nave which has scenes from *Pilgrim's Progress.*

★ *Setting, away from roads.*

PUDDLETOWN (E) is the Weatherbury of Hardy's *Far from the Madding Crowd.* Along the main road the village was substantially rebuilt by a reforming squire during the 1860's, but around the church the earlier houses survive, some thatched, some colour-washed. The church is attractive inside and out, and mostly dates from the 12th-15th centuries. The chancel and north-east chapel are of 1911 – Thomas Hardy led the unsuccessful fight against the demolition of the small original chancel. A memorial in the chancel reads: 'Over Charlotte's Dust there needs no pious care/To raise the Pageant Marble in the Air/Her modest mind/Her unassuming Heart/Despised the Pompous Piles of human art . . .' (1804). The woodwork dominates the interior – the box pews, communion rails, font cover, pulpit and so

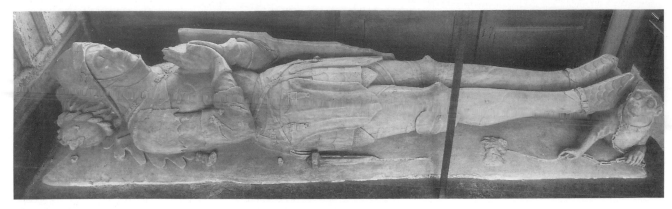
Knight in armour, Puddletown

forth all date to around 1635, the date carved on the fine west gallery. This was where the musicians and singers of the village band sat, including occasionally Thomas Hardy's grandfather before he moved to Stinsford. Two clarinets and a flute belonging to the Puddletown band are preserved in the church and are sometimes on display, as are the canvas fire buckets issued by an insurance company in the 19th century. The south chapel contains several full-size effigies, most notably a beautiful alabaster of a knight in full armour, once thought to be Sir William Martyn (d. 1503) who built Athelhampton (see entry) but actually of about 1470. The other alabasters are of another Martyn and his wife. His wasp-waisted armour-clad figure of *c.* 1460 has lost both arms and a leg: elaborate alabaster angels below him. Good brasses (also Martyns) of 1524 and 1595, beside other 13th and 14th century effigies. The heraldic stained glass window gives the owners of Athelhampton to the

Puddletown

late 19th century. The Norman font is carved all over with a pattern like a cloth design and has a nice plain 17th century wooden cover.

★★★ *Church, particularly for the 17th century woodwork, effigies, Thomas Hardy connection.*

Islington House east of the church (fee: lists), is where the reforming squire lived. His 1860s stables (straight ahead) are now houses. Luckily he left the house pretty well alone. The back (entrance front) looks entirely early 19th century (although long and low for that period), when indeed the house was refronted. Inside the hall has panelling partly dating from the original late 17th century house, and a fine 18th century staircase. Upstairs are the main rooms, the best being the Drawing Room, with early 19th century detailing and fireplace. These alterations were made for General Garth, an equerry to George III. He seems to have been the father of the illegitimate child of one of the King's daughters, Princess Sophie. The child was adopted by Garth and took his name, but the full details of this extraordinary scandal are still not clear.

The 'Princess's Bedroom' is shown, and downstairs a nice dining room overlooking the Rose Garden. Interesting collection of paintings.

★★★ *House and gardens.*

PULHAM (E) Very dispersed, and largely modern. Blackmore Vale dairying country. The church and Georgian rectory stand apart. The church of St Thomas Becket is largely of the 15th century. Good 16th century gargoyles reset in the parapet. Inside, mostly Tudor with at the western end fine corbels with slight Renaissance influence — eg cherubs rather than angels holding the shields. The superb 15th century niche in the chancel is not in its original position. The north aisle and parts of the south were rebuilt in the 19th century. Norman font. Fine Tudor porch.

★ *Landscape* ★★ *Village church.*

PUNCKNOWLE (D) Pronounced 'Punnle', a handsome village with lots of stone cottages and farm buildings, and trees in the middle. A ridge of scrubby downland topped by the Knoll shelters one side of the village from the sea. On the other side is the Bride Valley.

The church of St Mark feels ancient, although only the tower arch and tiny chancel arch remain from the Norman church. The rest is mostly later 19th century. Robert Napier who lived in the Manor House paid for the rebuilding of the tower (dated 1678 on the arch and with RN in nails on the door) and perhaps also for the nice wooden font cover. Good 17th century monuments, one with Greek. The 12th century font sits on another of the same date. Interesting 1960's iron screen. In the churchyard is a fine 15th century cross which originally stood in the village. Behind the church is the manor house, partly 19th century but the front wing of 1650 with a lovely porch. Round headed windows and door. Henry Shrapnell (1761-1842) who invented the shell lived here for a short while, and his friend William Barnes, the Dorset poet, visited him and helped with the mathematical calculations.

Between Puncknowle and Litton Cheney the road runs right through the farmyard of Looke, with its handsome farmhouse with a chimney in each corner, dated 1700.

★★ *Village, church.*

PURSE CAUNDLE (A) A small stone-built village, a backwater with an attractive church and a superb manor house (fee: lists). Projecting over the village street is the lovely little oriel window which marks the wing of the 15th century house. A fine iron gate leads to the forecourt and the main facade. Inside the great Hall of the 15th century with its lovely roof is the core from which the house has grown. The fireplace and door close to it were inserted in the 16th century, but several original doorways survive. The great west

window was reconstructed this century. Off the room is a bay with 16th century fireplace, ceiling and window. All the 17th century panelling was brought here this century. Apparently a staircase behind the fireplace was built over a well in order to imprison a fairy. The fairy escaped and annoyed those who used the stairs, which were demolished to thwart it. The present staircase is 17th century. The best room upstairs is the Great Chamber, part of the 16th century house, with its barrel roof, oriels and marvellous wallpaper. Pretty garden.

The church of St Peter has a north chapel probably built early in the 16th century by William Long (d. 1524) one of the builders of the manor house. His elaborate tomb (from which the effigies have been removed) lies between the chapel and the chancel, and the chapel still has windows, pretty door, doorway, and arches to the chancel all probably built by him. Beside his tomb is a tiny brass with a simple figure of a woman – William Long's daughter and heir who died in 1527. The chancel was rebuilt in 1731 (Victorian windows) and the nave in 1883. The seating is made from cut-down 18th century box pews. Elaborate 15th century font with 17th century cover. 15th century west tower. Oak bier dated 1733.

★★ *House, Village.*

RADIPOLE (H) Although so close to Weymouth its setting remains rural, although split by a fast busy road. The church, school and manor house stand apart from the rest of the village, and form a fine group. The school is pretty 1840's 'Gothic' and the charming stone manor house is 16th and 17th century. The church of St Ann has an unusual Italianate bellcote,

ABOVE *Looke farm, Puncknowle*
RIGHT *Oriel window, Purse Caundle manor*
BELOW *Purse Caundle manor*

probably 16th century. The body of the church is a mixture of dates from the 13th-18th centuries, with a porch dated 1733. In the graveyard are some victims of local shipwrecks (see Wyke Regis).

(Radipole Lake see: Weymouth)

RAMPISHAM (E) rambles, small and secluded, through a well-wooded valley with some thatched stone cottages and a deeply-bedded stream flowing below the

manor house and church. The church of St Michael and All Angels has a late 15th century tower, a chancel rebuilt by Pugin in 1845 with contemporary stained glass perhaps also by him, and a nave rebuilt in 1860 by John Hicks. By the pulpit are two small brasses of 1523. Outside there is the massive base of a churchyard cross, late 15th century with very worn figures and inscriptions. Pugin also designed the village school (now a house) and the Rectory

ABOVE *The post office stores, Rampisham*

(crosses on the gables), both early vernacular revival 1845.
★★★ *Landscape.*

RAWLSBURY (E, west of Bulbarrow) A small Iron Age hillfort in a superb position. The entrance faces the ridiculously narrow neck of land which joins the little spur of chalk the hillfort occupies to the main ridge. The neck has views north to the Blackmore Vale and south over more complex topography. A variety of tracks and hollow ways run to the fort, mangling the original entrance. The thick hedge bisecting it is a parish boundary. A large rough cross is now set up inside it. The prettiest of the small hillforts.
★★★ *Hillfort, landscape.*

The RIDGEWAY is the chalk ridge which runs for 12 miles east-west to the south of Dorchester, and is famous for the quantities of barrows built on it in the Bronze Age – one of the highest concentrations in the country. There are (or have been) more than 230 on the main ridge with at least another 200 on spurs projecting from it. On the south the edge of the ridge is dramatically abrupt. The barrows are positioned so as to be impressive from the lower ground, which is why much of the skyline is still pimpled by the survivors. Agriculture has been cruel to these burial mounds: less than 15% survive intact, and many have been ploughed away. Both ends of the main concentration are marked by a Neolithic bank barrow, like elongated long barrows both 600 ft long. At the west end the Long Bredy bank barrow is seen very clearly on the skyline from the main Dorchester-Bridport road. The Broadmayne bank barrow at the east end can be seen from the side road beside Came Wood. These large earlier monuments must have been deliberately used to define the main limits of the cemetery. A footpath, track or road exists along the whole length of the Ridgeway, and it makes a fine high level walk, with good views south over the coast and north inland. The barrows survive best on the gravels, as for example at Bronkham Hill, near Hardy's Monument (see entry).
★★★★ *Landscape, barrows, walks.*

RINGSTEAD (H) Toll Road. A few modern houses and caravans (with a tiny block of three earlier buildings. Shingle beach, but good swimming. Once renowned for red mullet. Spectacular view of White Nothe (see entry) – 500 ft of crumbling chalk cliff and undercliff with

LEFT *Stone and thatch barn near Rodden*

more complex geology including clay below and on top a tiny capping of geologically recent gravel. Good walking both along the shore and on footpaths inland. National Trust car park to the east, at Falcon Barn. See also Holworth. ★★★

RODDEN (H) is a few cottages, a couple of farmhouses and a lovely Portland stone Georgian house, all rather isolated just back from the Fleet.

ROCKLEY SANDS (F, west of Hamworthy) is Poole's seaside, with a good sandy beach. Although backed by development, the outlook is rural, with Poole Harbour and lots of boat traffic. At the west end is a huge caravan park, with amusements and shops (car park fee). There is another car park (fee) to the east, where the beach is backed by a fringe of sandy heathland, Ham Common Nature Reserve, with ponds and a marked trail.

★ *Safe swimming.*

RYME INTRINSICA (A) must have the oddest name in Dorset, which is saying a lot, considering the competition. It means the in, or home, part of the Ryme manor as opposed to the out part, once called Extrinsica. Nice stone cottages. The church is dedicated to St Hypolite (a bishop of Ostia, near Rome, martyred in the 230's) – only one other church in England is dedicated to him. The chancel and nave are basically 13th century, but the interest of the church lies in the unusual 17th century work – the east window, most of the windows in the nave (including the little round placed high to light the pulpit) all early 17th century, comparable to Folke church. The tower is early 17th century too, with an intricate profile caused by the projecting stairway.

★ *Church, name.*

SADDOROW (D, south of Thorcombe) is a handsome 1770's mansion, just visible from the road. The attractive gardens are sometimes open.

ST ALDHELM'S HEAD (J) is worth the 2 mile walk from Worth Matravers (see entry) or the mile from the car-park at Renscombe Farm west of the village. The heavy square Norman chapel, dramatically isolated on the headland was not a parish church or a chantry chapel, and the difficulties of explaining it have led to several legends, one that it was built by a man in memory of his daughter and her husband whom he saw shipwrecked and drowned on the rocks below. In the 19th century it was used by the coastguards

The Chapel and coastguard cottages, St Aldhelm's Head

stationed nearby, as a store. Wishes were believed to be granted to those who dropped a pin in a hole in the central pier. On Whit Tuesday the villagers from Worth Matravers decorated the chapel with flowers, and danced there. Beyond is a modern coastguard look-out and a range of coastguard cottages built in 1834. Fragmented undercliffs. From 1940-2 radar research was carried out here; a few concrete footings survive. TRE Worth Matravers was an important research station employing 2,000 people by 1942. The best of St Aldhelm's Head is the

view all along the coast to Portland in the west and Isle of Wight in the east. By walking a little way west along the coast path the closer cliffs of Emmett's Hill and Hound's Tout come into view. The path along the top of the cliff continues to Chapman's Pool, and on to Kimmeridge (see entry) for the energetic.

★★★ *Landscape.*

ST IVES, *see* **ST LEONARDS**

ST LEONARD'S (G) is on the edge of the New Forest, and is virtually all modern

The old Coastguard Station, Sandbanks (see entry on following page)

development amongst the trees and rhododendrons. St Ives merges with it.

SALWAY ASH (D) Spreads along a road, with the small church of 1887 to the north of the village. Outside the church is stone, inside it is lined with three different coloured bricks, brought from Poole, Broadmayne and Fareham (Hants). Much woodwork made by the vicar himself at the time the church was built.

SANDBANKS (K) was wild sand dunes like Studland just across the mouth of Poole Harbour until 1900 with only a hotel, one house and the Coastguard station – which between 1910/1930 was housed in a beached Crimean gunboat. When a new station was built, the gunboat was relaunched by an enterprising Poole shipbuilder. Since 1910 Sandbanks has been totally built up. A car ferry runs throughout the year across the narrow mouth of the harbour to Studland, and boats also go to Brownsea from April to September (see entry). The harbour behind Sandbanks is full of pleasure boats.

SANDFORD ORCAS (A) An attractive stone village in a secluded setting north of Sherborne with small high-hedged fields and a fine 16th century manor house (fee: lists). The entry is through a gatehouse with separate arches for pedestrians and wheeled traffic; the little projecting roof covered a garderobe or lavatory. Round the corner the garden and house form a classically English picture. Stone monkeys surmount the gables, and the elaborate porch has pinnacles and a decorated lozenge typical of the period, here with arms inside. The house dates from the 1530's, when the medieval two-storied hall was giving way to a single storey hall with a great chamber over, the pattern found here, but with unusually large windows. Lots of good woodwork in the hall – the best the early 17th century screen, and some original heraldic glass. Two circular stone staircases lead to a warren of rooms upstairs. Well worth seeing.

Next door is the church of St Nicholas, late medieval, but internally looking Victorian after a restoration in 1871. Good monuments in the south chapel, mostly to the families who lived in the manor house, including a fine one of 1607 to William Knoyle, with his two wives and eleven children, seven of whom kneel: the other four are shown dead in swaddling clothes.
★★★ *House.*

SANDSFOOT CASTLE (H) is on the north side of Portland Harbour and was built in 1541 to pair up with Portland Castle on the far side (which see for history) to defend Weymouth. Sandsfoot was always smaller than Portland Castle, and erosion has made it smaller still. The octagonal gun room on the front has almost completely disappeared. The quarters behind for the garrison survive, but are roofless. The remains of the dry moat in front were probably dug in 1623, and the castle was held for the King in the Civil War. Smallish formal garden behind, and just along the road to the west is a small partly sandy beach. Good views from the castle over the coast east and Portland Harbour.
★ *Castle.*

SEABOROUGH (D) is an attractive tiny village on the River Axe close to the Somerset border. The church of St John was almost entirely rebuilt in 1882, apart from the north chapel, which is dated 1729 externally, and has a strange imitation medieval window. The nave retains its 1882 pitch-pine fittings, and has elaborate columns symbolically dividing the nave and chancel. In the north chapel is a super monument of 1738 with a bust above, and a tiny, rather battered early 13th century effigy of a knight. On two sides of the church are modern farm buildings. Seaborough Court is a stone mansion of 1887.
★ *Village.*

SEATOWN (D) A small village right on the sea, reached by a very narrow lane. Car park near the shore (fee). The little river percolates through the shingle bank. To the west towers the great bulk of Golden Cap (see entry).

SHAFTESBURY (B) A real hill-town sitting 700ft up on a Greensand spur overlooking the Blackmore Vale, with steep 100 ft slopes on every side except the narrow north-east one. A burh (a defended settlement) and a nunnery were here from the 9th century: the nunnery was founded by King Alfred for one of his daughters, and he also probably founded the burh as one of the series of fortesses he built or restored around the boundaries of Wessex. It was probably on the western, best protected part of the promontory, the area called Bimport, now a leafy suburb since the main town has developed on the flatter ground to the north and east. Geoffrey of Monmouth, the imaginative early medieval historian, was convinced that the town was founded in 950 BC by a grandfather of King Lear.

Hardy described Shaftesbury in *Jude the Obscure* as 'one of the queerest and quaintest spots' with the 'limitless landscape' of the Blackmore Vale around it. 'Vague imaginings of its castle, its three mints, its twelve churches, its shrines, chantries, hospitals, its gabled freestone mansions – all now ruthlessly swept away – throw the visitor, even against his will, into a pensive melancholy'. Hardy correctly blamed the Dissolution of the monasteries in the 1530's for all this

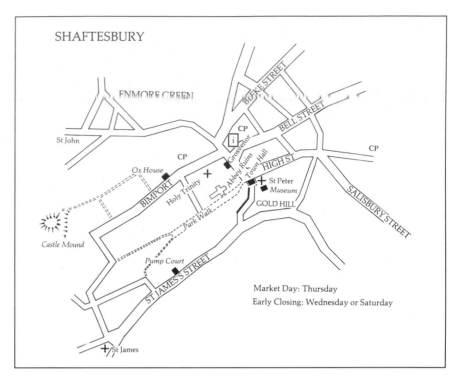

SHAFTESBURY

Market Day: Thursday
Early Closing: Wednesday or Saturday

ABOVE *The porch vault, St Peter's church, Shaftesbury*
BELOW *Gold Hill, Shaftesbury, wood engraving by John R. Biggs*

impressive early 19th century Grosvenor Hotel is large and rather plain. (In the first floor lounge of the Grosvenor is a huge and horrible piece of mid 19th century furniture – The Chevey Chase sideboard, representing the battle of 1388, an absolute brute which has been admired by visitors since it was bought by the hotel in 1919; apply to reception to visit). At the southern end of the market place is the Town Hall, (1826), better from the back as the front is rather marred by the 1879 clock tower. The lower storey all round was originally open for market stalls. Nice 'Gothic' windows on the first floor. Next door is the church of St Peter, with in the west porch a pretty late 15th century stone vault. The church is a funny shape, probably because the site was restricted. Mostly of the 14th-16th centuries, with 16th century wooden roofs. No separate chancel, so the altar area is taken out of the nave. This makes a happy composition, with 15th century arches either side, black and white stone floor, 17th century communion rails, 1631 altar, 18th century tables of the creed etc, and a fine pair of 19th century 'Gothic' chairs. Several 15th century niches around the walls and a good font of the same date.

At the top of **Gold Hill** is the museum, (fee: lists). Five rooms with good displays of the archaeology and history of Shaftesbury, including local industries like button and lace-making; bygones such as a serpent (musical not venomous), photographs and so on, all well worth seeing. Lovely views from the little garden and the first floor. Gold Hill is the most photographed part of Shaftesbury: a steep cobbled hill below the Town Hall, lined on one side with 18th century small houses and cottages, and with the green fields of the Blackmore Vale beyond. The right-hand side is a huge stone retaining wall, the most impressive surviving part of the Abbey, dating from *c.* 1400 although perhaps on the line of an earlier precinct wall. The street leads down to St James.

To the west of the Town Hall is Park Walk, originally laid out in 1753. Stupendous view and seats to admire it from. Off Park Walk is the entrance to the **Abbey Ruins** (fee, lists). The abbey is so ruined (and has been used as a quarry for building stone) that only the footings remain, outlined in lawns. This is not the Saxon church, but its Norman successor. Excavations have taken place several times, and in the 1930's a lead coffin containing what may be the bones of St Edward, King and Martyr (d. 978) was found (see Corfe Castle). Besides the footings there are small areas of late 13th century tiles in a local style, and a small museum filled with fragments from the abbey buildings.

destruction. Shaftesbury was the most populous town in Dorset in the 14th century, and because the nunnery had the bones of Edward the Martyr from the year after his death in 978, a great place of pilgrimage. It became the richest Benedictine nunnery in the country, with more than 120 nuns in 1326. There were twelve medieval churches and chapels in the town of which only one (St Peter's) survives with medieval masonry; three as 19th century rebuilds (St James', St Rumbold's and Holy Trinity); and one, the abbey church, only as footings.

The town often seems to be cold and windswept and is occasionally in the clouds, comfort having been sacrificed in the original foundation for its splendidly defensive position. The **Market Place** is merely a widening of the west end of the High Street and 18th century brick and Victorian buildings mix pleasantly. The

ABOVE *Bell Street, Shaftesbury* BELOW *Pump Court, St James, Shaftesbury*

The town centre, particularly High Street, but also Bell Street and Salisbury Street leading down to Cann, has pretty green-sand houses and cottages mixed with a few 18th century brick ones, and others in less attractive 19th century brick. In Salisbury Street is St Rumbold's church, 1840 and redundant. Holy Trinity, Bimport, 1840 by Gilbert Scott, is also no longer a church. Further west along the road is Ox House,

of *c. 1600* but restored. It was used by Hardy in *Jude the Obscure* as the house where Sue lived with Mr Phillotson after their marriage. The school opposite, where perhaps Phillotson taught, is converted to housing. A path leads out towards Castle Hill, giving wide views. The earthworks of the 12th century castle are muddly.

Running along the foot of the escarpment on the south-east is the suburb of **St**

James, and it is a good walk down Gold Hill, along through St James to the church, back up the steep hill via a footpath and so to Park Walk. St James has lots of Green-sand cottages, mostly of the late 18th or early 19th century, some thatched. Half way along is Pump Court, set back from the road and still with the pump in the middle. Larger houses at the west end by the church, some Georgian and one early 17th century, with transomed and mullioned windows. St James was a medieval suburb, and had a medieval church, but this was demolished in the 1860's and replaced. Big and decorative with lots of leafy corbels and capitals, and a particularly pretty tower. The 12th century font (from St Rumbold's church) has a huge inscription of 1664 on the bowl, presumably recording a repair. In the tower is a fine carved stone Stuart coat of arms.

Enmore Green is almost a suburb of Shaftesbury to the west, down the steep Tout Hill. Until the 19th century Shaftesbury's water had to come from here because this was the closest spring to the town. Hardy claimed that in Shaftesbury 'beer was more plentiful than water and . . . there were more wanton women than honest wives and maids', but didn't link the two facts. An annual procession of the Mayor and burgesses (assisted by the population) ritually visited Enmore Green carrying the Byzant, to confirm the town's right to water from Enmore, which was outside the town's jurisdiction. The Byzant was probably originally a besom (broom) but the 18th century version carried up to 1830 (when the town got its own water supply) is in the museum, an exotic object of gilded wood, shaped as a palm tree with a scrolly lid. The church of St John the Evangelist at Enmore is Neo-Norman of 1843, by the same architect as East Stour, but smaller and simpler with nice 1843 glass in the chancel and galleries. The 15th century font has an unusual wooden cover, probably of the same date. The church is on a shelf cut into the hillside, surrounded by overgrown Victorian evergreens.

SHAPWICK (F) In the flat valley of the River Stour, and still with many thatched cottages of brick or cob, including one towards the church chequered with greensand and brick. The church of St Bartholomew is right down by the river, an odd position to choose as it can flood (and now has flood banks and gates). In 1870 a flood rose during a funeral and the coffin was assumed to be washed out to sea, as it was never seen again. The whole church (even the Victorian bits) is a mixture of small stone and flint. All later medieval

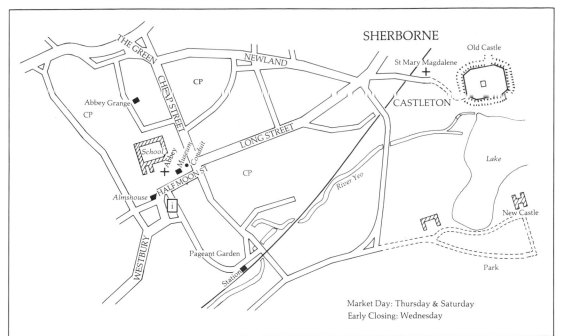

SHERBORNE

Old Castle

St Mary Magdalene

CASTLETON

Lake

New Castle

Park

Abbey Grange

School
Abbey
Museum
Conduit

Almshouse

Pageant Garden

Station

NEWLAND

THE GREEN

CHEAP STREET

LONG STREET

HALF MOON ST

WESTBURY

River Yeo

CP

Market Day: Thursday & Saturday
Early Closing: Wednesday

apart from the Norman arches to the
north chapel and the chancel 1878 , when
the rest of the church was restored. Reset
in the floor is a slate gravestone inscribed
'Anne Butler here beneath is laid, a pious
prudent modest maid 1659'. By the altar is
a brass with the figure of a priest, Richard
Chernock, who died in 1538. Other good
brasses, monuments and a table tomb. In a
case towards the east end of the nave is
an 18th century clarinet once used in the
church band. The six thick bench-ends are
16th century. The Norman font has a
remarkable high iron cover of 1870,
which includes iron water-lily flowers.

N. Colling, church

SHERBORNE (A) The most attractive
town in the county, with stone buildings
of all dates from the 15th century onwards, and Dorset's most beautiful church.
Very varied shops, lots of places to eat,
and lush green surroundings, with many
trees, especially on the hills.

Sherborne has often been described as
being like a small cathedral town, and
indeed it once was – from about 700 AD
to 1085 it was the seat of the Bishop of
Wessex, with St Aldhelm as Bishop from
c. 705-10. There was a monastery from
998 until the dissolution in 1539, and
two Saxon Kings were buried here in
the 9th century. The settlement probably
only became a town in the 12th century.
In the same century a very expensive
Castle (now the Old Castle) (cont p.138)

RIGHT *Sherborne Abbey*

Geology and Scenery

Dorset has no great lakes or mountains, but it does have a remarkable variety of scenery, ranging inland from chalk downs to heathlands, and on the coast a superb diversity from sand dunes to high cliffs. The basis of all this is the geology, which structures the inland areas and whose swift changes on the coast (where almost every type of rock outcrops) make it so spectacular and interesting to explore.

Two-thirds of the county consists of chalk, clay, or the mixed sands, gravel and clays known as Tertiary deposits. The remaining third is far more complex and contains most of the hard building stones.

The Chalk produces undulating upland with wide rounded valleys and sparkling clear streams. The hills can be quite high, and the escarpment on the north edge of the Chalk can be exceptionally steep. The second highest point in Dorset – Bulbarrow 902 ft – is on this chalk escarpment. A narrow but high ridge of chalk forms the northern boundary of Purbeck, and produces chalk cliffs at Swanage, and on either side of Lulworth.

The Clay Vales are also very distinctive, and were once marshy areas covered with forest, now cleared and drained. Only the quantities of hedgerow oaks are a reminder of their former state. They are and have been great dairying areas. Blackmore is the larger, running from the Chalk across the north of the county, on two bands of different clays separated by a narrow belt of limestone. In the west of the county is the little vale of Marshwood, much smaller and on the Lias clays.

The Tertiary deposits cover much of the east of the county, and continue on through Hampshire where they underlie the New Forest. In Dorset they are undulating lowlands, and where not reclaimed have the characteristic heathland vegetation of heather and gorse, now often intermingled with rampant rhododendron (only introduced in the 18th century) or plantations of conifers. The river valleys with their rich

Quarry near St Aldhelm's Head

alluvium contrast with the poor heathlands they run through.

The heathlands were seen as dreary primeval wastes by unromantic farmers, and they were steadily reclaimed from the 17th century onwards. In fact they were not primeval, but created in the Bronze Age nearly 4,000 years ago when the woodland which was their original vegetation was cleared, destroying the natural balance of soil and vegetation and producing very poor, acid soils.

The division of the county into these three types of land is obvious and has long been recognised, but the untangling of the geology of the rest of the county is far more difficult. It is easier to consider the areas separately. Purbeck appears moderately straightforward, with the beds running east-west. On the north it is bounded by a narrow ridge of hard Chalk, inside which is a wide valley of the softer Wealden clays and sands. The southern part consists of a wide ridge formed from the Portland and Purbeck Beds (mostly limestones). These, along with the Kimmeridge strata of shales and clays, form the diverse and beautiful coastline. This description is, in fact, over-simplified, and glosses over the complexity of the geology. The Purbeck Beds for example consist of a varied sequence of limestones, muddy limestones, calcareous clays, clays and shales.

West Dorset is yet more intricate, with many small hills and swift changes from one type of rock or clay to another, partially caused by a network of faults.

Broadly there is more sandstone, and many of the higher hills such as Shipton Hill in the Bride Valley,

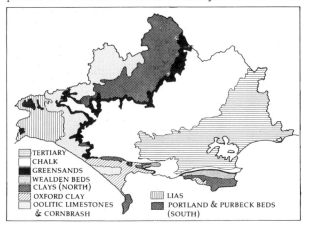

TERTIARY
CHALK
GREENSANDS
WEALDEN BEDS
CLAYS (NORTH)
OXFORD CLAY
OOLITIC LIMESTONES
& CORNBRASH
LIAS
PORTLAND & PURBECK BEDS
(SOUTH)

The Lulworth crumple, West Lulworth

Golden Cap and Hardown Hill in the west, are of the Upper Greensand with its protective capping of Chert. The extreme west has high cliffs but towards Portland these die out. Portland consists almost entirely of Portland stone. The area to the north of Weymouth is also complicated, with intermingled sand, clay and harder rocks.

Fossils are plentiful in many of the Dorset strata, and although flying reptiles have been recovered from the Lias at Lyme, elephants from the Dewlish Elephant Trench, and crocodiles and dinosaur footprints from the Purbeck Beds, one is unlikely to see those outside of museums. Ammonites, belemnites and bivalves are among the commoner fossils of the Dorset coast, and these may be found in rock exposures. Only professional geologists should hammer specimens from the Dorset cliffs because it is dangerous. The beaches below the cliffs are good places for amateurs to search for fossils or samples of rock, as the unstable cliffs are continually eroding onto them.

Chesil is perhaps the most unusual geographic feature in Dorset – a large gravel ridge some 8 miles long joining Portland to the rest of Dorset, with a partly fresh, partly salt water lagoon behind it.

The discovery and exploitation of the oil (and gas) deposits in south east Dorset is only the most recent aspect of economic geology in the county. Building stone has been quarried since Roman times, and chalk, gravel and sand extracted. Various clays have been used for making tiles, bricks and earthenware pottery. Fine white ball-clay has been exported from Purbeck first for clay pipes in the 17th century and for fine pottery manufacture from the 18th century. This still continues, but there is only one brick yard still working at Godlingstone, Swanage. Of the less economically important deposits, the Kimmeridge Shale has perhaps the most varied history, having been used *inter alia* for bangles and furniture inlays in the Roman period, and as a source of a rather poor quality oil in the 19th century.

Clavel Tower on top of Kimmeridge Shale cliffs, Kimmeridge

was built on the outskirts of the town. Only ruins remain. The New Castle was built nearby from the 1590's.

The church of St Mary ★★★★ was the abbey church, and is considered to be the most important piece of architecture in the county, famous for its elaborate 15th century fan vaulting. This rather complex building is described from west to east. To the west of the church was Sherborne's parish church and the springing for the arches is still to be seen, with the boundary wall on the north being the north wall of the church. Externally the south side of the abbey church facing the Green is almost all 15th century ie Perpendicular, except for the south porch the lower floor of which is reconstructed 12th century, and the upper floor work of the 19th century to match (the lovely iron gates are of *c. 1750*). The eastern end of the church is dated 1561 on the east wall and has characteristic flat-headed windows and much decoration on the south wall. Inside, the west wall is still largely Saxon, partly refaced and with more recent windows and doors, except for the doorway in the north aisle, which has Saxon 'long and short' work. Its external tympanum is 12th century and retains a little painted plaster of that date.

The nave is gorgeous, with fan vaulting all through, all of the last quarter of the 15th century, although the odd spacing of the piers at the western end suggests that earlier piers were re-used and cased. Lovely pillars, panelled all around, with windows above leading into the vaulting. Vaulting of the same date in the aisles. Off the south aisle is St Katherine's chapel, remodelled in the 15th century with a

vaulted roof. The monument to John and Joan Leweston (1584) is lovely, with good fluted Corinthian columns. Many fragments of mainly 15th century glass are collected, in the windows here, including small figures. The whole west wall of the south transept is taken up by an impressive monument to Lord Digby (d. 1697) and he stands in full wig with his hand on his hip, looking sophisticatedly heavenwards (he hopes), flanked by his two wives (who have enough drapery for six) holding what look like flaming carrots. Superb.The crossing under the tower is basically Norman, with three plain 12th century arches surviving: the third to the presbytery was replaced in the 15th century when it was vaulted. The horrendous pulpit is 1899. The large (restored) 15th century south window has fine stained glass designed by Pugin (1851) and he probably also designed the similar west window.

The north transept is virtually filled by the organ. Off it is the Wykeham chapel, with a much restored 12th century arcade on the lower part of the wall, and a tiny vault above. Good monument to Sir John Horsey and his son, 1564, both in armour of almost 100 years earlier. Sir John bought the abbey at the dissolution. The (punning) horse heads on the corners look like chess pieces, and the whole design is very formal, apart from the putti on the back who are having a job to hold up the achievement of arms. Around the crossing and in the presbytery are areas of reddened stone, caused by the fire of 1437, which happened during a riot when people of the town opposed the Abbot. The church was being altered at the time,

and work resumed after the fire, producing the lovely vaulting and so on at this eastern end. The presbytery has an enormous stone reredos of 1884. The east window is splendid, continuing to the floor with blank panels otherwise identical to those of the window. Superb fan vault again. All the painted decoration is mid 19th century, producing a very rich effect. Behind the Victorian choir stalls are, on either side, five bays of restored 15th century stalls, with misericords and carvings on the elbow rests.

The south aisle around the presbytery has a good 15th century vault, and an effigy of a 13th century abbot in Purbeck marble. At the east end is the chapel of St Mary le Bow, rebuilt in 1561 as part of the school, and not taken back into the church until the 1920's. It is said that the headmaster and his family could hear all the church services, and that the clergy could hear the headmaster's wife playing polkas on her piano! This is the only modern stone vault in the building.

The first part of the Lady chapel is 13th century, Early English, with a simple vault, and pretty capitals (modern corbels). The eastern-most part of 1920 is rather strange imitation late Perpendicular. The engraved glass reredos (1968) is by Lawrence Whistler. In the north aisle of the presbytery are two coffins, both probably 13th century, one still in the ground. Another 13th century Purbeck marble monument to a priest, and the head only of another very handsome one with inscriptions around, Abbot Clement,

c. 1160, one of the earliest surviving in the south-west.

On the south-west of the green outside the church is the **Almshouse of St John.** The church side is part of the extension of 1858 designed to match the original. On the east wall is an oriel, and round the corner a cloister, both of 1858 too. The original block is that on the street, remarkably pretty, with an elaborate doorway, lots of chimneys, and continuous mouldings over the lower windows. Good iron railings to the road, topped with mitres. The almshouse was refounded in 1438, and complete by 1448. It is possible to go into the original part of the almshouse (fee: lists).

The chapel is strange because it has a full height arch, cut off by the upper floor of the almshouse. Very fine, with original screen. The south window has 15th century glass, but the treasure is the very fine triptych, almost certainly purchased for the almshouse soon after it was painted in the late 15th century. It may be from Cologne. The body of the building was for twelve poor men and four poor women, but with the expansion of 1858 the rest of the ground floor is now used for a dining room. Nice wooden partition (16th century with a modern top), with a good doorway.

The Close, to the west of the almshouse, is now open, giving a good view of the abbey: until 1884 the town hall filled much of the area. Mock-medieval memorial to a Digby of 1884, and right on the road a tiny semicircular 18th century building still containing part of a 19th century weigh-bridge. Adjoining the Close, east along Half-Moon Street is a range of shops, originally with one long room over, built early in the 16th century. This is a rare survival. The upper storey was used as a church house (a sort of church hall) and the lower parts were let out as shops. These have been altered, but the upper storey has its original curved headed windows. The taller building on the corner is 1890's mock-medieval much more complicated. On the opposite corner is a real period piece – an 1870's shop front.

Just up **Cheap Street** is the Conduit, built as a lavatorium or washing place in the cloister of the Abbey in the early 16th century, and moved here after the dissolution in 1539 to form a small market house. It has been used to house a water supply, as a reading room, a police station and a penny bank. Along the pathway towards the abbey church is a 15th century gateway, also part of the Abbey. Just beyond on the left is **Sherborne Museum**, with displays on the abbey, almshouses, castles, school, silk mills, archaeology, natural history, super books of old photographs of the town, and photographs of the Sherborne Missal of *c.* 1400. Temporary exhibitions as well (fee: lists). All of Cheap Street (cheap meaning market or fair; the shops are smart) is worth exploring, with most buildings in the local stone. It is a mixture of dates from the 16th century onwards, with some pretty 19th century shop-fronts surviving; one has original 16th century posts, and its neighbour, Abbeylands, a jettied-out first storey with timber framing, and a stone wing with the porch dated 1649. Towards the top of the street are two red brick houses of the late 18th century. On the right is the Digby Estate Office, a slightly strangely proportioned house of *c.* 1800, with two good bow windows. More timber framing and the Julian, three-storey stone. The road curves to The Green, and finishes with lovely calm and regular early 19th century stone houses, three storeys high.

Just to the east is Priory House, with 17th century windows, but odd crenellation on top and an elaborate doorway, both probably of the 1830's. Just along Newland is Sherborne House, a lovely building constructed as a big private house about 1720, and further along the street the Manor House, with an elaborate oriel window of *c.* 1500, moved from round the corner and used as the centre piece for an early 19th century medieval front, which is far too symmetrical to be real. The whole of the centre of the town is exciting to walk, with buildings all still on a human scale, and in great variety. Newlands, Westbury and Long Street (leading out to Castleton) are all worth exploring, with many stone buildings.

The famous boy's public school uses buildings all over the town (including the Digby down by the station, built as an hotel in 1869) but the main school is north of the Abbey. The entrance is in Abbey Road, through a large mock-Tudor block of *c.* 1920. Restored and altered abbey buildings survive right down by the church, and a few small school buildings of the early 17th century, but the bulk of the buildings date from after 1850, and are imitation Tudor. The school expanded from 40 boys in 1850 to nearly 300 in 1877, with more than 600 today. Round the corner in Hospital Lane is Abbey Grange, a house converted early in the

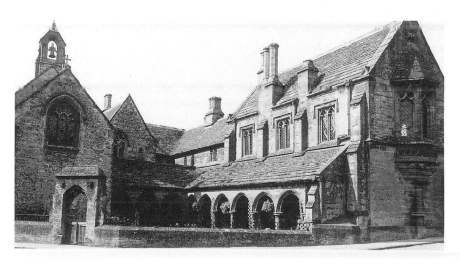

Sir Walter Raleigh by Nicholas Hilliard
The New Castle, Sherborne

19th century from part of an abbey barn of *c.* 1400. A very odd house dominated by buttresses.

On the south of the town is the trim railway station, with a lovely grassy hill behind topped with trees.

At the end of Long Street, on the east of the town, is **Sherborne Old Castle** ★★★ – really a fortified palace built between 1107-35 by Roger, Bishop of Salisbury (fee: lists). Although the castle was used during the medieval period, the original buildings were little altered until the late 16th century, when it was bought by Sir Walter Raleigh, who started converting it into a house (see New Castle). It was held by the Royalists for the whole of the Civil War, unsuccessfully beseiged by nearly 6,000 Parliamentary soldiers in 1642, and taken after another siege in 1645 conducted by Cromwell himself who called it 'a malicious mischievous Castle, like the owner'. The walls were beaten down with gunfire and undermined, and the Royalists were only saved from butchery by the quantities of loot in the castle, which distracted the soldiers. The castle is entered over a modern bridge which has the piers of the medieval one beneath. This gatehouse is 12th century, apart from the flat-topped 16th century windows. Originally there was a curtain wall all round: the earthwork to the west probably dates from the Civil War seiges. The foundation of the north gate survives as a long passage, and there are the remains of another bridge beyond the north-east gate. The buildings in the centre are mainly 12th century, apart from the bayed part to the north of the keep, vaulted with a re-used Norman pillar as support. This

may be part of Raleigh's alterations. The original plan was unusual – a keep adjoining four wings around a small courtyard: a combination of military and domestic, all very high quality, in ashlar, with the main rooms around the courtyard on the first floor. Some Norman detailing survives around the windows and arcading. The Castle hill has old beech trees and gives good prospects.

At the entrance to the Old Castle is a fine row of large stone houses, one with latticed windows and an 18th century 'Gothick' porch, and all with hood moulded and transomed windows of the 17th century. The Castle end one is 19th century, the rest 17th. Opposite is the church of St Mary Magdalene, Castleton, the second to occupy the site, replacing one built by Raleigh in the 1590's. Alexander Pope, the poet, admired the new church as 'a neat chapel' even before he knew that his friend Lord Digby (of the New Castle) had designed it. It was finished in 1715, virtually a square building with a tiny chancel. Simple, but pretty, with plain glass in the windows making it very light. Many of the fittings (not the seating) are early 18th century – the gallery, the pulpit, reredos (1733) the rather odd font, and a fine brass candelabrum dated 1714.

Raleigh had acquired the Sherborne Castle estate in 1592, and soon afterwards he fell out of favour with Queen Elizabeth, because she discovered he had married secretly and had a son. He and his wife (after a short period in The Tower) retired to Sherborne. His wife spent a lot of time there, but Raleigh was often away seeking the gold of Eldorado or fighting.

He regained Elizabeth's favour, but was sent to The Tower by James I, and lost the castle. It was bought in 1616 by the Digbys shortly after Raleigh's execution. **The New Castle** (fee: lists) ★★★★ is a strange building externally. It is rendered, and at first sight it is difficult to guess its dates. In fact the centre block was built by Sir Walter Raleigh (on the site of a smaller earlier house) after he had given up trying to convert the old Castle, in the 1590's. In 1600 he added the eccentric polygonal corner turrets. Wings with more turrets were added at each corner by the Digbys in about 1625, in a style similar to the original house. Finally in 1860 a wing was added on the west and many of the interiors altered. A romantic building, and with good furniture and superb paintings.

The front courtyard is barred by an elaborate stone gateway of the 17th century, framing a doorway of similar date added to the main block of the 16th century building. The ostrich with a horseshoe in his mouth is the heraldic beast of the Digby family, found all around the building. The entrance for visitors is through one of the 17th century turrets, lined with contemporary panelling. The library is delicious – 18th century 'Gothick' with serious looking busts in the niches of frivolous panelling. The 1860 ceiling does not detract. The solarium is a superb Victorian scheme, with a monstrous alabaster fireplace, and a clock made as a model of Sherborne Abbey tower (1890). This was part of Raleigh's house. The Red Drawing room has an intricate 17th century ceiling and a fireplace of similar date with recent paint. Famous painting of the procession of

Queen Elizabeth I, *c. 1600*. The Green Drawing room has three 17th century fireplaces, a huge one in the main room and smaller ones in the flanking turrets. The ceiling has the arms of Raleigh. The rich decorations are 1600's, as are those in the Blue Drawing room. Lady Bristol's room has a 17th century ceiling and doors. The hall, downstairs, feels much simpler than the rest of the house, stone with white walls and some original detailing. The long Oak room is lined with Jacobean panelling, and has two beautiful wooden lobbies, with crested tops, heraldic beasts and pretty original doors. These and the stone arch at the other end of the room are also early 17th century. In the cellars, mostly of the original house, are displays of household utensils, weapons etc.

Close to the house are two large wooden game larders, and the entrance to the icehouse. Beyond is a lovely classical orangery (teas) of 1779 with a frieze of beautifully carved garlanded ox-skulls! and a Gothick dairy of similar date, with charming mock-medieval facade and original fittings, very fanciful, with a re-laid Roman mosaic on the floor. This is the central part of a mosaic excavated nearby in 1836. Walks through the landscape created by Capability Brown and along the lake. At the entrance to the Castle is a little Victorian Lodge, and the huge stable blocks.

SHILLINGSTONE (B) has a good view of Hambledon Hill (see entry), across the River Stour. The village is large with some nice cottages and houses, but it is not picturesque. Until early this century an unusual remnant of Christmas mumming was kept here. The Bull, along with his 'keeper' (both probably 'drinky') might appear uninvited at any party, and had to be allowed into every room of the house and to frighten everyone present. At the junction of the main road and the turning to the church is the village cross – 15th century base and shaft of 1903, reconstructed as a memorial. In the first six months of the 1st World War 90 villagers enlisted, the highest number of any village in England. The church of the Holy Rood has Norman walls to the nave and chancel, but the only windows of that date surviving are the small ones re-set above the arches of the 1888 north aisle. The sophisticated 17th century pulpit is supposed to have been given by a London merchant who took refuge in the village during an outbreak of plague. Pretty painted roofs of 1902.

SHIPTON GORGE (D) is rather hilly,

and has good views, particularly from the churchyard over the Bride Valley, and up to Shipton Hill on the north-east. There is no gorge – the village belonged to the de Gorge family in the 13th century. The church of St Martin has a nice tower of c. 1400 with an elaborate doorway, but the rest of the church was rebuilt in 1862 in a rather cold style. The architect was John Hicks of Dorchester, for whom Hardy was then working. Boldly carved capitals in the north aisle and a rather horrid stone pulpit (both 1862), all by Benjamin Grassby, the Dorchester stone-carver. The 13th century font is odd because it has seven sides. Just below the church is a fine 18th century thatched stone cottage, one of several in the village.

★ *Setting.*

Sir Hugh Wyndham, Silton Church

SHITTERTON, *see* **BERE REGIS**
SHROTON, *see* **IWERNE COURTNEY**

SILTON (B) In the north of the county, a scattered small village surrounded by flattish pastures. Next door to the church is Manor Farm, a lovely mixture of stone buildings from the 17th century onwards. Good views west from the churchyard. The church of St Nicholas is basically 15th century but once inside the porch with its pretty doorway it is the magnificent memorial to Sir Hugh Wyndham of 1684 which dominates. It is huge, very Charles II, despite not being erected until 1692, with barley twist columns, attenuated but theatrical curtains forming bows over his head, and the centre-piece of Sir Hugh himself flanked by those of *(cont p.144)*

History

Dividing Dorset's archaeology and history from one another is fairly arbitrary (and arguable anyway as to exactly where this should be done). The period between the Romans leaving Britain (c. 410 AD) and the late 7th century when Dorset had been settled by the Saxons is a little-understood era, commonly known as the Dark Ages. Scattered documentary references (mostly in later sources), a few burials and other archaeological material are all the evidence we have. It is difficult to interpret: romantic legends of King Arthur mingle with the more solid fact that life must have continued in the county. The towns and the larger settlements may have been deserted but agriculture continued.

The Saxon period sees the establishment of the rural settlement pattern which still survives: most of today's villages (and even towns) are found listed in the Domesday book (1086) which although made for a Norman invader is a record of Saxon England.

Saxon Dorset was the scene of one of the first visits of Viking ships in the south in about 790. They killed the King's official who came from Dorchester to find out who they were. From the 830's Viking raids on the coast were frequent, until finally they were defeated by a combination of King Alfred and a storm which wrecked a large number of their longships in Swanage Bay.

The Norman Conquest had more effect on the ruling classes than the peasants of the countryside, with Saxon overlords being replaced by Normans. Castles were built in Dorchester and Wareham (these do not survive) and at Sherborne and Corfe, with smaller motte and baileys elsewhere. Dorset had its part in the troubles of the mid 12th century – the Anarchy – when the throne was disputed by Stephen and Matilda.

The bubonic plague – the Black Death – reached England through the port of Melcombe Regis (Weymouth) in June 1348, and although it is difficult to be precise in the absence of contemporary statistics probably between a quarter and a half of the population of the county died from it. We know from the records of clergymen that more than half the livings in the country became vacant during 1348-9, surely in most cases because the priest had died of the plague.

In the 1530's the monasteries were dissolved. Most of the Dorset houses had been founded in the 10th century, but some were older yet. Shaftesbury's rich nunnery was founded by King Alfred in 888 with one

ABOVE   *Toller Fratrum, Norman font*
BELOW   *Corfe Castle from the west*

ABOVE *Lady Bankes with the key of Corfe Castle (Kingston Lacy)*
RIGHT *Effigy of abbot, Abbotsbury*

of his daughters as the first abbess and became the richest Benedictine nunnery in the country, but there were also many smaller ones like the nunnery at Tarrant Crawford whose rule was laid down by a bishop early in the 13th century and included the charming injunction 'Ye shall not possess any beast, my dear sisters, except only a cat'.

Many of the monastic buildings were demolished, but some were converted to secular use, like Forde Abbey. Some churches survived because they were taken over by the parishes like Christchurch, Sherborne, and Milton Abbas.

The county was divided in the Civil War of 1642-6, with Dorchester, Lyme Regis, Poole and Weymouth on the side of Parliament, and the great castles of Corfe and Sherborne for the King. The Royalists took most of the county in 1643, and thereafter places like Dorchester changed hands several times. Poole and Lyme Regis managed to survive sieges by the Royalists, and Corfe was defended for the King by Lady Bankes, who successfully kept the Castle through two sieges, and finally lost it through treachery. Charles II tried to escape to the Continent by ship from Charmouth in 1651 after he had been defeated at the Battle of Worcester, but the mariner's wife locked her husband in his bedroom to prevent his being involved with such a dangerous enterprise.

Many Dorset men were involved with the revolt of the Clubmen, who in the last year of the Civil War opposed both sides because they were fed up with the war. They were routed by Cromwell on Hambledon Hill.

In 1685 the Duke of Monmouth, one of Charles II's illegitimate sons, landed at Lyme Regis to claim the throne in opposition to his uncle, James II. Many people from Dorset supported him, and after the defeat of Monmouth's army at Sedgemoor, were executed, like Monmouth himself. Judge Jeffries held the 'Bloody Assizes' at Dorchester when 74 of the rebels were hung, drawn and quartered and the pieces distributed to the towns around to be displayed as warnings.

Dorset missed out on the Industrial Revolution. During the medieval period the county was probably average in its emphasis on agriculture, with some industries such as cloth manufacture and quarrying. With the introduction of machinery and factories in the midlands and north, Dorset was left behind, and almost all its cottage industries were ruined. The button industry is a late, but otherwise typical, example. Up until 1851 many people were employed producing buttons by hand, especially in east Dorset, where one firm employed a thousand workers. A button-making machine perfected in 1851 destroyed the Dorset industry in five years, driving many of the erstwhile workers to emigration. Cloth manufacture had ceased to be of any significance by 1800, and even such a traditional local task as corn milling was under threat by the late 19th century because large mills at the ports, using imported grain, were cheaper. Dorset still has little industry.

The one increasing trade was tourism. Lyme and Weymouth were rescued from decay as ports in the 18th century by the growth of sea-side holidays, as was Swanage in the later 19th century. Bournemouth is totally a creation of the later 19th century holidaymaker and rich invalid. From the late 19th century and increasingly from 1920, the whole county became involved, but the main focus of tourism is still the coastline.

The Royal bathing machine at Weymouth

his wives who predeceased him, weeping. Superb. The pretty stencilled decoration all over the church was designed in 1870 by Clayton and Bell, the well-known church designers — all the stained glass here is also by them. Alfred Bell was born in 3ilton, and some of the glass was a gift from him. The brass candle holders (coronas) may also be by them. The late 12th century arcade to the south aisle is simple: the church was heavily restored in 1869. The odd chair in the chancel was assembled in the 19th century from 16th century woodwork, and the tables with the creed either side of the altar are unusual, Purbeck marble with incised lettering dating from c. 1700. They were found under the vestry floor in 1937.

★★ *For monument and stencilled decoration.*

SIXPENNY HANDLEY (B)

SIXPENNY HANDLEY (B) (or as the older signposts still have it 6d Handley) is quite a large, well-wooded village in Cranborne Chase with lots of recent development. Much of the old village was destroyed by a fire of 1892 which began in a wheelwright's shop when the wells were low and left 100 homeless. The church of St Mary was rebuilt in 1877, apart from the 14th century chancel and the strong, heavy porch of the same date. In the porch is a very battered Norman carving of Christ in Majesty. Banded flint and greensand, rather plain inside and with a monstrous pulpit of 1877. Nice plain 16th century table tomb in the south aisle.

SMEDMORE, *see* KIMMERIDGE

SOUTHWELL, *see* PORTLAND

SOUTH PERROTT (D)

SOUTH PERROTT (D) Still attractive despite the main road. Streams, small bridges and lots of 17th and 18th century stone cottages. ¾ mile south is Pickett Farm, large parts of which date from the 15th century. The arched and traceried 15th century window is visible from the road. From the entrance path the church of St Mary is an oddly complex mass, short and heavy. Inside it all fits simply together. The central tower has four identical arches of the early 13th century, and the north transept, nave, and plain but pretty font are all a little later. The chancel and south chapel were rebuilt in 1907-13. Good corbel heads in the nave and south transept. Behind the church is a dry moat now surrounding nothing, dating from the medieval period.

★★ *Village, church.*

SPETISBURY (F)

SPETISBURY (F) Long thin village, cramped on the bank of the River Stour, almost a continuation of Charlton Marshall. Many of the cottages are colourwashed, and there is quite a lot of recent building. Cedar Court, once the vicarage, is one of the handsomest in the county, prim symmetrical brick, and was built in 1716 for Dr Charles Sloper, who paid for the rebuilding of Charlton Marshall church. Crawford Bridge over the River Stour is stone and partly medieval. At the south end of the village is Spetisbury Rings, a simple Iron Age hillfort with a single bank and ditch. When the railway cut through it in 1857 more than 80 skeletons were found in the ditch,

probably killed at the Roman invasion as part of a Roman shield was found with them. The church of St John is not exciting: it mostly dates from the later 19th century, with a tower of about 1500. Fine 1591 table tomb and early 17th century pulpit. In the churchyard the impressive pyramidal tomb of Rev. Thomas Rackett (1833).

STALBRIDGE (A)

STALBRIDGE (A) Rather plain, old-fashioned very small town or large village in the Blackmore Vale with a variety of buildings. A few cob cottages have stone slated roofs, but most of the buildings are in the local greyish stone. Some of the 19th century houses and nonconformist chapels are stone with either pale brown or hot red brick used for window and door surrounds. Towards the north end is the best market cross in Dorset, later 15th century with a new top of 1950 and an even more recent final. Behind it is the Old Rectory of 1699. At the south end are many well-spaced pairs of houses mostly of the mid 19th century, and fronting a little triangular park 5 pairs of small early 19th century mock-Tudor cottages. On the outskirts particularly to the north and east are many stone walls, some drystone, including the remains of the 5 mile wall around Stalbridge Park. The house, once the home of the mathematician Robert Boyle (1627-91), was demolished in 1822 and only a pair of gate piers surmounted by lions remain. The church of St Mary was basically rebuilt in the 1860's and 70's although small parts of the medieval church remain. Large, with a monumental tower, but not

Crawford Bridge, Spetisbury

The lodge, Stanbridge

particularly attractive. In it are several good monuments, including one of *c.* 1500 with a rather gruesome cadaver effigy. Some good Victorian woodwork including the font cover.

★★ *Old fashioned flavour.*

STANBRIDGE (F) Also known as Hinton Parva: is a tiny parish in the Allen valley, with few buildings. Two are of great charm – the cottage right on the road, built as a deliberately rustic lodge in 1809; and the church (now redundant) which was rebuilt in a light-hearted imitation Norman in 1860. Reset inside the porch a 12th century carved panel shows St Kenelm, probably a Saxon King's son, murdered when he was only 7. The church is dedicated to this saint, a rare dedication with only 8 others in the country. Opposite the church is a huge late 19th century rectory, and just to the north Victorian almshouses in a style similar to the church.

STANTON ST GABRIEL, *see* **GOLDEN CAP**

STAPEHILL (G) Mostly recent, but woody. The Cistercian nunnery, founded in 1808, has been transformed into **The Stapehill Experience**, a tourist attraction combining the abbey buildings, new gardens and a superb farming display. The plain and simple nunnery buildings (chapel, cloister, parlour and so on) are mostly mid-Victorian, and were used up to 1990. Incongruously, craftsmen now fill the upper floors. Three rooms of the 18th century farmhouse preserved by the nuns have been furnished as they might have been in the late 19th century. Large gardens including a huge rockery, formal garden and a lake, have been constructed, but the best part is the large exhibition called 'Power to the Land', which is the best farming display in the county, with reconstructed workshops, many tractors, stationary engines, hand tools –virtually everything which has powered farming. The centre piece is a gigantic gyrotiller of 1934, the largest tractor ever made in Britain.

★★★★ *For the whole 'experience', the gardens on their own* ★★★

STEEPLE (J) is tiny, on a little ridge in the band of Wealden beds which runs through the middle of Purbeck, and has a lovely view to the east. The medieval village was much larger, as humps and bumps of deserted medieval settlement around the church demonstrate. The houses and cottages are all of local limestone, and most have limestone roofs. The church of Saint Michael is not particularly distinguished, but has a lovely isolated position. Austere 16th century tower, and the rest, apart from the plain 12th century doorway and the 1850s chancel, is 16th or 17th century. In the porch, on the roof bosses and above the east door (some dated 1616) are carved the coat-of-arms of the Lawrence family, whose ancestors were allied to those of George Washington. The stars and stripes of the Lawrence arms are thought to have inspired the American flag. The barrel organ bought for the church in 1853 has been restored. In isolated areas without an organist these were often used to replace the traditional rustic church bands which Victorians regarded as improper for church services, but few survive. Half a mile north-west of the village up on the ridge is a picnic site with good views over the coast and inland.

★★ *Landscape.*

STINSFORD (E) A pleasant hamlet with an undistinguished medieval church, visited because of its Hardy associations. Although he was a famous agnostic, Hardy loved this church. He attended services here in his youth, and visited it regularly, walking or cycling over from Max Gate, after his parents, sister and first wife were buried at Stinsford. His heart is buried in his first wife's grave, while his ashes were buried at Westminster Abbey. The church of St Michael is small and homely, ranging in date from the 13th to the 17th century, with a 14th century tower. Several Victorian restorations. A late Saxon carving of an angel is re-set in the tower externally. The wooden gallery where the musicians and singers of the village choir or band sat has been removed (a larger example and some instruments can be seen in Puddletown church). Hardy's plan of the gallery is displayed. The Stinsford band consisted of three violins and a 'cello, and was organised by Hardy's grandfather and then his father from about 1801 until 1842, after which they only played for weddings and other country parties. As a young man Hardy joined them, playing the violin, and the Stinsford band is affectionately recorded in his third novel *Under the Greenwood Tree* (1872). Stinsford House, close to the church tower is mostly of the 19th century, with some 17th and 18th century features. A path leads out of the churchyard down to the River Frome, with good views of the watermeadows. The riverside path leads to Lower Bockhampton, or Dorchester, both interesting walks. It is also possible

ABOVE *Church and farmhouse, Stockwood*

LEFT *Coronation lion head, Stoke Abbott*

to walk south across the watermeadows towards Max Gate. By the roundabout for the Dorchester by-pass, is a circular stone pillar, some 4ft of which shows out of the ground. It may be a Roman milestone.
★★★★ *For Hardy fans.*

STOCK GAYLARD (A, west of Lydlinch) has an immense deer-park, well stocked with fallow deer, which the main Sherborne/Blandford road runs right alongside. Stock House (*c.* 1720) is visible through the trees. Close by is the church of St Barnabas, 1884.

STOCKWOOD (E, between Chetnole and Melbury Osmond) A tiny hamlet at the foot of the chalk downs in a superbly woody area, with many hedgerow oaks. It has the smallest church in Dorset, the second smallest in England — 29ft 3in by 12ft 9in — dedicated to the Saxon saint Edwold, the hermit brother of an East Anglian King, who died in 971 and was buried at Cerne Abbas. Although this suggests that there was a Saxon church here the present building mostly dates from the 15th century. The tiny elaborate porch is dated 1636 and the odd little bellcote is the same date. The key for the church is kept at the lovely late 18th century brick farmhouse right beside the church.
★ *Setting.*

STOKE ABBOTT (D) Charming, a big unspoilt village in a lumpy beautiful valley

with cottages of every sort from 17th century to Victorian, all very rural and unassuming. In the centre is an oak tree planted in 1901, a trough fed by a spring for the horses, and another little spring fed through a lion's head (of 1953) for humans. To the north of the village are the heights of Waddon and Lewesdon (894 ft). The

approach to the church from the north is past a thatched farmhouse dated 1751 and 1762, looking as though it should be 17th century. Its only concession to the 18th century is to be symmetrical. Beyond a farmyard is the church of St Mary, of a great variety of dates. Part of the chancel is 12th century, and a little window of that date survives in the middle of the north wall. In the nave the restoration of 1878 dominates, with the new roof and north aisle of that date. Jacobean pulpit, and high class 12th century font with arches enclosing heads, and patterns all over. Local club staves displayed at the back of the church Bright little mosaic memorial by the doorway to a matron of Beaminster Union (the workhouse) who died in 1920. The Workhouse still survives as Stoke Water House on the road to Beaminster — now flats. The road from Broadwindsor enters the village through a tiny wooded gorge.
★★★ *Village.*

STOKE WAKE (E) clings to the side of a hill near Bulbarrow, and the road through is overshadowed by a variety of trees. Miniature village, in which the church of 1872 has been turned into a farm store.
Lovely view (see also Rawlsbury).

STONEBARROW, *see* GOLDEN CAP.

STOURPAINE (F) like so many villages is not pretty on the main road, but the village centre just beyond it is, with lots of thatched

difficult date to guess because of the 19th century additions and alterations to the roof
★ *Village.*

STOUR PROVOST (B) Pretty village, with 18th and 19th century local limestone cottages, some still thatched, and a couple of 17th century farmhouses. The church of St Michael has lovely trees in the graveyard and is a medley of dates from the 14th-17th centuries, all restored: chancel 1845.
★ *Village.*

STOUR ROW (B) has a few stone houses and a little simple church of 1867.

STOURTON CAUNDLE (A) Some fine stone buildings at the church end of the village, and the church itself is surrounded by farmyards. The landscape is flat and agricultural with lots of willows and alders: like bits of Normandy. The medieval church of St Peter was sensitively restored in the late 19th century, after a survey showed that only the chancel had decent footings – even the tower had only 1 ft of masonry below ground. Several of the walls remain at odd angles. The chancel is 13th century with original windows apart from the eastern one. The fine memorial tablet to Aylen Fernandes (1921) is by Eric Gill. The font is of the early 18th century garden-ornament type. Next to the extremely pretty 16th century pulpit (which has crocketed finials and tracery, like stonework) is a very nice 15th century tomb, with an alabaster effigy. The tower is earlier than most – 14th century, as is the porch which has a reset 13th century lancet window like those in the chancel.
★★ *Village, church*

STRATTON (E) A small village, now bypassed, containing a mixture of houses

LEFT   *Two porches, Stourton Caundle*
BELOW   *The Manor House Hotel, Studland*

and cottages from the 17th century to the present in a variety of materials. St Mary's church was drastically restored in 1891. Thomas Hardy and others opposed this, and succeeded in having some of the original doors and windows reset in the new building and preserving the 15th century tower. The interesting feature of the church is the early 16th century tower staircase which is enclosed with linen-fold panels and supported on an elegant newel post via ribbed wooden vaulting.

STUDLAND (K) A miniature sea-side town: its tiny centre mostly Edwardian, but with older cottages particularly around the church, and an extraordinary 'Marine Villa' (now Manor House Hotel) built in 1825 with later 19th century alterations. The village is full of trees and hedges and all fits happily together. Much of the area, including the heath, now belongs to the National Trust.

The church of St Nicholas is both high quality and early. The tower and chancel, built in the 11th century just before the Norman conquest, were remodelled in the mid-12th century, and the arches and decoration date from this period. Both have heavy vaulted ceilings with thick ribs, supported on columns and round-headed arches. The east window in the chancel and the south windows of the tower crossing are more recent, but the tiny deep windows are 12th century. The nave was rebuilt in the late 11th century: its windows are original in the west wall, as are the plain and attractive north and south doorways. Fine 1987 lectern. Externally the corbel table (at the junction of the wall and roof) with human and animal heads and other decoration was added to the nave in the mid 12th century, at the same time as the remodelling of the chancel. Heavy unfinished tower. The gravestone of Sergeant William Lawrence to the south-west of the porch records his exploits in the Peninsular War: 'medal with

cottages and leafy gardens. Several late Victorian buildings on the road to the church. The church of Holy Trinity has a greensand 15th century tower, while the body of the church is of 1858, with some original windows re-set. Pretty late 19th century tiles behind the altar. In the tower is a kneeling figure of a vicar, c. 1670, erected by the man himself some years before his death. To the north of the village is Fontmell Parva House whose central five bays are of 1665, a

ten clasps'. He fought at Waterloo, married a French girl in Paris soon afterwards, and retired to Studland in 1821 to keep a pub. His wife's memorial is on the back of his. To the south of the church on a hump beside the road is a new village cross, carved in 1976 with Concorde, 'spaceship earth' and so on. The long sandy beach is full of shells (hence Shell Bay) and runs right round the bay and on for 2½ miles to South Haven Point, where a chain ferry runs across to Sandbanks. The road through is private, and a toll is charged. Most of the promontory is a National Nature Reserve, with a car park by the beach just north of Studland village. With the recent addition of Godlingston Heath to the west into the Reserve there are 1500 acres. The promontory has grown seawards over the last 400 years, with sand-dunes now enclosing the Little Sea, once part of the main ocean, but now a land-locked lake. The reserve has heathland woodland and sand dunes with nature trails laid out on the hummocky dunes and in the wood. Studland and Godlingston Heath are good walking areas, but the notices at the entrances to the reserve should be read and their instructions followed. Godlingstone Heath is less sandy, and carries traditional heath vegetation. In the middle of the eastern part is the **Agglestone,** a vast lump of sandstone (estimated as 500 tons) sitting on a knoll: . . . *'the famous Agglestones, Said to be by Satan, thrown/ At Corfe Castle in the night, / From the neighb'ring Isle of Wight'* (John Webber, 1853). And as so often, despite his daemonic powers, he missed. Until the later 19th century ravens bred here. In the Arctic February of 1986 the dry heath caught fire, and a huge swathe right round the Agglestone and up to 1½ miles beyond burnt, destroying all the vegetation. A furze bush and part of a holly were all that survived on the Agglestone's knoll.

Good views from the beach towards

ABOVE *The beach, Studland*
BELOW *Studland church and a detail showing the corbel table*

the chalk stacks of Old Harry Rocks on the south, and east to Bournemouth. The Isle of Wight can usually be seen, and another viewpoint one-third of the way to Corfe from Studland on B3351 has a small car-park which gives a most marvellous view out across the heath and the conifer plantations (concealing oil wells) to Poole Harbour, up west to Wareham, including Brownsea Island. On the east are Studland and Sandbanks at the entrance to Poole harbour, and beyond the coastline to Bournemouth, Hengistbury and even further if it is clear.

★★★★ *Landscape, beaches, heath.* ★★★ *Church, because so early.*

STURMINSTER MARSHALL (F)

A big village in the Stour river valley, with two triangular greens in the middle, one with the maypole (restored 1986), the other with the village stocks. The village is a mixture of modern houses, and cob or brick thatched cottages mostly of the 18th century. The modern predominate. Fine (restored) long thatched row opposite the church. The church of St Mary has a mock-medieval tower of 1805, built after the medieval tower collapsed and altered during a severe restoration in 1859. Although the aisle and nave walls are medieval most of the windows are 1859, and the 12th century piers were encased in stone and made square at the same time. The round arches above them survive. A small brass of a vicar who died in 1581 is in

ABOVE *White Mill Bridge, Sturminster Marshall*
BELOW *Market day, Sturminster Newton*

BELOW *The maypole, Sturminster Marshall*

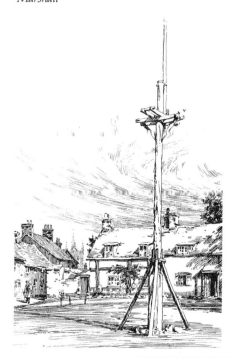

the chancel (under the carpet) and set in the second pier of the nave (beside the altar in the north aisle) is a large silver seal dated 1688. In the north aisle is a monument commemorating King Alfred's millenium in 1901 – not a common thing to be celebrated. Nearby is a 17th century helm. The very Norman arch to the tower is 1859. In the autumn there are dozens of cyclamen under the yew by the path, by an unusual modern table tomb. In the porch are two early 14th century coffin lids, one with an inscription. To the north of the village is the long and handsome White Mill Bridge, basically late medieval with eight arches and big cut-waters with refuges for pedestrians. White Mill (fee: lists) picturesque on the far side, was rebuilt in 1776. Now restored, with all the mill machinery on view.

★ *Village, church.* ★★ *Mill.*

STURMINSTER NEWTON (A/B)

Known locally as 'Stur', and traditionally the capital of the Blackmore Vale. A small town, pretty but sleepy every day of the week except Monday when there is a huge cattle market and the streets are awash with lorries and farmers. William Barnes, the Dorset poet, was born at Bagber in 1801, a mile and half west of Sturminster, and went to school here until he was 13, working as a solicitor's clerk in the town until 1818, when he left the Vale of Blackmore, never to return. Much of his poetry celebrates the slow rural life of this small area, especially Pentridge Farm, where his uncle and aunt lived; *Pentridge! – oh! my heart's a-zwellen / Vull o'jaÿ wi' vo'k a- tellen / Any news o' thik wold pleäce, / An' the boughy hedges round it, / An' the river that do bound it / Wi' his dark but glis'nen feäce. Vor there's noo land, on either hand, / To me lik' Pentridge by the river.*

The town has buildings in great variety, ranging from stone to timber framing, many of which date from just after a disastrous fire of 1729. The central market place has the stone Assembly Room of *c.* 1800, with a wide carriage entrance and

next door the 18th century Swan Inn, with elaborate and pretty brickwork. Beyond the stump of the 15th century market cross are a couple of 16th century houses, one very restored. Many other good 18th century brick buildings in the town, particularly in Church Street, Tanyard Lane and Bridge Street, mixed with some stone and timber-framing, occasionally still thatched. The town centre has several attractive late 18th and early 19th century shop fronts, and the side streets are worth exploring. Huge market area to north-east.

The greensand church of St Mary was greatly extended in 1872, but the extensions were based on the late 14th century nave, so that everything matches. The west tower has an original first stage

and rather odd 1827 above. Door dated 1728 in nails. The chancel and transepts are all 1827, with remarkably modern-looking stained glass in the east window of the chancel, in fact dating from 1865. In the east window of the south aisle is a very unusual stained glass of 1921. The nave has pretty clerestory windows, and a very good altar, 15th or 16th century wooden roof with angels, and pretty bosses. This is imitated in the 1827 chancel in plaster. Barnes was christened here and the lectern is a memorial to him. Lots of 20th century (but traditional) woodwork. Behind the church is the late 18th and early 19th century school and school house of stone and brick.

About 1¼ mile up the Bath Road are the

remains of the Workhouse, with a little detached chapel sometimes housing **Sturminster Newton Museum** (fee: lists).

A fine stone bridge, built in the 16th century and widened in the 17th leads across the river to Newton. Sturminster Newton Mill, ★★★ is open to visitors. The attractive austere building is partly 17th century (stone) and partly 18th century brick. A visit is highly recommended to see all three floors of the mill and its machinery working (fee: lists). Displays on local history, crafts, archaeology, etc. Picnic area, and it is possible to walk upstream across the meadows to Riverside Villas, where Thomas Hardy lived from 1876-8 whilst writing *Return of the Native*. The house he lived in is the far one furthest from the recreation ground.

Newton consists almost entirely of really pretty buildings, in brick, stone, timber-framing or a combination. Fine rendered Georgian house with a porch, and even some thatch. On a little spur is Sturminster Newton 'Castle', described by Leland in the 1540's as 'an hille made stepe rounde by mannes hand'. In fact it is probably the earthworks of an Iron Age fort, re-used from the 10th century for a manor house. The ruins of part of a 14th century building are all that remain.

SUTTON POYNTZ (H) Right up under the hills. Its large mill-pond has been a beauty spot since visitors first came to Weymouth in the 18th century. The mill and village in Hardy's *Trumpet Major* are partly based on Sutton Poyntz, and photographs taken before most of the cottages on the far side of the pond were altered and re-roofed show it was then one of the prettiest spots in Dorset. Still good, with willows fringing the water and ducks waddling about. A footpath leads down along the mill stream past the big brick mill of *c.* 1820. Almost all the other buildings in the centre are of local limestone.

Above the pond is the **Wessex Water Museum** (free: list; car park inside), based in the solid little stone buildings erected from 1856 to supply Weymouth with pure water. Still used, but the modern equipment only needs one building. The rest contain earlier pumps, turbines etc, and displays on water and so on. The water comes from a large spring up under the chalk down, well worth walking up to the reservoir and spring, which can supply 2.8 million gallons a day. The filter in the reservoir was originally one of the funnels on Brunel's ship *Great Eastern*.

★★ *Village.*

SUTTON WALDRON (B) is in nice hummocky landscape and has some pleasant mock-Tudor brick almshouses of 1830 in the middle of the village, and a pair of prim Victorian cottages dated 1857 built in chequer work of flint and stone – a late revival (or survival) of an earlier style. The surprise is the church of St Bartholomew, built in 1847 for the rector Anthony Huxtable (a pioneer scientific farmer) and his wife. The old church was completely demolished, and this graceful replacement built. The tower with its small steeple and flying buttresses is most attractive, and the whole church has been described as recapturing the medieval style as successfully as any 19th century church in the county (RCHM) and by John Betjeman as 'one of the best and most lovely examples of Victorian architecture'. The interior is even better than the exterior. Owen Jones (1809-74), a designer better known for decorating houses and designing parts of the Great Exhibition of 1851, and interested in Arabic ornament and the careful use of colour, designed the painted interior of the church. His elaborate scheme is slowly being uncovered: much of it had been painted over. The chancel arch is gorgeous, and the chancel itself has inscriptions and borders on a severe maroon ground. The arches in the nave are also beautifully painted, and when it is fully restored the effect will be magnificent. The chancel is floored with small, intricate tiles of many colours, and has stained glass of the same date as the church. The font has a wonderful, lacy wooden lid, and a high

cruciform stand. Very plain 'Arts and Crafts' benches. The stone gatepiers and cast-iron railings at the entrance are presumably of 1847, and very attractive. Anthony Huxtable's rather odd tomb can be seen outside the north east of the chancel. A church well worth seeing, both as a marvellous building of 1847 with splendid decoration, and as an example of how painted churches must have felt in the medieval period.

★★★★ *If you can stand 19th century churches.*

SWANAGE (K) Up to the early 19th century, Swanage was a small fishing port, which also shipped stone from the nearby quarries. In the 1820's William Morton Pitt of Encombe (see Kingston) bought the estate and tried, with limited success, to develop Swanage as a seaside resort, like

The Wellington clock tower, Swanage

the already successful Weymouth and Lyme Regis. It grew slowly during the 19th century, but after the railway came in 1885 the resort really expanded, so that today Swanage is full of buildings dating from the late 19th and early 20th centuries. Treves recorded that in the 1870's Swanage was 'a queer little town' all of stone but by 1905 'it was the scene of a furious struggle between rival builders, who fight to cover the land with copious red brick'. Thomas Hardy lived here for the winter of 1875/6, and the town is described in his *Hand of Ethelberta* (1876) as Knollsea, where 'everybody in the parish who was not a boatman was a quarrier.' The wide bay gives good views, to the Isle of Wight in good weather with the chalk cliffs leading to Old Harry Rocks (see entry) to the north and the sweep of the downs inland.

The main beach is on the (cont p. 154)

Mansions and Manor Houses

Unlike churches and villages, many of the larger houses are not accessible, or even visible. This brief survey only refers to those which are open to the public, or whose gardens are open. Those which can be glimpsed from the road are mentioned in the Gazetteer.

Dorset has many fine manor houses, which grow from their landscapes in a comfortable, homely manner. Three are surprisingly early examples, the central part of Cranborne Manor, built about 1207 – Fiddleford Manor of the 1370s, and a tiny complete house of the late 14th century, Lodge Farm, Kingston Lacy. Cranborne can only be admired externally but the other two are open. Most of the manor houses are late medieval or 17th century, and many are on the medieval pattern with a hall with a high roof as the main room. The later 15th and early 16th century ones have particularly rich halls, with elaborate wooden roofs. Purse Caundle is a smallish example of the late 15th century. The finest is Athelhampton, of about 1500, which has a two storey oriel window at one end of the open hall as well as a good roof. The abbots halls at Forde Abbey and Milton Abbey are similar to those in houses, but finer and grander still – Forde with a very showy and enormously high three storey porch 1520s), and Milton (1498) with a superb wooden roof and screen.

Sandford Orcas, probably built in the middle of the 16th century, has a single storey hall with another chamber over it, moving decisively away from the medieval style of house. Wolfeton, early 16th century gatehouse has towers intended rather to impress than defend, but most of the house is late 16th century, with many fashionable large and elaborate plaster, stone or wood chimney pieces of about 1600. Lulworth Castle, now an established ruin, is an early 17th century mock castle, originally a palatial hunting lodge. Early 17th century additions were made to Sherborne New Castle, the core of which was built by Sir Walter Raleigh in the 1590's.

Later additions have turned some of the houses already mentioned into great houses or mansions, but with Kingston Lacy we move to a house built all at once on the great scale. Although the 1650's house has been altered inside and out, in shape and size it is still the same, and still classical as it was intended to be.

Milton Abbey is an early example of a Gothic large house, built in the 1770's. The mock-medieval style was adopted to blend with the church and the remains of the abbey, and in form the house is really a classical symmetrical design with small–scale Gothic detailing. In the early 19th century several far more correct imitation Tudor houses were built, but none of them except Parnham are open. Parnham is a picturesque mixture of

FROM THE TOP   *Athelhampton, Sandford Orcas, Wolfeton House*
OPPOSITE   *Kingston Lacy, Sherborne Castle, Chettle*

real 16th and 17th century with imitation early 19th century all fitting together to produce a lovely house.

Smedmore, a quietly classical stone house of the 17th and 18th centuries, and Chettle, an unusual brick house of 1710's are good examples of the smaller houses.

Part of the delight of visiting houses is the fittings and furniture: Athelhampton, Forde, Parnham, Purse Caundle, Sandford Orcas, Sherborne New Castle, Smedmore and Wolfeton all have much to offer, and Kingston Lacy has the most superb collection of pictures.

The large houses spread their influence into the landscape. Even today they are the centre of great areas

of trees which were planted over the last couple of centuries as much for ornament as use. Avenues and parkland are only part of it: around Melbury are woodlands and a deer-park. The same is true, to a greater or lesser degree, of all the big houses. Milton Abbey is the most famous case of deliberate creation of a beautiful landscape, including the removal of a small town and the flooding of a valley to make a lake. Extensive woodlands still ornament the whole area. Owners of other houses managed even to remove public roads from their parks; main roads at Iwerne Stepleton and Charborough still make the long loops made necessary by the diversions.

There are only two town houses open to the public, and they could not be in greater contrast. The Tudor House, Weymouth is a pair of simple late 16th century houses, while the Russel-Cotes Museum, Bournemouth is partly in the donor's house, a rich mixture of the late 19th century.

★★★★: Athelhampton; Fiddleford; Forde Abbey; Kingston Lacy; Milton Abbey; and Sherborne New Castle.
★★★: Parnham; Wolfeton; Smedmore, Kimmeridge. Sandford Orcas; Lulworth Castle; Merley House; Islington House, Puddletown.
★★: Chettle; Russell-Cotes Museum, Bournemouth; Tudor House, Weymouth; Edmonsham House; Purse Caundle; Upton House; Lodge Farm Kingston Lacy. (See also Gardens).

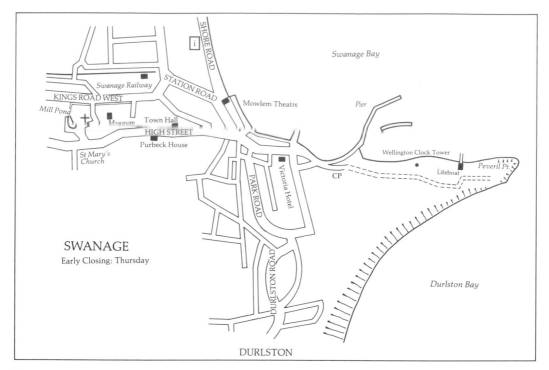

SWANAGE

Early Closing: Thursday

DURLSTON

north side of the town, along Shore Road, with an amusement park, recreation ground and bandstand behind it (also the Tourist Information Office). The Mowlem, at the south-east end of Shore Road, commemorates John Mowlem (1788-1868), the successful stone and building contractor. He, and more particularly his successor in the firm, his nephew George Burt (1816-94), were very influential in Swanage, despite the firm being based in London. Along the shore between the Mowlem and the stone quay was where the stone was 'banked', that is stored

waiting to be transported to the ships. After the arrival of railway stone went out by train, and the Bankers were built over with typical seaside lodgings and shops with 'Dutch' gables. The block is dated 1896.

At the east end of the **High Street** is what was the Royal Victoria Hotel – the centre is mid-18th century (rather masked by a 19th century glazed portico) with large 19th century wings. This was the manor-house, turned into an hotel by Pitt in the 1820's, who also built the little stone quay opposite. The hotel was renamed

after Princess Victoria spent one night there in 1835. In the quayside are tram tracks – the remains of a line which ran out onto the pier to carry stone.

From the Royal Victoria Hotel eastwards are the sailing and diving clubs, sailboarders etc. The Pier of 1896 is currently closed because of storm damage. To the south of it are the remains of the earlier pier of 1859, and on the shore to the south of both is a plain building, Marine Villas, built in 1825 as a cold salt-water baths, with billiard and coffee rooms above.

Further west the High Street has good

ABOVE *Purbeck House, Swanage*
LEFT *The Town Hall, Swanage*

The mill pond, Church Hill, Swanage

early 19th century houses, some with pretty wrought iron balconies. Several 18th century pubs, and some 18th century cottages with the heavy local stone roofs, are mixed with more seasidey architecture of the later 19th century and 20th centuries. Along the High Street and up the hill are two of the curiosities of Swanage. The Town Hall (1872) on the right was designed by Crickmay, the Weymouth architect, in fairly typical later 19th century style, but up the centre of the building is an elaborate façade taken from the Mercer's Hall in Cheapside, London, and placed here in 1883. It dates from 1670, and is high quality 17th century classical, with fat putti, a bust of a rather seedy looking Flora, and intricate carving. The iron balustrade is the same date. The façade was acquired by George Burt, who transported much unwanted stonework and ironwork (particularly bollards and lamp-posts) from London to Swanage in his sailing ships, some of it as ballast and some simply because he wanted it. Behind the Town Hall is a tiny lock-up of 1802, inscribed 'For the Prevention of Vice and Immorality by the Friends of Religion and Good Order'. It was originally in the churchyard. Just beyond on the left is George Burt's house, Purbeck House, now a convent. This amazing building was also designed by Crickmay in 1875. The walls are of large chips of different coloured marble, waste from the steps of the Albert

Memorial in London which Mowlem's were building. The rich porridge effect is laced in by the mercifully plainer corners. The octagonal tower, and the gazebo in the garden wall are splendid. The house was described in a 1920's sale catalogue as being of 'superb massiveness . . . very striking architecture after the style of the Scottish Country Mansions'. The stable yard (visible from the road) shows a good sample of Burt's scavenging – the stone bollard is from Millbank Prison, the iron panel in the wall and the pillar supporting the two-storey wing are from Billingsgate Market, and a reproduction of part of the Parthenon frieze adorns the upper storey.

On up the hill is the plain 1837 and 1901 United Reformed Church, and opposite is the large Methodist church 1886. On the right is Church Hill, with some pretty 18th century houses. Here is the most photographed part of Swanage, the spring-fed mill pond, surrounded by stone buildings. The mill house at the bottom has a superb datestone of 1734, but the building has been altered.

St Mary's church is close to the millpond and apart from the 14th century tower, heightened in 1620, is 19th or 20th century. Tremendous arrangements of the wooden roof over the east ends of both nave and aisle. Good memorial tablets and a modern font made from a huge block of Purbeck marble. Almost all the glass is recent because the church was damaged by bomb blast during the war.

The Tithe Barn Museum has good displays on local themes, particularly the stone industry, including photographs of the quarries, samples of the stone and so forth (fee: lists).

On the bay, half way to **Peveril Point** is the Wellington Clock Tower, prominent from all around. This had been erected in London in 1854, and after being removed as a traffic hazard Burt brought it to Swanage in 1866. Now surrounded by Spanish style development. In the grounds of the Grosvenor Hotel above are two huge Ionic pillars, also brought from London by Burt. Further along is the Lifeboat station, where the lifeboat can usually be inspected. Peveril Point gives good views back across the bay, over the race caused by rock ledges in front of the Point, and along the small bay to the west towards Durlston Castle.

Burt bought the Durlston Estate, south of Swanage in 1862, hoping to develop it as a suburb. He drew up elaborate plans, but only the roads and a few buildings were constructed in his time. The Durlston Water Tower, looking medieval can be seen from Swanage Bay. On Durlston Head he and his architect Crickmay built in 1887-8 a super mock castle – used as a restaurant then as now. According to Treves in 1905, Durlston Castle 'combined the architectural features of a refreshment buffet, a tram terminus, and a Norman keep'. Now part of the **Durlston Country Park**, run by the Dorset County Council – 260 acres of wild countryside, with the Anvil Point Lighthouse (sometimes

The Globe, Durlston Country Park, Swanage

open), a visitor centre with displays on the local quarries and wildlife; and the castle itself. Splendid views, especially from the Castle area. Below the Castle is a huge globe made out of Portland stone, weighing 40 tons, put there by Burt (of course), who had it made. All round the castle are inscriptions, some giving height above sea level, some giving geographical information and others improving quotations. Large car park (fee).

The railway to Swanage closed in 1972 but is being remade by the Swanage Railway Company, who will run trains from Wareham to Corfe soon. Steam engines run trips (fee: lists) at weekends and daily in the peak season. Nordon, just north of Corfe, has large car parks for passengers, and the train will be the best route to Swanage. Well worth paying the supplement on the fare to ride in the 1930s Pullman car which was once part of the Brighton Belle, and has good Orient Express style interior with veneer panels and so on. Display in a 1916 goods wagon, and one can look into the workshop.

SWYRE (D/E/H) Although originally a fishing village, set back from Chesil Beach, sheltered on the east by Pins Knoll, which has a little coastguard house on top. Much of the village was rebuilt by the owners, the Dukes of Bedford, from the middle of the 19th century, and many of the cottages are dated. Now mixed with modern. The church of Holy Trinity retains its 15th century tower. The rest was rebuilt in 1843, with amusing plasterwork inside like 18th century 'Gothic' work consisting of an elaborate frame around the door, and an oddly supported ceiling. Good Napier family monument of 1692 and on either side of the doorway are brasses to the Russell family, from whom the Dukes of

ABOVE *Sydling St Nicholas*
RIGHT *Two cottages, Sydling St Nicholas*

Bedford are descended. The family were originally from Swyre. John Russell was rushed to Wolfeton House in 1506 because he could speak Spanish, needed because the Archduke of Austria and his Spanish princess bride had taken refuge there, having been forced to land at Weymouth by bad weather. He went on to court with them, thus initiating the rise of the Russells, Dukes of Bedford.

SYDLING ST NICHOLAS (E) Stunningly and unaffectedly picturesque village, with lots of really good quality thatched cottages, mostly banded flint and stone, in a lovely setting. Lots of small bridges over the Sydling Water, and profuse gardens. At the south end is East House, the only brick house, handsome and *c.* 1790. Next door is a stone and flint banded house in a very old-fashioned style dated 1733 on the front. South-east of the path to the church is a fine stone and flint Elizabethan barn which has lost part of one end, leaving it lop-sided. Fronting the churchyard on the north is Court House, an early 19th century Gothic remodelling of an earlier house. The church's setting is park-like, and it is basically rather plain, of the late 15th – early 16th century, with its chancel remodelled about 1750, and a 15th century tower with an 18th century top. Lots of good Georgian monuments, for example a large one in the chancel of 1766. Good woodwork – the seating is made from 17th century panelling, and a few 18th century box pews survive. By the 18th century

screen under the tower arch are three chests – very plain medieval one, an early 17th century one with carved decoration, and another panelled, late 17th century.
★★★ *Village.*

SYMONDSBURY (D) A secluded, village, beautifully situated among small hills west of Bridport, with the church, school of 1863, cottages (many 17th century) and larger

Tarrant Crawford church

Georgian houses all built from the lovely local golden sandstone. Lots of greenery. The church of St John the Baptist is mostly of the 14th century, with a huge 15th century window at the west end. The tracery in this, and almost all the other windows, is 20th century. The 14th century tower crossing is unusual because it has huge corbels to carry the weight and preserve space at floor level. Good multi- coloured marble monument of 1782 in the north transept, looking like Wedgewood pottery.
★★ *Village, setting.*

TALBOT VILLAGE *see* BOURNEMOUTH

The little **TARRANT (F/B)** river, a tributary

Cottages at Tarrant Gunville

of the Stour, has eight villages in only 10 miles. There were nine churches in the medieval period, and seven survive. The valley is shallow and wide, with chalk on either side. Like apparently every other Dorset river name Tarrant means . . . river, being an elegant variation of Trent.

TARRANT CRAWFORD (F) is the most southerly, close to the junction of the Tarrant and Stour. Best approached on foot along the path from Tarrant Keynston e. Now only a house, a farm and a small church, it was once one of the richest nunneries in England. The vanished convent church was the burial place of Richard Poore, Bishop of Salisbury (1217-28), who moved the see from Old Sarum to Salisbury, and commenced the building of the present cathedral. He was the illegitimate son of a previous Bishop of Salisbury, and founded the convent at Tarrant Crawford. Queen Joan of Scotland, sister of Henry III was buried in the convent church in 1238. The only possible remnants of the convent buildings are parts of Tarrant Abbey House (mostly 18th century brick), and the stone bits of the well-buttressed barns beyond. The tiny tower of the parish church of St Mary is of *c.* 1508 and like the rest of the building consists of big lumps of brown heathstone and greensand lacing together flint. The rest is 12th and 13th century, with a good series of wall-paintings all of the 14th century, rather faded, although there are many outlines of elegant figures. On the south wall the upper part shows the acts of St Margaret of Antioch, with the allegory of the three living and three dead below. The seating was made from 17th century box pews, more of which are used around the altar as panelling. 17th century pulpit and communion rails. The thin font is 16th

century, and it seems likely that the wooden cover is original, a rare occurrence.
★★ *Church, setting.*

TARRANT GUNVILLE (B) had (briefly) the largest and finest mansion in the whole of the county – Eastbury Park designed by Vanbrugh and built in the 1720's and 30's for George Bubb Doddington, 1st Baron Melcombe, a flamboyant figure whose friends ranged from the Prince of Wales to Voltaire. Eastbury Park was so large that after his death and that of his nephew no-one would live in it, even though the heir offered £200 per annum to any gentleman who would occupy and keep the mansion in repair'. Three-quarters of it was demolished, using gun-powder, in the 1770's and 80's, and all that remains is part of the stable block, converted to a house, and the fine classical gateways. The house can be seen from the road through the village, as can the entrances, one with a little bridge. The whole area is prettily wooded, and the village has several pretty, rather prim, 19th century banded brick and flint cottages, alongside earlier cob buildings, many still thatched. One farmhouse is flint chequered with fine greensand blocks doubtless taken from Eastbury. To the east of the church is the Old Rectory of about 1800, plain but enlivened by flint banding, and to the west of the church Gunville House of much the same date. Both of these probably used materials from Eastbury too. Stubhampton, just to the north, is similar to Tarrant Gunville but rather more sparse.

The church of St Mary has a 15th century tower, but much of the rest was rebuilt in 1843. The chancel has stencilled decoration with inscriptions. In the little windows above the chancel arch is 16th century stained glass with the arms of Henry VIII in one which we

Eastbury Park, Tarrant Gunville

with the arms of Katherine Howard his fifth wife and the other of Katherine Parr, his sixth and last wife, both of whom held the manor. A rather dull tablet records Thomas Wedgewood, the son of the great potter, who lived in Eastbury after it had been reduced in size. Outside the church is a nicely lettered gruesome inscription of 1567 'HERE LITHE S.T.D. PARSON: ALL FOWRE BE BVT ONE, EARTHE, FLESCH, WORME AND BONE'. The church contains many memorials to the Farquharson family, descendants of the famous hunting squire

Tarrant Hinton

who used Eastbury from 1805-37 to house one of his three packs of hounds. Squire Farquharson hunted throughout Dorset at his own expense, and was master for Dorset's greatest run (in 1825) when a fox led the field for 30 miles and was finally killed in the yard of the Plume of Feathers, Dorchester.

★★ *Landscape.*

TARRANT HINTON (B) Off the main road there are several picturesque cob and thatch cottages around the pleasant medieval church (St Mary). The 15th century tower has enormous gargoyles, and the greensand and flint banding of the church is pretty. The real treasures are inside – a gorgeous Art Nouveau lectern of brass and iron (1909), and

an Easter sepulchre of *c.* 1536 in a remarkably classical style for such an early date. Two angels set above it (originally part of the same scheme) have classical drapery. The well-carved communion rails were made in about 1665 for Pembroke College Chapel, Cambridge, and were moved here in about 1880. Fine memorial to a Second World War pilot. The chancel was rebuilt in 1874, and the rest of the church dates from the 14th-16th centuries with soft pretty greensand windows.

★★ *Church, village.*

TARRANT KEYNSTON (F) Quite a large village, with lots of trees. The church of All Saints was totally rebuilt in Perpendicular style in 1852, preserving only the medieval tower. By the tower is a table-tomb to members of the Bastard family including Thomas (died 1731) brother of the Bastards who rebuilt Blandford in the 18th century.

TARRANT LAUNCESTON (F) has cob or brick cottages like the other Tarrants, but no church because it was demolished in 1762.

TARRANT MONKTON (F) Lots of cob and thatched cottages, and a few brick ones, forming a pretty village centre. Nice humped bridge and a ford. The rather austere church of All Saints has a 15th century tower and nave. The chancel and the chancel arch are 14th century, and very unusually the chancel was restored in the 18th century. The simple east window and the other lancet windows are all of that date. Rest 1873. Nice late 17th century pulpit and 12th century font.

★★ *Village and church.*

TARRANT RAWSTON (F) A large farm and a small church, on the side of the shallow

Tarrant Monkton, bridge and ford (above) and cottage (below)

Venn chapel, near Thorncombe

valley in the prettiest part of the Tarrant, with lots of trees and pasture. The church is now privately owned, but visitors are welcomed. The farm's show front is 18th century, brick with greensand pilasters (which once supported a pediment) and green sand corners. Handsome. The church of St Mary's entrance is nice, with the little porch and south chapel (both 16th century) chequered in greensand and flint. Most of the inside is 18th century, with a mock medieval east window. The building has recently been thoroughly restored, and the interior is thus rather austere. Medieval tiles re-set around the 1868 font.
★★ *Church, setting.*

TARRANT RUSHTON (F) is small, with the mostly cob or brick cottages on a surprisingly steep little slope on the side of the valley. The small airfield was created in the Second World War: the gliders for D-Day were towed from here. The church of St Mary is an unusual shape – an equal-armed cross, The tower hardly rises above the nave roof, Although there are parts of 12th century walls surviving the bulk of the church is 14th century. Inside, above the main doorway, is an early 12th century carving of the lamb of God (centre), a figure either side, one probably St Gregory (the book is inscribed GREGOR). The carving has been cut to fit a door, probably in the 16th century. The chancel arch is 12th century too, simple and round. On either side, are unusual openings lined with decorated stones, almost grilles. All different, and all three 14th century. Up in the east side of the chancel wall are two big medieval cooking pots, apparently set there to improve the acoustics. Elegant medieval piscina and niche in the chancel. ★★ *Church, setting.*

THORNCOMBE (D) is close to the borders with Somerset and Devon (and was in Devon until 1838): the clusters of cottages and houses in its few steep streets have more in common with Devon than Dorset. Most of the buildings, including the church, are of chert, an unusual building stone. The church of St Mary was unexcitingly rebuilt in 1867. Two large brasses of 1437 are the best in Dorset – a man and woman in civil dress, with dogs at their feet. The restored pulpit has 16th century linen-fold panelling, and the vicar's pew includes early 17th century panels and figures. Two brothers, Samuel *(cont p.161)*

Museums

Dorset has museums in great variety. Many towns have one devoted to their history and that of the area around, while other places have more specialised displays.

Poole has two museums in historic buildings – the 15th century town cellars on the Quay, and Scallen's Court, a medieval and later town house. The Town Cellars and a huge warehouse are the Waterfront Museum, certainly the most attractive display in the county, showing the maritime history of the town and harbour. Bournemouth has a large museum (Russell-Cotes) in the town centre partly housed in a strange and exotic 1880's house, overpowering but fascinating. Priest's House Museum, Wimborne is a much earlier house. A small museum is dedicated to the poet Shelley at Boscombe. Christchurch has the Tricycle Museum, and a rare (for Dorset) industrial museum, The Southern Electric Museum. Wessex Water Museum is at Sutton Poyntz.

Dorchester has three museums – the Dorset County Museum with extensive displays on the archaeology, history, geology and natural history of the whole county, and on Hardy and Barnes. The Keep Military Museum shows the long history of the Devon and Dorset Regiments. The Dinosaur Museum is dedicated to those seemingly legendary beasts, and is very attractive to children who appear to take to them.

Weymouth has very modern displays at Timewalk. The Tank Museum at Bovington and the Army

Signals Museum at Blandford are obviously specialised but nonetheless interesting.

Bridport, Corfe, Blandford, Christchurch, Gillingham, Lyme Regis, Portland, Shaftesbury, Sherborne, Swanage, Wareham, Weymouth and Wimborne all have museums, several of them in interesting buildings. Displays of bygone farming implements at Abbotsbury Tithe Barn, Milton Abbas and Burton Bradstock, and a superb huge new display 'Power to the Land' at Stapehill Experience, one of the best in the county.

At Weymouth the superb Sea Life Park, has huge displays running up to shoals of fish in huge tanks. Merley Bird Gardens has a great variety of tropical and other birds, and vast horses can be admired at the Heavy Horse Centre, Holt and at Weymouth. Monkey World at Wool is interesting.

Most of the Dorset villages had mills in the medieval period, but few survive with all their works. Newton Mill at Sturminster Newton , Melbury Abbas, Mangerton and Place Mill, Christchurch are open to the public.

★★★★ Bovington Tank Museum; Dorset County Museum, Dorchester; Waterfront Museum, Poole; Russell-Cotes, Bournemouth; Stapehill Experience; Timewalk, Brewer's Quay, Weymouth; Deep Sea Adventure, Weymouth.
★★★ Red House, Christchurch; Dinosaur Museum, Dorchester (especially for children); Military Museum, Dorchester; Lyme Regis Museum; Scaplen's Court, Poole; Portland Museum; Priest's House Museum, Wimborne; Mill House Cider and Clock Museums, Owermoigne; Wessex Water Museum, Sutton Poyntz; Southern Electric Museum, Christchurch.

ABOVE *Bridport Museum*
ABOVE RIGHT *Outside Sherborne Museum*
LEFT *The Waterfront Museum, Poole*

and Alexander Hood, born here in the 1720's. Both became admirals and Viscounts.

THORNFORD (A) has an amazing (and ugly) stone tower with a clock in the centre, a memorial to the 1897 Jubilee. Quite a large village, with several fine 17th century stone farmhouses, Victorian estate cottages and so on, but Yeovil's proximity has led to recent building. Opposite the Victorian school, up by the church is Glebe Cottage, thatched and with a rustic porch of branches. The church of St Mary was greatly extended and restored in 1866, when the north aisle was added. The chancel and nave are later medieval, and the stone screen survives between the two, albeit with a 19th century chancel arch above. Rich late 19th century pulpit of inlaid marble, and behind the altar the old wooden pulpit, set as panelling.

THORNHILL (A) The house built near Lydlinch by the famous painter Sir James Thornhill (1675-1734) after he bought back the family estate in 1725. He probably designed it himself. Not open, but visible from the road, as is the thin obelisk he had erected in 1727 to commemorate George II's accession. The best visible example of Thornhill's work in Dorset is the altarpiece in St Mary's, Weymouth (he was born in the town) and his most famous are his paintings in the dome of St Paul's Cathedral and at the Royal Hospital, Greenwich.

TINCLETON (E) consists of a few houses dotted about amongst the meadows of the Frome valley, with in the middle the church (1840) by Benjamin Ferrey and distant views of Clyffe House (1842) a splendid mock-Tudor mansion by the same architect. The pretty school with schoolhouse adjacent could be by him as well.
★ *Setting.*

TODBER (B) Mostly modern development although there are a few cottages in the local stone. The short cliffs around some fields are the remains of quarrying. The little church was virtually rebuilt in 1876. Inside it is pleasant and plain. Nice 1879 screen and 17th century pulpit (whose sounding board is set behind the altar). During the rebuilding several large fragments of a decorated stone cross of c. 1000 were found, and they are now reassembled inside the church. Pretty interlace decoration.

TOLLER FRATRUM (E) Sits isolated on a little promontory in a river valley, and the

Toller Fratrum church

road up to it goes no further. The 'village' consists of a few cottages. One 17th century range is thatched and partly built of clunch (hard chalk). The Fratrum or 'brothers' were the Knights of St John of Jerusalem, who owned the manor in medieval times. Little Toller Farm was built in the 1540's, and although parts have been altered, the decorative chimneys with a freestanding figure of a monkey holding a mirror and all the round-headed windows are original. The outbuildings are also fine: the thatched stable block to the east is superb, and there is a large barn with a granary on staddle stones in front. The entrance to the church is off the farm courtyard. Dedicated to St Basil, the small church was virtually re-built in the 19th century. It has the oddest font, covered

Martyr's tree and shelter, Tolpuddle

with simple figures and a two-bodied monster. This is 12th century, as is the fragment which shows Mary Magdalene washing the feet of Christ.
★★ *Church, farm.*

TOLLER PORCORUM (E) (the toller of the pigs) is a small village set in a valley, split in half by the track of the disused Bridport-Maiden Newton railway. A mixture of buildings including thatched cottages. The church of St Peter stands on a hillock, and is a typical village church with walls of the medieval period, but windows altered or restored in the 19th century. The south aisle was added in about 1830 and has large windows with clear glass, low sills and odd tracery. The font is double – a small 15th century one sits on a large Norman one looking rather like a capital, with ram's heads at the corners. Small 1990 village tapestry. Nice plain 14th century tower.
★★ *Village, setting.*

TOLLER WHELME (D) Tiny, lots of trees and hedges. Only a few farms, the mostly 17th century manor house, and the little church of St John, a new church of 1870.

TOLPUDDLE (F) is famous for its Martyrs, six farm labourers who were transported to Australia in 1834 for trying to set up a tiny agricultural trades union. Trades Unions were not then illegal, so they were prosecuted for having administered an illegal oath. Five of them were Methodists, and experience in preaching doubtless helped George Loveless to compose his defence in words

which thunder across the years 'My lord, if we have violated any law, it was not done intentionally, we have injured no man's reputation, character, person or property; we were uniting together to preserve ourselves, our wives and children from utter degradation and starvation'. After a public outcry at the persecution of the men, they were pardoned and returned to England in three or four years. Five of them emigrated to Canada. In late July every year a Trades Union rally is held here.

The village (which has far too much traffic) centres around a small green on which is a very old and ill-looking sycamore under which the Martyrs used to meet, and a thatched shelter erected by Sir Ernest Debenham (see Briantspuddle) as part of the centenary celebrations in 1934. Happily a young sycamore was planted in 1984, to replace the old one when surgery can do no more. Below the green the River Piddle, bridge and meadows are serene despite the traffic. There are good brick or cob houses and cottages, many of them thatched, all through the village, and at the east end a plain Methodist chapel post-dating the Martyrs, but with an arch of 1912 commemorating them. On the west side of the village are the TUC Memorial cottages, built in 1934 with a small museum devoted to the Martyrs and the history of Trade Unions. The church of St John Evangelist is of most dates from the 12th century. The main doorway is of that date, the tower up to corbels and the north transept are 13th century, the porch and north aisle 14th century, and the tower was heightened in the 15th century. The chancel looks mostly 1855, when the 14th century original was remodelled. Leafy corbels and elaborate tiles. The sturdy roof in the nave is 14th century, a rare survival, and in the north transept is a Purbeck marble monument to a 12th century priest called Phillip, with inscription. In the graveyard, to the north-west of the tower is the gravestone of the only Martyr who returned to live in Tolpuddle – James Hammett who died in 1891. The rather dull gravestone was lettered by Eric Gill and put up in 1934.

★★ *Village and associations.*

TRENT (A) A village whose golden orange stone buildings, several of them late medieval, somehow fail to coalesce into the picturesque, despite many trees and a rural setting. Scattered around the church are superb stone buildings of the 15th-17th centuries, with no modern development obtruding. Perhaps the best is on the north-east side of the churchyard, probably a priest's house of *c.* 1500, tall with some original cusped windows. To the south-

ABOVE *Notice in porch, Trent church*   BELOW *Priest's House, Trent*

west is Church Farm of the 15th-17th centuries, with on the churchyard side a heavy 17th century classical window and a re-set 15th century one. From the north of the churchyard are glimpses of the manor house where Charles II was concealed for nearly 3 weeks after escaping from the Battle of Worcester. He was disguised as a servant, and once attended church to disarm suspicion. On the road south is yet another 16th century house with an elaborate window in the gable wall and a nice 17th century front. At the road junction are almshouses built in 1846 in Tudor style. The village is rather denser towards the west, with more 16th and 17th

century stone farmhouses and cottages, some of them dated and some thatched, but there is no real village street.

Externally the church of St Andrew is very pretty, with a little 14th century octagonal stone spire, rebuilt in 1925. On top is a copper weathercock dated 1698. The porch is 14th century, but the rest is 15th, with a lovely frieze on the top of the walls. Inside the porch is a good wooden roof support, a medieval door to the church and a 17th century one to the tower. An early 19th century painted notice states: 'All persons are requested to take off, Pattens and Clogs before entering the Church'. Inside it is the fittings which

Jacobean bench end, Trent

dominate – lovely chunky benches some Jacobean, some 1840's when the church was heavily restored. Of the same date are the set of stained glass windows, the odd ceilings and the placing here of the heavy Dutch pulpit of *c.* 1600 and the patchwork of Continental glass in the east window. All this, and the almshouses, the work of the Rev W. H. Turner, whose effigy is in the north chapel. The 15th century wooden screen in front of the chancel must be the best in Dorset, with its superlative fan vaulting and tracery below. The eastern side (or back) was made classical in the 17th century. A little staircase still leads to the top of the screen. The north chapel has a heavy looking mid-17th century screen, but far more prominent is the memorial to Ann Gerard (d. 1633) which, unusually, uses the arch as part of the monument, with her family tree painted along it. Very stylish angels hold up her achievement of arms. The monument was restored and repainted in 1792. In the 1620's Ann Gerard's husband wrote the first book on Dorset. Inside the north chapel (largely rebuilt in the 1860's) are two fine stone effigies, one a knight in armour and the other in civil costume. Under the tower is a 19th century font with a fine lacy wooden font cover of the 15th century – usually it is the medieval font which survives, not the cover.

★★★ *Village, church.*

TUCKTON (G, west of Christchurch) has grown up around the lowest bridging point of the River Stour, but perhaps inevitably the original village has pretty well disappeared under the expansion of Bournemouth. The water works, built in 1875, have an unlikely literary association. Russian exiles, including a friend of the novelist Tolstoy, took them over as a printing works in 1897, and until 1908 printed (in Russian) the works of Tolstoy which were forbidden in Russia. They called themselves the Free Age Press, as a plaque on the building records.

TURNERS PUDDLE (F) is a tiny hamlet whose small disused church (rebuilt after a storm 'unroofed' it in 1758) and overgrown graveyard sit on a hillock beside water meadows and a ford over the River Piddle. Good walk to Throop and on to Briantspuddle.

TURNWORTH (F) Deeply rural in a wooded valley, and although most of the buildings are 19th century, an attractive hamlet. Turnworth House (now demolished) was the model for Hintock House in *The Woodlanders*, and the church at Turnworth is also associated with Hardy. The church of St Mary has a tower of *c.* 1500, but the rest was rebuilt in 1869, and the assistant to the architect was Thomas Hardy. He may have designed the large low capitals to the pillars, with lizards and birds in amongst the foliage, in French Gothic style of the 14th century, and the good large heads of prophets on the corbels opposite. The font, reredos and pulpit are of 1869 and the greatest elaboration. Hardy was great friends with Thomas Perkins the vicar of Turnworth 1893-1907, and sometimes, after cycling the 17 miles from Dorchester with his wife, read the lesson here.

Tyneham in the late 19th century

Wide views from the top of the hill to the north of the village, with a car park and Okeford Hill picnic site to admire it from. A footpath leads from the car park to **Ringmoor,** 134 acres of downland and woods owned by the National Trust. In the middle is a Roman or Iron Age settlement with its fields and trackways preserved as shallow hollows and bumps in the turf. A super area for walks.

★★ *Hardy connection and general area.*

TYNEHAM (j) The deserted Purbeck village at the centre of the 7,500 acres used by the Army as a firing range. The village was evacuated in 1943, and no-one has lived there since, but the valley is open when the firing range is not in use (usually week-ends and holidays). The villagers left a touching note on the church door asking the Army to take care of their village, its homes and church which they thought they had given up only for the duration of the war. They were never able to come back, and the village is now ruined. A detailed account of the life and people of the Tyneham valley was written by one of the exiles, Lilian Bond – her *Tyneham, A Lost Heritage* is a fascinating book. The valley is lovely, with the limestone ridge to the south and another of chalk to the north, but it is now only used for rough grazing and the land, as well as the buildings, seems derelict and forlorn. The large boards with numbers on along the hillside are part of the firing range. Car park beside the village, with its stark walls of the ruined cottages. The church (which is basically 19th century with a 13th century north transept) is used for a good display on the geology, archaeology and history of the area, with lots of photographs of the village before it was deserted. In the little school of 1860 is a display on the wildlife of the ranges, much of which has benefited from the lack of modern intensive agriculture.

Worbarrow Bay before the Army

Half a mile walk from the car park leads to the beautiful **Worbarrow Bay,** a fine shingle beach curving round. Short colourful cliffs of Wealden Bed sands and clays, with beyond, huge chalk cliffs. At the top of the first chalk cliff the ramparts and ditches of Flower's Barrow, an Iron Age hill fort, can be seen. Portland lies across the horizon. The little bay to the east is still protected by large concrete blocks, put there during the war to prevent tank attacks. On either side of the small bay the Portland and Purbeck beds (stone and clays) tilt, and on one side form the knoll of Worbarrow Tout. From the top of the Tout (once used by coastguards and fishermen as a look-out) are good views back to St Aldhelm's Head, Kimmeridge and so on. Until 1911 there was a Coastguard station on the bay, and until the army took over there were several fishermen's cottages.

To the north of the Tyneham valley are Povington and Whiteway hills, with a car park and superb views north over the heathland and south to the coast. When the army ranges are open a footpath leads west along the top of the hill to Flower's Barrow, actually a hill-fort not a barrow. Clifftops are an unusual position for hillforts; its southern side has fallen into the sea and erosion continues. There are two banks and ditches, with a distinct change of direction in the outer at the east end, suggesting an extension. The fort is further protected on the east, the only side without a steep slope, by a cross-ridge dyke. The path continues down to Arish Mell (no access to the sea) and steeply back up again to Bindon Hill and so on to West Lulworth.

★★★ *Landscape, bay, rural history.*

UP CERNE (E) is a tiny hamlet in a lovely setting of chalk hills and park land, with lots of trees. 17th century manor house and mostly 1870 church. Superb walking country.

★★★ *Landscape*

UPTON (F) has developed as a suburb to Poole: the few Victorian houses were swamped by development this century.

Upton House and Country Park. The park is slightly municipal, but has a heather garden, lots of azaleas and camellias, a good herbaceous border and so on. The wilder parts run down to the mudflats of Poole Harbour with Poole itself away in the background, and a hide to watch the birds on the marshes and mud-flats. The Countryside Heritage Centre in the stables has displays on Poole Harbour, the geology, archaeology and natural history of the area, etc., and a cafe. A small Romano–British Farm is being reconstructed in the grounds. Upton House (early 19th century) is pretty inside, with lots of plaster friezes, elaborate door surrounds and so on. The hall is charming, with a galleried circular central opening, with a lantern over it, all highly decorated. Pretty colonnades to the side wings and intricate 'Gothic' glazing to the lower windows.

★★ *Good place for an afternoon out with children.*

UPLODERS (D) is not really a separate parish, but part of Loders (see entry). However it feels separate, and has a superb selection of stone buildings, mostly of the 18th and 19th centuries. The best of all is Upton Manor Farm at the eastern end of the village: a huge quadrangle of farm buildings and house, all of stone with thatched or pantile roofs. A plain Wesleyan chapel with some classical detail is dated 1827.

★★ *Village*

UPWEY (H) Many good cottages, and a charming setting in a little wooded valley with high bare downs above. The spring known as the **Wishing Well (fee: lists)** has been visited since tourists started coming to Weymouth in the later 18th century. A sizeable stream emerges from the ground in two springs because the permeable Portland sand and stone meet the impermeable Kimmeridge Clay. The springs are over-shadowed by trees, and have a small water-garden. Upwey Mill is a large Portland Stone building dated 1802, Hardy knew the family who lived here, and it is probably the mill he described in *The Trumpet Major,* where Bob Loveday escapes the press gang by going up through the mill on the sack hoist. In front of it, on the road is the early 19th century mill house. All along the road are pleasant stone cottages and houses dating from the 17th to the early 18th centuries. The little school by the Wishing Well was built in 1840, and a matching school-house is further along the road to the church. Opposite the well is a small early 19th century stone granary, and a late 17th century cottage with characteristic mouldings round the windows. The church of St Lawrence is pretty. The north aisle, the windows on that side and the porch are late 15th century, and were neatly matched on the other side when the south aisle was built in 1838. Heavy but attractive 1841 roof. Nice woodwork – medieval porch door, 17th century pulpit and panelling at the east end of the north aisle. The three wooden panels with carved figures hanging on the walls are figures of saints, probably 17th century and from another pulpit. 15th century font and several good 18th and 19th century monuments. Wall-paintings of texts and flowers.

★★ *Village, setting, well.*

VERWOOD (C) Like Alderholt, is mostly heathland, and until recently only had scattered small farms and cottages. The local smallholders earned their living partly by farming and partly by making brooms and earthenware pottery. The bowls, jugs and pancheons made here were originally cheap and commonplace, but are now collectors items. The heathy ground has always been too poor for good farming. The village is even less attractive than Alderholt with the few late Victorian or Edwardian buildings swamped by recent development, which includes huge estates and acres of bungalows. The church of St Michael and All Angels was built in the 1870's, but has been recently enlarged by the addition of aisles and a porch which totally encase the old nave. The new work is plain and attractive. Elaborate late 19th century font and cover, and alabaster and wrought iron screen to the chancel.

Dorset Heavy Horse Centre is a modern stable block where the large breeds of working horses can be seen, at close quarters. Very impressive. Carts and other farm implements are on display in a cart shed, and there is a pets corner with ornamental birds and so forth (fee: lists). 1½ miles north west of Verwood, well signposted. ★★★

HOLT HEATH, *see* **WHITE SHEET HILL**

WADDON (H) A superb house of *c.* 1700 (not open), tucked under the ridge just east of Portesham. From the road the tall classical Portland stone main house with attached outbuildings can be seen. The barn is dated 1702.

WALDITCH (D) just outside Bridport, has some good stone cottages, some still with hood moulds round the windows, alongside quite a lot of modern development and some rather overpowering Victorian buildings. The little church of St Mary was totally rebuilt in 1863. Just along the road to the west at The Hyde is a huge chapel-like building, actually built in the later 19th century as an (indoors) Royal tennis court, soon to be restored. It belonged to the large 1853 mock-Tudor house next door to it, which has large stone gate pillars, nice park and avenue. ★ *Village.*

WAREHAM (i) A small riverside town, with much to interest the visitor, lying between the rivers Piddle and Frome, with surviving earthen defences around three sides dating from the time of King Alfred (later 9th century). Captured by the Vikings in 876, who overwintered here. The town seems to have developed inside the defences from the 10th century. Until the 14th century Wareham was a port, but

ABOVE *The Wishing Well, Upwey*
BELOW *Waddon Manor*

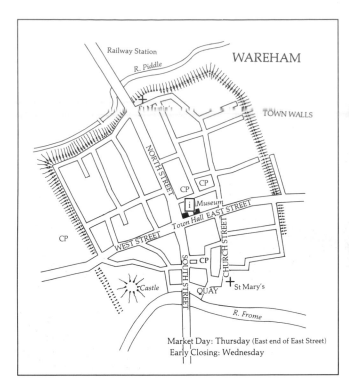

Wareham: (top) St Martin's, *and (bottom)* the Frome and Wareham from Redcliffe Farm

the increasing size of ships and the silting of the river led to the use of Poole at the expense of Wareham. Most recent development is over the river valley to the north, so that the town is still bounded on the east, north and partly on the west by the Saxon banks, which were refurbished in the Norman period, and heightened on the west during the Second World War. It is possible to walk around the town on these grassy banks (called the Town Walls) which give good views, especially on the north.

Many later 18th and early 19th century houses line all the main streets, dating from after a bad fire in 1762, and two thatched cottages survive in the town. East Street has fine almshouses of 1741, with an interesting little bell cote. Opposite is Wareham Town Museum (lists), a large room containing local and natural history exhibits. Further east the street is mostly residential, with a small market at the end. The horrid town hall in the centre is of 1870, by Crickmay, and particularly unfortunately it faces The Red Lion and other fine 18th century buildings. West Street has many good houses and the Rex, a gas-lit early cinema, and South Street has the elegant three storey stone manor house, with opposite, set back from the street, the rather odd facade of the Unitarian Chapel of 1830, now the Conservative Club. Further down is the Black Bear Hotel with superb 3-storey bow windows, and a huge bear. Trinity church's 16th century tower can be seen below — the church is now used as a picture gallery.

Right on the river is the **Quay**, a pleasant 2-sided square where the river can be admired, boats hired, or boat trips taken. Immediately to the east is Church Green, and south of the church is The Priory (now an hotel) a 16th and 17th century building with later alterations on the site of the medieval priory.

St Mary's church (lists) preserved until the 1840's a large late Saxon nave, which was then demolished to make way for a very plain new one. It would be difficult to forgive the new nave even if it was charming, and it is not. The chancel is basically 14th century with a fine east window and two 13th century Purbeck Marble effigies of knights. To the south is the little medieval chapel of St Edward (martyred at Corfe in 978 – his body was here for a year), with 13th century vaulting and window, Norman doorway. Plaque to the Rev. John Hutchins, the county historian who was Wareham's rector from 1744 and died in 1773. He was away when the great fire of Wareham (1762) broke out and but for 'the care and presence of mind of Mrs Hutchins, who preserved his MS not without hazard to herself' his great history would have been lost. In the north-east corner of the nave, some loose, and some set in the wall, are rather insig-nificant looking scratched carvings, memorials, in Latin and a strange script dating from between the late 7th and early 9th centuries, a tenuous link with the Celtic population of Dorset, as their form is purely Celtic. The superb lead font is 12th

Wareham: (top) the Quay, and (bottom) East Street

century, and probably shows the Apostles. The fine tower is 15th century, on top of which is a weather vane of a salmon (still caught in the river).

In the middle of North Walls, in North Street is **St Martin's** church, ★★★ the only Saxon church in Dorset surviving in anything like its original state. Well worth visiting, both for the building of 1030 and the superb full length marble effigy of T.E. Lawrence (died 1935) in Arab dress, by Eric Kennington (see Moreton). The entrance is through the 16th century tower (top rebuilt in 1712, as a datestone records). The interior is difficult to define. The building has been adapted and enlarged but the nave with its cutabout chancel arch, a tiny window in the north side of the chancel and very clear 'long and short' work on the corners outside are all of c. 1030. The north aisle was added in the 12th century, but alterations have left it with a variety of supports ranging from a 12th century capital with stiff-leaf to an 18th century fluted pillar. The church is full of fragments of wall-paintings *(cont p. 171)*

167

Thomas Hardy

Thomas Hardy, the novelist and poet, was born in the hamlet of Upper Bockhampton, 3 miles east of Dorchester in 1840. His father was a small builder, and his mother had been a general servant and cook. Thomas was their first child. He went to school at Bockhampton, and then Dorchester, and was articled to John Hicks, a Dorchester architect, in 1856. From 1862 he worked in a London architect's office, and when, due to ill-health, he returned to Hick's in Dorchester in 1867 he started to write fiction. His first novel (which he later destroyed) *The Poor Man and the Lady* (1868) was rejected, but *Desperate Remedies* set at Kingston Maurward, was published in 1871, and *Under the Greenwood Tree* (Stinsford and Bockhampton) in 1872.

Hardy was commissioned to produce *A Pair of Blue Eyes* (1873) as a serial for a magazine, and this gave him enough money and confidence to give up architecture for full-time authorship. With the commissioning of *Far from the Madding Crowd* (1874) (set at Puddletown) for another magazine he felt he had a large enough income to marry Emma Gifford, whom he had met four years earlier while working on the restoration of the church at St Juliot, Cornwall.

The Hardys lived for short periods in South London, Swanage and elsewhere while Hardy wrote *The Return of the Native* (1878), *The Trumpet Major* (1881) and three other novels. In 1883 they moved back to Dorchester, where Hardy (now a successful novelist) designed and built Max Gate, the house on the outskirts of the town where he lived from 1885 until his death in 1928. In 1886 *The Mayor of Casterbridge* was published, set in the Dorchester of the 1850's, the period when he was at

ABOVE *Thomas Hardy at 16*
BELOW *Hardy's birthplace, Upper Bockhampton*

ABOVE *Max Gate.* BELOW RIGHT *Hardy in his study at Max Gate. Study now in Dorset County Museum*

school and starting work there. *The Woodlanders* (1887) is set in central Dorset, and *The Well-Beloved* (1897) on Portland. With the publication of *Tess of the D'Urbevilles* (1891) and *Jude the Obscure* (1895) Hardy became even more famous. These two controversial novels, regarded by some at the time as obscene and immoral, were Hardy's last fiction apart from a couple of short stories. He had been writing poetry since his late teens, although his first volume of poetry was not published until 1898. Six more volumes followed. His wife Emma died in 1912, and in 1914 he married Florence Dugdale. Hardy died in 1928, Florence ten years later.

When Hardy started writing about the Dorset countryside in the 1870's it was a little known county, attracting visitors only to its seaside resorts. Even in the 1880's Hardy and his friend Henry Moule, a watercolourist, decided there was not enough interest in the county for them to produce a book on it. From the 1890's Hardy's novels made the Dorset countryside famous. He claimed that his 'Wessex' was not confined to Dorset, but the bulk of his prose and poetry is set within the county. Some novels and poems record the Dorset of his childhood or even earlier, drawing on his parent's and grandparents memories, while others were contemporary. His powerful, realistic descriptions of the landscapes drew, and still draw, visitors to the country,

and innumerable guidebooks to his Wessex have been published since 1900. The small town of Beaminster, and some Dorset villages like Melbury Osmund, where his parents were married and which he used in *The Woodlanders*, still seem unchanged. Max Gate and the Upper Bockhampton cottage are both open to the public.

Thomas Hardy's Dorset Names

AREAS

Valley of the Great Dairies: the Frome Valley

Vale of Little Dairies: Blackmore Vale

PLACES

Abbot's Beach, Abbotsea: Abbotsbury

Abbot's Cernel: Cerne Abbas

Anglebury: Wareham

Athelhall: Athelhampton

Broad Sidlinch: Sydling St Nicholas

Budmouth Regis: Weymouth and Melcombe Regis

Casterbridge: Dorchester

Chaldon: Chaldon Herring

Chalk Newton: Maiden Newton

Chaseborough: Cranborne

Corvsgate: Corfe Castle

Creston: Preston

Dead Man's Bay: West Bay

Durnover: Fordington

East Egdon: Affpuddle

East Quarriers: Easton

Eggar: Eggardon

Emminster: Beaminster

Estminster: Yetminster

Evershead: Evershot

Flintcomb-Ash: perhaps Plush or Dole's Ash, Milton Abbas

Froom-Everard: West Stafford

Greenhill: Woodbury Hill

Haggardon Hill: Eggardon Hill

Havenpool: Poole

Hintock House: Turnworth House (demolished)

Kingsbere: Bere Regis

Kingscreech: Steeple

King's Hintock: Melbury Osmund or Minterne Magna

King's Hintock Park: Melbury Park

Knapwater House: Kingston Maurward

Knollsea: Swanage

Leddington: Gillingham

Little Hintock: amalgam of Hermitage, Melbury Osmund and others

Lower Longpuddle: Piddlehinton and Puddletown

Lower Mellstock: Lower Bockhampton

Lulstead or Lulwind Cove: Lulworth Cove

Mai Dun: Maiden Castle

Marshwood: Middlemarsh

Martlott: Marnhull

Melstock: Stinsford

Middleton Abbey: Milton Abbas

Millpond St Jude: Milborne St Andrew

Nether Moynton: Owermoigne

Newland Buckton: Buckland Newton

Nuttlebury: Hazelbury Bryan

Oakford Fitzpiers: Okeford Fitzpaine

Overcombe: Sutton Poyntz

Oxwell Hall: Poxwell Manor

Pebble Beach: Chesil Beach

Port Bredy: Bridport

Po'sham: Portisham

Pummery: Poundbury

Ringsworth Shore: Ringstead Bay

Sandbourne: Bournemouth

Shaston: Shaftesbury

Sherton Abbas: Sherborne

Shottsford Forum: Blandford Forum

Springham: Warmwell

Stancy Castle: perhaps Corfe Castle

Stapleford Park: Stalbridge Park

Stourcastle: Sturminster Newton

Street of Wells: Fortuneswell

Sylvania Castle: Pennsylvania Castle

Tolchurch: Tolpuddle

Traunton: Tarrant Hinton

Trantridge: Pentridge

Upper Longpuddle: Piddletrenthide

Warborne: Wimborne Minster

Weatherbury: Puddletown

Welland House: Charborough House

Wellbridge: Wool

Wyndway House: Upton House, position only

Yalbury Wood: Yellowham Wood

Greenhill (Woodbury Hill), scene of the fair in Far from the Madding Crowd

— 12th century figured ones in the chancel, outlining in imitation of stone coursing in several places of the 13th century, black letter inscriptions of the 16th or 17th centuries and even a florid memorial inscription of about 1800.

In the south west quarter of the town is a large mound with a Victorian house on it. This was the castle, but no medieval buildings survive. It was probably built soon after the Norman conquest, but was overtaken in importance by Corfe.

Stoborough is almost a rural extension of Wareham, just across the river valley. The road crosses this on a causeway.

WARMWELL (H) has early 19th century farm buildings in the middle, including a brick granary raised on arches (now a shop). A main road dashes through the village, and there are hardly any pavements. The church of Holy Trinity has a little plain 17th century tower (with a sundial on the north side dated 1646), medieval nave, and a huge chancel of 1881 paid for by the Rev E. Pickard-Cambridge, and built by him with the assistance of his gardener Charles Bushrod and two parish masons, all in a rather anaemic Early English style. In the graveyard are the gravestones of 24 Air Force men of the Second World War, here because they were killed while stationed at Warmwell Airfield. The manor house, which is just visible from the main road beyond the village, was the home of the eccentric 17th century prophet John Sadier, who predicted the Fire of London and the Monmouth Rebellion.

★ *Village.*

WEST BAY (D) An odd place, difficult to define. A village-sized seaside resort, in a fine situation with a miscellaneous collection of buildings and a proper harbour. To the east is a vertical sandstone cliff, while on the other side the slippery Fuller's Earth is actively eroding. Beyond is Golden Cap. The views along the shore are beautiful. Until 1884 this was Bridport Harbour, a small port improved by the construction in the 1770's of the harbour with its moles sticking out into the sea. The river is held back by sluices under the road bridge to scour the harbour at low tide. To the west great lumps of Portland Stone protect it, and inside the harbour are huge double T shaped concrete blocks for the same purpose. A few buildings survive from this commercial port, probably including the thatched cottages on the east,

ABOVE *The Harbour, West Bay*

BELOW *West Bay in the 1890's*

with the shingle beach right at their doors. In 1884 the railway was extended to what was then re-named West Bay (station now being restored). Attempts were made to turn it into a resort, but West Bay is still small. Little paddle-boats on the river, and fishing trips from the harbour. The largest building is the terrace in the centre with its three different pitches of roof, designed in 1885 by the Arts and Crafts architect E. S. Prior (see Bothenhampton). He also designed the Georgian-looking house to the north of the church with the little look-out on top. The church of St John was built in 1930, and is plain and white inside and out.

Just over the sluices is **The Harbour Museum**, with displays on West Bay, and the rope and net making industry (fee: lists).

WEST BEXINGTON (H, west of Abbotsbury) has a farm at the centre, with a little modern development and 1930s bungalows leading down to the sea. Attempts were made in the 1930s to develop it as a resort, and chalets,

Looking east from above Durdle Door in winter

bungalows and the car park date from this period. Good area for birds, with a Dorset Trust for Nature Conservation reserve including reed bed, wet meadows and scrub. On the shingle bank are plants which enjoy that strange situation, like horned poppy and a sort of cabbage. No cliffs but the land slopes steadily upwards with lots of scrub which is good for birds.

WEST CHALDON (H) is only a farm and a few cottages, but the narrow roads to it have fine views.

WEST CHELBOROUGH, *see* **CHELBOROUGH**

WEST COMPTON (E) Remote, with good scenery. Tiny stone village with a little redundant Victorian church.

WEST KNIGHTON, (H) Hidden by woodland close to the heath east of Dorchester. Several good cottages, especially a group opposite the school (now converted to a house). The medieval church of St Peter is a handsome small-scale example of a church which has grown slowly over the centuries. A sensi- tive restoration in 1893-4 was overseen by

Thomas Hardy, by then famous and writing *Jude the Obscure*. His brother Henry was the building contractor. Opposite the church is West Knighton Farm, dating from the late 17th century, but altered later.
★ *Village*

WEST LULWORTH (J) A popular spot for visitors who come to see the cove, and in the summer it can be overcrowded. Quite a few cafes and so on, but it is beautiful all the year round, and perhaps best seen in the winter. Wonderful walking country, and good grassland and flowers. The cliffs are dangerous and can slip at any time. The road down to the village and the cove is between two great chalk ridges – Bindon Hill on the east and Hambury Tout on the west. The main village, a mile back from the sea, is mixed stone and thatched cottages and Victorian villas, built to accommodate visitors. The church of Holy Trinity is in this part, slightly isolated, having been built on a new site in 1870 to the designs of John Hicks, the Dorchester architect. The only feature preserved from the earlier church is the east window in the north chapel which has a disjointed inscription 'Robiertus Lulleworthi'. The rest is characteristic of the 1870's, with finely

carved capitals by the Dorchester carver Grassby.

Large car park (fee) just back from the cove. Close by is **The Lulworth Heritage Centre** (fee: lists). Smallish exhibition, good on oil exploration in Dorset. Also smuggling, local history etc. The street leading down to the sea has some good cottages, the best of which are on either side of the spring – one with arched Gothic windows and the other more conventional. Both are thatched. Just below is a good duck pond, and the stream then sets off for its short journey to the sea. An effusive Guide of 1864 described Lulworth as 'one of the most perfect and romantic little coves . . . the high towering cliffs and hill rise behind . . . east and west the coast presents a rapid succession of the capricious forms of deep inlets, sharp promentories, insulated rocks, deep inverns, stormy heights and sheltered nooks; and landwards of swelling downs, verdant-glades, and luxuriant plantations'. With the alteration or excision of a few Victorian adjectives this serves as a description today. The geology dramatically dominates the landscape. The Purbeck beds, mostly limestone, guard either side of the entrance to the bay, but a small gap has let the sea in to erode the softer Wealden beds and formed the cove. The chalk behind has started to erode and forms a 300 ft irregular cliff at the back of the cove. The coastal path goes up over this hill, and gives a fine almost aerial view of the cove from the top. Rowing boats can be hired in the summer, and there are lobster pots and other fishing tackle on the shore. The water in the cove is very cold, partly because freshwater springs enter the sea here.

Immediately to the west of the Cove is Stair Hole, where the sea has broken through the almost vertical Portland stone, cutting small arches underneath, smaller

versions of Durdle Door. The sea is eroding the Wealden beds, just as it has done at the cove, and eventually the two will join. The Purbeck Beds stand as an almost vertical cliff on the east side, showing a cross-section of the 'Lulworth Crumple' – a great bend in the rocks. About 15 million years ago they were subjected to such forces that they folded over.

A well-worn path leads west from Lulworth over Hambury Tout to Man-of-War Cove and the famous Durdle Door, a great natural arch of limestone through which the sea passes.

Lulworth is just to the west of the Army Ranges, and makes a good starting point for walks within them (when open). Notice boards show large-scale maps of the area, and all the footpaths are well signposted. Just to the east of the Cove (and inside the Ranges) is the so called Fossil Forest, a ledge in the Purbeck limestone sea-cliff with fossilised remains. The strangely lobster-pot shaped fossils are the lumps of algae which accumulated around the bottom of trees some 135 million years ago. The trees are only represented by the hole down the middle, but a specimen from here on display in the Dorset County Museum has fossilised wood surviving.

★★★★ *For the Cove, and for a really good walking area.*

WEST MILTON (D) Lots of houses and cottages in the local yellowy stone, sitting on one side of a tiny valley. The church of 1873 has been demolished, but the late 15th century tower of its predecessor still stands, looking very odd and truncated. Good view of Eggardon (see entry) hillfort from the top of the graveyard and a nice stone farmhouse next door. Very attractive countryside around the village.

★★ *Landscape.*

WEST MOORS (G) is one of the east Dorset villages which have expanded enormously recently. It was originally heathland, and there are still lots of trees and rhododendrons. Two small late Victorian churches, one stone, one timber.

West Moors Country Park and Forest, Ashley Heath (north of West Moors, west of Ashley Heath). Coniferous forest with many marked trails. The Play Trail with Loggosaurus and many other adventure structures is superb, and the Treetop Trail is just that. Lakes and meadows too, and a superbly detailed Moors Valley miniature railway (fee: lists). Visitor centre.

★★★ *Adventure playground, especially for children.*

WESTON, see PORTLAND

WEST ORCHARD (B) has a few stone and brick farms, and a church mostly of 1876. Inside it is all smooth white ashlar with rather odd lean-to transepts. Typical Blackmore Vale landscape-grass and cows.

WEST PARLEY (G) Now sprawls, with modern development stretching north to join up with Ferndown. The old church of All Saints is right down to the south, by the River Stour, away from the modern part. Occupation is more sparse here, with some nice 18th century brick houses. The church is a mixture of dates with an unusual survival – a wooden porch of *c.* 1500. The nave is the earliest part, 12th century, with the doorway of that date but all the windows 18th century. The lower part of the font is 12th century too. The seating in the nave is 1841, with some of the pews still labelled FREE. Fine 17th century double-decker pulpit, with a sounding board and brass candlesticks added in the 18th century. 16th century roof, with some of the original decorative roof bosses are displayed in a case. The chancel is 1890. Reset externally in a niche in the east wall is an earthenware cooking pot of the 14th or 15th century, which was dug up during the 1896 restoration, and is believed to have contained the heart of the 'Lady of Lydlinch'. By romantic legend she was a West Parley girl who married and had to live at Lydlinch, north Dorset, but instructed that her heart should be buried in West Parley as it had been there all her life. Nice little 18th century wooden bellcote.

★★ *Church*

WEST STAFFORD (E) A small village in the Frome valley with many thatched cottages: even the bus shelter (cont p.176)

Other Dorset Writers

The Dorset poet, William Barnes, was born near Sturminster Newton in 1801, the son of a small yeoman farmer. He lived near Pentridge, and went to school in Sturminster Newton, the closest town. From 1835-62 he ran a school in Dorchester, and became quite famous with the publication of *Poems of Rural Life in the Dorset Dialect* in 1844. From 1862 until his death in 1886 he was rector of Winterborne Came, a scattered hamlet on the outskirts of Dorchester (see also Whitcombe). He married in 1827, and had five children. He wrote poems in both dialect and standard English, most of which are rural, idyllic, and nostalgic, with strong simple emotions, harking back to the contented times of his youth in the Blackmore Vale with its 'elems woaks' and the slow Stour river. His most famous poem is probably 'Linden Lea':

'Ithin the woodlands, flow'ry-gleäded,
  By the woak tree's mossy moot,
The sheenen grass-bleädes, timber-sheäded,
  Now do quiver under voot;
An' birds do whissle over head,
An' water's bubblen in its bed,
An' there vor me the apple tree
Do leän down low in Linden Lea.'

Although Barnes was a generation older than Hardy, they were friends, and Hardy admired Barnes' verse, which is still read with pleasure today, while his prose, much of it academic study of language, is forgotten.

Henry Fielding's house at East Stour, engraved by Barnes

The literary persona of the county is dominated by Hardy, but many other writers have lived here, or visited, and some have used the county as the setting for their works.

Henry Fielding (1707-54) grew up at East Stour, North Dorset, and although his works do not contain specific descriptions of places, much of *Tom Jones* (1749), for example, is set in Dorset, and contains characters known to have been based on people he knew in Dorset. William Wordsworth (1770-1850) lived at Racedown in west Dorset from 1795-7, and many other poets, such as Keats, visited the county. Rupert Brooke (1887-1915) spent several holidays at Lulworth, and wrote his famous 'If I should die, think only this of me: / That there's some corner of a foreign field / That is for ever England' at Canford and Blandford Camp.

William Barnes (seated) with his family at Winterborne Came rectory

T. E. Lawrence's effigy by Eric Kennington (St Martin's Wareham)

T. E. Lawrence (of Arabia) (1888-1935) did not write about Dorset, but his last home, the little cottage at Cloud's Hill near the Army camp at Bovington is open to the public. He was buried at Moreton, and there is a fine effigy of him in Arab dress in St Martin's Church, Wareham.

T. F. Powys by Elizabeth Muntz (Dorset County Museum)

Boscombe, Bournemouth, has a posthumous connection with the poet Shelley (1792-1822). His son, Sir Percy Florence Shelley, lived at Boscombe Manor from 1851 until his death in 1889, and there is now a Shelley museum in part of the building. A monument to the poet, which should have gone to St Peter's, Bournemouth, where his heart is buried, is in the Priory church Christchurch.

There were several writers amongst those who visited or lived in Bournemouth from the 1800s. It was thought particularly suitable for those with TB, and Robert Louis Stevenson who lived there for a couple of years in the 1880's (whilst writing *Kidnapped)* and Aubrey Beardsley, in the 1890's both suffered from that disease.

The Shelley Memorial (Christchurch Priory)

The poet and novelist Sylvia Townsend Warner (1893-1978) lived at East Chaldon and Frome Vauchurch. East Chaldon is more closely associated with the Powys brothers. T.F. Powys (1875-1953) lived there for many years, and many of his allegorical novels like *Mr Weston's Good Wine* (1927), are set in the area around. Late in life, he moved to Mappowder, and was buried there. Llewelyn Powys (1884-1930) also lived at Chaldon for some time and his ashes are buried on the cliff top there. Llewelyn's *Dorset Essays* (1935) give brilliant word-pictures of several parts of Dorset. John Cowper Powys (1872-1963), the most famous of the brothers, set three of his early novels in Dorset – *Wolf Solent* (1929), *Weymouth Sands* (1934) and *Maiden Castle* (1936). He spent less time in Dorset than his brothers, but after his death his ashes were scattered off Chesil Beach.

A charming vignette of Lyme, which Jane Austen had visited in 1803 and 1804, is given in *Persuasion* (1819) and a much broader picture of the town in the 1860's is given in John Fowles *French Lieutenant's Woman* (1969). The best of the smuggling tales is John Meade Falkner's *Moonfleet* (1898) set in Fleet and Purbeck in the 18th century.

has a thatched roof, as does a huge 18th century barn with brick and timber walls now converted for commercial use. Rather stiff stone school of 1846. The church of St Andrew has a small 16th century tower: the nave seems to have every possible style of window, all dating from the 16th to 17th century. The nave is dated 1640 on the porch and elsewhere. Despite the later addition of a chancel the church is still dominated by 1640 fittings: the barrel-vaulted ceiling, the nice wooden screen and benches (restored) and probably the pulpit. Small areas of painted inscriptions of the same date at the west end of the nave. The fine quality candelabrum with six arms hanging in the nave, the sconces either side of the archway through the screen and the double candlestick on the side of the pulpit were all given by John Gould in 1713, and are inscribed to that effect. John Gould's large monument of 1727 is on the north wall, with a classical monument of 1674 opposite. In the chancel is a life-size marble effigy of 1898, and some strident Victorian and later stained glass. The gallery at the west end is 18th century.

★★★ *Because unusual date for church.*

WEST STOUR (B) is mixed limestone and later brick cottages in the middle of the Blackmore Vale. The limestone church of St Mary sits on a prominent little knoll. The tower and nave were rebuilt very plainly in 1840, but the chancel is 13th century, restored and with a new east window of the late 18th century, an unusual period and an odd window. The pulpit is 17th century, and on the 1840 west gallery is re-set 16th century decoration, probably from a screen. ★ *Church*

WEYMOUTH (H) A bustling town which attracts thousands of holiday-makers to its sandy beach. The settlement is in three parts – a working harbour, tucked in behind the town centre proper, a wide bay lined with fine late 18th and early 19th century terraces, and the resort.

Weymouth began as two separate medieval towns (both ports) which developed from the 12th century on either side of the mouth of the River Wey. Weymouth was on the far (south) side of the river, mostly alongside the harbour under a steep cliff. Melcombe Regis was the north part of the town, where the present shopping centre is. It seems to have been through Melcombe Regis that the Black Death came to England in 1348. In 1571 the two towns, which had competed for years, were united, and in 1597 the first bridge was built across the harbour between them. Despite Melcombe Regis having the larger area, the town took the name of Weymouth.

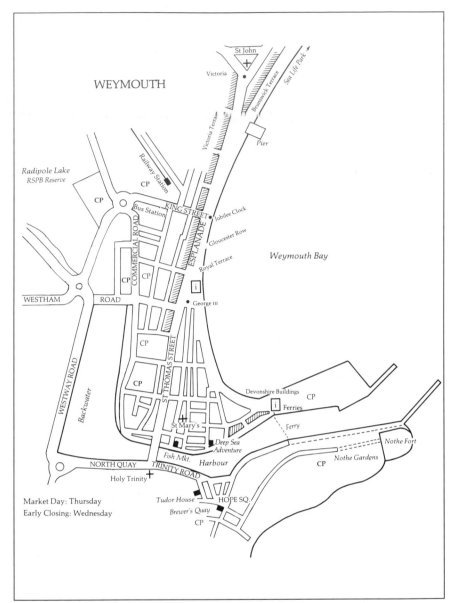

Market Day: Thursday
Early Closing: Wednesday

The decline of the port's trade was more than compensated from 1760 by its development as a resort where visitors could undertake the newly fashionable sea-bathing. A local doctor, Dr Crane, published a book in 1795 called *Cursory Observations on Sea-Bathing; the use of Sea-Water Internally* . . . (drinking a pint a day was thought to be beneficial) which extolled Weymouth: 'The Sea-Water of this fine Bay is quite pure, of a beautiful azure Colour, perfectly clear and transparent; the Sands under Foot are soft, yet firm: entirely clear and free from Sea-Weeds, Rocks, Slippery Stones or any Kind of Obstruction whatever. The Declivity is so gradual, as to be almost imperceptible; a great Security to the weak and fearful'. From 1789 until 1805 George III visited the town almost every year for long summer stays, making it fashion-

able. From 1780 until 1850 elegant terraces were built to house summer visitors, particularly along the Esplanade extending east along the bay, away from the medieval town. The 18th century visitors to Weymouth did not simply rush into the sea and swim, or even paddle along the edge, as we would today. Sea resorts were like inland spas: bathing and drinking the sea water was medicinal, not for entertainment. Dr Crane explained that 'staying too long in the water may sometimes occasion a temporary Depression of the Spirits and bring on a chillness or shivering'. Bathing machines were used – huts on wheels which were drawn by horses into deeper water where the bather was supervised by an attendant. Immersion was carefully timed, and female bathers voluminously clad. When George III bathed the loyal

Weymouth, with the Nothe Fort on the left

town employed a band to play 'God Save the King' from the bathing machine behind him.

Although the Royal family did not return after 1811, the town continued to flourish as a resort, and the arrival of the railway in 1857 was an added stimulus. The town today has hundreds of late 18th or early 19th century houses, mostly in terraces and fairly simple, but beautiful. They display bow or bay windows of every type, sometimes on the first storey only, sometimes through two or three storeys. Like many sea-side towns, Weymouth divides itself up into the seafront proper (the holiday part); the town centre; and a picturesque harbour. Although the three parts are immediately adjacent, they are very different.

The Harbour is always busy, with commercial fishing and crabbing vessels up by the bridge and pleasure craft of all sorts everywhere. The Trawler Race and Regatta held late May is a great attraction. The harbour has been extended out to the east, with ferries for the Channel Islands running from opposite the Nothe. The seasidey Pavilion is of 1955. Row-boat ferry across to the Nothe. The north side of the harbour, along from the ferries, is the more commercial with many warehouses. Towards the bridge is first the fine brick Custom House and later the Harbour Master's office in Portland Stone, both early 19th century. Unusual 1850s Fish Market, a heavy stone building, still selling fish.

Deep Sea Adventure (fee: lists). In a huge early 19th century brick warehouse right on the quay. The history of diving from the 17th century, illustrated by life-size reconstructions of early apparatus, and the real thing (including modern diving bells) for more recent times. Very interesting even for the non-diver, as all is well explained. Also displays on shipwrecks, some local like the *Avalanche* and the *Earl of Abergavenny*, others from further away. Good view of the harbour from the top floor. Big displays, well worth seeing. ★★★

The opposite (southern) side of the harbour is more domestic, lined with charming early 19th century houses. On the south side of the bridge Holy Trinity church, which looks quite small from the outside, is actually huge. Built in the 1830's (Wyke Regis was the parish church of Weymouth until then) and greatly extended in 1887 when the altar was moved to the south, an

The Esplanade, Weymouth

ABOVE *Devonshire Buildings* (top) *at the south end of the Esplanade and Brunswick Terrace at the northern end*

unusual position forced by the lack of land. Very high, with lots of 1887 woodwork and elaborate windows. To the west of the church quantities of good buildings were demolished to make way for new municipal offices in 1970. The best place to see what the pre-18th century buildings of Weymouth looked like is Trinity Street, leading off the harbour. Two late 16th century buildings survive, both of Portland stone, having mullioned windows and hood-moulds. The Old Rooms was used in the 18th century as an assembly rooms. Further along nos. 2 and 3 (Tudor House) were saved from demolition in the 1930's and restored after the war. Originally two cottages with one room on each of the three floors (fee: lists). The rooms are well-furnished, mostly with 17th century furniture, and worth seeing. just around the corner Hope Square is dominated by the Victorian buildings of Devenish's brewery (Brewer's Quay), now converted to shops, workshops and so on, and **Timewalk** (fee: lists), Weymouth's museum, with displays, temporary exhibitions and the Timewalk, a modern exposition of the history of Weymouth, with fourteen or so impressive set pieces with commentary, noises, smells, lights and so on: the Plague, Armada, Civil War, Georgian Weymouth, Smuggling etc. Very good. Some of the building's original brewing equipment is incorporated into displays. ★★★★ *Timewalk*.

The Devenish Shire Horse Stables (fee: lists) have large and small horses and Discovery has science for children (fee: lists).

The Nothe ★★★★ is the headland which protrudes from the south side of the harbour mouth. The town's guns had been stationed here since the 17th century, and

there was considerable fighting in this area during the Civil War. It continued as a gun emplacement all through the 18th and early 19th century and the present fort was built from 1860-72 as part of a series (known as Palmerston Follies after the Prime Minister of the time and because they were never used in war) built along the south coast to defend harbours and naval installations. The Nothe fort was positioned to defend both Weymouth and Portland Harbours. The latter was under construction from 1849-1903 (see Portland). The fort on the Verne and a small fort actually on the breakwater of Portland Harbour completed the defences. The Nothe fort was for artillery, built to house and protect huge guns along with their gunners and ammunition. The entrance, under an embankment (and originally over a drawbridge), is impressive and so are the internal Portland stone openings. Originally 12 gun emplacements, not divided as they are now, but open. The power of the large guns was such that the rear windows and doors started to disintegrate when trial firings were carried out, so that they had to be removed before the guns were used. The guns recoiled at great speed back into the emplacement, filling the area with smoke and fumes. The fort was modernised in 1905 with new guns fitted on the top level, and was used in the Second World War as an observation point and for anti-aircraft guns. Wonderful view of Portland Harbour, just around the corner, from the upper level. The under-ground corridors and rooms beneath the fort, used mostly for the storage of ammunition, seem to go on forever. Some of the gun emplacements have guns, and some have displays showing the subse-

The north side of Weymouth harbour

quent uses of the building, adding to the main displays near the entrance. In the 19th century 200-400 men formed the garrison (fee: lists). The Nothe gardens to the west of the fort have recently had a waterfall added on the harbour side. They are worth exploring, and are a good place to see the ferries dock or embark. The jetty beyond the fort is so long that from the end one feels at sea, and gives lovely views in all directions.

The Georgian sea front turns its back on the medieval town, and curves round the bay, which is lined for its whole stretch with fine terraces, and on the sands are donkeys and other traditional seaside entertainments including sand sculptures. Devonshire Buildings form the start, partly on reclaimed ground, and facing the sea rather than the harbour. Lovely curved end, good red brick and two-storey bow windows, all of *c.* 1805. To the west the late 18th and early 19th century buildings have been rather altered, but Johnson Row, which continues round the corner, is very good. This and the matching block opposite date from around 1810, and provide the perfect backdrop for the Coade stone statue of George III put up by 'the *grateful* Inhabitants' to celebrate 'his entering the 50th year of *His REIGN*', in 1809. The King never saw it as he stopped visiting Weymouth in 1805, but it doubtless served to impress visitors with Weymouth's Royal past. The Esplanade, the road curving round the sea-front, was laid out about 1800. In 1803 a Guide said that 'but a short time ago it was nothing but a place where the inhabitants deposited all the rubbish of the town . . . now converted into one of the most charming promenades in England.' Frederick Place of

the 1830's extends back into the town proper, and the first sea-front terrace is Royal Terrace of *c.* 1815, in what was the shrubbery to Gloucester Lodge, where George III stayed. Now much altered and with an additional storey, but retaining the original Venetian windows on the ground floor. This was the first house in Weymouth to face the sea, built by the King's brother the Duke of Gloucester about 1780, and so is the seed from which Weymouth as a resort grew. This house and all those along the Esplanade are on reclaimed ground. The only break in the Georgian terraces is the Royal Hotel of the 1890's, big and brash, and towards the eastern end the stone Victoria Terrace, carefully composed with higher parts at each end and in the centre, a quiet building of the 1850's, in harmony with Waterloo Place to the north (1830's), and Belvidere to the south (1820's). The latter has pretty cast-iron balconies. Halfway along is the elaborate cast iron clock commemorating Victoria's jubilee in 1887. The earlier terraces along the front have iron balconies whilst the later (1820's) ones have bay windows. The sea front curves round separately from the main road at the north end, and Brunswick Terrace of the 1820's completes the Georgian seafront. Rather altered, but shows its fine bones nevertheless.

The bronze statue of Queen Victoria sits in the middle of the road staring right along the Esplanade to the (much better) statue of her grandfather George III. Appropriately, behind her is the large Victorian church of St John, built in the 1850's. Portland Stone with a handsome steeple.

The town centre runs between the Harbour and the sea-front, mostly to the east of St Thomas Street where the streets

are narrow and linked by alleys. Some early 19th century houses, particularly off the main streets, but on the shopping streets these are mixed with plain and elaborate later 19th century buildings and a sprinkling of more modern ones. St Edmund Street has the mixture in very pleasant fashion: the large and classical Portland Stone Guildhall of 1836 and the brick and stone Methodist chapel of 1870 dominate, but there are several plain early 19th century houses, and at the east end an earlier survival – a 17th century Portland stone house, with some original windows above the ground floor. The church of St Mary was totally rebuilt in 1815 and has a classical front to the street, with a pretty cupola on top. The interior has been recently altered, with the insertion of a porch and the conversion of the aisles to a hall and vestries. The curtains masking this give the interior a rather theatrical feel. The dominating feature is the reredos, a huge painting of the Last Supper by Sir James Thornhill, dated 1721 and moved here from the earlier church. The pillars supporting the roof and galleries are stone, but very similar to the wooden ones in St James Church, Poole (1820). St Mary's is an interesting provincial classical church. ★★ *(lists)*.

Just to the north, beyond Westham Bridge, the backwater widens. This is known as **Radipole Lake,** and is an RSPB reserve. Very good for waders and warblers, and in winter, wildfowl. Car park with information centre at the south end, east side, and in the southern part two hides with public access. Along the public paths are listening posts, with recorded information about the reserve and its birds. The area is also good for flowers and butterflies in summer. The display in the information centre greatly helps with identifying the birds, and the reserve is interesting even for those who know little about ornithology.

The Sea Life Park ★★★★ at Lodmoor on the east of Weymouth is very good, with individual fish and other sea creatures such as the malignant conger eels in smaller tanks, but the most impressive and fascinating parts are the large tanks with quantities of different sorts of fish looking natural. The flat fish like nosey rays or the lazier flounders and plaice are marvellous to see; the fishier-shaped ones like the herring or mackerel are beautiful to watch as they move around the huge tanks in shoals. Far too many varieties, besides displays on the life of the sea, to describe. A very good visit, for all ages (fee: lists).

In summer there is a miniature railway and small fun fair at Lodmoor and other amusements, including a 'Tropical Jungle'. The further parts are an RSPB Nature Reserve, with public hides.

WHATCOMBE (F) is an 18th century house substantially altered in 1802. Its drive swings off the road, and there is little else in the park-like valley but its lodges and a few pretty cottages.

WHITCOMBE (H) A compact, unspoilt hamlet consisting of a large thatched 17th century stone barn, seven or eight thatched 18th century cottages and a large early 19th century farmhouse, all beautifully preserved. Set apart just to the north is the church. The village was larger in the medieval period and the earthwork remnants can be seen to the east of the churchyard. The church, whose dedication has been lost, is redundant. It has a fairly plain but attractive tower which is dated 1596 on one of the pierced stones in the bell openings. The north wall of the nave and the tiny doorway are 12th century. The pleasantly empty interior has wall paintings surviving so well that one can actually see what they are. On the east is St Christopher carrying Christ, 15th century, and the other is early 14th century arcading. Two pretty fragments of 10th century crosses with interlace pattern. Outside, by the porch is a shapely table-tomb of 1680 to a man with a splendid name Melchisedeck Gillet. William Barnes, the Dorset poet, took his first service here in 1847 and his last in 1885, a year before he died. Racing stables here.
★★ *Hamlet*

WHITCHURCH CANONICORUM (D) A mixture of farms and cottages, some 17th century, some still thatched, scattered over an attractive landscape on the southern edge of the Marshwood Vale. Sir

ABOVE   *Melchisedeck Gillet's tomb, Whitcombe*
LEFT   *Whitcombe church*
BELOW   *St Wite's shrine, Whitchurch Canonicorum*

George Summers, a famous sailor popularly thought to be the discoverer of the Bermuda Islands, owned a large estate here and was buried here. In fact the islands had been discovered years before he was shipwrecked on them in 1609, but they were still uninhabited.

The church is known locally as 'the cathedral of the Marshwood Vale' and is a fine building in an attractive setting. There was a Saxon church here, but the earliest surviving masonry is the slightly-battered looking 12th century south doorway, the two fat circular pillars inside, one with strange modern-looking leaves on the capital. Apart from modern bits (the north

aisle, some of the windows in the south aisle, the clerestory windows, the vestry and the north and east wall of the chancel), the body of the church is mostly early 13th century, with many beautiful stylised capitals. The chancel arch with its clustered pillars and capitals, and the whole of the north transept are particularly fine. Within the north transept is the reason for the unusual dedication of the church – to St Candida, otherwise known as St Wite – and possibly the reason also for the Whitchurch part of the village name. The 13th century shrine of St Wite is a simple stone chest (containing her skeleton) with three large oval openings below for pilgrims to put their afflicted limbs into, so that close contact with the relics could cure them. This is a rare survival as during the Reformation all shrines were ordered to be destroyed. The identity of St Wite is a mystery: there is a St Wite's well about a mile from the church which was also a place of pilgrimage. The arches between the nave and transepts, and the tower arch are 15th century, with panelled decoration. In the chancel is a splendidly elaborate, frantically carved wall monument of 1611 with an effigy. The smaller stone monument next to it is of 1584-5 and much simpler. Jacobean oak pulpit. The stalls in the chancel are 19th century incorporating some French 16th century carved panels. Fine early 15th century tower with a nice west doorway.

★★★ *Village, church, setting.*

WHITE NOTHE (H, Ringstead) is the highest of the chalk cliffs which run from west of Durdle Door to Ringstead (see entries). The National Trust car park just off the Ringstead Road at Falcon Barn has a glorious view across Weymouth Bay and Portland. A good walk across to the Coastguard Cottages on the top of White Nothe from which it is possible to see the coast along to St Aldhelm's Head in the east. Other paths from the car park lead down to the beach. A very steep zig-zag 'smugglers' footpath down the face of White Nothe to the beach. Part of White Nothe is a Dorset Trust for Nature Conservation Reserve, and the whole area has good chalkland flowers and butterflies in late spring and summer. See also Ringstead and Holworth.

★★★★ *Landscape.*

WHITE SHEET HILL (C) has a Forestry Commission car park on the edge of the forest, and gives good views on the south and east. This is the best place to gain access to the National Nature Reserve of Holt Heath, 1200 acres of woodland and heathland. Some of the latter is very boggy and walkers are advised to keep to the tracks and paths so as to avoid the wetter areas. Good for heathland plants, reptiles and birds.

★ *Heath.*

WIMBORNE MINSTER (F/G) A very attractive town, whose long history begins in the early 8th century with a double monastery – one for nuns and one for monks. This was probably destroyed in the late 10th century and no vestige remains. By Domesday (1086) Wimborne was a small market town, and it has been expanding ever since. The beautiful substantially Norman Minster church is

East Street, Wimborne Minster

well worth visiting. Today Wimborne is a thriving shopping centre, with a large market a little way east of the town centre on Friday, Saturday and Sunday mornings.

West Street, High Street and East Borough all contain good 18th and early 19th century buildings, but perhaps the best street is West Borough, with at the south end an elegant stone building, once the Wimborne Club, of about 1830 set back from the street, and opposite the early 19th century brick Conservative Club. Most of the smaller houses are 18th century, and one fine larger town house of the second half of the 18th century has suffered a dreadful fate – in the 1970s its lower half was removed to form shops and what was a cinema. A thatched cottage survives towards the north end of the street.

Cornmarket, to the north-west of the Minster is attractive, with a nice plain market house of 1758, originally with an open ground floor. In High Street, close to the Minster, is the Priest's House Museum of East Dorset Life (fee: lists), interesting both as a building and for what it contains. The street front is mostly 18th century infilling (1756 on waterspout), but the stone gable wall is early 17th century, with moulded windows in the two upper stories. Inside is the centre of the original front wall, set back from the street, with a fine early 17th century window and a reset door of the same period. The parlour at the back of the house has an early 17th century plaster ceiling, and around the tops of the walls a lovely plaster frieze with the inscription AL PEOPLE REFRAYN

FROM SYN. Reconstructed Victorian shops, and many rooms including a Georgian parlour, 17th century hall and Victorian kitchen. More material is displayed in the amazingly long and very good garden, including bygones in what was a tinner's workshop. Very good displays. ★★★

The minster church of St Cuthberga is dedicated to the sister of Ine, King of Wessex, who was its abbess in the early 8th century, in charge of both the monastery and nunnery. No masonry survives from her time – the main part of the church is Norman of high quality and the most magnificent work of that date in Dorset. The first six bays of the nave from the tower are 12th century, with arches having deep chevron decoration. Above is a Norman clerestory with small deep windows (restored in the 19th century). The upper clerestory is later. The 1857 roof has 17th century carved corbels. The central tower is open inside the church for three stages, each showing characteristic 12th century decoration. The lower has high round arches with plainish capitals, the next arches enclosing arcading with Purbeck marble shafts, and the top deep windows with arches between. The north and south transepts are 14th century. At the tower end of the north transept is a recess which preserved a succession of superimposed wall-paintings, the earliest 13th century. Nearby is the elaborate and rather horrific pulpit (1868). Above the south vestry is the chained library, (fee: lists) established in 1686, dark and crammed with books which are all chained to the shelves. A rare survival. In the south chapel is the brightly painted sarcophagus

ABOVE   *18th century cottage, East Borough, Wimborne Minster*
RIGHT   *The Cornmarket, Wimborne Minster*
BELOW   *St Edmund Uvedale, Wimborne Minster*

of Anthony Ettricke, lawyer, antiquary and friend of John Aubrey. He believed he would die in 1691 because of the magical quality of the figures (the same either way up), and had this date inscribed on his tomb, which had to be altered when he survived until 1703. He is known as 'the man in the wall' because he is supposed to have sworn that he would not be buried in the church or in the churchyard, and with a lawyer's cunning fulfilled his vow by being buried actually within the wall. The chapels on either side of the medieval chancel were rebuilt in the 1850's. The chancel has a lovely east window and a good 14th century sedilia. Close by is a superb tomb with two alabaster effigies of the Duke and Duchess of Somerset, 1444. The lower part of the chancel has interesting woodwork of 1608, remodelled in the 19th century. Beneath it is the crypt. In the north chapel

is the gorgeous monument of Sir Edmund Uvedale (1606) who lies at the conventional uncomfortable angle looking very alive in armour: superb alabaster surround, touched with colours. The nave was extended to the west in the 14th century, and the west tower is mid 15th century with a stone vault. The astronomical clock in the tower is of re-used 17th century materials, with additions, and shows both the sun and moon circling the earth. Good monuments all around the church. Outside the central tower is Norman, apart from the prominent battlements and pinnacles which date from 1608, after the spire fell in 1600 during a 10 o'clock service. Protruding from the west side of the north transept is a circular stair tower, possibly Saxon but re-faced in the Norman period. The mid 15th century west tower is a great contrast to the central tower as it is not of various

coloured stones, but of all one sort. On the north side is the Quarter-jack, a Napoleonic figure of a soldier, who strikes the bells on the quarter hour.
★★★★ *Church.*

Wimborne Model Town to the west of the Minster, on King Street, shows the town as it was in the 1950's, at one-tenth scale. Surrounded by gardens, and with views over the water meadows.

Deans Court has a large, mostly informal, garden open to the public (fee: lists), seemingly far too rural to be so close to Wimborne. Some very fine specimen trees (amongst them a vast tulip tree), many labelled. The River Allen runs through the garden and feeds a large fishpond. The handsome classical square part of the house was built in 1725, and the part with mullioned windows in 1868, (not open but wholemeal teas in basement). Good herb garden and an enviable walled kitchen garden, where everything is grown organically and one side is bounded by a crinkle-crankle wall, built early in the 18th century ★★★ Garden.

On the other side glimpses can be had of the fine Victorian imitation Tudor grammar school, now flats.

Off the Cranborne road, on the northern outskirts of the town is Walford Mill, run by the Dorset Crafts Guild with a shop and workshops open to the public.

WIMBORNE ST GILES (C) A small village, scattered about in the lush well–wooded landscape of the edge of Cranborne Chase. Although the mostly

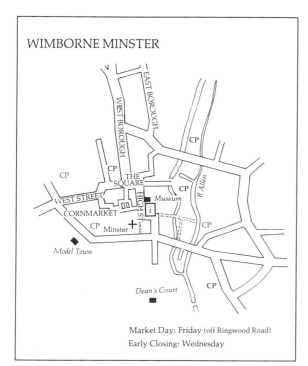

WIMBORNE MINSTER

WEST BOROUGH
EAST BOROUGH
CP
CP
CP
THE SQUARE
R Allen
WEST STREET
HIGH ST
Museum
CP
CORNMARKET
i
CP
CP
Minster
Model Town
CP
Dean's Court

Market Day: Friday (off Ringwood Road)
Early Closing: Wednesday

brick cottages are of a variety of styles, this is the estate village at the centre of the Shaftesbury estate. St Giles House, the home of the Ashley Cooper family since the 15th century, is completely hidden by trees. The centre of the village is decidedly odd, with a green partly surrounded by large brick buildings. The long row of almshouses of 1624 are of small bricks with stone detail, including a weathered loggia. Inside an elaborate oak door is visible. The weathered remains of the village stocks survive on the side of the road, preserved under a little roof inside iron railings. Opposite is a large 17th century

brick mill house on the River Allen.

The attractive church of St Giles is of only two dates. It was rebuilt in 1732, probably by the Bastards of Blandford, architects and builders, and the tower, the south side and part of the east side survive from their church. Very fine, seriously classical, with the south side continuing the pretty greensand and flint chequering of the lower part of the tower. The interior is totally different – the church (which had already been altered in the 19th century) was badly damaged by a fire in 1908, and the distinguished architect Ninian Comper was employed by the

Shaftesburys to rebuild. His interior is quirky and individual, wonder- ful or ghastly according to taste. Both aisles are his, and all the fittings and decoration. The first impression is theatri- cal, with the tall painted font just inside. The church seems square, with the tall elaborate wooden screen reflected by the rather stouter west gallery. The screen's square extension on the south is the Shaftesbury pew. The plaster ceiling is *(cont p. 188)*

ABOVE *The chained Library, Wimborne Minster* BELOW *Almshouses and church, Wimborne St Giles*

Villages

Dorset's villages are famous. Four are particularly popular — the stone villages of Abbotsbury and Corfe; the 18th century 'model' village at Milton Abbas, and Cerne Abbas, which is almost a small town. These are all visited both for their attractive village centres and for other things — the gardens, barn and Swannery at Abbotsbury: the castle at Corfe; the church and mansion at Milton Abbey; and the giant, church and remains of the abbey at Cerne. All are in attractive landscapes. Two other villages equal these, although in very different ways. Pamphill, near Wimborne, now belongs to the National Trust, and is a spread-out brick built village where very little seems to have changed in the last 100 years. Little Bredy has a superb setting at the head of the Bride valley, with lots of trees, and the village itself is a deliberately picturesque fake constructed in the middle of the 19th century.

Others are recommended below, but all selections are personal and very fallible. The well-visited villages are more likely to have tea-shops and be generally equipped to handle visitors, but the more isolated, less popular ones may feel more real. There are nearly as many varieties as there are villages, ranging from those which have been consumed by neighbouring towns, to quiet pretty places like Stoke Abbott, Netherbury, Evershot or Melbury Osmund. The best key to visiting any of them is the village church, which makes a good reason to walk the paths, enquire directions and so on. The church itself carries the history of the village and reflects its present. Very few are dull.

In most villages the buildings are more recent than is generally assumed, but the settlement itself is older.

A typical Dorset village has its roots back at least as far as the 10th century, when surviving Saxon land charters detail the boundaries of parishes or parts of parishes. It is difficult to see how this Saxon pattern of land division relates to anything earlier, for example the Roman period, but it is possible that there was some continuity. Some villages have grown from single farmsteads. Only a few settlements had churches before the 11th century, and a typical, smaller village may have had a stone cross where services were held. On the chalk lands the usual village would have had one street, parallel with the stream, a pattern still discernible today in, for example, the Piddle valley. On the heavier clays the pattern would have been more dispersed. Although the development of open fields is unclear, by the 11th century our typical village would have been working these communally-held large fields. By the 12th century this imaginary village would have had a church, probably small and simple like the surviving one at Winterborne Tomson. Expansion of arable farming or problems with the fertility of the fields, probably in the 12th or 13th centuries, led in some areas to the creation of lynchets, strips running along the side of steep hills. More farmland was also obtained by clearing forest, particularly on the heavier clay areas.

LEFT *Corfe Castle*
BELOW *Winterborne Tomson*
OPPOSITE ABOVE *Lynchets near Uploders*
OPPOSITE BELOW *Sydling St Nicholas*

(**Villages** *continued*)

Many villages had problems in the 14th and 15th centuries, and some failed altogether, and were deserted. The Black Death of 1348-50 was part of the cause, as was the growth of sheep-farming at the expense of arable, but other factors were also involved. Our imaginary village shrank a little, but survived. Some enclosure of open fields or pasture probably took place from the 14th century onwards, and in the 15th or 16th century the church would have been altered and added to. Typically in Dorset it would have been given a fine new tower. Some farmhouses, belonging to emerging yeoman farmers or landlords, were becoming larger and more substantially built in the later 14th and 15th centuries, although they are more likely to survive as 17th or 18th century rebuildings on the same site. The privatisation of monastic lands in the 1530's speeded up this process, so that instead of churches and monastic buildings, money was spent on private houses. As a result, perhaps a fine stone house was built in our village in the later 16th century. Enclosure, especially of downland, continued, with even more emphasis on sheep for wool production.

Piddletrenthide

TOP *Winterborne Houghton.*   BELOW *Farnham*

In the river valleys water-meadows were created to provide early grass, and forest and heathland were enclosed too, a process which continued until the later 19th century, although some common land and heath-land remains unenclosed. A very few cottages survive from the 16th century: the majority are those built in traditional manner between the 17th and 19th centuries. The typical village probably gained some estate cottages during the second half of the 19th century built in less traditional style, perhaps of brick. The spiritual mastery of the church was almost certainly challenged early in the 19th century by the construction of a non conformist chapel, probably quite small and severe. Between 1833 when public funds were made available for schools and 1880 when education was made compulsory, our village gained a school, but only for the under 11s. From about 1860 the village probably had a little general shop. Up to about 1850 the village grew and developed, but after that date the typical picture is one of decline. In 1801 four-fifths of England's inhabitants lived in villages or

Milton Abbas

tiny towns, by 1851 it was only a half, and by 1901 three quarters of the inhabitants lived in large towns or cities. Some of Dorset's larger villages had cottage industries like button or glove making, but by the middle of the 19th century these were ruined by mechanisation. Many villages declined in population, with people moving to the towns or emigrating, and our typical village probably lost some of its worst cottages in the later 19th and earlier 20th centuries. Possibly a few bungalows were constructed between the wars, and certainly after the war some council houses. Probably in the 1920's the village hall was built. From the 1950s a few 'executive houses' were added on the outskirts, and in the last ten years barns and farm buildings may have been converted to housing or for holiday accommodation. Vernacular (local-styled) housing may have been recently built. The medieval church, a hotch-potch of styles and periods may have survived the 19th century, but it is equally possible that it was demolished (apart from the tower) and a more 'correct' one built.

This hypothetical village has three constants, the first, farming the land, the most important and until recently its very life-blood; the church, and (to a lesser degree) the pub. Although in Dorset today the majority of the buildings may be legacies from its agricultural past – the farmhouses, cottages, barns and even the larger houses of the landlords   the majority of its current inhabitants will have no direct involvement with farming. Many are retired people. The small school has probably closed and there may be no shop. The self-sufficient village has totally disappeared, and the village which up until this century grew its own wheat, ground it in its own mill and baked it in its own bakery, now has the bread delivered from the town.

★★★★ Abbotsbury, Cerne Abbas, Corfe, Little Bredy, Milton Abbas and Pamphill. ★★★ Ashmore, Briantspuddle, Evershot, Marnhull, Melbury Osmund, Netherbury, Okeford Fitzpaine, Stoke Abbott, Sydling St Nicholas, Trent, Worth Matravers and Yetminster.

Mill house, Wimborne St Giles, with the roof sheltering the village stocks just visible

supported by thin angels with wings like seagulls', and the altar is superlatively elaborated, with a gorgeously painted 'tester' high above, the window carved and painted. An inscription near the altar records the robin who nested in the church during the rebuilding. Many good monuments – the 14th century knight in armour is a 1908 reproduction as the original did not survive the fire, but there is a wonderful series of Shaftesbury monuments starting with a gaudily painted tomb with two good effigies of 1628, with a daughter kneeling outside. The first Earl, Anthony Ashley Cooper, (1621-83) who changed over to Parliament in the Civil War, was one of the cabal cabinet of Charles II, and prominent in national politics all his life (a turbulent period) is commemorated by a distinguished portrait bust by Rysbrack (made in 1732). The fourth Earl (d. 1771) has an elaborate monument by Scheemakers. The main memorial to the famous philanthropist 7th Earl (1801-85) is Eros, in Piccadilly Circus, intended to show the Christian virtue, love, and whose arrow is aligned with Wimborne St Giles. In recognition of his work he was offered burial in Westminster Abbey, but he refused and is buried here.

★★★ *Church.*

WINFRITH NEWBURGH (J) Attractive, with a cottagey main street, and some large Georgian houses. The church of St Christopher has a handsome early 13th century chancel arch with scallops, an intricate north doorway, part Norman,

part 1854, and a pretty 15th century hamstone window in the south aisle. Concealed inside the Jacobean south porch is a plain Norman doorway. Apart from the 15th century tower the rest of the church is Victorian. The village is surrounded by farmland, apart from the north, where Winfrith Heath is dominated by the Atomic Energy Establishment, unattractive buildings which sometimes steam. The heathland is bleak and open, but good for wildlife and plants.

THE WINTERBORNE VILLAGES
There are 15 villages (or remains of villages) whose names are prefixed Winterborne in the county. They are named after streams which only flow in the winter, when the water-table rises because the chalk is saturated. Traditionally they are secretive, and allow no-one to observe the first running of the waters in the autumn. The north Winterborne now runs all year because deep wells have been dug. The villagers of Winterbourne Abbas kept watch for a fortnight on theirs, but one night the watchmen nipped along to Bridehead Lodge to get a light for his pipe and (of course) while he was gone the stream broke. The South Winterborne has a chain of villages to the south of Dorchester, while the River Winterborne (sometimes called the North Winterborne) is right in the middle of the county. Despite varying from small fast streams in the winter to dry beds and stagnant pools in the summer they have a rich, sometimes marshy, vegetation.

WINTERBOURNE ABBAS (E) Yet another pleasant village ruined by the main road which runs through it. The Winterborne runs alongside the road with little bridges to the houses and there are many stone, brick or flint-banded cottages of the 17th-19th centuries. The church of St Mary has a 16th century tower and a 17th century porch. The elaborate stone spiral stair originally led to the top of the rood screen between the nave and chancel. A small tablet on the south wall of the chancel records the last member of the last church band to survive in Dorset – William Dunford, who played the bass viol at the Harvest Thanksgiving in 1940. The gallery is dated 1701 with later iron pillars. The complicated and unusual roofs date from 1894, as does the seating. The painted Royal Arms are dated 1661.

Just west of the village, on the main road, is a small stone circle, known as the Nine Stones, probably of the early Bronze Age, on the edge of a beech wood. A little further along the road is a little castellated lodge built in 1837 (and later extended). Two miles west of the village on the main road, close to the junction running north to Compton Valence, the Poor Lot barrow group lies on both sides of the road. 44 barrows in all (some have been ploughed out recently) including several of the unusual 'disc' barrows with a small central mound and a ditch and bank of large diameter around it.

★★ *Village* ★★★ *Stone circle.*

WINTERBORNE CAME (A/H) is in the shallow valley of the South Winterborne, with parkland all around. Came House, a handsome plain classical building, was designed by Francis Cartwright (see Blandford St Mary) in 1754. The church is close by the house, down an overgrown path through a thicket. Just to the south of the tower a large mock Saxon cross marks the grave of William Barnes (1801-86) the Dorset poet, rector of the parish from 1862 until his death. He was well loved by his parishioners, and took his parochial responsibilities very seriously. He lived in the delightful early 19th century cottage orné rectory (a mile to the north on the A352) which still looks exactly as it did when he lived there, with thatched verandas and complicated glazing. The little church is mostly 15th century, and has some good fittings. The screen is early 16th century, much repaired and restored, and the Jacobean pulpit matches the communion rails. The main door is 17th century. In contrast to these is the elaborate lectern of 1892. Either side of the altar are good monuments: to the north recumbent effigies of

The Nine Stones, Winterborne Abbas

William Barnes's rectory, Winterborne Came

1610/11, with small figures of children in the base; and on the south an altar tomb of 1591 with brasses. The big armorial hatchments are 19th century, and there are other interesting memorials, including one to Colonel Dawson Barnes who was with the Russians during Napoleon's retreat from Moscow and had two horses shot from under him at Waterloo.

★★★ *Setting & Barnes connection.*

WINTERBORNE CLENSTON (F) is in a lovely small wide valley which has lots of trees. The hamlet is small, and scattered

up the valley away from the church. The manor house's outbuildings are more prominent from the road than the house, with two barns, one thatched, the other of the late 16th century in banded flint and stone with a Victorian roof of chequered black and red tiles supported by a later medieval timber roof, perhaps from Milton Abbey. The church of St Nicholas is one of the neat romantic buildings of the period 1830-40. It was totally rebuilt in 1840 (dated on the tower), and sits looking like a model in the lush green landscape. Banded flint and stone, with a

pretty spire – fanciful, playful Gothick revival rather than the heavier later variety. On the tower, above the entrance is a panel of Coade stone with very 1840 romantic armour. Inside the ceiling is heavy, but most of the fittings are 1840 and amusing including the extraordinarily thin font and the communion rails. Nice arms of Queen Victoria in glass in the north transept.

★★ *Church, setting.*

WINTERBOURNE FARRINGDON (E/H) lies west of Winterborne Came and

Came House, Winterborne Came, with the church visible in the trees on the left

189

The church of St Nicholas, Winterborne Clenston, with the fine Coade stone armour clearly visible above the entrance

is a completely deserted medieval village, with extensive earthworks. One wall of the church just about survives, (seen clearly from the road) and was used by Hardy in *The Trumpet Major*.

WINTERBORNE HERRINGSTON (E/H) is a large house and a few cottages just to the south of Dorchester. In February millions of snowdrops flower up the drive and even in the fields. The main front of the house is early 19th century Gothick, concealing much earlier parts behind.

WINTERBORNE HOUGHTON (F) is in a remote fold of the chalk downs, with several whitewashed thatched cottages. The flint and stone church of St Andrew was rebuilt in 1861. The pretty 15th

century font with its 18th century domed cover came from the earlier church.

WINTERBORNE KINGSTON (F) has some good thatched brick or cob cottages, but they are swamped by more recent development. The medieval church of St Nicholas was drastically restored by Street in 1871, and a new north aisle added. The nicest fittings are the early 17th century pulpit and the stone font, dated 1736, a rather low-slung baluster with a pretty pinneapple finialled wooden lid.

WINTERBORNE MONKTON (H) A hamlet set in the valley to the south-east of Maiden Castle, consisting of a large farmyard and a few houses and cottages. The cottages were all rebuilt by the Church Commissioners, who owned the village, in the 1870's. The small church stands apart, nicely positioned on a hump. William Miles Barnes, one of the poet's sons, was the Rector from 1866-1908 and

his father (Rector of the adjoining parish) often visited. The church of St Simon and St Jude is of the 13th century, although most of the windows and the tower are 16th century, when the arcade was also rebuilt.
★ *Hamlet.*

WINTERBORNE ST MARTIN (E/H) (also known as Martinstown) has a pleasant wide street with the Winterborne alongside, and some good 18th and 19th century cottages and houses. The church of St Martin has a lovely setting on the side of the little valley, and a typical attractive 15th century tower. The rest is a mixture of dates— the south wall of the nave was rebuilt in the late 19th century with large odd pillars of that date supported on earlier bases. Most of the rest of the church is 15th century, as is the roof of the nave (the boss dated 1626 probably relates to a repair) and would originally have been plastered, with just the ribs and bosses showing. Just inside the door is a monument with a mourning widow leaning on a pillar which looks to be Georgian, but is in fact of 1859. Many of the monuments in the church are similarly rather later than their style might suggest – rural conservatism perhaps, or a mason who continued working in an earlier style. (See also Maiden Castle).
★★ *Village.*

WINTERBOURNE STEEPLETON (E) Consists of several 17th and 18th century thatched cottages built of stone, or stone with flint banding, with a few larger later houses, and Manor Farm at the west end which is 16th-18th century and very fine. The 18th century mill retains its wheel. The church of St Michael has re-set inside a carving of an uncomfortable-looking angel, an important piece dating from the first half of the 11th century. The nave of the present church retains the corners of the pre-Conquest church to which the angel belonged: the characteristic long and short stones on the corners can be best seen on the north-west. The nave was rebuilt in the 12th century – the doorways survive. The 15th century chancel has a rather odd arch, rebuilt in the 18th century. The pretty if squat steeple and pinnacles on top of the 14th century tower probably date from the 18th century, although the *Steepleton* part of the village name implies that there was a medieval steeple. Fine woodwork includes the pulpit with 17th century carved panels, the main door of *c.* 1700 and the west gallery dated 1708.
★★ *Village, church.*

WINTERBORNE STICKLAND (F)

Quite large, with thatched cottages of a variety of materials, mixed in with more modern houses including some Victorian villas. The church of St Mary has the usual late 15th or early 16th century tower, but the body of the church is an unusual combination of dates – basically 13th century (eg the east window, chancel arch, etc) altered in the 18th century. All the windows in the nave are 18th century, and rise at the back to accommodate a gallery, now gone. Outside they have plain classical surrounds. The font, its cover and the main wooden door are the same date, and in 1756 a 'tomb chamber' with doors was added to the north of the chancel to house a large sarcophagus. The later medieval tower arch was altered, probably in the 18th century, to make it look more classical. In the chancel is a really odd memorial of 1653 – a black marble column complete with corbel below, entablature above, and the inscription on the column. In the porch is a carved medieval stone panel showing the crucifixion, rather battered.

★ *Village, church.*

WINTERBORNE TOMSON (F, Anderson)

consists of a fine farmhouse with good farm buildings, a 17th century cottage and the tiny church, which because its simple apse is the same width as the body of the church, looks like an upturned boat. The church once formed one side of the farmyard and is basically 12th century, with 16th century windows and an 18th century doorway. Inside is a completely unspoilt rustic interior of about 1720 with pews, pulpit and small gallery painstakingly restored by A R Powys, the architect brother of the novelists John Cowper and T. F. Powys in 1930, using the money raised by the sale of Hardy's correspondence with the Society for the Protection of Ancient Buildings. A finely lettered Purbeck marble wall tablet by Reynolds Stone records this.

★★★ *A rare survival.*

WINTERBORNE WHITECHURCH (F)

The village is now grouped round the main road, but it once ran along the River Winterborne, and the channels that used to flood the water-meadows can still be seen either side of the village. George Turberville, the Elizabethan poet, was born here about 1540. In 1568 he went to Russia, describing the inhabitants as 'a people passing rude, to vices vile inclinde'. The church of St Mary is tucked just off the main road, with an avenue of six yews leading up to it, some of which

The mill, Winterbourne Steepleton

we know were planted in 1768. The chancel is the earliest part, dating from the 13th century with plain lancet windows. The crossing and all its arches are later. Two of the arches have strange carved heads with foliage. The main body of the church, the nave and aisles, was totally rebuilt in 1844, with Benjamin Ferrey as architect. The pretty stencilled decoration was added in the 1860's. A good group of late 17th century monuments, an elaborate 15th century stone font with a pretty 17th century cover, and a heavily restored painted wooden pulpit (said to have come from

Winterborne Tomson church

Milton Abbey) of which three panels (not the figures) are 15th century. Externally the flint and stone banded tower is very pretty.

★★ *Setting, church.*

WINTERBORNE ZELSTON (F) Far

enough off the main road to have preserved its seclusion. Lots of thatched cottages and trees, and takes its winter-flowing stream very seriously, with a double arched bridge and a pond with ducks. The church of St Mary follows a classic pattern – the tower is 15th century, and the rest of the church 1865. All banded flint and heathstone, with good stone only for the dressings.

WITCHAMPTON (F)

Unusually for Dorset, a village built of brick. The little bridge over the River Allen is brick (1795) and there are (restored) 17th century timber-framed, thatched brick cottages. The village is linked together by small lanes, still with fields between the houses and running down to the river. The best building is Abbey House (really a manor house) surrounded by a 16th century brick wall, with darker patterning. One wing of the house is also Tudor (Victorian restoration) with little arched windows – one of the earliest brick buildings in Dorset. The church is not brick, but flint and stone banding for the body of the church which is of the 1830's and 40's, and a miscellany of stones in the 15th century tower. Good wall monument to John Cole of 1636 in the south transept, and a brass of 1572 in the north transept with a figure. The lily-bedecked lectern of 1912 contrasts with the plain and simple

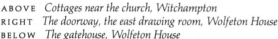
ABOVE *Cottages near the church, Witchampton*
RIGHT *The doorway, the east drawing room, Wolfeton House*
BELOW *The gatehouse, Wolfeton House*

early 18th century pulpit. The ornate gates at the north end of the village lead to Crichel House, the grandest of Dorset's Palladian houses.

★ *Village.*

WOLFETON HOUSE (E) is a rambling stone manor house to the south of Charminster, set on the edge of the watermeadows. A romantic fragment of a Tudor house, well worth visiting. Sir Thomas Trenchard, who paid for the splendid tower of Charminster church, continued the construction of the house started by his father. The massive gatehouse is the earliest part surviving, dating from about 1500. Oddly lop-sided, because the elaborately moulded gateway is off-centre and one of the two round

towers is larger than the other. The windows are original with stylised flowers in the corners, although some of them have been re-set. Inside the smaller tower (now a chapel) are an interesting series of early 16th century small carved panels with signs of the Zodiac. Most of the rest of the early 16th century house was demolished in the 19th century, but the surviving great hall, the octagonal stair tower (apart from its battlements of 1862) and the projecting garderobe further along the south front are part of it, although all the fittings in the great hall date from 1862, as do the plaster ceilings in the other rooms. Inside the heavy mid-19th century porch, the passage contains an amalgam of 16th and 17th century woodwork, placed here in the

19th century. The woodwork in the east drawing room is even more magnificent, with an elaborately carved door, and a doorcase which runs right up to the ceiling. The chimney piece is of similar style and proportions, and all date from the early 17th century, elaborate and exotic. They were moved to this room from other parts of the house in the 19th century, and the panelling in this and the west drawing room is of that date. The west drawing room has a fine plaster overmantel and wooden surround of the early 17th century. The later 16th century staircase is handsome as is the almost classical stone doorcase of the same date at the top. A ghostly coach and four is supposed to be seen going up this staircase in emulation of the feat of a long-dead Trenchard. The recently revealed long gallery has the original late 16th century stone chimney piece: although as extensive as the wooden ones below, it is more restrained. The rest of the house dates from the 17th-19th centuries, with 18th century stables. Some 100 yds north of the house is a riding house, a rare survival, dating from the very early 16th century (not open, but possible to see from the path).

★★★ *House.*

WOODLANDS (G) Well wooded, with brick cottages dating from the 18th century onwards. Lots of market gardening. The little village was given the church of the Ascension in 1892 by the

Countess of Shaftesbury. Outside it looks like a chapel, brick and stone, but inside it not only has elaborate High Church fittings, but also is odd because it was designed by Bodley to have two naves. Right up the middle of the building runs an arcade of pillars such as one would expect to support an aisle. The result is unfortunate — the arcade blocks the view of the rood and the altar, and gives the whole interior a peculiar feel of being cut into halves.

Henry Hastings, squire of Woodlands until his death aged 99 in 1650, is remembered because the first Earl of Shaftesbury left a famous description of him and his (now demolished) house: 'the great hall strewed with marrow bones, full of hawks perches, hounds, spaniels, and terriers . . . hung with the fox skins of this and last years skinning . . .'

At the T-junction to the north-west of the village (Remedy Gate) is an ancient oak with a plaque recording that in the 16th century 'According to tradition King Edward VI sat beneath this tree and touched for the King's Evil.'

WOODSFORD (E) In the Frome valley; a rare survival —one side of a medieval fortified manor house, built in the middle of the 14th century. The remains are impressive: a large 3-storey stone building with a huge thatched roof. In 1630 it was described as 'almost ruinated'. Not open, but can be seen from the road. The church of St John the Baptist was rebuilt in 1863 re-using a little 13th century masonry including the doorway into the tower from the nave.

★ *House.*

WOOL (J) has recently grown enormously, and the road through it is dominated by modern housing estates. Set apart, yet amongst them is one of the few interesting modern buildings in rural Dorset – the Roman Catholic church of St Joseph, built in 1972 and designed by Anthony Jaggard. The old village is best seen in Spring Street, where a little stream runs alongside the road. Lots of late 18th and 19th century cottages, either cob or a mixture of heathstone, limestone and brick. The cottages continue round to the church of the Holy Rood which has a 15th century tower and north aisle, with the south aisle a copy of 1862. The arcades are 13th century on the north, again with a faithful imitation of 1862 on the south. The slightly irregular medieval masonry feels very different to the smooth copies. The 15th century font attached to a pillar in the north aisle belongs to this church, whilst the second 13th century one was brought here from Coombe Keynes. The amazing stone pulpit is 1862, as are the rather good head-corbels in the aisles, the leafy ones in the nave and the weaker angel corbels in the chancel. The pulpit with its passion flowers and the foliage corbels are by Grassby, the Dorchester stone carver.

To the north of the village is **Woolbridge**, a fine 16th century stone bridge with a cast-iron notice threatening transportation to anyone damaging it, and Woolbridge Manor, in a lovely position beside the river on the water-meadows. Fine early brick front with stone dressings, which dates from the early 17th century. Three charming small barns range in date from 16th-18th centuries. The manor house was where Hardy's Tess spent her sad honeymoon. The ghostly Turberville coach is supposed to drive across the bridge, a bad omen only visible to those with the blood of the family.

East Burton is almost a suburb of Wool, with a few thatched cottages and farms, engulfed in modern development. The little church looks like a chapel. Built in 1840, it is now redundant.

Bindon Abbey to the east of Wool is the ruins of a Cistercian Abbey (not open). Visible from the road is the fanciful Gothick gatehouse of the 1790's.

Monkey World, 1 mile north of Wool on Bere Regis Road (fee: lists). Half a dozen varieties of monkey in large

Henry Hastings, squire of Woodlands

Woodsford Castle in the late 18th century

Wildlife

Despite the changes in agriculture over the last forty years Dorset is still a very good county for birds and flowers because of its great diversity of landscapes. The visitor is less likely to see wild animals except rabbits and hares. Badgers are quite common but being nocturnal they are rarely seen. At the right times of day (early morning and dusk) deer can be seen, especially on the margins of woods. Roe deer are the variety most common, but sika are found particularly on the heathlands. The tiny Chinese Muntjacs are apt to be mistaken for large dogs because they are so small. The easiest place to see deer is Stock Gaylard Park, where there is a large herd of spotted fallow. Foxes can occur everywhere, but the most likely place to see grey squirrels is in the parks and chines of Bournemouth and Boscombe. Red squirrels are only found on Brownsea Island.

More than 360 species of birds have been recorded in the county, a large number due to the variety of countryside and the coastline, with the harbours of Poole and Christchurch particularly attractive to over-wintering wildfowl. All the undeveloped coastline has many birds, and at Radipole (Weymouth) there is a large RSPB reserve with public access where many varieties of wildfowl, waders and sea birds can be seen.

The county is also good for butterflies, with 48 species breeding. The surviving downlands like Hod Hill and unspoilt coastal areas like Golden Cap or on the edge of woodlands such as the Powerstock Common Nature reserve, are good places to see them on fine days in the summer.

Generally, where butterflies are found, there are flowers, trees and a generally 'natural' environment. Despite the prairie effect of modern agriculture, with huge areas of corn and never a flower in sight, there are still bits of inland Dorset with a varied, alluring flora. Purbeck and West Dorset are the least changed areas, where fields are still hedged and the verges in late spring are a garden. The surviving heathlands are good too. Away from the towns most of the coast is wild.

Much of the coast is good for wildlife, but Arne, Black Ven, Brownsea, Chesil, Fleet, Durlston, Golden Cap Estate, Hengistbury Head, Ringstead, Radipole Lake (Weymouth), the Spittles (Lyme Regis), Studland Heath, West Lulworth and White Nothe are some of the best places. Poole Park has a good variety of birds, and the Swannery at Abbotsbury is fascinating, especially in the spring. Inland, good areas include the reserves at Powerstock Common, Hod Hill, Thorncombe Woods (Bockhampton), Avon Forest Park, Bride Valley, Bulbarrow, Fontmell Down, Hambledon Hill, Kingcombe, Wootton Hill forest walk, Winfrith Heath. See lists for addresses.

LEFT *Fallow deer at Stock Gaylard Park* TOP *The Swannery, Abbotsbury* BOTTOM *St Aldhelm's Head, a typical coastal habitat for a whole range of flora and fauna*

Woolbridge and the manor, Wool

enclosures, but easy to see. Can be watched for hours. ★★★
★★ *Bridge, the old village.*

WOOLLAND (E/F) has masses of trees, even on the chalk escarpment behind it. A tiny hamlet with large church which the landowner built in 1856, and which he tried to keep from the bishop's jurisdiction. The architect was Sir Giles Gilbert Scott. The polygonal chancel apse is sumptuous, with leafy capitals and pillars in three different marbles. The severe pulpit is approached by a little tunnel. The nave is plainer, but has a large tower arch with no tower behind. In the north chapel is a brass of 1616 with a figure of a kneeling woman with a verse starting 'Here lyeth our Landladie, loved of all' [landlady of the manor of Woolland of course, not a pub]. 'her prayers to God she never neglected / Her life with Infamye never detected'. Many carved inscriptions around the church, and in the porch the stone top of the collecting box is labelled 'FOR THE POOR' and 'COUNTY HOSPITAL' a reference to the hospital being built in Dorchester at the same time as the church. The bell tower is decidedly perverse, slender and elaborate. Most of the hamlet consists of pretty Victorian buildings.
★★ *Hamlet, church*

WOOTTON FITZPAINE (D) A rather straggly village in the Marshwood Vale. The village hall is a First World War Memorial, with a clock. The church is within the grounds of Wootton House (south front *c.* 1765 – the northern parts, seen from the church, 1896). The church is

of chert and dates from the 13th-15th centuries, with the north transept and the vestry of 1872, and a chancel that seems larger than the nave. The pulpit has early 17th century carved panels. Pretty position. ★ *Setting.*

Wooton Hill Forest Walk to the west of the village is set in an area partly beech forest and partly conifers. There is a car park and picnic site, with signposted ½m or 1½m walks giving good views, and in spring,

WORTH MATRAVERS (J) Famous and popular, one of Dorset's beautiful Purbeck stone villages, set only a little way back from the sea, but still bleak. Best to use the car park at the entrance to the village. Although most of its stone houses and cottages date from the later 18th or 19th centuries, there has been a quarrying settlement here since the medieval period, with stone being extracted both from inland and the quarries on the cliff. At the centre of the village is a fearfully neat and tidy duck pond, with a charming, small public garden below. The pond is the best view point for the marvellous series of strip lynchets, the result of medieval agriculture, which cover the hills between the village and the sea. Good walks down to the sea at Seacombe, or Winspit (1½ miles), a tiny rocky bay, with deserted quarries on either side, including shafts running back inland, like the one the hero of *Moonfleet* hid in (see Fleet). The limestone was loaded directly on to boats from the quarries, the last of which ceased working in the 1930's. The coast path leads west to St Aldhelm's Head (see entry), or eastwards along the cliffs towards Durleston (see entry).

The church of St Nicholas is in the middle

of the village, and very pretty. Unusually for Dorset it is virtually all early medieval, dating from around 1100. Even the 18th century porch is decorated with re-set Norman zig-zag decoration, and inside it has a fine complex doorway of about 1160, with a very mutilated carving over it. This and the spectacular chancel arch inside of the same date are not original to the church, but inserted, possibly in the 16th century. Where they come from is not known. The nave retains the tiny high windows of the 12th century, supplemented by larger later medieval ones. The north doorway is also original. Most of the fittings are 19th century. Outside under the roof is a corbel

Worth Matravers church in 1934 by Paul Nash. Reproduced by permission of the Paul Nash Trust

ABOVE *Cottages, Worth Matravers*
LEFT *The duck pond, Worth Matravers*
BELOW *The Jesty gravestones, Worth Matravers*

RIGHT *Higher Wraxall manor house*

table, a characteristic feature of Norman churches, with animal and human heads. In the grave- yard to the north are the grave-stones of Benjamin and Elizabeth Jesty. He was 'the first person (known) to introduced the Cow Pox by innoculation' in 1774 and Elizabeth was one of the people he tried it on. (Happily she survived, outliving her husband and reaching the age of 84.)

★★★ *Village, church, landscape.*

WRAXALL (E) is divided into two little hamlets – Higher Wraxall has a fine large stone manor house of *c. 1630* (extended in the 19th century), a few cottages and a farm. Lower Wraxall has a charming tiny church of St Mary, just a nave and chancel. The chancel arch and doorway are late 12th century, but the rest is much restored with a 19th century east window and bell cote. Good monuments in the chancel particularly those to the Lawrences, late 17th century with affecting verses. Intricate wrought iron gate to churchyard, which is surrounded by farm buildings. The little hamlet has houses of flint, brick and stone, sometimes all three used together.

★ *Setting, hamlets.*

196

WYKE REGIS (H) is almost engulfed by Weymouth, and is surrounded by recent housing and so forth. In the middle, to the south-west of the church, is the pleasant village centre, with many early 19th century houses. The church of All Saints is remarkable because it all dates from the mid-15th century. It was re-dedicated in 1455, and although the structure has been repaired and the furnishings altered, externally it is much the same today as it was then. All of white Portland limestone, high, light and spacious inside, with plain arcades and a huge east window. The angel corbels are good, and the two large corbels with serene heads probably carried the rood beam. The Victorian seating is pretty, as is the 15th century font, of unusual shape; but the most attractive fitting is the vigorously and deeply carved stone Tudor coat of arms over the main door, which was probably taken from Sandsfoot Castle. Lots of 18th and early 19th century monuments because until 1836 this was Weymouth's parish church. Many victims of ships wrecked off Chesil Beach are buried here, including Captain John Wordsworth, brother of the poet, who was drowned along with 300 others when his ship *The Earl of Abergavenny* was wrecked on the Shambles in 1805, due to an error by the pilot.
★★ *Church.*

WYNFORD EAGLE (E) lies between two chalk ridges, is small and particularly empty in the centre, with meadows between the few buildings. The manor house, rebuilt in 1630, has a most impressive west front topped by a large stone eagle. It was the home of the Sydenham family: Thomas Sydenham (1624-89) fought for Parliament in the Civil War, and became 'the father of British medicine' (Treves) applying 'sound commonsense' to the study of diseases and publishing his observations. The last of the Sydenhams was far less worthy – being short of money he put the estate up as a lottery (not uncommon then) and fiddled the result. The arranged winner refused to return the estate, as she had promised, but sold it and married. The last Sydenham died in Dorchester Prison in 1709.

The church of St Lawrence sits on its own, and was rebuilt in 1840 in rather mean manner, re-using the 15th century chancel arch from the earlier church. Set in the wall beside the porch is a late 15th century tympanum (the stone which filled the head of an arch, in this case a doorway) showing two confronted wyverns. The interest of the piece lies in the inscriptions, reading 'Mahald de l'egele' for Matilda Eagle who presumably paid for it, and 'Alvi me feci', for the sculptor, Alvi, who made it.
★★ *Setting.*

WYNYARD'S GAP *see* **CHEDINGTON**

YETMINSTER (A) Architecturally one of the most important villages in Dorset, and well worth visiting. Its sleepy old-fashioned feel is mostly due to a fortunate lack of through traffic. The village is on the happily named River Wriggle. Everything in the centre is built from local yellowy orange limestone, including a remarkable number of 17th century buildings, originally farmhouses. To the south of the church is the earliest – Upbury Farm, with two 15th century cusped windows and a doorway of the same date. The rest is 17th century. Running north from the church, the school and old library of the late 19th and early 20th centuries have distinctive round-headed windows.

On the little triangle at the end of the road

Wyke Regis in the late 18th century

is Manor Farm, with a three storey gable to the street, and mullioned windows with hood moulds to each floor. This is 17th century, as is the cottage beyond the shop, dated 1607. Many of the houses in Yetminster are dated, and there are more good 17th century buildings alongside 18th and 19th century ones, in High Street, Chapel Lane and Queen Street. At the west end of the village is Boyle's School, built in 1697. The doorway has a huge apron over it which looks as though it should have an inscription. The founder of the school was Sir Robert Boyle, famous for Boyle's law of gases.

This village of fine stone houses also has a fine stone church. St Andrew's is almost all of one build, with the nave and its aisles, the tower and even the porch dating from c. 1450. Rarely does one find so uniform a church. Outside there are big battlements, in the tower a huge window and 10 incised consecration crosses. Inside is high and light with tall thin arches. Figures in the capitals include a goose hanging a fox. At the back of the nave are several 15th century benches, some with square ends and others with poppy-heads. These may have been the seating for the new church. The roofs are also c. 1450. Some of the original painted decoration survives on the walls and arches. The font is built into one of the pillars. The long thin chancel is 13th century, with greatly restored lancer windows. Good selection of memorials including brasses to Sir John Horsey and his wife, 1531, and a wall monument with a kneeling figure of Bridget Minterne 1649. Six times a day the faceless clock chimes the National Anthem, a memorial to 1897 Jubilee.

★★★ *Village, church.*

TOP RIGHT *Yetminster, Upbury Farm*
RIGHT *A house in the village*

Afterword

Dorset County Museum, Dorchester, the 1881 gallery

I have greatly enjoyed my journeyings around Dorset for this book, and also my travels in the writings about the county, usually in the Dorset County Library (to whom many thanks). I have discovered of course that I knew nothing about Dorset, particularly the little-visited north and east. My constant companions have been the eight volumes of the Royal Commission on Historic Monument's superb survey of Dorset (to which readers are referred for more information on buildings and archaeology); *The Buildings of Dorset* by John Newman and Nikolaus Pevsner, and *Victorian Stone Carvers in Dorset* by Joan Brocklebank which gives much information about the Victorian churches.

George Ellis, who published a *History of Weymouth* in 1829, comments on the position of a local author, who 'is fully aware that he incurs fearful responsibility, as the most ungrateful task which any writer can undertake, is that of a work of entirely a local character, for with whatever discretion he may proceed, he must offend that mighty phalanx who think they cannot be too lightly censured or too highly praised; and the Author is placed between the perilous alternative either of drawing down hatred on himself, or of sacrificing his duty'.

I am particularly conscious of the 'drawing down of hatred' having found parish or church guides in my travels still smarting under uncomplimentary remarks made by Sir Frederick Treves in his *Highways and Byways in Dorset* — published eighty years ago! I have felt that I must describe and evaluate buildings, villages, and landscapes for the intending or actual visitor, and that a colourless unopinionated description would not do. I apologize to any places I have thereby offended. I hope with Ellis that this book will be of use to 'the great influx of migratory characters annually resorting to towns seated on the sea coast' (or indeed inland) and 'satisfy the inhabitants of various local particulars with which they were either imperfectly acquainted, or had allowed to lapse from their memory'.

Ellis regretted 'that the subject of the following sheets, has not devolved upon a more efficient individual'. I cannot concur in this view (although the reader may well) — I have enjoyed producing the book too much!

TEN YEARS ON

After ten years (and five small revisions) this book has been totally revised. I have revisited the entries, adjusting the text to changes both in the places and in my reaction to them. I have regretted small losses — the only artificial thatch in the county, and the conversion of many sets of farm buildings to housing.

Some places seem not to have altered by a blade of grass in ten years: others have seen many changes. Most are in between, but generally rural buildings seem in better repair than ten years ago, with very few neglected or derelict cottages for example and much more thatch in good condition. New vernacular locally-styled housing has become much more convincing, with the best examples at Broadwindsor, Abbotsbury and Poundbury (Dorchester).

A few small churches have closed, but some have acquired fine new fittings, like the sculptures on Durweston tower and the lectern at Studland. Sculptures have been added in both town and countryside. I am very grateful to all those who communicated with me about omissions and mistakes in earlier editions, and will be grateful to hear about this new one.

Acknowledgements

I am very grateful to the staff of the Dorset County Library (both reference and lending) for all their patience; to Christopher Chaplin for all his help and the maps; to my mother for reading typescript and proofs; to Roger Peers, curator of the Dorset County Museum, for kindly ploughing through the whole typescript; to Paul Ensom for his geological advice; to the Dorset Trust for Nature Conservation and the Dorset Environmental Records Centre for advice on natural history; to Roland Tarr, Dorset Coastal Heritage Officer, for reading the coastal sections and offering many useful suggestions; to Barry Cunliffe for his advice and company visiting the hillforts; to Richard Bradley for archaeological advice and showing me Wessex Guidebook; to Alan Roberts, secretary of the National Farmers Union, Dorchester, for help with the farming section; to Sheena Pearce for all the typing; and to John Fowles for the Foreword.

I would like to thank the following for providing the photographs: Aerofilms Ltd, 49 top left, 108 top; Douglas Allen Photography, 42 top left, 78 top; John Bailey, 96 top left; Bournemouth Corporation, Tourism and Publicity Department, 36 top right and centre right; Bridport Museum, 43 bottom, 97 top, 171 bottom; Grace Burnett, 186 middle right; Thomas Burnett, 151 top, 158 bottom; Ian Chapman, 43 top, 81; Common Ground, 50 bottom; Compton Acres, 120; Patrick Cooke, 152 top; Dorset County Council, 38 top; Dorset County Museum, Dorset Natural History and Archaeological Society, 67 left, 163 bottom, 168 top, 169 bottom, 175 top, 199; Meriel Ensom, 18; Fay Godwin, 10 top, 20; Martin Green, 40 top; HMS *Osprey*, 19; Jude James, 182 top left and right, 192 top left; A. F. Kersting, 13 top, 21 bottom right, 22, 24 top left, 26, 31 top right, 32 top, 33 bottom, 35 top, 45 bottom, 52 top, 61 bottom, 62, 64 top, 73, 77 bottom, 80 bottom, 91 bottom, 99, 106 top, 110 top left, 122 top left, 142 bottom, 169 top, 194 right, 195; Kitchenhams Ltd, 45 top, 58 top right, 64 bottom, 85 top, 92 bottom, 177; Litton Cheney Parish Council, 96; John Makepeace, 115; Paul Mellon Collection, 79; Museum of English Rural Life, 104 top, 105 top; Paul Nash Trust, 195 bottom; National Portrait Gallery, 140 right; The National Trust, 59 bottom, 77 top, 153 top, 137 bottom; Paul Penrose, 48 top, 98, 126; Poole Museums, 160 bottom; Stan Price, 75 top, 76 centre, 89 bottom right, 91 top, 95 top, 128 bottom, 173, 174 bottom right, 189 top right, 191 bottom, 194 bottom right; Royal Commission on Historical Monuments (England), 11, 23, 25 top left, 27 bottom, 31 bottom, 36, 41 bottom, 48 bottom, 51 top, 52 centre left, 58 top left, 58 centre, 59 top right, 66, 72 bottom right, 74 bottom right, 75 top left, 76 top, 78 bottom, 83 top, 83 bottom, 85 bottom, 93 bottom, 97 bottom, 103 bottom, 105 bottom, 106 bottom, 107 bottom right, 110 top right, 111 top left, 118 top, 133 top, 135, 138, 139 top, 141. 143 top left and right, 163 top, 175 right, 180 bottom, 182 bottom, 190; Royal Society for the Protection of Birds, 25 right; Russell-Cotes Museum, 38 bottom; Dr Peyto Slatter, 69 top; the Estate of the late Alan Sorrell, 101; Roland Tarr, 137 top; University of Cambridge, Department of Aerial Photography, 28 bottom, 41 top, 71 top; John Wilson, 113 top, 172, 187; Rees Winston, 156 top right. All the remaining photographs were taken by David Burnett of the Dovecote Press.

For the colour photographs I would like to thank: David Burnett, front cover; Bournemouth Corporation, 3 top; Dorset County Library, 1 bottom right, 3 bottom, 7 bottom; A. F. Kersting, 2 top right and bottom left, 6 centre right, 8 top; The National Trust, 6 top right; John Wilson, back cover, 1 top, 2 bottom right, 6 bottom right, 7 top; George Wright, 1 bottom left, 6 centre left and bottom left, 8.

I am grateful to those who have written to me about the first edition of this Guide, and particularly indebted to those who have sent in corrections. They include: Joan Arnholt, B. Basil, John Bugler, Rev. H. Carter-Lloyd, W. O. Copland, B. G. Cox, Brigadier S. N. Floyer-Acland, Captain I. G. H. Garnett, Viola Hall, Paul Joliffe, Alex Kent, H. J. Knott, Polly Legg, Rev. Alex Martin, Mrs John Montagu, Judy Morris, Mrs J. D. Pinnock, G. W. Pritchard, A. J. Ralph, Rev. Andrew Salmon, Rosa Smith, Dr Nigel Webb.

The Lists

Contents

These are not lists of what you can see in Dorset, but lists of the places which have opening times or events which occur at certain times of the year. Further descriptions of most of them can be found under their entry in the Gazetteer, where their map reference letter is also given. Landscapes, villages and towns are not included, but are found in the Gazetteer, and if especially good they are also mentioned in Praise o' Dorset and in the various double page spread sections on specific subjects. In all cases their map reference letter is given at the start of their entry in the Gazetteer.

Unless otherwise stated the months in the Lists are complete, e.g. March-Sept means March 1st to September 30th. All the information given was correct when this edition of the Guide went to press, but phone numbers are given wherever possible and we would suggest you check opening times in the winter or if you are making a long journey. A lot of work has gone into the Lists but we have had to rely on advance information, some of which may prove inaccurate. Tourist Information Offices are a good standby and will be happy to help: all of them are shown on the town maps and phone numbers are given in the Lists. We apologize for any mistakes or omissions.

Price Guide: A: less than £1, B: less than £3, C: less than £5, D: £5 and over. The key gives the price of a single adult ticket, but most places give reductions for children and Old Age Pensioners, and some offer family tickets. Please remember that not all the places charge admission.

Animals, Fishes, Butterflies, Birds

Abbotsbury Swannery. Nesting swans and duck decoy. 9.30am-5pm daily April-Oct (after the swans have started nesting). Price B. Abbotsbury (01305) 871684.

Bournemouth Water Zoo, Pier Approach. 10am-6pm daily winter, 10am-10pm summer. Price: B. Bournemouth (01202) 295393.

Dorset Heavy Horse Centre, Verwood. Large horses, interesting. Cafe. 10am-5.pm daily, mid-April-Sept. Rest of year 11am-4pm (closed Mons). Parades of horses 11.30, 2.30, 4.15. Price C. Verwood (01202) 824040.

Kingston Maurward Park, near Dorchester. Lots of animals and wonderful gardens. 1-5pm daily, Easter-mid-Oct. Price B. Dorchester (01305) 264738.

Merley Bird Gardens, Merley, south of Wimborne. Lots of exotic birds. Good Cafe. 10am-6pm, Mar-Oct, 10am-dusk winter, daily. Price C. Wimborne (01202) 883790.

M.G.F.T. Animal Sanctuary, Church Knowle. Ponies and other animals. 11am-4pm daily. Price A. Corfe Castle (01929) 480474.

Monkey World, a mile north of Wool. Primates in the heathland. Good. Cafe. 10am-6pm daily in summer, winter shorter opening. Price C. Bindon Abbey (01929) 462537.

Natural World (Poole Aquarium and Serpentarium), Poole Quay. Lots of fish snakes, crocodiles, etc. 10am-5pm Nov-March; 9.30am-9.30pm June-Aug. Daily except Christmas. Price C. Poole (01202) 686712.

Putlake Adventure Farm, Langton Matravers. Farm animals. Cafe. 11am-6pm daily, Easter-October (closed Sats.). Price C. Swanage (01929) 423751/422917.

The Rare Poultry, Pig and Plant Centre, Long Ash Farm, Milton Abbas. Teas. 10am-6pm daily except Weds, Easter-October. Price B. Milton Abbas (01258) 880447.

Sea Life Park, Lodmoor, Weymouth. Extremely good. Cafe. Car Park. 10am-6pm daily; mid-July-Aug 10am-9pm. Price D. Weymouth (01305) 761070.

Shire Horse Centre, Brewer's Quay, Weymouth. Horses large and small. 10am-5pm daily March-Sept. Price: B Weymouth (01305) 760149.

Upper Farm, Edmonsham, Farm animals and so on. Cafe. 10am-5pm daily, March-October. Price: B. Cranborne (01725) 517784.

Worldlife, Compton House, west of Sherborne. Butterflies in exotic variety and silkworms. Conservation displays. Cafe. 10am-5pm daily, April-October. Price C. Yeovil (01935) 74608.

Annual Events

Only the larger events which are held on the same day each year are listed here; for fetes, flower shows and festivals, temporary exhibitions, Morris Dancing, craft and antique fairs, vehicle or steam rallies and many other events see the local weekly paper *The Western Gazette* or the daily evening papers, *The Dorset Evening Echo* and *The Bournemouth Echo*.

March-April: Point-to-points at Badbury Rings (three), Milborne St Andrew and Toller Down Gate, Beaminster.

May: Portland Fling, Beaminster Fair, Blandford Georgian Fayre, Weymouth Water Regatta and Trawler Race, Blandford Festival, Verwood Carnival.

June: Wimborne Folk Festival, Dorchester Carnival, Bournemouth Festival of Flowers. Swanage Arts Festival.

July: Puddletown Carnival, Shaftesbury Festival Week, Wareham Carnival, Burton Bradstock Festival (music), Swanage Jazz Festival, Tolpuddle Martyrs Trades Union Rally (3rd Sun), Milton Abbas Street Fair, Poole Regatta, Lyme Regis Lifeboat Week.

July/August: Brownsea Island Open Air Theatre, Mudeford Trawler Race.

August: Gillingham and Shaftesbury Show, Swanage Carnival and Regatta, West Bay Regatta, Hurn Air Show, Dorset County Arts and Crafts Exhibition, Corfe Carnival, Lyme Regatta and Carnival, Christchurch Carnival and Regatta, Bournemouth Carnival and Regatta, Bridport Carnival, Sherborne Carnival, Weymouth Carnival, Milton Abbas Music Festival, Melplash Show, Sturminster Newton Carnival.

Late Aug/September: Dorset Steam Fair, Blandford Carnival.

September: Dorchester Shows (1st Saturday in month), Swanage Folk Festival, Shaftesbury Carnival (end of month).

October: Dorchester Sheep Fair, Gillingham Carnival, Sherborne Pack Monday Fair (First Mon after the 10th).

November: Portland Fair.

Castles and Forts

Corfe Castle (National Trust). One of the finest castles in England. Cafe. April-October, 10am-5.30pm daily; Nov-Feb, daily, noon-3.30pm, March 10am-4.30pm. Price B. Corfe Castle (01929) 481294.

Nothe Fort, Weymouth. 1860s, large and interesting. Teas. May to mid-Sept daily, 10.30am-5pm. Other months Sunday afternoons. Price B. Weymouth (01305) 787243

Portland Castle (English Heritage) Complete Henry VIII Castle. Very good. April-Sept, 10am-1pm & 2-6pm daily, October 10am-1pm, 2-4pm. Price B. Weymouth (01305) 820539.

Sherborne Old Castle (English Heritage). Ruined but interesting. April-Sept daily 10am-1pm, 2-6pm, Nov-Mar, Wed-Sun 10am-1pm, 2-4pm. Price B. Sherborne (01935) 812730.

Churches

A few churches advertise opening times and are listed here. The majority of Dorset churches are either open or the keys can be borrowed from an address indicated in the church porch.

Bournemouth, St Stephens, open weekdays, closed Sats.

Gillingham, St Mary, 11am-12, 2.30-3.30pm. Mon-Sat; 2.30-3.30pm Suns.

Marnhull, 2.30-4pm Fris, 10.30am-12 Sats.

Melcombe Horsey, 9am-4pm daily.

Poole, St James, 11am-4pm Mon-Fri, 9am-12 Sat, Spring Bank Holiday-Sept.

Reforne, Portland, St George, 2-5pm daily, May-Sept.

Wareham, Lady St Mary, 10am-3pm winter, 10am-5pm summer, Mon-Sats, Suns pm summer only.

Weymouth, St Mary, 10.30am-12.30pm Thurs-Sat.

Gardens

An annual list of Dorset Gardens open to the public, including lots of smaller gardens and those only open for a very few days, is published annually and is available from Tourist Information Offices or libraries. Most of the smaller or infrequently open gardens are not listed here. Sometimes lots of gardens in one village have a joint open day (see the local papers). Only the most spectacular gardens to houses which are open to the public are listed here, but several others on the Houses list have nice gardens.

Abbotsbury Sub-Tropical Gardens. One of the best. Big. Cafe. 10am-6pm daily,

March-October. Shorter opening in winter. Price B. Abbotsbury (01305) 871387.

Athelhampton (see also Houses). Very good. Cafe. 12-5pm, Easter-Oct Weds, Thurs, Suns and Bank Holidays; also May-Sept Tues; and July and Aug, Mon and Fri. Price B, for gardens only. Puddletown (01305) 848363.

Bennetts Water Gardens, Weymouth. Lakes with waterlilies. Cafe. 10am-5pm Easter-Sept (closed Mon) 10am-5pm. Closed Suns in Sept. Price B. Weymouth (01305) 785150.

Compton Acres, Canford Cliffs, Poole. One of the best. Formal. Cafe. 10.30am-6.30pm daily (or dusk if earlier), March-October. Price C. Canford Cliffs (01202) 700778.

Cranborne Manor, Cranborne. Superb, but infrequently open. Teas. Mar-September, Weds only 9am-4.30pm; occasionally other days (see local paper). Price B. Cranborne (01725) 517248.

Dean's Court, Wimborne. Smaller, good organic veg and herb gardens. Teas. 2-6pm Easter Sun; end of May-Sept, Sun last week in month only; 10am-6pm Bank Holidays and some other days. Price B. All enquiries written.

Edmonsham House, near Cranborne. Big walled garden etc. See Houses list for opening times etc.

Forde Abbey, Thorncombe (see also Houses). One of the best. Cafe. Gardens daily, 10.30am-4.30pm (last admission). Price B. Chard (01460) 220231.

Horn Park Gardens, near Beaminster. Good gardens, wonderful setting. 2-6pm, Tues, Weds, Sun and Bank Holidays, April-Sept. Price B. Beaminster (01308) 862212.

Kingston Maurward, near Dorchester. Superb formal gardens, and landscape with lake. See Animals etc list for opening times.

Knoll Gardens, Hampreston, Nr Wimborne. Smallish. Car park. Cafe. 10am-6pm March-Oct daily. Price C. Wimborne (01202) 873931.

Mapperton, near Beaminster. Formal and fine. March-Oct Daily 2-6pm. Price B. Beaminster (01308) 862645.

Melbury Sampford. Rarely open, but very fine park etc. 2pm-6pm. Some Thurs and occasional Suns June-Sept. (See local papers). Price B.

Minterne, Minterne Magna. Large and good. Rhododendrons. 10am-6pm daily. April-October. Price B. Cerne Abbas (01300) 341370.

Stapehill Experience, Stapehill, Nr Wimborne. Big new gardens. See Misc.

Houses

Athelhampton. Tudor manor house with lovely gardens. Cafe. 12noon-5pm Easter-Oct, Weds, Thurs, Suns and Bank Hols. Also May-Sept, Tues; and July and Aug, Mon and Fri. Price: B house, C house and gardens. Puddletown (01305) 848363.

Cloud's Hill, near Moreton (National Trust). T. E. Lawrence's retirement cottage. Small. April-October Suns, Weds, Thurs and Fri, Bank Holiday Mons, 2-5pm. Price B.

Thomas Hardy's Birthplace, Bockhampton (National Trust). Charming cottage. Occasionally open, or by appointment, phone Dorchester (01305) 262366. Price B. Garden open April-October, 11am-6pm, free.

Russell-Cotes Museum, Bournemouth. A good museum and an extraordinary late Victorian house (see also Museums). Teas. All year, Tues-Sun 10am-5pm. Free. Bournemouth (01202) 551009.

Chettle House, Chettle. Fine 1710 brick. Easter-early Oct every day except Tues and Sat. 11am-5pm. Price B. Tarrant Hinton (01258) 830209.

Edmonsham House, Edmonsham, near Cranborne. Interesting gardens, 16th-19th century house. House 2pm-5pm Easter Sun, Bank Holiday Mons, Weds in April & October. Garden: when house is open plus Wed and Sun, 2-5pm. April-October. Teas in village hall on house open days. Price: A garden only, B house and garden. Cranborne (01725) 517207.

Fiddleford Manor (English Heritage). Very fine, late 14th and 16th century. April-Sept daily 10am-6pm, Oct-Mar 10am-4pm. Free.

Forde Abbey, Thorncombe. Superb mixture - 15th-17th century. Large. Cafe. (See also Gardens). 1pm-4.30pm, Suns, Weds and Bank Holidays, April-October. Price C. Gardens only B. Chard (01460) 220231.

Kingston Lacy, near Wimborne (National Trust). Stately mansion. Fine paintings. 12noon-5.30pm, April-October, daily except Thurs and Fri. Park same days but 11.30am-6pm. Price D house and park. Wimborne (01202) 883402.

Ilsington House, Puddletown. Interesting house, paintings and gardens. 2-6pm Weds, Thurs, May-Sept, also Aug. Suns and Bank Hols. Price C. Puddletown (01305) 848454.

Lodge Farm Kingston Lacy. A little medieval house. Open occasionally or by appointment. Price B. Enquiries to Lodge Farm, Wimborne, BH21 4DZ.

Lulworth Castle, East Lulworth (English Heritage). Shell of early 17th century imitation castle. Good park and 1786 chapel. April-Sept, 10am-6pm daily, rest of year 10am-4pm. Price B. (01929) 400510.

Max Gate, eastern outskirts of Dorchester (National Trust). The house Thomas Hardy designed for himself in 1885. 2-5pm Suns, Mons and Weds, April-Sept. Price B (01305) 262538.

Merley House & Model Museum, off Wimborne by-pass. Many models & fine house. 10-30am-4.30pm daily, Easter-Oct. Price B. Wimborne (01202) 886533.

Milton Abbey, Milton Abbas. Fine Georgian mansion and 1498 Abbot's hall. Teas summer only. 10am-6.30pm daily, part of Easter and summer school holidays. Price B. Milton Abbas (01258) 880489.

Parnham House, near Beaminster. Picturesque Tudor house and The John Makepiece Furniture Workshops. Restaurant. April-October, Weds, Suns, and Bank Holidays, 10am-5pm. Price C. Beaminster (01308) 862204.

Purse Caundle Manor. 4m east of Sherborne. 15th and 16th century, fine house. 2-5pm, Easter-Mon; May-Sept, Thurs, Suns and Bank Holiday Mons. Price B. Milborne Port (01963) 250400.

Sandford Orcas Manor House. 4m north of Sherborne. 1530s manor house and gatehouse. Very fine. 2-6pm Sundays, 10am-6pm Mondays, Easter Monday May-Sept. Price B. Corton Denham (01963) 220206.

Sherborne New Castle. Extraordinary un-military Castle, 1600 on. Very fine furniture etc. Cafe. 1.30-5pm (grounds open from 12.30), Easter-September, Thurs, Sats, Suns, Bank Holiday Mons. Price C. Sherborne (01935) 813182.

Smedmore House, Kimmeridge. 18th century house, fine position. 2.15pm-5.30pm, May-mid Sept, Weds. Price C. Corfe Castle (01929) 480717.

Tudor House, 3 Trinity Street, Weymouth (Weymouth Civic Society). Two late 16th century town houses, furnished. June-September, Tues-Fri 11am-3.45pm and 1st Sun in month Oct-May 2-4pm. Price B. Weymouth (01305) 782925/788168.

Wolfeton House, Charminster. 1500 gatehouse; fine house, wonderful woodwork. 2-6pm, May-Sept, Tues, Thurs & Bank Holiday Mons. Price C. Dorchester (01305) 63500.

Upton House, Upton, Poole. Good gardens (free); The Country Heritage Centre 10am-5pm every day except Mon (free). The house itself open some Suns pm. Price B. Poole (01202) 675151, ext. 3514.

Mills

Mangerton Mill, Loders. Collection of Agricultural items etc. All the mill machinery. Teas. 2-5.30pm (closed Mondays) May-Sept, plus Easter week. Price B. Bridport (01308) 485224.

Place Mill, Christchurch Quay. Restored mill with machinery. 10am-5.30pm; Easter, Spring Bank Holiday to mid-July and September weekends only; mid-July to early September daily. Price B. Christchurch (01202) 487626.

Sturminster Newton Mill, Sturminster Newton. See Sturminster Newton Museum.

White Mill, Sturminster Marshall (National Trust. 11am-5pm Sats and Suns. Easter-September.

Museums

Abbotsbury Barn. Collection of agricultural bygones in a superb setting. 10am-6pm daily April-October; Suns only in winter 10am-dusk. Price C. Abbotsbury (01305) 871817.

Blandford Museum, Bere's Yard, off Market Place, Blandford. April-Sept 10am-4pm weekdays. Price A. Blandford (01258) 451115.

Royal Signals Museum, Blandford Camp. History of Army Signalling. Medium size. 10am-5pm, all year Mon-Fri (not public holidays). Weekends and holidays June-Sept. 10am-4pm. Free. Blandford (01258) 482248.

Bournemouth Museums
Russell-Cotes Museum, Bournemouth. Quirky late Victorian House, huge collections. Teas. 10am-5pm Tues-Fri, all year. Free. Bournemouth (01202) 551009.
Bournemouth Transport Museum, Tram, trolley and diesel buses. Currently by appointment only.
The Shelley Rooms, Boscombe Manor (Bournemouth Art College). Smallish, devoted to the poet Shelley. 2-5pm Tues-Sun. Free. Bournemouth (01202) 303571.

Expo Centre, Old Christchurch Lane. Changing exhibitions. Price D. Bournemouth (01202) 293544.

The Tank Museum, Bovington Camp. 150 Tanks, armoured cars, etc., very good. Cafe. 10am-5pm, daily. Price D. Bindon Abbey (01929) 405096/463953.

Bredy Farm Old Farming Collection, between Burton Bradstock and Litton Cheney. Implements, wagons, saw-mills. 10am-5.30pm, weekdays, late May-Sept. Price B. Burton Bradstock (01308) 897229.

Bridport Museum, South Street. History of the town, bygones etc. 10am-5pm daily except Suns which are 2-5pm, April-October, winter Weds & Sats 10am-5pm, Suns 2pm-5pm. Price A. Bridport (01308) 422116.

Christchurch Museums
Christchurch Motor Museum, Matchams Lane, Hurn. Vintage cars and displays. 10am-late daily. Price B. Christchurch (01202) 488100.
Red House Museum, Quay Road, Christchurch. Archaeology, natural history, costume, bygones, etc 10am-5pm, daily April-Sept, winter 10am-5pm Tues-Sats and Bank Holidays. Every Sunday 2-5pm. Price A. Christchurch (01202) 482860.
Tricycle Museum, The Quay, Christchurch. About 30 tricycles. 10am-5pm, daily June-Sept; and weekends April, May, Oct. Price A. Christchurch (01202) 479849.
St Michael's Loft Museum, above the Priory church. Summer only, Suns pm and some other days. Price A.
Southern Electric Museum, Bargates, Christchurch. Very good, everything to do with electricity in an old Power Station. 1.30-4pm Mon-Fri Easter-June; 10am-4pm July-Sept. Car Park. Price B. Christchurch (01202) 480467.

Corfe Museum, West Street. Small. 9am-5pm daily April-October. Free.

Dorchester Museums
Dorset County Museum, High West Street. The largest museum in Dorset, a must. 10am-5pm Mon-Sat and Suns 10am-5pm July and Aug. Price B. Dorchester (01305) 262735.
Dinosaur Museum Icen Way. Middle size. 9.30am-5.30pm, daily. Price C. Dorchester (01305) 269880.
The Keep Military Museum, Bridport Road. Large and interesting. 9.30am-5pm Mon-Sat (closed 1-2pm Sats) July-Sept; shorter winter opening. Price B. Dorchester (01305) 264066.
Tutankhamun: The Exhibition, High West Street. Smallish. 9.30am-5.30pm daily. Price C. Dorchester (01305) 269571.

Dorset Collection of Clocks, Owermoigne, see Mill House Cider Museum.

Gillingham Museum, Chantry Fields, Gillingham. Small, local history. Mon, Tues, Thurs and Fri 10am-5pm, Sats 10am-12noon. All year. Price A. Gillingham (01747) 822810.

The Harbour Museum, West Bay. Local history & rope & net manufacture. 10am-6pm daily April-Sept. Price A. Bridport (01308) 420997.

Langton Matravers, Coach House Museum, Langton Matravers. The stone industry. 10am-12 noon, 2-4pm, Mon-Sat. Price A. Swanage (01929) 423168/423866.

The Lyme Regis Museum, Bridge Street, Lyme Regis. Medium size, interesting, especially good for fossils. 10am-5pm daily (closed Sunday lunchtimes) April-Oct. Price A. Lyme Regis (01297) 443370.

Dinosaurland, Coombe Street Chapel, Lyme Regis. Dinosaur models and fine local fossils. 10am-5pm daily, Easter-Nov plus winter weekends and half-terms (August open 9am-8pm). Price B. Lyme Regis (01297) 443541.

Mill House Cider Museum, Owermoigne. Cider making in season, display all year. 9am-1pm, 2-5pm daily, all year. Price B. Dorchester (01305) 852220.

Park Farm Museum, west of Milton Abbas. Farming bygones. 10am-6pm daily, April-Oct. Price B. Milton Abbas (01258) 880704.

Poole Museums
Waterfront Museum, 4 High Street. Maritime, reconstructed streets etc. Very good. Price B.
Scaplen's Court, High Street. Good building plus domestic life. Price B.
Both Poole Museums 10am-5pm Mon-Sat, 2pm-5pm Suns, closed weekdays part of the winter. Poole (01202) 683138.

Portland Museum, extreme south end of Wakeham. Local history, geology and so forth. Very good. 10.30am-1pm, 1.30-5pm daily Easter-Oct, rest of year Fri-Tues only. Price B. Portland (01305) 821804.

The Priest's House Museum of East Dorset Life, High Street, Wimborne. Archaeology, local history, bygones. 10.30am-5pm Mon-Sat, April-Oct. Bank hols and Suns June-Sept 2-5pm. Price A. Wimborne Minster (01202) 882533.

Shaftesbury Local History Museum, Gold Hill. Medium sized, local history bygones. 11am-5pm daily, Easter-Sept and some winter weekends 11am-4pm. Price A. Shaftesbury (01747) 852157.

Shaftesbury Abbey Ruins, Park Walk. The foundations of the abbey and a small museum. 10am-5.30pm daily, April-Oct. Price A. Shaftesbury (01747) 852910.

Sherborne Museum, Abbey Gate House. Medium sized, interesting, local history etc. 10.30am-4.30pm Tues-Sat, Easter-Oct. Price A. Sherborne (01935) 812252.

Stapehill Experience, Stapehill, superb farming displays. See Miscellaneous.

Sturminster Newton Museum, now in the Mill, with local displays as well. Well worth a visit. 11am-5pm Sat, Sun, Mon, Thurs, Easter-Sept. Car Park. Price B. Sturminster Newton (01258) 472325.

Tithe Barn Museum, Church Hill, Swanage. Local History, geology, etc. 10.30am-12.30pm, 2.30pm-4.30pm, 7.30pm-9.30pm, daily (not Sunday mornings) Spring Bank Holiday to mid-Sept. Price A. Swanage (01929) 424566.

Tolpuddle Martyrs Memorial Museum, TUC Memorial Cottages, Tolpuddle. Agricultural Trade Unions and the Tolpuddle Martyrs. 10am-5.30pm, Tues-Sun, April-Oct, Shorter winter opening. Free. Puddletown (01305) 848237.

Wareham Museum, East Street. Small. Local History etc and Lawrence of Arabia. 10am-1pm, 2pm-5pm, Mon-Sat, Easter-mid Oct. Free. Wareham (01929) 553448.

Wessex Water Museum, Sutton Poyntz, nr Weymouth. Water supply from 1856 to present, plus local history. Mons-Fris all year (phone for times). Free. Poole (01202) 671144.

Weymouth Museums
Deep Sea Adventure, Custom House Quay. Large and interesting. 10am-6pm daily, open until 10pm in July & August, closes 4.30pm Nov-Feb. Cafe. Price C. Weymouth (01305) 760690.
Timewalk, Brewer's Quay, Hope Quay. Very modern displays: Weymouth history and brewery. 10am-9pm summer, to 5.30pm winter, daily. Price C. Weymouth (01305) 777622.
Discovery, Brewer's Quay. Science for Children. 9.30am-9pm daily school summer hols, winter: 10am-5.30pm Weds-Sun; rest of year daily. Price C. Weymouth (01305) 789007.

World of Toys, Arne. Good. 1.30-5pm April, May, June and Sept. (closed Mon and Sat) plus 10.30am-5.30pm July & Aug daily. Teas. Price B. Wareham (01929) 552018.

Nature Reserves, Country Parks, Walking

Most of Dorset is good for walking and seeing plants and wildlife. This list gives only the larger reserves and the country parks. The Ordnance Survey maps show thousands of miles of footpaths, and visitors using them will find good countryside and walking. The coast is all good walking but is under-represented here, as apart from the Army Range there are no restrictions on access. Smaller nature reserves, and those with no public access are not listed here. Many of the Dorset hillforts have public access and make good walks, quite apart from their archaeological interest. Eggardon, Maiden Castle, Pilsdon Pen, Rawlsbury, Lambert's Castle and Coney's Castle are all good.

The Dorset Heritage Coast organises many guided walks at Easter and in the summer: lists from libraries or Tourist Information Offices.

English Nature, Slepe Farm. Arne, Wareham, Dorset BH20 5BN.

Dorset Wildlife Trust, Brooklands Farm, Forston, Dorchester DT2 7AA

Royal Society for the Protection of Birds, Radipole Lake Nature Centre, Swanner Car Park, Weymouth.

Unless otherwise stated the places listed below are open all year, free.

Arne and Shipstall Point . Huge R.S.P.B. heathland reserve bordering Poole Harbour. Birds, especially Dartford Warbler. Nature trails and bird hides. Car Park.

Avon Forest Park, south-west of Ringwood. (Dorset County Council). Heath and pines on the edge of the New Forest. Car Park. Ringwood (01425) 478082.

Black Ven and the Spittles, just east of Lyme Regis. (Dorset Wildlife Trust). Landslips, meadows and scrub. Small car park.

Blue Pool, north of Corfe Castle. Lake in old clay-workings. Heathland and pines. Cafe. Open Easter-Oct from 9.30am. Car Park. Museum. Price B. Wareham (01929) 551408.

Bockerly Dyke, Good downland walking and archaeology. Car park and even larger nature reserve in adjacent Martin Down, Hants.

Brownsea Island, Poole Harbour, (National Trust). The largest island in the harbour. Heath and woodland. 10am-8pm, April-Oct, Price B, plus boat fare from Poole Quay or Sandbanks. Boats are infrequent. Canford Cliffs (01202) 707744.

Bulbarrow. Good walking. Views. Picnic site and car park.

Charmouth Heritage Coast Centre, on the beach. 10.30-5pm school holidays except Xmas. Price A for audio-visual. Charmouth (01297) 560772.

Cranborne Common, south-west of Alderholt (Dorset Wildlife Trust). Access by footpath to this wet heathland reserve.

Duncliffe Hill, west of Shaftesbury. Fine wooded hill, with footpaths leading up from several directions.

Durlston Country Park, South of Swanage. (Dorset County Council). Large, cliff top. Cafe. Car park (fee). Display on wildlife in information centre which is open Easter-end October, 10.30am-5.30pm. Park open all year. Swanage (01929) 424443.

Fontmell Down, between Blandford and Shaftesbury (Dorset Wildlife and National Trust). Chalk downland. Tiny car park.

Hardy's Monument, west of Dorchester. Fine view point and good walks to Bronkham Hill or along the Ridgeway.

Hengistbury Head, Bournemouth. Sand spit and headland, heathy. Small ferries run round the harbour to Hengistbury and Mudeford, Tuckton and Christchurch.

Hod Hill (National Trust). Large hillfort with good chalkland flowers and butterflies.

Holt Heath (English Nature). Heathland (mostly very wet) and woodland. Access from Forestry Commission White Sheet Plantation, east of Holt.

West Moors Country Park, north of the village. Pine Forest with play trail, lake, miniature railway (see Misc.) and so on. Tea Room, visitor centre. 9am-dusk all year except Xmas day. Parking fee: B. (01425) 470721.

Kingcombe, (Dorset Wildlife Trust). Unimproved pastures, woodland etc. Car Park.

Purbeck Marine Reserve, Kimmeridge (Dorset Wildlife Trust). Information Centre at Kimmeridge Bay. Car park. Toll road.

Powerstock Common, Powerstock. (Dorset Wildlife Trust). Very mixed nature reserve. Small car park.

Portland, bleak, good marine views, limestone quarries. Best car parks for walking Portland Heights and Church Ope.

Radipole Lake Weymouth. R.S.P.B. bird reserve. Hides, information displays. Open 9am-5pm all year. Car park (fee). Weymouth (01305) 778313.

Golden Cap, Stonebarrow Hill and Stanton St Gabriel (National Trust). Nearly 2,000 acres of coast, farmland and small woods. Car parks at Stonebarrow Hill (side road just west of Charmouth) and a small one at Langdon Hill, along a side road off the A35 between Chideock & Morecombelake.

Thorncombe Woods, east of Dorchester. Dorset County Council. Woodland and heath running up to Hardy's birthplace. Nature trails, car park.

Studland and Godlingston Heath, Studland (English Nature & National Trust). Huge heathland reserve. Nature trails. Sandy beach and dunes. Car park.

Tyneham. The deserted village in the Army ranges. Displays on wildlife, the village, etc., in the church and school. See Army range walks for opening times. Free.

Army Range Walks, 5 miles of the coast from just east of Lulworth to Kimmeridge are used as a tank firing range, and the roads within it, as well as all the footpaths, are closed when the range is in use. But open most weekends and school holidays. For checking times ring Bindon Abbey (01929) 462721 extn 4819.

Ringmoor, Turnworth (National Trust). Downs and woodland. Okeford Hill picnic site adjoins, with car park.

Upton House, Upton, near Poole. Both wild and formal, with domestic animals, and a hide to see the birds on Poole Harbour.

Wootton Hill Forest Walk, Wootton Fitzpaine. Car park, picnic site.

White Sheet Hill, east of Holt. Car park and access to Holt Heath.

The Working Woodland, on B3163 between Beaminster & Hooke. Woodland walk & experimental buildings. Times & dates as Parnham. Price B.

Tourist Information Centres

Blandford Forum, Marsh & Ham Car Park, West Street. 10am-5pm Mon-Sat, Suns and Bank Holidays 11am-3pm. Blandford (01258) 454770.

Bournemouth, Westover Road. 9.30am-7pm summer, 11am-3pm Suns. Earlier closing winter. Bournemouth (01202) 789789.

Bridport, 32 South Street. 10am-1pm, 2pm-5pm during summer. Oct-Easter 10.30am-12.30pm. Closed on Bank Holidays. Bridport (01308) 424901.

Christchurch, 25 High Street. Easter-October 9.30am-5pm, Oct-Easter 9.30am-4.30pm except Sats. Christchurch (01202) 471780.

Dorchester, Antelope Yard, off Trinity Street. 9am-5pm Mon-Sat. Dorchester (01305) 267992.

Lyme Regis, The Guildhall, Bridge Street. 10am-1pm, 2pm-5pm Mon-Fri, all year and Sats during summer. Lyme Regis (01297) 442138.

Poole, Poole Quay and Dolphin Shopping Centre, Quay; 9am-5pm Mon-Fri, closed 4.30pm Sats and Suns. Open July and August 9am-9pm. Winter weekends 10.30am-4.30pm. Dolphin Shopping Centre 10am-4.30pm Mon-Sat. Poole (01202.) 673322.

Shaftesbury, 8 Bell Street. 10am-5pm, Easter-October. Shaftesbury (01747) 853514.

Sherborne, 3 Tilton Court, Digby Street, 10am-6pm every day except Sunday. Closed Oct-Easter. Sherborne (01935) 815341.

Swanage, White House, Shore Road. 10am-12-45pm, 2.15pm-5pm Mon-Sat, 10am-12 noon, 2pm-4pm Sun. Swanage (01929) 422885.

Wareham, Town Hall, East Street. Mon-Sat Easter-Oct, Suns also in June-Aug. Winter Tues, Thurs, Fri am. Wareham (01929) 552740.

Weymouth, King's Statue, The Esplanade; 9am-5pm daily. Weymouth Pavilion; 9.30am-4.30pm Mon-Fri. Lodmoor Country Park; 10am-4-35pm daily. Weymouth (01305) 785747.

Wimborne, 29 High Sheet. 10am-5.30pm, Mon-Sat. Wimborne (01202) 886116.

Miscellaneous

Alice in Wonderland Maze and Family Park, opposite airport, Hurn. Alice-theme park, some farm animals. 10am-5pm daily April-Oct. Price B (01202) 483444.

Anvil Point Lighthouse, Swanage. Easter-Sept, 11am-one hour before sunset. Closed in fog or during maintenance work. Best to ring day before. Swanage (01929) 422246.

Cerne Abbas Abbey Buildings. Fine porch to the Abbot's hall. 11am-5pm. Tues-Thurs, Sat and Sun, April-October. Price A. Cerne Abbas (01300) 341284.

Corfe Castle Model Village. 10am-6pm daily, Easter-September. 11am-4pm Sun-Thurs October. Price B. Corfe Castle (01929) 481234.

Cranborne Ancient Technology Centre, Cranborne Middle School, Damerham Road. Iron Age round houses etc. Really for schools so by appointment only. (01202) 888992.

Dorchester Crown Court, High West Street, Late 18th century courtroom. 9am-12noon. 2pm-4pm, weekdays. Free, entry through West Dorset District Council Offices. Guided tours and cells 2-4pm, August. Price B. Dorchester (01305) 252241.

Hurn Airport, Hurn, north of Bournemouth. Observation area. Cafe. Open all year. Bournemouth (01202) 579751.

Knights of Christchurch, Stony Lane, Christchurch, Jousting. Most days April-Sept, performances 3pm. Price D. (01202) 483777.

Lifeboats: the lifeboats can be seen at Swanage, Lyme Regis and Mudeford. Old Lifeboat House, East Quay, Poole, has an old Lifeboat on display (10-15am-12.30pm, 2.15pm-5pm Easter-Sept daily, but dependent on volunteers so occasionally closed). Small museum at RNLI headquarters, West Quay Road, Poole, (9.30am-4.30pm weekdays only, not Bank Holidays, all year). Royal National Lifeboat Institution, Poole (01202) 671133.

Model Town, 16 King Street, Wimborne. The town in the 1950s, at one-tenth scale. 10am-5pm daily, April-Sept. Teas. Price B. Wimborne (01202) 881924.

Moors Valley Railway 7¼in gauge steam railway, very good layout, in West Moors Country Park. 10.45am-5pm School holidays, most weekends and daily Spring Bank Holiday to mid-Sept. Weekends March-Oct; Suns Nov-Feb; daily two weeks over Easter, Spring Bank Holiday to mid-Sept; Half-Term holidays; Boxing Day-end school holiday. Price B. (01425) 471415.

Moore's Dorset Biscuits, Morcombelake. Making Dorset knobs and other biscuits. 9am-5pm Mon-Fri. Free (01297) 489253.

New Barn Field Centre, Bradford Peverell. Iron Age homestead. 10am-5pm daily. Price: B. Dorchester (01305) 267463.

Poole Model Railway, The Quay, Poole. Supposedly the largest oo gauge model railway in the world. Times etc as Natural World (see Animals etc.).

Poole Pottery, The Quay, Poole. Good small museum and very good guided tours of the factory. Cafe. 10am-12.15pm, 1.15-3.45pm, daily, all year. Price B. Poole (01202) 666200.

Portland Lighthouse, Portland Bill. 10.30am-4pm, every day except when fog-horn sounding, Easter-Sept. Free. Portland (01305) 820495.

Poundbury Centre, Dorchester. Energy Conservation Displays. 9.30am-5pm Mon-Fri, all year. Free. Dorchester (01305) 250533.

Sherborne, Almshouse of St John, Half Moon Street. 15th century, and still in use. 2pm-4pm daily except Mon and Weds Easter-end Sept. Price A. Sherborne (01935) 813245.

Stapehill Experience, Stapehill near Wimborne. Big new gardens, 19th century nunnery and the best farming display in the county. 10am-5pm, Easter-October, rest of year 10am-4pm Weds-Suns. Price: D. Wimborne (01202) 861686.

Sunnydown Farm, Langton Matravers. 140 million year old dinosaur tracks. Opening 1995. Price: B. Corfe Castle (01929) 439385.

Swanage Railway, Swanage Railway Station. Trains run every weekend, with daily running June-Sept. Santa specials for a month before Christmas. Suns Easter-September & school summer hols daily. Opening soon to Corfe Castle and Norden (car parks at Norden). Price B-D. Swanage (01929) 425800.

Upwey Wishing Well, Upwey. Cafe. 10.30am-6pm, daily Easter-Sept. Price A. Upwey (01305) 814470.

Wimborne Minster Chained Library, in the minster church, founded 1686. 10am-4pm Mon-Fri, Easter Mon-Oct. Price: A.